THE JOHN PHILLIPS COMMENTARY SERIES

Exploring

EPHESIANS & PHILIPPIANS

An Expository Commentary

JOHN PHILLIPS

kregel
PUBLICATIONS

Grand Rapids, MI 49501

Exploring Ephesians & Philippians: An Expository Commentary

Exploring Ephesians © 1993 by John Phillips
Exploring Philippians © 1995 by John Phillips

Published by Kregel Publications, a division of Kregel, Inc., P.O. Box 2607, Grand Rapids, MI 49501.

ISBN 978-0-8254-3476-1

Printed in the United States of America

07 08 09 10 11 / 8 7 6 5 4

Exploring

EPHESIANS

CONTENTS

PREFACE

In some ways the city of Ephesus is unique in the New Testament. It was not a religious center like Jerusalem, a cultural center like Athens, or a political center like Rome. It was a Christian center.

Pagans knew the city as a center of heathen activities. Its famous temple of Diana (Artemis) was one of the seven wonders of the ancient world and a source of terrible moral and spiritual pollution. But Ephesus is known around the world today not because of the temple that attracted thousands to its courts and courtesans, not because of its trade, but because of the Biblical truth that was taught there. Ephesus is known to all who know the Bible.

Paul spent several years in Ephesus and a truly great church resulted from his ministry. Paul's final farewell words to the Ephesian elders reveal how diligently he had preached and pastored there (Acts 20). Mark and the apostle John also ministered in Ephesus. Timothy is believed to have been martyred there for denouncing the licentiousness of a feast of Diana.

It was from Ephesus that John was exiled to the offshore island of Patmos. During that exile he wrote to Ephesus one of the letters to the seven churches. In that letter, dictated personally by the ascended Lord, he exposed the church's lack of love for the Lord Jesus (Revelation 2:1-7). Their labors were commended, their loyalty was praised, but their lack of love was lamented. The Lord took this lack of love for Himself so seriously that He warned that if there were no repentance and revival, He would remove the lampstand. Light without love is a barren thing. The Lord has no use for a church that no longer loves Him.

When Paul wrote his Ephesian letter, the events foreseen by John were still over the horizon. Yet the warnings Paul had issued several years before in his farewell to the Ephesian elders at Miletus show that he had his own private fears. The onslaught of a cult at nearby Colossae alerted Paul to growing dangers, but what destroyed the Ephesian church in the end was not falsehood, but formality. It became, so to speak, a cold, fundamental, orthodox, evangelical,

Bible-believing church that lacked even a spark of its original love for Christ.

As we read this Ephesian letter, what impresses us is Paul's emphasis on love. He told us about our blessings, he talked about our behavior, and he warned us about our battles. But it is our Beloved—Christ—who dominates it all.

Come, then; join me in a tour of this letter, perhaps the grandest of all Paul's Epistles. Doctrine will thrill us in the book of Romans and discipline will confront us in Corinthians. We will read of deliverance in Galatians, deception in Colossians, discord in Philippians, duty in Philemon, and discovery in Thessalonians. But in Ephesians devotion is the theme. There Paul was saying, "Take another look at the Beloved. Fall in love with Him afresh. He is the chiefest among ten thousand, the altogether lovely One, fairer than the fair, the glorious Bridegroom of our hearts."

In His matchless love,
John Phillips

COMPLETE OUTLINE
OF THE EPISTLE TO THE EPHESIANS

I. Introduction (1:1-2)

A. Greetings from Paul (1:1)
1. The Author (1:1a)
2. The Audience (1:1b-c)
a. The Local Church (1:1b)
b. The Larger Church (1:1c)
B. Grace for All (1:2)

II. The Christian and His Blessings (1:3–3:21)

A. The Realities of the Christian Life (1:3-23)
1. Where We Stand: Basic Principles (1:3-14)
a. The Will of the Father (1:3-6)
(1) The Source of Our Blessings (1:3a)
(2) The Sphere of Our Blessings (1:3b)
(3) The Scope of Our Blessings (1:4-5)
(a) We Have Been Chosen (1:4a)
(b) We Have Been Changed (1:4b-5)
i. God Has Removed All Our Sins (1:4b)
ii. God Has Remade Us As Sons (1:5)
(4) The Significance of Our Blessings (1:6)
(a) The Father's Benevolence
(b) The Father's Beloved
b. The Work of the Son (1:7-12)
(1) Redemption (1:7)
(a) The Person Involved (1:7a)
(b) The Price Involved (1:7b)
(c) The Pardon Involved (1:7c)
(2) Revelation (1:8-9)
(a) The Divine Perception (1:8)
(b) The Divine Purpose (1:9)
(3) Royalty (1:10-11)
(a) For the Christ (1:10)
(b) For the Christian (1:11)
(4) Rejoicing (1:12)
c. The Witness of the Spirit (1:13-14)

(1) His Word: A Witness to the Christ (1:13a)
(2) His Work: A Witness to the Christian (1:13b-14)
   (a) The Proof of Our Faith (1:13b)
   (b) The Pledge of Our Future (1:14)
2. Why We Stand: Believing Prayer (1:15-23)
  a. A Church-centered Prayer (1:15-16)
    (1) The Cause of It (1:15)
    Paul had heard how they:
    (a) Trusted the Savior (1:15a)
    (b) Treated the Saints (1:15b)
    (2) The Constancy of It (1:16)
  b. A Christ-centered Prayer (1:17-23)
    Paul wanted them to know more of:
    (1) The Person of Christ (1:17)
    (2) The Portion of Christ (1:18)
    (a) Our Hope Is in Him (1:18a)
    (b) His Heritage Is in Us (1:18b)
      i. The Fact of It
      ii. The Fame of It
      iii. The Fullness of It
    (3) The Power of Christ (1:19-21)
    (a) The Direction of It (1:19a)
    (b) The Dimensions of It (1:19b)
    (c) The Demonstration of It (1:20a)
    (d) The Distinction of It (1:20b-21)
      i. All Seats of Power Are Beneath Him (1:20b-21b)
       a. Where He Is Seated (1:20b)
       b. What He Has Subdued (1:21a-b)
        1. All Spiritual Seats of Power (1:21a)
        2. All Secular Seats of Power (1:21b)
      ii. All Spheres of Power Are Before Him (1:21c)
    (4) The Position of Christ (1:22-23)
    Paul wanted us to consider:
    (a) The Lord's Feet (1:22a)
    (b) The Lord's Fullness (1:22b-23)
      i. The Church Finds All Its Fullness in Him, the Head (1:22b)
      ii. The Christ Finds All His Fullness in Us, the Body (1:23)

B. The Revolution of the Christian Life (2:1-22)
1. The Great Dispositional Change (2:1-10)
  a. The Past (2:1-3)
  We were:
  (1) Dead (2:1)
  (2) Deluded (2:2a)
  (3) Disobedient (2:2b)

        (4) Defiled (2:3a)
        (5) Doomed (2:3b)
     b. The Present (2:4-6)
        (1) God's Love Shown to Us (2:4-5a)
          (a) Its Richness (2:4)
          (b) Its Reality (2:5a)
        (2) God's Love Shared with Us (2:5b-6)
          (a) It Plucked Us from the Tomb (2:5b-6a)
          (b) It Placed Us on the Throne (2:6b)
     c. The Prospect (2:7-10)
        (1) Unstinted Grace (2:7-9)
          (a) Eternally Revealed Through Us (2:7)
          (b) Eternally Revealed To Us (2:8-9)
        (2) Unstunted Growth (2:10)
  2. The Great Dispensational Change (2:11-22)
     a. The Blood That Invites (2:11-13)
        (1) Our Natural State (2:11-12)
          (a) No Covenant Relationship with the God of Israel (2:11)
          (b) No Commonwealth Relationship with the God of
             Israel (2:12)
        (2) Our New State (2:13)
     b. The Body That Unites (2:14-18)
        (1) Peace Procured for Us (2:14-16)
          (a) The Old Barrier Abolished (2:14-15)
          (b) The New Bond Established (2:16)
        (2) Peace Proclaimed to Us (2:17-18)
          (a) All Difference Gone (2:17)
          (b) All Distance Gone (2:18)
     c. The Building That Delights (2:19-22)
        (1) The New Household (2:19)
        (2) The New Habitation (2:20-22)
          (a) The Foundation of the Building (2:20)
          (b) The Framework of the Building (2:21)
          (c) The Function of the Building (2:22)

C. The Revelations of the Christian Life (3:1-21)
  1. Our Enlightenment (3:1-9)
     a. Paul as a Prisoner for the Truth (3:1)
     b. Paul as a Pioneer of the Truth (3:2-4)
        (1) The Truth Entrusted to Him (3:2)
        (2) The Truth Enlightening to Him (3:3-4)
        How it was:
          (a) Communicated To Him (3:3a)
          (b) Communicated By Him (3:3b-4)
     c. Paul as a Partner in the Truth (3:5-6)
        (1) How the Truth Was Concealed (3:5a)
        (2) How the Truth Was Revealed (3:5b-6)

b. What Light Repudiates (5:11-12)
   What is done in darkness is not:
   (1) Something with Which We Can Compromise (5:11)
   (2) Something about Which We Can Converse (5:12)
c. Why Light Regenerates (5:13-14)
   It has to do with:
   (1) The Work of the Spirit (5:13)
   (2) The Work of the Savior (5:14)
8. A Conscious Decision (5:15-17)
   a. Concerning Time (5:15-16)
      We are to be:
      (1) Wise concerning Our Ways (5:15)
      (2) Wise concerning Our Days (5:16)
   b. Concerning Truth (5:17)
9. A Captivating Discovery (5:18-21)
   a. How to Be Filled with the Spirit (5:18)
   b. How to Be Thrilled in the Spirit (5:19-20)
      (1) Joyful Acclamation in Song (5:19)
      (2) Joyful Acceptance of Wrong (5:20)
   c. How to Be Drilled by the Spirit (5:21)

C. In His Marital Relationships (5:22–6:4)
1. As a Partner (5:22-33)
   a. Some Priorities of the Marriage Relationship (5:22-29)
      (1) The Wife: Loyalty Revealed in Surrender (5:22-24)
         (a) The Exhortation (5:22)
         (b) The Example (5:23)
         (c) The Expectation (5:24)
      (2) The Husband: Love Revealed in Sacrifice (5:25-29)
         (a) The Exhortation (5:25a)
         (b) The Example (5:25b-27)
            i. Love That Travails (5:25b)
            ii. Love That Transforms (5:26-27)
         (c) The Expectation (5:28-29)
            i. The Self Motive (5:28-29a)
            ii. The Supreme Motive (5:29b)
   b. Some Principles of the Marriage Relationship (5:30-33)
      (1) The Concept (5:30-32)
         (a) A Man and Christ's Body (5:30)
         (b) A Man and Christ's Bride (5:31-32)
      (2) The Conclusion (5:33)
2. As a Parent (6:1-4)
   a. The Child's Simple Task (6:1-3)
      (1) The Principle (6:1)
      (2) The Precept (6:2)
      (3) The Promise (6:3)
   b. The Father's Sublime Trust (6:4)

PART I

Introduction

Ephesians 1:1-2

INTRODUCTION

The city of Ephesus was large and important in Paul's day. It had a population of some 350,000 people. Centrally located on the western coast of Asia Minor, Ephesus was positioned midway between two continents. Here east met west. Here oriental luxury, extravagance, and sensuality met occidental enterprise, discipline, and ambition. Here sensual oriental religion blended with lofty and progressive Greek culture and firm, but on the whole fair, Roman government. Here crowds of government officials, Roman soldiers, and Jewish businessmen rubbed shoulders with Eastern pilgrims flocking into Ephesus to worship at the notorious temple of Artemis.

The city was famous for the great arterial Roman road that linked it with the world, for its markets and warehouses, and for its administrative buildings and schools. But above all Ephesus was famous for its temple of Diana (Artemis). Heralded as one of the wonders of the world, it was the sacred shrine of the repulsively ugly image of the mother goddess Artemis—an image reputed to have descended from the sky. In that temple worshipers enacted the licentious rites characteristic of many Eastern religions.

Ephesus was Paul's headquarters during his third missionary journey. He stayed in the city for nearly three years and established a large, influential church. His colleagues and converts fanned out from Ephesus to evangelize the hinterland. They planted churches in city after city, including Smyrna, Pergamos, Thyatira, Sardis, Philadelphia, Laodicea, Colossae, and Hierapolis. Names associated with the church at Ephesus include Paul, Aquila, Priscilla, Apollos, Tychicus, Timothy, and the apostle John. The church there enjoyed the prolonged ministries of two apostles and was the only church in the New Testament to receive letters from two apostles.

The letters to the Ephesians and the Colossians are complementary Epistles, written to address a heresy that had raised its head in the churches of the Lycus valley. Paul seems to have written the

Epistle to the Colossians first, to emphasize the deity of Christ and His *headship* over the church, His body. In Colossians he set forth a cosmic Christ, the Creator of Heaven and earth. In Ephesians, on the other hand, he emphasized the church as the *body* of Christ. The mystical relationship between Christ and His church—between the head and the body—is so real, however, that the church shares in Christ's exalted position on high.

It is not surprising, therefore, that Ephesians introduces us to the most sublime themes that have ever occupied the human mind. Expositors have likened the Ephesian letter to the Grand Canyon and the European Alps. Vista after vista appears. In Ephesians we get the eagle's view of things. We see the eagle rising and wheeling, then soaring off into the high vault of Heaven. We trace the apostle Paul's thoughts as they wheel and as they soar above the confines of time and space beyond the mundane thoughts of ordinary men. We marvel at Paul's command of language, only to discover that even his eloquence is inadequate to convey the concepts of eternity completely.

I. INTRODUCTION (1:1-2)

A. Greetings from Paul (1:1)

1. The Author (1:1a) "Paul, an apostle of Jesus Christ by the will of God."

The name *Paul* at the head of this letter commanded immediate attention. Paul's name had power in Ephesus. He had won large numbers of people there to Christ. As he reminded the Corinthians, a person might have ten thousand teachers in Christ, but he does not have many fathers. So a letter from the one who led them to Christ would always be cherished.

At the end of his second missionary journey, on his way to Jerusalem, Paul paid a brief visit to Ephesus. He stopped at the local synagogue and made a friendly contact with the Jews and rabbis. He declined an invitation to stay in Ephesus because of his desire to be at Jerusalem for the feast. However, he left Aquila and Priscilla in Ephesus to cultivate the spiritual ground there in preparation for his return.

During Paul's third missionary journey, Ephesus became the center of a spiritual awakening that embraced the whole area. The Jews as usual soon turned hostile but Paul, undaunted, turned to the Gentiles and the revival thrived. Miracles were performed. Paul's converts built a public bonfire to destroy their books of magic—books that were worth a small fortune. The Holy Spirit's power was poured out in ways that put the fear of God into those who tried to counterfeit His work. Describing this revival Luke wrote, "So mightily grew the word of God and prevailed" (Acts 19:20).

Possibly it was at Ephesus that Paul suffered one of his many imprisonments, for this spectacular spread of the gospel did not go unhindered (2 Corinthians 11:23). In 1 Corinthians 15:32 he spoke of fighting with wild beasts at Ephesus. In the end Paul was forced out of the city by a riot instigated by Demetrius the silversmith. When the mob seized Gaius and Aristarchus, Paul would have rushed to the support of his companions since he was well used to hazarding his life for the gospel. But he was restrained by believers who were concerned for their beloved apostle's safety.

After he left Ephesus, Paul went to Europe. Then he made his last, fatal visit to Jerusalem. On the way to Jerusalem he stopped at Miletus, a city close to Ephesus. The elders of the Ephesian church met Paul at Miletus where he gave them his last charge and warned them of doctrinal heresies he could foresee.

2. The Audience (1:1b-c)

a. The Local Church (1:1b) "To the saints which are at Ephesus."

The local church in this case was probably not just the church in Ephesus itself, but all the local churches in the area.

To be a saint at Ephesus was to be like a lovely lily in a stagnant pond. Ephesus rivaled Corinth as the "filth capital" of the Roman world. People from all over the world came to Ephesus to see the temple of Artemis and to patronize the sacred prostitutes whose services were offered as the consummation of worship. Sin was at the very heart of religion in Ephesus, as it is to this day in Hinduism and other Eastern religions.

In contrast, God's people were to be saints—called-out ones— cleansed and made holy, separated unto the true and living God and His Son by the power of the indwelling Spirit of God. The true temple of God at Ephesus was to be found in the bodies of the believers where Jesus was enshrined as Lord. It was to these people— God's people—that Paul addressed his letter.

b. The Larger Church (1:1c) "And to the faithful in Christ Jesus."

In some original manuscripts the words "at Ephesus" are not found in Ephesians 1:1. The writings of such early fathers as Origen and Basil intimate that their copies of the Epistle also omit these words. The usual explanation is that this Epistle was a circular letter; the words *en Epheso* were omitted so that the names of the various churches to which it was sent could be written in the blank space. In Colossians 4:16 Paul asked the Colossians to share their letter with other churches. He also told the Colossians to read the letter from Laodicea (some think he was referring to the letter to the Ephesians).

If the letter to the Ephesians was encyclical and the actual name of the church was left blank, we can write the name of our church in the blank and read the letter as if Paul addressed it to us. This is true of course of all the Epistles, but especially the encyclical ones. The salutation encourages us to adopt such an attitude even if we reject the idea of a blank space since the letter is addressed to "the faithful in Christ."

The Ephesian saints were to be faithful amid much temptation, and so are we. Pollution, perversion, and pornography were accepted norms in their world and in ours. Our calling is to be "faithful in Christ Jesus" in our corrupted world. How did Jesus react to the corruption of human life and society? He loved the sinner and hated the sin. So must we.

B. Grace for All (1:2) "Grace be to you, and peace, from God our
     Father, and from the Lord Jesus Christ."

The word "grace" occurs a dozen times in this letter. Paul customarily replaced the regular Greek salutation "Rejoice" (*chiare*) with the phonetically similar word "Grace" (*charis*). The regular Jewish salutation was "Peace" (*shalom*). Paul joined Jews and Gentiles in the bond of love in his greetings.

But he did more. He customarily lifted the salutation even higher. It came from "God *our* Father" (italics added), indicating that Jews and Gentiles in the church are members of a common family—children of the same Father.

And then Paul added, "From the Lord Jesus Christ," equating the Lord Jesus to the Father. Thus Paul emphasized the deity of Christ. Jesus is coequal, coeternal, and coexistent with the Father. The greeting comes from "God our Father" *and* from "the Lord Jesus Christ." Thus "Grace and peace" is elevated from a marketplace salutation to a benediction and an affirmation of faith.

PART II

The Christian
and His Blessings
Ephesians 1:3–3:21

II. THE CHRISTIAN AND HIS BLESSINGS (1:3–3:21)

This section of the book of Ephesians introduces us to the unscalable heights and unfathomable depths of the Christian life. The Bible contains no greater truths than those written here. As we examine this great segment we will look at the realities, the revolution, and the revelations of the Christian life.

A. The Realities of the Christian Life (1:3-23)

1. Where We Stand: Basic Principles (1:3-14)

a. The Will of the Father (1:3-6)

(1) The Source of Our Blessings (1:3a) "Blessed be the God and Father of our Lord Jesus Christ."

The paragraph opening up before us is probably the longest single sentence of unbroken discourse in ancient literature. Ephesians 1:3-14 is really one long sentence. It winds around and about, here and there, climbing higher and higher. In some ways it baffles analysis because its thoughts are complex and interwoven. We have to read it over and over before we can grasp the overall significance of its complex themes. Before going a step farther, let's look at it in its entirety:

> Blessed be the God and Father of our Lord Jesus Christ, who hath blessed us with all spiritual blessings in heavenly places in Christ: According as he hath chosen us in him before the foundation of the world, that we should be holy and without blame before him in love: Having predestinated us unto the adoption of children by Jesus Christ to himself, according to the good pleasure of his will, To the praise of the glory of his grace, wherein he hath made us accepted in the beloved. In whom we have redemption through his blood, the forgiveness of sins, according to the riches of his grace; Wherein he hath abounded toward us in all wisdom and prudence; Having made known unto us the mystery of his will, according to his

good pleasure which he hath purposed in himself: That in the dispensation of the fulness of times he might gather together in one all things in Christ, both which are in heaven, and which are on earth; even in him: In whom also we have obtained an inheritance, being predestinated according to the purpose of him who worketh all things after the counsel of his own will: That we should be to the praise of his glory, who first trusted in Christ. In whom ye also trusted, after that ye heard the word of truth, the gospel of your salvation: in whom also after that ye believed, ye were sealed with that holy Spirit of promise, Which is the earnest of our inheritance until the redemption of the purchased possession, unto the praise of his glory.

Now let's read it in modern English, in J. B. Phillips's translation:

Praised be the God and Father of our Lord Jesus Christ for giving us through Christ every spiritual benefit as citizens of Heaven! For consider what he has done—before the foundation of the world he chose us to be, in Christ, his children, holy and blameless in his sight. He planned, in his love, that we should be adopted as his own children through Jesus Christ—this was his will and pleasure that we might praise that glorious generosity of his which he granted to us in his Beloved. It is through him, at the cost of his own blood, that we are redeemed, freely forgiven through that free and generous grace which has overflowed into our lives and given us wisdom and insight. For God has allowed us to know the secret of his plan, and it is this: he purposed long ago in his sovereign will that all human history should be consummated in Christ, that every-thing that exists in Heaven or earth should find its perfection and fulfillment in him. In Christ we have been given an inheri-tance, since we were destined for this, by the One who works out all his purposes according to the design of his own will. So that we, in due time, as the first to put our hope in Christ, may bring praise to his glory! And you too trusted him, when you had heard the message of truth, the gospel of your salvation. And after you gave your confidence to him you were, so to speak, stamped with the promised Holy Spirit as a pledge of our inheritance, until the day when God completes the redemption of what is his own; and that will again be to the praise of his glory.

When I was a little boy, my aunt and uncle took me to see Hampton Court, a famous palace built on the outskirts of London by Cardinal Wolsey in the days of Henry VIII. When the palace was finished, Wolsey made the mistake of inviting Henry to come and see his magnificent new home. The king cast covetous eyes upon it. "This," he said, "is a palace fit for a king." Ever jealous of any rivals to his power and glory he added, "I think you'd better give it to me." Valuing his head more than his home, the cardinal did just that, but he lost his head a few years later anyway.

On the grounds of Hampton Court is a maze of hedges and for a penny or two, visitors could have the privilege of getting lost in that maze. My uncle and I went in. The paths were narrow and the hedges high. All the paths looked the same and after a few turns we were lost. Eventually we wandered into the middle of the maze where the authorities had thoughtfully provided a seat so that one could sit and think things over and try to unravel the maze's mystery before setting out again. But the maze simply defied analysis. I don't know how long we wandered around in there before an attendant took pity on us and showed us the way out.

Although the maze defied all our attempts at analysis, it is not merely a jumble of hedges; it has been laid out according to an orderly plan. For those who know its secret, for those who have seen the blueprint, the maze is no mystery. It is only puzzling to those who are content with casually attempting to find a way through it.

It is the same with Ephesians 1:1-14. This passage is not just a jumble of words. It is laid out according to a definite plan: verses 3-6 describe *the will of the Father*; verses 7-12 describe *the work of the Son*; and verses 13-14 describe *the witness of the Spirit*. These three main divisions can be separated phrase by phrase into their component parts to display the intricate mosaic of Paul's thoughts.

It is the will of the Father to bless us and that is where Paul begins. He directs our attention to the source of our blessings.

The supreme revelation of God in the Bible is that He is the *Father* and that He is the God and Father of our Lord Jesus Christ. The concept of God as Father scarcely appears in the Old Testament. God is revealed there as the creator, *Elohim*; as the God of covenant, *Jehovah*; and as the Lord, *Adonai*. He is *El*, the almighty; *El Shaddai*, the gracious giver; *Jehovah Jireh*, the Lord who provides; *Jehovah Nissi*, the Lord our banner; *Jehovah Shalom*, the Lord of all peace; *Jehovah Sabaoth*, the Lord of hosts; *Jehovah Tsidkenu*, the Lord our righteousness; and *Jehovah Shammah*, the Lord who is there.

Not until Jesus came was God fully revealed as the Father. Jesus' first recorded words enshrine this truth: "Wist ye not that I must be about my Father's business?" (Luke 2:49) In the greatest of Christ's parables—the parable of the prodigal (Luke 15:11-32)—the word *father* occurs a dozen times. That name was on the Lord's lips as He prayed in dark Gethsemane, as He hung on the cross, as He greeted His loved ones on the resurrection morning, and as He walked on the road to Olivet on the day of His ascension.

God is the Father. What a wonderful truth! He is the God and Father of our Lord Jesus Christ. What a blessed fact! He is just like Jesus, who could say as He walked among us, "He that hath seen me hath seen the Father" (John 14:9). Jesus was "the visible expression of the invisible God" (Colossians 1:15, J. B. PHILLIPS). And together the Father and the Son (along with the Holy Spirit) are the source of all the abundant blessings mentioned in this opening statement of Ephesians 1.

(2) The Sphere of Our Blessings (1:3b) "Who hath blessed us with all spiritual blessings in heavenly places in Christ."

There are two spheres of blessing. Our blessings (and our battles) are *"in heavenly places"* and also *"in Christ,"* in whom "we live, and move, and have our being" (Acts 17:28). We meet these two expressions repeatedly in this Epistle.

The heavenlies (heavenly places) at the present time are Satan's sphere of operations. He holds them as "the prince of the power of the air" (Ephesians 2:2) and he is aided by countless hosts of spirit beings who accept his lordship and follow his lead. So we have to take the heavenlies by storm. Later chapters in the Epistle tell us how to arm ourselves and how to fight victoriously against these entrenched foes who try to deny us our inheritance and keep us out of our rightful sphere.

Ephesians is the New Testament counterpart of the book of Joshua. Just as Israel's blessings were found *in Canaan,* so ours are found *in the heavenlies.* Just as the Israelites had to battle many enemies in Canaan in order to possess all that God had promised them, so we have to battle Satan and his army in order to enter into all that is ours in heavenly places. Just as Israel's inheritance in Canaan was fiercely contested by the foe, so our inheritance in the heavenlies is also strongly contested. Just as Joshua led God's chosen people into victory, so Jesus leads us.

If our blessings are in heavenly places, they are also in Christ. Satan and his evil hosts may haunt the heavenlies, but Christ has conquered them.

The Israelites only had to trust and obey in order to enter into all the blessings God had in store for them in Canaan. The Canaanites, despite their formidable appearance, were already defeated. Yet

the Israelites did not believe God's promises. We recall how ten of
the twelve spies discouraged the people:

> The people is greater and taller than we; the cities are great
> and walled up to heaven; and moreover we have seen the sons
> of the Anakims there (Deuteronomy 1:28).
> And they brought up an evil report of the land which they
> had searched unto the children of Israel, saying, The land,
> through which we have gone to search it, is a land that eateth
> up the inhabitants thereof; and all the people that we saw in it
> are men of a great stature. And there we saw the giants, the sons
> of Anak, which come of the giants: and we were in our own
> sight as grasshoppers, and so we were in their sight (Numbers
> 13:32-33).

How different was the minority report of Joshua and Caleb in
Numbers 14:7-9:

> And they spake unto all the company of the children of Israel,
> saying, The land, which we passed through to search it, is an
> exceeding good land. If the Lord delight in us, then he will
> bring us into this land, and give it us; a land which floweth with
> milk and honey. Only rebel not ye against the Lord, neither
> fear ye the people of the land; for they are bread for us: their
> defence is departed from them, and the Lord is with us: fear
> them not.

Their report was confirmed later by Rahab's testimony: "I know
that the Lord hath given you the land, and that your terror is fallen
upon us, and that all the inhabitants of the land faint because of
you" (Joshua 2:9). All the Israelites had to do was enter the land and
possess their possessions. The Canaanites were already thoroughly
demoralized.

All Israel had to do was go forward in faith and obedience, and
the same is true of us. The heavenlies are occupied by the foe and
there can be no blessings without battles, but the foe is already
defeated. Christ, our heavenly Joshua, leads us into victory and into
the actual possession of all that has been promised to us in Him.

(3) The Scope of Our Blessings (1:4-5)

(a) We Have Been Chosen (1:4a) "According as he hath chosen us
in him before the foundation of the world."

There is a mystery here that centers in the fact that we are finite and God is infinite. We are creatures of time; God inhabits eternity. We express our mode of being in three tenses of time—I was, I am, I will be. God expresses His mode of being in the eternal present—I am, I am, I am. Thus Jesus did not say, "Before Abraham was, I was" (which in itself would have been an astonishing statement expressing a longevity of life His enemies would have found bewildering). Jesus said, "Before Abraham was, I am" (John 8:58). He was claiming eternity of being and coexistence with the Father, and His enemies considered His statement blasphemous.

We are hindered in experience and understanding by the limited nature of our being. As finite creatures we live in the here and now and can deal with only one thing at a time. Life is presented to us, so to speak, in tiny little packages. We live it moment by moment. The future lies before us, but we cannot experience it until it touches us in a fleeting moment of the present before it recedes instantly into the past. We can anticipate the future and recall the past, but we live in the flickering moment we call the present. In God's mind, however, the past, present, and future are swallowed up in the all-embracing present.

Thus when we read that we were chosen in Him "before the foundation of the world," we must realize that the Holy Spirit has stated the issue from our perspective. Since God lives in the present tense, there is to Him no time difference between the moment He chose me and the moment I chose Him. The perception of time difference is ours alone. From the standpoint of God's eternal present tense, both acts are simultaneous. That explanation does not, however, lessen the mystery of God's grace. With the chorus writer we still wonder:

> Why did He love me? I never can tell;
> Why did He suffer to save me from Hell?
> Nothing but infinite grace from above
> Could have conceived such a story of love.
>
> (G. R. Harding)

Spurgeon said, "If God hadn't chosen me before the foundation of the world, He wouldn't choose me now!"

(b) We Have Been Changed (1:4b-5)

i.   God Has Removed All Our Sins (1:4b) "That we should be holy and without blame before him in love."

God saves us, sanctifies us, and sees no blemish in us. His love can be content with nothing less than our complete Christlikeness. This is the practical purpose of His grace. The full realization of Christlikeness awaits a coming day when "we shall be like him; for we shall see him as he is" (1 John 3:2). Meanwhile the indwelling Holy Spirit is at work in our hearts to produce in us—here and now—the same quality of unblemished holiness that characterized the Lord Jesus when He lived on earth. God already sees us positionally as holy and without blemish because He sees us in Christ. That is, when He looks at us, He sees Christ. The work of the Holy Spirit is to make us holy and without blame in the everyday aspects of life. Because God is so pleased with Jesus, He wants everyone to be like His Son. The Holy Spirit is here to begin the process of bringing my imperfect state into line with my position, which is perfect. As the apostle John stated in nine apt monosyllables, "As he is, so are we in this world" (1 John 4:17). Christlikeness is our goal, and the driving force is love—His infinite love for us and our increasing love for Him.

ii.   God Has Remade Us As Sons (1:5) "Having predestinated us unto the adoption of children by Jesus Christ to himself, according to the good pleasure of his will."

Some have rephrased Ephesians 1:5 as "Having fore-ordained us unto adoption as sons through Jesus Christ unto himself." That is an important change. There is all the difference in the world between *children* and *sons*. The word *children* has to do with our membership in God's family. For example, I became a member of that family by virtue of the new birth, by being born into it. The word *sons*, on the other hand, has to do with maturity in the family. It refers to the position we occupy in God's family as adult sons.

If we see a sign on a business that reads Henry Brown and Sons, we know that Henry Brown's sons are partners in their father's business. They have grown up and assumed positions of authority and responsibility in their father's business. We never see a sign that reads Henry Brown and Children!

God has predestinated us to maturity. Those who are saved are predestinated. The word *predestinated* is not used in connection with the lost. God does not predestinate certain people to go to Hell and others to go to Heaven. The concept of predestination is reserved in Scripture for those who are in God's family. We might say that election has to do with the past and predestination has to do with the future. Election has to do with what we were chosen from;

predestination has to do with what we were chosen for. It is God's intent to bring us to spiritual maturity so that we can become partners with Him in His eternal purposes.

We were chosen for spiritual maturity "according to the good pleasure of his will." The Father's pleasure is best illustrated by the story of the prodigal son. When the wayward boy returned, repentant and remorseful, he found his father waiting for him. The son had his speech all ready. He was going to say, "Father, I have sinned against heaven, and before thee, And am no more worthy to be called thy son: make me as one of thy hired servants" (Luke 15:18-19). But before he ever reached the part about being made a hired servant, his father interrupted and called for the ring, the robe, the shoes, and the fatted calf. The father had everything ready for the prodigal's return.

Like the father in the parable, God is waiting for us. It is the pleasure of His good will to have everything ready so that in the ages to come the Christian might wear the ring, the robe, and the royal sandals and take his place at God's table as His son.

(4) The Significance of Our Blessings (1:6) "To the praise of the glory of his grace, wherein he hath made us accepted in the beloved."

(a) The Father's Benevolence

To be accepted is one of man's greatest psychological needs, and our psychological needs are echoes of far greater spiritual needs. Our need to be accepted by other people is nothing compared with our need to be accepted by God.

People go to extraordinary lengths to gain the acceptance of those they admire. Many teenagers will do almost anything to be accepted by their peers. They wear outlandish clothing, dye their hair, pose as scholars, or act like slobs—they do whatever is the "in" thing with the group they want to join. Adults do the same, but they are usually more subtle.

Remember, if you will, the story of Oliver Twist. The poor orphan boy was made of tough fiber and refused to do anything to gain acceptance. He would not allow the bully Noah Claypole, for instance, to malign the memory of his mother. Nor would he steal to win the approval of the artful Dodger and old Fagin. The wily Jew, however, knew human nature. He had a plan to wear down Oliver's resistance. He would leave Oliver alone—leave him to his own devices, leave him to wander aimlessly hour after hour in the old house he used as a den. Fagin counted on the natural need for acceptance to wear down Oliver's resistance, so that Oliver would finally seek the approval of the petty thieves and burglars among whom he had fallen, deeming it better than no acceptance at all.

We need acceptance from other people, and we desperately need God's acceptance. But our sinful nature is wholly unacceptable to God. His burning holiness rejects what we are by nature and what we consequently do.

(b) The Father's Beloved

Yet God does accept us! The reason lies in the phrase *the Beloved*. He accepts us, not because of our prayers and promises, not because of our resolves and efforts to be good, not because of our zeal, but because of Jesus. We are accepted in the Beloved.

What a lovely name for Jesus! It was spoken first by the Father when John baptized Jesus in the Jordan. "There came a voice from heaven, saying, Thou art my beloved Son, in whom I am well pleased" (Mark 1:11).

Jesus is Heaven's Beloved, the altogether lovely One, the chiefest among ten thousand (Song of Solomon 5:10,16). God's smile of approval rested on Him throughout His earthly journey. He always did what pleased the Father (John 8:29).

It was God's eternal counsel that the Lord Jesus should first give His life *for* us at Calvary and then give His life *to* us. When we accept Him as personal Savior, the transaction is complete. "For Christ also hath once suffered for sins, the just for the unjust, that he might bring us to God" (1 Peter 3:18). "For he hath made him to be sin for us, who knew no sin; that we might be made the righteousness of God in him" (2 Corinthians 5:21). God now sees us in the Beloved. He looks at us and sees Christ. No angel among the heavenly hosts has more acceptance than we.

An acquaintance of mine who was born in a foreign land became a United States citizen. Once he was accepted, his standing as an American citizen was perfect. I heard him say to an American audience, "I am just as much a *citizen* as your president." Likewise, God placed us in His sight in such a way that we can be perfectly accepted, perfectly at home, perfectly at ease.

Our acceptance by the Father in the Beloved is "to the praise of the glory of his grace." God's glory is greatly enhanced by the grace He has shown to us. It was His idea, not ours. It was His plan to seek us, save us, sanctify us, and seat us in glory. The endless ages of eternity will prove to be all too short a time to sing His praise for such matchless love and grace.

b. The Work of the Son (1:7-12)

(1) Redemption (1:7)

(a) The Person Involved (1:7a) "In whom we have redemption."

We can be accepted by God because of the work of the Lord Jesus Christ. A price had to be paid to redeem us. As the hymn says:

> There was no other good enough
> To pay the price of sin;
> He only could unlock the gate
> Of heav'n and let us in.
> (Cecil F. Alexander)

The price Jesus paid was astronomical—beyond human comprehension. In his short masterpiece, "The Reason Why," Robert Laidlaw faced the question, "How could the Lord Jesus Christ's one life be considered the substitute for the lives of so many, so that God offers salvation to whosoever repents and believes in Christ?" Laidlaw answered:

> That seems a fair question—a problem in arithmetic that can be demonstrated on paper. Christ was God manifest in the flesh—Divinity in humanity—so that the life He gave was an infinite life, which can meet the needs of any number of finite lives. Get a sheet of paper and write down all the big figures you can think of—millions or more—add them up. Now you have a big number; then multiply it by 10—100—by a million if you like—cover sheets of paper, and after all you still have a finite number—a number that has bounds set about it—it has a beginning and an end, however far it may extend. No, by adding finite things together no man has ever been able to make that which is infinite. The *infinite life* of Christ given for sinners is more than sufficient to save all who accept Him as the One who died in their room and stead.[1]

That's the person involved! No wonder our redemption is so great.

(b) The Price Involved (1:7b) "We have redemption through his blood."

In the Old Testament there were two means of redemption—by power and by purchase. The book of Exodus illustrates redemption by power; the book of Ruth illustrates redemption by purchase. It is significant that the first time the kinsman-redeemer Boaz is introduced in the story of Ruth, we are told that he was "a mighty man of wealth" (Ruth 2:1). Only a rich man could redeem. Redemption is a costly business.

Paul wrote, "For ye know the grace of our Lord Jesus Christ, that, though he was rich, yet for your sakes he became poor, that ye through his poverty might be rich" (2 Corinthians 8:9). To secure our redemption, Jesus had to leave the glory of Heaven, enter human life by means of the incarnation, live a perfect life, and then die. He had to suffer the agony of crucifixion, the heartbreak of rejection, betrayal, and abandonment, the sting of ridicule and shame, the horror of being made sin, the torment of God's wrath, and the indignity of death. His blood had to be shed. That was the price. Peter said that we "were not redeemed with corruptible things, as silver and gold . . . But with the precious blood of Christ" (1 Peter 1:18-19). Only God can know how "precious is the flow / That makes me white as snow" (Robert Lowry).

(c)   The Pardon Involved (1:7c) "The forgiveness of sins, according to the riches of his grace."

Grace—there it is again! Redemption is by grace. Grace is unmerited favor. It is getting something we don't deserve. Paul strikes this note over and over.

Years ago a converted derelict called Sam Duncannon lived in Scotland. Old Sam haunted the Glasgow mission where he had found the Savior and where his life and soul had been redeemed. He was not an evangelist or a great soul-winner, but he loved his new-found Lord and wanted to brighten the drab lives of the down-and-outers who drifted in and out of the mission. He collected colored pictures, found appropriate verses of Scripture or gospel hymns, and framed the pictures and verses together; then he gave these illustrated verses to people who came to the mission. He hoped the pictures would add a little color to their lives and the verses would bring a little comfort to their souls.

One day Sam found a picture of Niagara Falls that greatly impressed him. He loved the sense of power and inexhaustibility conveyed by the rush of the water over the falls, but for a long time he could not find a verse to go with the picture—a verse that said what he wanted to say.

Then D. L. Moody and his song-leader, Ira Sankey, came to the mission. Mr. Sankey sang a solo and as soon as Sam heard that song,

he knew that he had found the words he needed for his picture of
Niagara Falls. He could see the finished picture in his mind's eye—
the endlessly rushing water and the words of this hymn:

> Have you on the Lord believed?
> Still there's more to follow;
> Of his grace have you received?
> Still there's more to follow.
>
> O the grace the Father shows!
> Still there's more to follow;
> Freely he his grace bestows,
> Still there's more to follow.
>
> More and more, more and more,
> Always more to follow;
> O his matchless, boundless love!
> Still there's more to follow.
>   (Philip Paul Bliss)

In Ephesians 1:7 Paul wrote, "The forgiveness of sins, according
to the riches of his grace." In a parallel passage in Colossians 1:14
he added the word *even*—"Even the forgiveness of sins." How
wonderful is that word *even*. We read of the Lord Jesus that He
"became obedient unto death, even the death of the cross"
(Philippians 2:8). Esau cried, "Bless me, even me also, O my father"
(Genesis 27:34). When we read, "We have redemption through his
blood, even the forgiveness of sins," we could think of the unclean
nature of our sins, of the uncompromising nastiness of our sins, of
the uncountable number of our sins. No wonder Paul would say,
"Even the forgiveness of sins, according to the riches of his grace."

We can thank God that He is rich in grace. What a horror it would
be if God had revealed Himself to be a God of infinite power, a God
of infallible wisdom, a God of inflexible holiness, and also a God
devoid of compassion and sympathy for lost and ruined mankind.
How we should praise Him for the riches of His grace!

(2) Revelation (1:8-9)

(a) The Divine Perception (1:8) "Wherein he hath abounded
toward us in all wisdom and prudence."

The words "wisdom and prudence" are full of significance. The
Greek word translated "wisdom" here is *sophia*, a great word that

embraced such ideas as "cleverness and skill in handicraft and art, skill in matters of common life, sound judgment, intelligence, practical wisdom, learning, speculative wisdom, natural philosophy and mathematics."[2] Archbishop Trench said that in the New Testament and Christian writing, *sophia* is reserved for the highest and noblest in wisdom and it is never used in Scripture except to describe God and good men (or in a sarcastic sense). When *sophia* refers to God, it refers to the omniscience that belongs to God alone. The Greek word translated "prudence" is *phronesis. Phronesis* is the product of *sophia*—right thinking leads to right actions. Prudence is the effective use of wisdom.[3]

The Greek word translated "abounded" means "more than enough." The word translated "wherein" refers to the grace in which God has superabounded toward us. This means that God's "more-than-enough" grace operates within the framework of His omniscient grasp of time and space and within the scope of His infallible will always to do what is right. In other words, God's unerring logic and unbounded love are behind His plan of salvation. What a revelation of God! But what He saw in us, so to plan for us and so to love us, is more than tongue can tell.

(b) The Divine Purpose (1:9) "Having made known unto us the mystery of his will, according to his good pleasure which he hath purposed in himself."

Do you recall Moses' explanation of God's love for the children of Israel? In his memoirs he wrote, "The Lord did not set his love upon you, nor choose you, because ye were more in number than any people; for ye were the fewest of all people: But because the Lord loved you" (Deuteronomy 7:7-8). In other words Moses was saying, "He loved you because He loved you!" That is the divine logic. We should not dissect God's love—just enjoy it.

But why did His heart overflow with love toward such graceless, unlovely, sinful people? Why did He use His wisdom to "devise means, that his banished be not expelled from him" (2 Samuel 14:14)? Why did He make a plan that did not violate His holiness or break His laws, yet involved enormous sacrifice and suffering for Himself? Why did He use His will to carry through a plan of salvation for the likes of us?

The answer can only be found in understanding the kind of God He is. He does what He does because He is who He is. He is a God of love, and He wants us to be loving like Him. Moreover, He will never rest until we are.

Even children understand that Jesus loves them. But the most mature will never completely unravel what Paul called "the mystery of his will." It will remain far beyond our understanding. All we know is that it was God's "good pleasure" to set His love upon us and make us the objects of such marvelous grace that even the angels must have gasped as they saw the plan unfold.

(3) Royalty (1:10-11)

(a) For the Christ (1:10) "That in the dispensation of the fulness of times he might gather together in one all things in Christ, both which are in heaven, and which are on earth; even in him."

No small part of the Father's eternal purpose, of "his good pleasure which he hath purposed in himself," is to glorify the person of the Lord Jesus. It was Jesus who came to earth, incarnated Himself in human flesh, lived a life wholly pleasing to God, and then bled and died in agony to make God's mercy and redemption available to us. God has no plan, no program, no purpose, that does not ultimately rest in the person of the Lord Jesus Christ.

That truth is evident in Ephesians 1:10. The word translated "gather together in one" can be rendered "sum it up" or "head it up." The same word occurs in Romans 13:9 where Paul listed five of the ten commandments then added, "If there be any other commandment, it is *briefly comprehended* in this saying, namely, Thou shalt love thy neighbour as thyself" (italics added). Our duties are *summed up* in the law of love.

God intends to sum everything up in Christ—everything in Heaven and on earth. Satan's rebellion brought in contamination. God's answer to the contamination is Christ. Satan no longer has his home in Heaven, although as the accuser of the brethren (Revelation 12:10) it would seem that he has admittance there. But Satan does have a hold on the heavens as "the prince of the power of the air" (Ephesians 2:2). In that sphere we as God's children, indwelt by His Holy Spirit, join the battle against Satan and his hosts. The Lord intends to clean up that sphere when He comes, just as He intends to clean up things here on earth.

Isaiah 24:21 casts a flood of light on this clean-up: "And it shall come to pass in that day, that the Lord shall punish the host of the high ones that are on high, and the kings of the earth upon the earth." The "high ones that are on high" are Satan's spirit rulers of this world's darkness, his principalities and powers, the wicked spirits in high places who lord it over the heavenlies and hold this world in bondage. All these will be cast down when Christ returns.

In Revelation 12:7-9 we learn that Michael the archangel will be sent to make war on Satan and his angels and to cast them down from the heavenlies. Satan will lose control over this sphere and will be confined to earth—to Heaven's rejoicing, his rage, and mankind's ruin (12:10-12). The kings of the earth who live on the earth will be dealt with at Armageddon (16:12-16; 19:11-21).[4]

During the millennial reign of Christ on earth, the believers of this present age—those who comprise the church, the body of Christ, and who are God's heavenly people—will reign with Christ on high. Our place will be in the heavenlies; our home will be the heavenly Jerusalem. From the heavenlies, we shall exercise enormous power and authority over the earth. In other words, we will be seated where Satan now sits as usurper. We will exercise for God a power for good on the earth just as Satan and his hosts today exert relentless power for evil.

In the same way and at the same time, Gentile world rule will end and the Jews (God's people) will replace the Gentiles in all the seats of power. The Lord Jesus will sit on the throne of David in Jerusalem; the twelve apostles will sit on twelve thrones and judge the twelve tribes of Israel; the Jews will govern the nations for God.

Such will be "the dispensation of the fulness of times," as Paul called it in Ephesians 1:10. Things will be summed up in Christ indeed.

(b) For the Christian (1:11) "In whom also we have obtained an inheritance, being predestinated according to the purpose of him who worketh all things after the counsel of his own will."

John Graham of Claverhouse was known as "Bonnie Dundee" and won his spurs as a handsome soldier of fortune in France and the Netherlands. He then led a Scottish uprising to support the deposed Roman Catholic monarch, James II of Britain.

On his return to Scotland he was made captain of the dragoons and was sent to suppress the Presbyterian Covenanters fighting for the right to worship God according to their own consciences. The Covenanters, however, came from a fighting breed. When the Claverhouse cavalry tried to break up one of their meetings, the Covenanters turned on their enemies and soundly defeated them. The enraged Claverhouse returned three weeks later and thrashed the Covenanters at Bothwell Bridge.

Scotland then experienced a wretched time. Claverhouse sent his dragoons to comb the heather and search the moss-hags for outlawed preachers. Some they shot on sight. Others they hauled to prison and treated with utmost barbarity. Not a week passed without the name of "Bloody Claverhouse," as he was called, being roundly cursed by Covenanters.

The Covenanters met for worship where they could—in dens, on the hills, in hideouts. One day a Scottish lass was making her way to one such meeting, following by-paths through the heather, when she was overtaken by a troop of Dundee's dragoons. The leader demanded to know where she was going so early on a Sunday morning. She knew her danger and the danger she posed to her fellow saints if she told the truth. But she could not lie. She looked the captain in the eye. "Sir," she said, "My Elder Brother has died and they're reading his will, ye ken. I want to be there to see what he has left for me."

It's great to have an inheritance, to be remembered in someone's will. Paul said that in Christ we have obtained an inheritance. Peter said that our inheritance is incorruptible and undefiled, that it will not fade away, and that it is reserved in Heaven for us (1 Peter 1:4). Paul told the Corinthians: "Eye hath not seen, nor ear heard, neither have entered into the heart of man, the things which God hath prepared for them that love him" (1 Corinthians 2:9).

From all eternity, God has had our well-being in mind. His eternal purpose was to bring into existence human beings upon whom He could bestow all the inexhaustible riches of His grace. No small part of that "counsel of his own will" is still in the future as far as we are concerned. What God has in store for us is beyond anything we can imagine. We find ourselves yearning for it at times with deep soul-longings that are beyond all utterance. We catch occasional, fleeting glimpses of that "sweet bye and bye" in a passage or two of Scripture, such as those in the closing chapters of the Apocalypse, although the reality will be far better, as Paul put it in Philippians 1:23. In the meantime we can rest assured that God has taken care of our inheritance. That part of our salvation is included in God's predestinating will.

(4) Rejoicing (1:12) "That we should be to the praise of his glory, who first trusted in Christ."

The Lord Himself gives us our first glimpse of rejoicing in Heaven. He tells us in His peerless parable of the Good Shepherd that when He finds His lost sheep, He brings it home rejoicing. So:

> All thro' the mountains, thunder riv'n,
> And up from the rocky steep,

There arose a glad cry to the gate of heav'n,
"Rejoice! I have found my sheep!"
And the angels echoed around the throne,
"Rejoice, for the Lord brings back His own!"
(Elizabeth C. Clephane)

As though the story of the lost sheep were not sufficient emphasis, the Lord then added the parables of the lost coin and the prodigal son. "They began to be merry" is the Lord's own description of the feast that was spread when the prodigal returned home (Luke 15:24). Music and dancing, the robe, the ring, and the fatted calf all contributed to the joyful celebration.

Not only do we have an inheritance in Christ; He has an inheritance in us and all Heaven joins in songs of happiness and praise over that. Just think, our salvation sets the joy bells of Heaven ringing and they echo in the everlasting hills. Our conversion causes joyful commotion in Heaven because the salvation of a sinner brings satisfaction to the Savior and glory to God. Eternal ages will be far too short to sing His praise and those anthems will never cease.

c. The Witness of the Spirit (1:13-14)

(1) His Word: A Witness to the Christ (1:13a) "In whom ye also trusted, after that ye heard the word of truth, the gospel of your salvation."

Paul was recalling his first cordial reception in the synagogue by the rabbis and the congregation and the division that followed when some trusted Christ after they heard the word of truth. Then revival broke out among the Gentiles, attracting the attention of the whole city, and Paul diligently went from house to house until he could say he was pure of all men's blood (Acts 20:26). The people in Ephesus to whom he was writing were the fruit of this ministry. The Holy Spirit had taken the gospel of Christ—the word of truth—and had so powerfully used it to witness to the Lord Jesus that multitudes had been saved.

Nobody can be saved apart from the word of truth. Human cleverness, persuasiveness, or eloquence cannot save souls, nor can oratory in the pulpit or artistry in the choir. God has not promised to bless programs or performances. He always blesses His Word. The witness of the Spirit is to the Son of God by means of the Word of God. Along the way God uses other vehicles, but His chosen channels for bringing light to an individual's soul and conviction to his conscience are His church and His saints who share His Word.

(2) His Work: A Witness to the Christian (1:13b-14)

(a) The Proof of Our Faith (1:13b) "In whom also after that ye
     believed, ye were sealed with that holy Spirit of promise."

Sealed! What a comforting word. It suggests a finished transaction, absolute assurance, eternal security.

An illustration of God's sealing is found in Revelation 7 where we read that during the postrapture judgment age 144,000 chosen Hebrew witnesses will be sealed by God to bear worldwide witness to the gospel of the kingdom. The beast—the devil's messiah—will be enraged, but he will not be able to harm them because they are sealed. They will spread the gospel from shore to shore with astonishing speed, and countless millions of Gentiles will be saved. These witnesses, a special and privileged company of God's people, will then be translated to Heaven (Revelation 14). The seal of God will have kept them safe. The beast's seal, marked in the flesh of his followers, seems to be a Satanic imitation of God's seal on the hearts of His people.

In this age we are sealed by the Holy Spirit—sealed not to escape life's perils and persecutions, but sealed against any possibility of losing our salvation after we respond to the word of truth, which is the gospel of salvation.

Seals are not used much these days except when a company uses its corporate seal to make documents official. Years ago, however, seals were commonly used. When I was starting out in the business world, I worked for a large multinational British bank. In those days when contracting parties entered into a legal agreement, the documents were "signed, sealed, and delivered." On numerous occasions the bank manager called for the sealing wax. Both contracting parties would sign the documents and the bank manager would sign as a witness. Then he would affix the heated sealing wax to the documents. After being signed and sealed, the documents were "delivered" to the contracting parties. The agreement, ratified by the seal, was then in force and was binding on all parties.

In a sense, salvation is a legal document. The Holy Spirit spells out the terms of the agreement in the "word of truth, the gospel of your salvation." In that gospel, everything is linked to Christ and His shed blood. The Holy Spirit makes it clear that our salvation is free and will last forever. All the doing has been done. All we have to do is by faith accept the Lord Jesus Christ as our personal Savior and Lord.

God has already signed the contract in the name of Jesus. The glorious name of Jesus is prominent everywhere: "Thou shalt call his name Jesus: for he shall save his people from their sins" (Matthew 1:21);

"Neither is there salvation in any other: for there is none other name under heaven given among men, whereby we must be saved" (Acts 4:12); "Whosoever shall call upon the name of the Lord shall be saved" (Romans 10:13).

When we hear the gospel, the Holy Spirit reveals God's terms of salvation to us, convicts us of our sin, and urges us to accept Christ— the One in whom God's offer of salvation centers. When we personally accept God's terms of salvation by receiving Christ as Savior, we in effect put our names on the contract. Immediately God applies the seal. He seals us with the "holy Spirit of promise." He gives us the Holy Spirit.

The gift of the Holy Spirit is God's seal on the document of salvation. He has signed it; we have signed it. The agreement is sealed; the contract of unconditional salvation goes into effect and is binding on all parties. Since God does all the doing, no failure on our part (all failure having been anticipated long, long ago) can invalidate the contract.

In my banking days, the manager would usually deliver the original contract to a bank officer who would place it in the vault for safekeeping. Everything that could be done was done to ensure that the contract was preserved and its terms were put into effect. We can rest assured that God has taken every precaution against His promise ever being broken. As far as we are concerned, God has sealed us with that Holy Spirit of promise. Our salvation is as certain as God's character and throne can make it.

(b) The Pledge of our Future (1:14) "Which is the earnest of our inheritance until the redemption of the purchased possession, unto the praise of his glory."

The Holy Spirit is not only the seal; He is also the earnest. He is not only the proof of our position in Christ; He is also the pledge of our possessions in Christ. He not only confirms our faith; He also confirms our future. He not only guarantees our eternal security; He also guarantees our eternal satisfaction.

We do not use the old-fashioned word *earnest* anymore in ordinary conversation, but real estate agents still use it in some business transactions. When my wife and I first came to the United States, we wanted to buy a house. The real estate agent showed us a number of homes, and we finally found a suitable one in our price range. We made our offer, and then the agent said, "I will need some earnest money." We had never heard that expression before and asked him what it meant.

"Well," he said, "I am going to take your offer to the owner of the house so that he can decide if he wants to accept it. I will need your check for one thousand dollars to show him that you are in earnest about this offer. Your check will prove to him that you really mean business and that you are not going to back out halfway through the deal." The check I wrote that day was not for the full amount of the offer. In fact it was only a token amount. I would have to pay much more money when it was time to complete the deal.

Similarly the Holy Spirit is the earnest of our inheritance as Christians. God gives the Holy Spirit to each believer as evidence that He is in earnest about our salvation. He means business. He is not going to back out. And there is much more to come. The great transaction is underway but is not yet completed. We are still waiting for the rest of it—"the redemption of the purchased possession."

Opinions differ over what Paul meant by the "purchased possession." Doubtlessly it includes the redemption of the body. One day we will have bodies "like unto his glorious body" (Philippians 3:21)—bodies free from disease, disability, defilement, and death. The believer's new body will be controlled by a human spirit that is fully yielded to the Holy Spirit. It will be a body in which the supernatural will be as normal as the natural.

The "purchased possession" may refer to this world, which is now under the curse but will one day be brought into the glorious liberty of the children of God (Romans 8:21). The glowing Old Testament promises of a global paradise will all be fulfilled at the second coming of Christ. God has no intention of leaving this world in its present ruined condition. The book of Ruth teaches us that our kinsman-redeemer has purchased not only the believer's person, but also his property.

The "purchased possession" may be the church. No one has ever seen the church as it exists in God's mind and heart. For the most part we see Satan's counterfeit. The church is torn and divided into sects and schisms, racked by heresy, and rendered powerless through apostasy. As the book of Acts and the Pauline Epistles show, it did not take long for dissensions and distortions to appear in the early church. The true church, however, is God's masterpiece. One day it will be displayed as such "unto the praise of his glory."

The "purchased possession" may include all of these and much more besides. In any case, the Holy Spirit is the earnest of it all. That alone should tell us how magnificent God's full and ultimate reality for us is going to be, and it will all be to the praise of God's glory. God always has an eye on His glory. That is the key to all hermeneutics, to all of God's eternal purposes. The unifying factor is God's glory.[5]

Thus Paul ended the first segment of this remarkable Epistle. He showed us where we stand. He dealt with basic principles: the will of the Father, the work of the Son, and the witness of the Spirit. And he left us nearly breathless with the wonder of it all, wanting to pray and praise God for His goodness and grace. Paul himself went on to pray, as we see in the next segment.

2. Why We Stand: Believing Prayer (1:15-23)

a. A Church-centered Prayer (1:15-16)

(1) The Cause of It (1:15)

(a) Paul Had Heard How They Trusted the Savior (1:15a) "After I heard of your faith in the Lord Jesus."

We must remember that this Epistle was most likely a circular letter. It was not just intended for the church at Ephesus where Paul knew most of the believers well. (Many of them had been won to Christ during his three-year stay in their city.) The letter was also intended for other churches springing up in the surrounding area. Although most of the believers in these churches would be strangers to Paul, he could properly speak of having heard of their faith in the Lord Jesus Christ.

Other people's converts were as precious to Paul as his own and after hearing of their faith, Paul began to pray for them. They too had come into the enjoyment of all the magnificent blessings he had just described. He poured out his heart in prayer for them, and what a model prayer this is! Because Paul was in prison, he could not visit these new converts, but he could write to them and pray for them. The devil had as much reason to fear Paul's prayers as he had to fear Paul's preaching and Paul's pen.

(b) Paul Had Heard How They Treated the Saints (1:15b) "And love unto all the saints."

Most of the Lord's people find it easy to love some of the saints, but it is not so easy to love all of the saints. How do we love the saints who disagree with us—saints who hold doctrinal positions radically different from our own? What about the saints whose dispositions and temperaments are the opposite of ours? And how do we love the saints whose culture clashes with ours?

It was easy for Paul to love Timothy—his son in the faith, his most ardent admirer and helper. It was also easy to love Luke, his physician. It was not too difficult to love Peter, even though he must have irritated Paul sometimes. On one occasion Paul had found it necessary to confront Peter face to face; yet there was much that was lovable about bighearted, impulsive Peter. But one wonders how easy it was for Paul to love James, who was stern, ascetic, legalistic, and narrow-minded.

Paul loved God's people, and his love was infectious. The believers at Ephesus had caught it, and so had their converts. Paul was delighted to hear that their love was overflowing to all those who loved the Lord. Love for God's people, after all, is one of the acid tests of genuine conversion. "We know that we have passed from death unto life, because we love the brethren" (1 John 3:14).

(2) The Constancy of It (1:16) I "cease not to give thanks for you, making mention of you in my prayers."

His prayers are among many evidences of Paul's love for all saints. We might wonder how he could find time to pray so consistently for such a large and growing circle of friends. His admonition to "pray without ceasing" (1 Thessalonians 5:17) strikes us as a great goal, but seems to many to be quite impractical. How did Paul find time to pray?

Paul was an active missionary—ever on the move, busy planting churches, evangelizing, soulwinning, counseling, training converts, writing letters, and planning new mission enterprises. Often he would put in a full day making tents to raise the funds he needed for his support. There he would sit with the stiff material, already cut out according to pattern, spread out before him. All he had to do was ply the needle—stitch, stitch, stitch—not an occupation calling for a great deal of mental activity. So he prayed! In and out of the cloth went the tentmaker's needle. In and out of the throne room of the universe went the great ambassador to the Gentiles.

Then, too, Paul could pray during his journeys. Driven out of Phillipi, he walked to Thessalonica, a 100-mile hike, and he prayed as he walked. Driven out of Thessalonica, he walked 40 or 50 miles to Berea. Driven out of Berea, he walked to Athens, a 250-mile hike. What precious time for prayer! Probably Paul never noticed the distances. His feet were tramping up hill and down dale, but his head was only mechanically noting the sights and sounds along the way because he was in Heaven, busy at the throne.

What an example for us! No time to pray? We could employ countless moments each day if we really cared.

b. A Christ-centered Prayer (1:17-23)

(1) Paul Wanted Them to Know More of the Person of Christ
    (1:17) "That the God of our Lord Jesus Christ, the Father of
    glory, may give unto you the spirit of wisdom and revelation in
    the knowledge of him."

Paul rarely prayed for the things that loom so large in our
prayers—better health, more money, job conditions, family problems, world crises. Paul prayed that people might know God better,
that they might become better acquainted with Jesus.

Knowledge of God must come from God. Paul described Him in
Ephesians 1:17 as "the God of our Lord Jesus Christ, the Father of
glory." In 1 Corinthians 2:8 Jesus is described as "the Lord of glory."
So God the Father is the Father of glory, and God the Son is the Lord
of glory. God the Holy Spirit is the revealer of glory (1 Corinthians
2:9-11). The spirit of wisdom and revelation that gives us the
knowledge of Him must come from the Holy Spirit.

A person can only be known through a process of revelation. A
clever Sherlock Holmes might be able to say, "Elementary, my dear
Watson," and proceed to produce a string of startling facts about
another person, but a process of reasoning cannot go much further
than that. Through reasoning we can learn *about* another person.
But if we are ever to know that person, that person must *reveal*
himself—show what he is like through words and actions, express
his thoughts and feelings, hopes and ambitions, likes and dislikes,
frustrations and fears, wants and wishes. Reason takes us just so far
on the road to knowing another person; self-revelation is essential
if we are to go farther.

Likewise God can be known in small measure through the
evidence we have of Him in creation—"even his eternal power and
Godhead," as Paul put it in Romans 1:20. We can know about God,
but we can only know Him in all the glory of His personality as He
reveals Himself to us.

He has revealed Himself in two ways—in the inspired Word and
the incarnate Word. He has *said* what He is like in the one, and He
has *shown* what He is like in the other. Our responsibility is to get to
know Him by getting to know the Scriptures and the Savior. There
is no greater or grander occupation here on earth.

Paul prayed that his fellow believers might have a spirit of wisdom
and revelation and that they might be occupied in gaining knowledge of God. "Get to know Him" is Paul's basic answer to all of life's
problems and perplexities. Knowing God would solve most of the

present-day problems that cause people to run to the psychologist or the family counselor. Knowing God would affect how people cope with all areas of life.

(2) Paul Wanted Them to Know More of the Portion of Christ (1:18)

(a) Our Hope Is in Him (1:18a) "The eyes of your understanding being enlightened; that ye may know what is the hope of his calling."

We enter into the "hope of his calling" by faith. That calling has its commencement in the council chambers of the living God in eternity past (Ephesians 1:4); it has its continuance in our coming to know Christ as Savior and the Holy Spirit as Comforter (1:13); and it has its completion in Heaven (1:14).

The "hope of his calling" embraces the wide sweep of God's eternal purposes in Christ. Our hope is in Him. We have not merely hitched our wagon to a star. We have been caught up in something so big, so basic to the universe, and so far beyond anything we could ask or think, that our minds simply cannot take it all in. No wonder Paul prayed that the eyes of our understanding might be enlightened.

We have become the objects of the triune God's attention and affection. Father, Son, and Holy Spirit are each interested in us and our eternal well-being. They have turned aside from their occupation with the details of the hundred billion galaxies to concentrate on us. Angels and archangels, cherubim and seraphim, "thrones and dominions" desire to look into these things (1 Peter 1:12). The sinless sons of light find human life more interesting than galactic life.

When God's Beloved stooped down from Heaven's heights to be born in that Bethlehem barn for us, it was an event so momentous that Heaven's hosts crowded down the skyways and starways to peer in wonder into that musty manger, adore the newborn babe, and shout the tidings across Judea's echoing hills. And God has not finished with us yet! Our hope in Him stretches out beyond our threescore and ten years to the endless ages of eternity. What awaits us on the other side is more than tongue can tell.

Paul wanted us to be occupied with thoughts about our hope in Christ. They help us put the mundane things of time and sense into perspective. Here is that fulcrum outside the earth for which Archimedes longed. Here is that lever, long enough to exert the pressure needed so that one lone Man could lift the whole wide world.

(b) His Heritage Is in Us (1:18b) "The riches of the glory of his inheritance in the saints."

God gets something out of our salvation too! What we get out of it defies description; what He gets out of it transcends comprehension. What we get is Him. What He gets is us. A poor bargain for Him, it would seem. But evidently He considered us eminently worth saving. The only explanation is His amazing, divine love—a love that is its own reason and logic.

We note the *fact* of His inheritance. Paul spoke of His inheritance in the saints; He has no inheritance in the sinner. His redemptive work gives us our value, which must be measured in terms of Christ's precious blood.

We note the *fame* of His inheritance. Paul spoke of the glory of His inheritance. It is the theme of seraph song, the wonder of all wonders in a land specializing in glory.

We note the *fullness* of His inheritance. Paul spoke of the riches of the glory. In some wondrous way we have become a source of untold wealth in the balance sheets of Heaven. We are assets of incredible worth to the living God—the brightest jewels in His diadem.

Such is the portion of Christ. We cannot understand it and can scarcely take it in. We can only marvel that the Holy Spirit tells us these things are so.

(3) Paul Wanted Them to Know More of the Power of Christ (1:19-21)

(a) The Direction of It (1:19a) "The exceeding greatness of his power to us-ward who believe."

We see something of the surpassing greatness of God's power when we turn our giant telescopes toward the sky. Our sun for instance is rated a star of only the fifth magnitude. It shines with a mild, yellow light and is 100,000 times less luminous than its brightest neighbor. Nevertheless the sun evokes our awe. It is 864,000 miles in diameter, consists of some 335 quadrillion cubic miles of violently hot gases, and weighs more than 2 octillion tons. It orbits the center of our galaxy, the Milky Way, once every 200 million years.

With the naked eye we can see only about 7,000 stars. The Milky Way, however, contains about 100 billion orbiting stars and is 100,000 light-years in diameter—an inconceivable 600 million billion miles of stars!

Astronomer Edwin Hubble calculated that there are as many galaxies outside the Milky Way as there are stars in it. Since the galaxies are moving farther and farther away from earth, the entire visible universe is expanding in every direction. The distance between the Milky Way and Hydra—a group of distant galaxies that are "as thick as raisins" and some 2.7 billion light-years away—is increasing at a speed of 38,000 miles per second. The Hydra galaxies are receding, in other words, at one-fifth the speed of light. Such is the exceeding greatness of God's power in the macrouniverse.

We see something of that power, too, in the microuniverse. Atoms are less than one-millionth of the thickness of a human hair. In the nucleus of the atom, numerous protons and neutrons are packed together in an inconceivably small space. Each proton and neutron consists of three even smaller particles called quarks. If a hydrogen atom were four miles in diameter, the nucleus would only be the size of a tennis ball! The remainder of the atom is mostly empty space in which electrons travel around the nucleus, making billions of trips each millionth of a second. Their incredible speed makes the atom behave as though it were solid. Facts such as these make our minds reel, but such is the exceeding greatness of God's power.

We see the exceeding greatness of His power *skyward* and *earthward.* In the redemptive process we see the exceeding greatness of His power *"us-ward."* It took as much power to effect our redemption as it did to effect creation. To create, God only had to speak. To redeem, He had to suffer. A seemingly endless universe is the demonstration of the one; an empty tomb is the evidence of the other. Paul reminded us here of the direction of God's immeasurable power. It is "to us-ward who believe." There's no excuse for any child of God to live a defeated, discouraged life. All the power of the godhead is directed toward us.

The book of Esther contains an illustration of directed power. Under the urging of Mordecai, Queen Esther agreed to approach the imperious King Ahasuerus on behalf of the Jews who were under dire threat of extermination. To approach this despotic monarch unbidden was to court death—even for Esther. Nevertheless, Esther walked that knife-edge of uncertainty. Arrayed in her royal robes, she approached and then stopped within sight of the king. "And it was so, when the king saw Esther the queen standing in the court, that she obtained favour in his sight: and the king held out to Esther the golden sceptre that was in his hand. So Esther drew near, and touched the top of the sceptre" (Esther 5:2).

All the power of the throne was suddenly turned toward Esther.

From then on, step by step, the power of that throne was exerted on her behalf and on behalf of her people. That is what has happened to us who believe. We have all the power of God who sits on the throne of Heaven directed toward us.

(b) The Dimensions of It (1:19b) "The working of his mighty power."

The Greek word translated "power" here, *kratos*, means "strength or power put forth with effect." We catch echoes of this word in several English words: "aristocracy" (government by the best), "democracy" (government by the people), and "theocracy" (government by God). The Greek word translated "might" is *ischus*, which means "strength as an endowment." *Ischus* is physical strength such as that mentioned in Mark 12:30: "Thou shalt love the Lord thy God with all thy heart, and with all thy soul, and with all thy mind, and with all thy strength." The word translated "working" is *energeia*, which means "strength put forth, energy." God made an enormous expenditure of His strength, power, and energy in the work of the cross and the subsequent emptying of the tomb in order to redeem us from sin.

(c) The Demonstration of It (1:20a) "Which he wrought in Christ, when he raised him from the dead."

Men had done their worst! They had beaten Christ until His face was scarcely recognizable and scourged Him until His back was as furrowed as a farmer's field. They had crowned Him with thorns so that blood ran in rivers down His head. They had wrenched His beard. Then they nailed Him to a wooden cross and hung Him up to die. Every bone in His body was out of joint; sheer physical exhaustion and raging thirst levied their toll. Agonizing minutes crept on until, after six hours of torment, He imperially dismissed His Spirit, bowed His head, and died. To make sure He was dead, a soldier took a spear and stabbed Him.

Christ was taken down from the cross. Loving hands bathed His mortal remains and swathed them in spices and bandages, layer upon layer. His body was put into a rock-hewn tomb and the entrance, closed with a massive stone, was secured with the Roman governor's seal. Then a guard was detailed to patrol the site and keep intruders away. That was that! Christ was dead and buried— or so men thought.

Soon it would be safe to remove the guard. The natural process of corruption and decay was at work. A little longer and the much-feared three days to His foretold resurrection would have come and gone. Then Jesus could be written off as a notable impostor. His story would be interred in the rubbish heap of history. Christ's claim to be God manifest in flesh would never survive the dissolution of His body in the tomb.

The hours passed slowly. His enemies bet that Christ would not rise again and that the Jesus movement would collapse. But God on His throne in Heaven was laughing and Christ was proclaiming His triumph to the souls of the departed in Hades. His body lay in stately grandeur on its granite slab, quietly sleeping, defying the ordinary processes of death.

Then when the third day dawned, Christ burst the bands of death, rose bodily through the hampering graveclothes, and marched out in the power of an endless life through the sealed door of the tomb. With a wild yell of mortal terror the soldiers fled for Jerusalem. Christ's resurrection appearances began, and the empty tomb became the evidence that He did rise again. Raising Jesus from the dead was the demonstration of God's energy.

(d) The Distinction of It (1:20b-21)

i. All Seats of Power Are Beneath Him (1:20b-21b)

a. Where He Is Seated (1:20b) God "set him at his own right hand in the heavenly places."

The same mighty power that raised Christ from the tomb would now raise Him to the heavenly throne. He stood there for a moment on Olivet to say a final fond farewell to those He had come to redeem, to look one last time into the faces of Peter, James, John, Thomas, Matthew, Philip, Andrew, Nathanael, and the rest of the disciples. He gazed one last time into the face of His beloved mother who now had joined the ranks of His own. Then raising His hands He summoned the angel escort and slowly rose toward the sky. The clouds wrapped around Him, the earth receded, the starry hosts rolled past in grand array, Heaven's gates appeared, and in He went.

Amid the hallelujahs of Heaven He made His way along the streets of gold, across the crystal stream, and up to the very throne of God. Then in a battle-scarred body of transfigured human clay, He sat down at the right hand of the Majesty on high.

That is where He is seated still, all other seats of power beneath Him. Around that throne are twenty-four other thrones, but those who sit on them cast their crowns before Him. At the four corners of His throne stand the four living creatures who only exist to sing His praise. Myriads of angels who fill Heaven's halls with ceaseless songs, hang on His words and rush to do His will.

b.   What He Has Subdued (1:21a-b)

1.   All Spiritual Seats of Power (1:21a) "Far above all principality, and power, and might, and dominion."

Principalities and powers are Satan's allies. Angelic beings of enormous power, they help him hold fast to his domains in the spirit world. They are his agents too in holding the world of men in subjection to him (Ephesians 6:12).

Sin did not begin on earth; it began in Heaven. Sin did not originate with the fall of man, but with the fall of Lucifer. Revelation 12 suggests that Satan's rebellion infected a third of the heavenly hosts. But not all the angels fell when Satan fell. The word *dominion* in Ephesians 1:21 may refer to the angelic rulers in the spirit world who side with God in the age-long battle against sin. *Might* and *dominion* here and *thrones* and *dominions* in Colossians 1:16 probably refer to the same ruling powers, and the thrones are probably the same as those mentioned in Revelation 4:4.

The Lord Jesus is enthroned far above all spiritual seats of power. Satan is no match for Him. Satan's hosts cannot hope to win. All they can do now is put on a brave show. As for Heaven's ruling hierarchy, they gladly acknowledge the vastness of the gulf that separates them from Christ by casting their crowns at His feet.

2.   All Secular Seats of Power (1:21b) "And every name that is named."

Whatever forms of government there are and whatever the names or titles of those in power may be, all are subject to Christ. Earthly kingdoms and empires wax and wane, coming and going like ocean tides. Christ reigns on high and overrules them all. All who govern must learn the lesson God taught Nebuchadnezzar: "The heavens do rule" (Daniel 4:26).

Babylonian despot or Persian satrap, Greek conqueror or Roman caesar, pope or prince, holy Roman emperor or Muslim sultan, British monarch or German dictator, American president or Russian commissar—all must learn that "the powers that be are ordained of God" (Romans 13:1). God has set *His* king on His holy hill of Zion. No power in Heaven, earth, or Hell can alter that. All secular seats of power are subservient to His.

Why has the invincible sovereign power that now rests wholly in Christ's hands seemingly been held back? That is part of the mystery of an age of grace.

ii.   All Spheres of Power Are Before Him (1:21c) "Not only in this world, but also in that which is to come."

In this age where sin abounds, grace much more abounds (Romans 5:20). Because we are living in an age of grace, injustice often seems to triumph and the abuse of power often goes unchecked. God deliberately holds back His arm of omnipotence—to the puzzlement of many thoughtful people. A young soldier on active duty with me asked, "Why doesn't God stop this terrible war?" My answer was glib: "Why should He? He didn't start it." But the truth is, He could have averted the war or stopped it, but He didn't because this is not the age of intervention.

An even greater mystery revolved around the cross. I think it was Archbishop Trench who said:

> He might have built a palace at a word,
> Who sometime had not where to lay His head;
> Time was when He who nourished crowds with bread
> Could not one meal unto Himself afford.
> Twelve legions girded with angelic sword
> Were at His back, the scorned and buffeted;
> He healed another's hurts, His own side bled,
> Side, feet and hands with cruel piercing gored.
> Oh wonderful the wonders left undone!
> And scarce less wonderful than those He wrought:
> Oh, self restraint, passing all human thought,
> To have all-power and be as having none;
> Oh, self-denying love, which felt alone
> For needs of others, never for its own.

If God stayed His hand at Calvary when twelve legions of angels arrayed for battle strained over the battlements of Heaven with drawn swords, it is no wonder that He stays His hand today. This is not "the day of vengeance of our God." The Lord Jesus made that abundantly clear when in the Nazareth synagogue He broke off His Scripture reading in the middle of a sentence (Luke 4:18-19; Isaiah 61:1-2). This is God's day of grace and man's day of opportunity.

The day will come, however, when His power will be displayed. Man's day will end and the day of the Lord will begin. Then it will be evident that the Lord Jesus is seated "above all principality, and power, and might, and dominion, and every name that is named."

(4) Paul Wanted Them to Know More of the Position of Christ (1:22-23)

(a) Paul Wanted Us to Consider the Lord's Feet (1:22a) "And hath put all things under his feet."

There is something gloriously appropriate in these words from Ephesians 1:22, since men once pierced His feet. Christ will put His feet on the necks of His enemies and the earth will be His footstool.

When John the beloved disciple saw the Lord he loved in all the splendor of His unveiled glory and majesty—His face shining like the sun, His feet glowing like burnished brass, His eyes flaming like fire—he fell at His feet as if dead! If such was the reaction of His closest human friend on earth, what will happen to His foes when they see Him? What about Caiaphas, the self-seeking, cynical high priest who so dreadfully disgraced what should have been the highest and holiest office in the land and used his position to manipulate Christ's unjust trial and bring about His death? What about Herod, who with his soldiers scoffed at Jesus? What about Pilate, who signed the death warrant of a man he knew was innocent? What about the man who punched Him in the face and said, "Prophesy unto us, thou Christ, Who is he that smote thee?" (Matthew 26:68) What about all the people who have cursed His name, spurned His grace, refused His salvation, or done despite to the Spirit of grace? They, like Satan, are under His feet. Christ will yet trample on that old serpent and crush his head.

(b) Paul Wanted Us to Consider the Lord's Fullness (1:22b-23)

i. The Church Finds All Its Fullness in Him, the Head (1:22b) "And gave him to be the head over all things to the church."

When many people think of the church, they think of the vast, organized system of religion that emerged in the second or third centuries of the Christian era. That system became the state religion of the Roman empire and today is represented by the Roman Catholic and Eastern Orthodox churches and the various Protestant denominations. This vast conglomeration is not the church; it is *Christendom*.

The *church*, on the other hand, consists of blood-bought saints of God who have put their personal faith in the Lord Jesus, who have been baptized by the Holy Spirit into the body of Christ, and who are now indwelt by Him. That is the church. Its members are found in all parts of Christendom. It knows no denominational boundaries. It is not limited by race or creed, color or class, time or space. (More of its members now live in Heaven than on earth.) Its unity is not an organizational unity, but an organic unity. The church is universal, mystical, invincible.

Christ, who is head over all things in the universe, is head over all things in the church. He is in Heaven, seated on high, enthroned at God's right hand. The head of the church is what gives the church its dignity and destiny. Members of the true church find their fullness in their relationship to the head.

ii.   The Christ Finds All His Fullness in Us, the Body (1:23) "Which is his body, the fulness of him that filleth all in all."

This statement should make us gasp. Indeed, we would consider such a statement to be blasphemy or the word of a madman if it were found anywhere but in the Bible. But this is the Word of the Holy Spirit, written in the Word of the living God.

We cannot comprehend this statement or exhaust it. It is God's solemn word that the Lord Jesus—who fills all in all, who is higher than the high, who conceived and created the universe through His omniscient and omnipotent power, who is the object of angelic worship and the ceaseless theme of seraph song—is incomplete without us. We can understand that we are incomplete without Him, but that He should be incomplete without us is incomprehensible.

This incompleteness is not a trivial thing, as when a man who dresses for a formal occasion forgets his top hat. Christ is as incomplete without us as a head would be without its body.

---

1. R. A. Laidlaw, "The Reason Why" (New York: Loizeaux, revised 1959), 31-32.
2. Liddell and Scott, quoted by Kenneth Wuest, *Ephesians and Colossians in the Greek New Testament* (Grand Rapids: Eerdmans, 1953), 42.
3. See Wuest, 42-43.
4. See John Phillips, *Exploring Revelation* (Neptune, NJ: Loizeaux, 1987).
5. See Phillips, *Bible Explorer's Guide* (Neptune, NJ: Loizeaux, 1987).

B. The Revolution of the Christian Life (2:1-22)

1. The Great Dispositional Change (2:1-10)

a. The Past (2:1-3)

(1) We Were Dead (2:1) "And you hath he quickened, who were dead in trespasses and sins."

This statement only deepens the mystery of God's dealings in grace. Those who are "the fulness of him that filleth all in all" were once "dead in trespasses and sins."

We were not just dead; we were dead in trespasses. The Greek word translated "trespasses" is *paratōma*, which means "a falling aside when one should have stood upright." This word conveys the idea of falling aside from truth and uprightness and is used to describe Adam's disobedience (Romans 5:15-18). The law was introduced so that this form of sin, *paratōma*, might be thought of as criminal in the mind of the sinner—just as it is in the mind of God.

We were also dead in sins. The word translated "sins" is derived from *hamartono*, which means "to miss the mark, to wander from the right path, to go wrong, to do wrong." Sin entered the world when Adam fell (Romans 5:12).

The natural consequence of falling aside, of missing the mark, was death. Thus, in our natural state, God sees us as dead in trespasses and sins.

When a man sets out to make something, he usually starts with the best possible materials—the purest clay, the finest marble, the choicest wood. But God goes to the refuse heap and selects materials that are worthless. He begins with people who are dead!

It is amazing what modern medicine can do for a patient. Doctors can remodel disfigured faces, transplant kidneys, implant lenses, bypass arteries—as long as the patient is alive. Once the person is dead, doctors can do nothing more than pull a sheet over the body and transfer the corpse to the morgue. But God begins with people who are dead in the fullest sense of the word—dead in trespasses and sins.

(2) We Were Deluded (2:2a) "Wherein in time past ye walked
according to the course of this world, according to the prince of
the power of the air."

Before we accepted Christ as Savior, our utter deadness to
spiritual things was evident in our behavior. We walked according
to "the course of this world." In other words, the spirit of the age
held us in its iron grip.

The word translated "course" is *aion*. This means an age or a period
of time during which certain things happen or a certain spirit or
attitude prevails. We live in a world that always displays a spirit of
hostility toward God. Whether the prevailing mentality is one of
adventure, persecution, discovery, or tolerance, the general spirit
will be worldly, fleshly, and devilish. Why? Because this world is the
sworn enemy of God. The Bible warns of this enmity repeatedly: "If
any man love the world, the love of the Father is not in him" (1 John
2:15). John summarized the spirit of the world as "the lust of the
flesh, and the lust of the eyes, and the pride of life" (2:16). The spirit
of the age is determined by the spirit of the world.

Once we walked according to the spirit of the age and our noblest
thoughts, our most generous impulses, our loftiest ambitions, and
our most religious aspirations were utterly devoid of spiritual
content. We were dead. The spirit of the air also had a hold on us.

The Bible clearly says that there are spirits in the unseen world of
the air. These spirits are fallen, malignant, and bitterly hostile to
man, and they are ruled by the dread prince of the power of the air.
This dark lord, who roams the heavenlies, is Satan. He is the one
who brings evil influences to bear upon the world of men. Our state
of spiritual death was demonstrated by the fact that we walked
according to the spirit of the power of the air. Satan had such
complete control over us that his influence was as all-encompassing
as the air. The air is all about us. It exerts constant but unnoticed
pressure on us. It can at times be felt, but in its essence it is invisible
and intangible. Such is Satan and his influence on the human race.

The reference to "the prince of the power of the air" in Ephesians
2:2 is deliberate and definitive. The Holy Spirit, who is Himself
likened to the wind (John 3:8), uses the title to depict Satan and his
sphere.

In our unregenerate state, we were completely deceived by Satan.
We walked according to the course *(aion)* of this world and according to the spirit of the power of the air. We were so devoid of spiritual
life that we were unaware of our deadness to spiritual things. The
fact that people are spiritually dead explains much that goes on in

the name of religion, philosophy, science, culture, and education even to this day.

Paul borrowed the terminology of the Gnostic heretics to expose who was really behind their anti-Christian ideas. The Gnostics taught that the universe was ruled by *aeōns,* emanations of deity. The prince *(archōn)* of the power *(exousia)* of the air ruled the air. The whole body of *aeōns* made up the fullness *(pleroma)* of the spirit world. These, according to the Gnostics, were the ultimate realities and they stood in contrast with the material world. The strength of Gnostic teaching lay in the fact that, although false and deadly in its hostility to Christianity, it was not altogether void of some vestiges of truth. All subtle doctrinal error contains a mixture of truth and error.

(3) We Were Disobedient (2:2b) "The spirit that now worketh in the children of disobedience."

The force of these words is far stronger than our translation suggests. Paul was not simply saying that we were disobedient children, for the Greek word rendered "children" is derived from *huios. Huios,* meaning "a son," has special reference to one's origin, nature, and relationship to his father. Therefore Paul was saying that we were sons of the disobedient one—Satan. We had the nature and character of that evil spirit who prompts people to disobey God. Through one man's disobedience sin entered the world, so we are heirs to a disobedient spirit.

One of the first behaviors a child displays, as soon as it is able to express its developing personality, is disobedience. No one ever has to teach a child to be disobedient. Rather, a child has to be taught to obey, and the lesson has to be reinforced often. Disobedience comes naturally. Satan has an enormous advantage—our fallen natures are allied to his.

God has to overcome this disobedient spirit in man. That is one reason He took redeemed Israel to Sinai, gave them the law, and instituted an age-long course of discipline. That is why He found such delight in His Son, who did "always those things that please" the Father (John 8:29), and why in this age He commands all men everywhere to repent (Acts 17:30).

So complete are the results of the fall that we have no natural interest in obeying the gospel; our first inclination is to disobey God. Even after we accept Christ, we find it difficult to tread the path of obedience, to believe that God's will for us is "good, and acceptable, and perfect" (Romans 12:2). All too often Satan still manages to persuade us that our own way is best, and that God's will is irksome, unpleasant, and even downright dangerous. "If you let God have His way," Satan whispers, "He'll send you to serve in a leper colony," or "He'll spoil all your fun." Satan slanders God with such suggestions. Our all-wise and all-loving God would never call us to do something for which He had not adequately prepared us and given the appropriate measure of His grace.

(4) We Were Defiled (2:3a) "Among whom also we all had our conversation [manner of life] in times past in the lusts of our flesh, fulfilling the desires of the flesh and of the mind."

Before we accepted Christ, we were controlled by natural desire. Natural desire is what Paul meant by "lusts of our flesh." The word "flesh" here refers to human nature. The Greek word translated "lusts" is *epithumia,* meaning "strong desire," not necessarily evil. For instance, Jesus said, "With desire I have desired to eat this passover with you before I suffer" (Luke 22:15). Paul wrote to Timothy, "If a man desire the office of a bishop, he desireth a good work" (1 Timothy 3:1). Even in unregenerate people, natural desire may produce some commendable results and fine endeavors, though devoid of spiritual worth. But there is a dark side to human desire. Paul had this side in mind when in Ephesians 2:3 he spoke of "fulfilling the desires of the flesh and of the mind."

We were also controlled by natural depravity. Fallen human nature gravitates to low things—to gross lusts of the body and contaminating lusts of the mind. Man may seek to disguise this depravity by culture and refinement, but underneath, these lusts burn like a seething volcano that from time to time erupts to his sorrow and shame.

(5) We Were Doomed (2:3b) "And were by nature the children of wrath, even as others."

The word translated "children" here means children by natural descent. We were born of sinful parents into a sin-cursed world. We were born possessed of a bent and inherently sinful nature, and exposed to God's wrath. Fortunately for the survival of the human race, God is rich in mercy, a theme Paul later developed with great delight. The fact remains, however, that wrath was all that we deserved. Wrath filled our horizon.

Sin has clouded our ability to think clearly about the nature of God. We have only the sketchiest notion of what God's blazing holiness is like. The shining seraphim who stand before His throne know. So bright is the effulgence of His glory, the burning brightness of His being, that they hide their faces in their wings and cry,

"Holy, holy, holy!" We have no real understanding of how outraged God is by our sin, what an insult sin is to His person, or how sin fires the flames of His wrath.

Such then was our past condition. We were without God, without Christ, without hope. We were sinners by birth, by choice, and by practice. Our lot was cast in a world controlled by the evil one, and our eternal destiny was to live forever under God's wrath and curse. But the Holy Spirit does not leave the matter there.

b.   The Present (2:4-6)

(1) God's Love Shown to Us (2:4-5a)

(a) Its Richness (2:4) "But God, who is rich in mercy, for his great love wherewith he loved us."

Thank God for that "But"! The *buts* of the Bible are always arresting; they are hinges on which great issues turn. Think for instance of the *buts* in the lives of Solomon (1 Kings 11:1), Uzziah (2 Chronicles 26:15-16), and the prodigal son (Luke 15:20,22).

Paul had painted a very black picture of human depravity and divine wrath. Now this glorious "But" draws our attention to God's mercy and love.

God is rich in mercy. It would have been cold comfort merely to be informed that God is rich. He *is* rich. We will never fully know how rich He is until we arrive at our heavenly home. Then we will see how He paves the streets of His city with gold, builds walls of jasper, makes foundations blaze with precious stones, and forms gates of pearl. Ten million times ten million million worlds are His. He makes the ministers of His throne a flame of fire and sits high and lifted up on a rainbow-circled throne bathed in the ringing anthems of celestial throngs. He is rich in wisdom, rich in majesty and might, rich in glory. And he is rich in mercy! He has lavished the vast treasures of His mercy on us. Blessed be His name.

> Oh for a thousand tongues to sing
> My great Redeemer's praise,
> The glories of my God and King,
> The triumphs of His grace.
> (Charles Wesley)

And our merciful God loves us. Paul wrote not of His love, but of "his great love." Only great love could embrace the sin-sodden wretches Paul described in verses 1-3. God does not just pity us. He loves us.

The grown daughter of a man I know is an alcoholic. I was visiting his home one day when she was delivered to his door in the grip of her terrible vice. She had drunk almost an entire bottle of whiskey. Her temper was flaming and abusive. Her face was flushed, her manner belligerent, her actions violent. I thought of the young girl I had met years before—before drink laid its devilish hand on her life. I looked at the picture of the young unspoiled girl that still hung on the wall of this man's home. I pitied the poor soul with all my heart for the terrible shipwreck she had made of her life, for the ruin of her womanhood, and for her slavery to such a cruel and relentless tyrant.

Her father took her gently by the arm, ignoring her abuse. He steered her unsteady footsteps to his car. He carefully settled her in, his face drawn and his eyes filled with pain. She thrashed around, but he patiently strapped her into the seat, drove her home, and put her to bed. I pitied her; he loved her. Multiply her wretchedness by all the misery sin has wrought in this world and multiply her father's love by infinity. Such is God's great love. He did not just pity me. He loved me. As Samuel Medley put it:

> He saw me ruined by the fall,
> Yet loved me notwithstanding all,
> He freed me from my lost estate,
> His loving kindness, oh how great!

(b) Its Reality (2:5a) "Even when we were dead in sins."

God in His great love did not shrink from us even when we were dead in sins.

Sir Henry Rider Haggard provided an illustration of such love in his novel, *Montezuma's Daughter.* His hero, Thomas Wingfield, found himself trapped among the Aztec Indians during the last stages of their empire. He married, half willingly and half by the sheer pressure of circumstances, the lovely daughter of Montezuma, the princess of the Otomie. He cared for her, admired her, and was more than half in love with her. But half his heart was far away in the England of his birth and with the sweetheart of his boyhood days.

Then the Spanish conquistadors forced the Indians into a desperate war. By virtue of his hatred of the Spaniards and his rank among the Indians, Thomas Wingfield was in the forefront of many fierce battles. The Spaniards, however, brought more than war, famine, and rapine—they brought the plague. Princess Otomie contracted it in its most terrible form, but fortunately escaped not only death but also the terrible disfigurement the plague so often left in its wake.

As her husband nursed her through her illness and ravings, he learned of the depth of her love for him and of her secret fear that he might leave her. When Otomie recovered, she asked her husband to give her a mirror and she breathed a great sigh of relief when she saw that she was still beautiful. In telling this part of his story Wingfield said:

> Supposing Otomie was now as many were . . . a mass of dreadful scars, hairless, and with blind and whitened eyeballs, should I then have shrunk from her? I do not know, and I thank heaven that no such trial was put upon my constancy. But I am sure of this; had I become a *leper* even, Otomie would not have shrunk from *me* (italics added).

God's love was put to an even greater test. He loved us when we were dead in trespasses and sins. The apostle's astonishment was expressed in that word *even*. "Even," he said, "when we were dead in sins."

(2) God's Love Shared with Us (2:5b-6)

(a) It Plucked Us from the Tomb (2:5b-6a) "Hath quickened us together with Christ, (by grace ye are saved;) And hath raised us up together."

The only thing to do with a dead person is to bury him. We have no other solution to the problem of death. The corpse can be washed and groomed, and the cosmetics and the skills of the embalmer can be employed. But the body is still a corpse, and the only place for it is the tomb.

God, however, is not daunted by death. Our trespasses and sins had brought us to the place of death, but then God acted in grace and power. He quickened us. He made us alive, plucked us from the tomb. The resurrection of Christ was the key. Since all our trespasses and sins were dealt with on the cross, when Christ arose it became possible for us to arise. God raised us from the tomb in which our trespasses and sins had placed *us*, just as He raised Christ from the tomb in which our trespasses and sins had placed *Him*. The debt was cancelled. Sin's penalty was paid. Death's hold was broken. We were quickened together with Him. Grace triumphed over guilt and the grave; God reached down into the corruption of death and raised us up.

(b) It Placed Us on the Throne (2:6b) "And made us sit together in heavenly places in Christ Jesus."

Imagine the awesome wonder of it: God has seated us on His glorious throne! In Christ we are already seated where He is. God has enveloped us in Christ so that when He looks at us, He always sees Him. No matter how or when God looks at us, He sees Christ— sees Him in all the beauty of His holiness, all the glory of His grace, and all the splendor of His person. We are like the boards of the tabernacle in the Old Testament that were hewn from gnarled, twisted acacia wood and then encased in gold. When people looked at those boards, all they saw was the gold. The same is true of us. When God looks at us, He sees Christ.

God has "made us sit together in heavenly places." If we could start at some point on earth and draw an imaginary line upward from earth to Heaven, up to where Christ sits at the right hand of God, at first we might draw our line up beyond the highest mountains. But the line would have to go higher than that. We might reach up beyond the clouds, beyond the stratosphere, beyond the radiation belts that girdle the globe. But our line would have to go still higher. We might trace the line on up until it is among the stars, climbing farther and farther into the starry heavens, leaving the Milky Way and our nearest neighbor galaxies far behind. But still we would have to go higher. At last we might leave behind the remotest star in space and cross the Great Divide between a space-matter-time dimension into an eternal, spiritual dimension. Our line might pass from star land into glory land, climbing past the shining sentinels at the gates of Heaven ever upward to the towering peak of the ultimate Zion. If we finally reached the dizzy peaks and pinnacles of glory, we would see the dazzling throne where God sits, where Christ sits, where He has "made us sit." We sit there together. This is a thought beyond all thought: He has raised us from the tomb and placed us on the throne. The verbs *quickened, raised,* and *seated* in Ephesians 2:5-6 are all in the aorist tense—it is already done.

c.   The Prospect (2:7-10)

(1)   Unstinted Grace (2:7-9)

(a)   Eternally Revealed Through Us (2:7) "That in the ages to come he might shew the exceeding riches of his grace in his kindness toward us through Christ Jesus."

Man's sin gave God the opportunity to display a side of His character that otherwise might never have been fully revealed. In His work of creation He displayed His wisdom and His power. (The more we learn about astronomy, physics, chemistry, biology, and medicine, the more we learn about God's infinite wisdom and power.) On the stage of redemption God demonstrated not just His grace, not just the riches of His grace, but the exceeding riches of His grace. As Robert C. Chapman put it:

> God is love I surely know
> By my Savior's depths of woe.

That grace will be eternally exhibited through the church—the ultimate vehicle of its expression—to an awed and admiring universe. All the varied ranks and orders of creation will see God's throne and will see Christ there, bearing in His body the scars of Calvary, the only marks of sin evident in glory. They will also see us there, trophies of God's grace.

(b) Eternally Revealed To Us (2:8-9) "For by grace are ye saved through faith; and that not of yourselves: it is the gift of God: Not of works, lest any man should boast."

Here is one of the great summaries of the gospel in the New Testament. Some argue over what the gift is, but it seems clear that it is neither grace nor faith. The gift is salvation, made available to us by God's grace and received by us through faith. Since salvation is a gift, it cannot be earned, merited, or otherwise purchased. The Holy Spirit emphasizes, "Not of works; lest any man should boast."

Suppose God were to take people to Heaven on the basis of their good works. It would then be possible for those people to boast, "I am here because I did this." "I am here because I did not do that." "I am here because of my sacrificial giving." "I am here because of my ascetic living." Boasting is an expression of pride and pride was the original sin, the sin that transformed Lucifer into Satan. Because of his pride, Satan was cast out of Heaven and the vast cycle of sin began. Boasting in Heaven about one's works would necessitate another expulsion and give rise to a fresh outbreak of sin, so God has put salvation on a basis that levels the axe at pride and completely eliminates boasting. Salvation is the gift of God. It is not of works.

Every false religion has at its heart the principle that salvation must be earned, merited, purchased at a price. The sinner must do something to deserve God's favor. The gospel strikes at the root of all false religions, for it declares that salvation is God's gift, available to sinners solely because of His grace and unmerited favor. Salvation can be obtained only by believing, but through all eternity the nail prints in Jesus' hands will remind us of the enormous cost of God's free gift.

(2) Unstunted Growth (2:10) "For we are his workmanship, created in Christ Jesus unto good works, which God hath before ordained that we should walk in them."

Good works are part of God's plan. They are not the *price* of salvation, but the *proof*. The believer is not saved as a result of good works; good works are the result of salvation. They are the result of God's working in the believer's heart. They are the evidence that he is alive from the dead. They are the proof of the glorious togetherness that exists between the believer and the Savior.

The Lord, when here on earth, lived a life of good works. He "went about doing good," Peter summarized (Acts 10:38). Now through His indwelling Spirit He continues to do His good works in us. This was all part of the eternal plan. The word translated "workmanship," *poiēma*, indicates that we are His poem, His masterpiece. Each of our lives is the canvas on which the Master is producing a work of art that will fill the everlasting ages with His praise.

A great dispositional change marks genuine conversion, so that a person who is still dead in trespasses and sins is in contrast to the believer who has been quickened together with Christ. If we profess to be Christians but our lives exhibit no evidence of behavioral change, we are self-deceived.

2.   The Great Dispensational Change (2:11-22)

a.   The Blood That Invites (2:11-13)

(1) Our Natural State (2:11-12)

(a) No Covenant Relationship with the God of Israel (2:11) "Wherefore remember, that ye being in time past Gentiles in the flesh, who are called Uncircumcision by that which is called the Circumcision in the flesh made by hands."

The Holy Spirit here emphasizes the great dispensational change brought about by Calvary and Pentecost. This change abolished the fundamental difference between Gentile and Jew.

Ever since the days of Abraham the rite of circumcision had served as a covenantal sign of the unique relationship that existed between God and the Israelites. The Jews gloried in this relationship and in their insular pride contemptuously referred to the Gentiles as "the uncircumcised." In the early church many Jewish believers felt that the church was merely an extension of Israel and insisted that Gentile converts to Christianity should be circumcised too as part of the process of coming into the good of the covenant. Gentile believers bitterly resented this requirement. The amount of space devoted to the subject in Acts and the Epistles demonstrates what a hot issue circumcision was.

Under the new dispensation, both circumcision and uncircumcision are without spiritual significance. Paul emphasized the obsolete nature of circumcision as a religious rite by referring to it as "the Circumcision in the flesh made by hands." True, circumcision was the sign of the Abrahamic covenant made with the nation of Israel—but the church is not Israel. The seal of those who are in the true church is not circumcision in the flesh, but the Holy Spirit in the heart (Ephesians 1:13). Gentiles are brought into a covenantal relationship with the God of Israel, not by becoming proselytes to Judaism, but by putting their faith in Christ. The same is true now of Jews. There is no difference. Calvary and Pentecost effected a remarkable change. Gentiles, who had no covenantal relationship with the God of Israel such as the one the Jews enjoyed and in which they made their boast, now have just such a relationship in the new covenant.

(b) No Commonwealth Relationship with the God of Israel (2:12)
        "That at that time ye were without Christ, being aliens from the commonwealth of Israel, and strangers from the covenants of promise, having no hope, and without God in the world."

This verse describes the natural state of the Gentiles. Prior to the great dispensational change that has now taken place, the only way a Gentile could partake of the spiritual blessings and covenantal benefits of Israel was to become a Jewish proselyte. Gentiles were natural-born aliens and had no part in the great covenantal promises God had made to Abraham, Isaac, Jacob, Moses, and David. Cut off from these covenants, the Gentiles had no hope and were without God. Their natural state apart from the gospel was deplorable; they were outside both the covenants and the commonwealth. (The Greek word translated "commonwealth" is *politeia*, "the body politic.")

The Gentile believers knew they had no hope. Pantheons in

Greece and Rome, Egypt and the East, were filled with gods made in the image and likeness of fallen men—gods who lusted and warred, gods who openly displayed vile and violent passions. The more sophisticated Gentiles may have paid lip service to such gods, but they knew these gods were obscenities.

No wonder so many Gentiles looked longingly at the Jewish religion. But at the same time they were attracted, they were repulsed by the hypocrisy, exclusivism, and pride of the Jews. The Gentiles were attracted by the Scriptures, but repulsed by the Mishna. They were drawn to the synagogue, but repelled by the thought of circumcision. They were attracted by the noble teachings—the moral, spiritual, and ethical content of the Bible—but dismayed by Jewish provincialism and intolerance.

Then the gospel came. No wonder hundreds of thousands of Gentiles instantly recognized its authority, its simplicity, its superiority over Judaism, its glorious availability, and its power. Now they no longer needed to belong to the commonwealth of Israel; they could establish a direct relationship with God themselves.

(2) Our New State (2:13) "But now in Christ Jesus ye who sometimes [once] were far off are made nigh by the blood of Christ."

As Catesby Paget put it:

> So near, so very near to God
> Nearer I cannot be;
> For in the Person of His Son
> I am as near as He.

God made this nearness possible through the shed blood of the Lord Jesus. What grace! Men put Him to death on a cross of shame. It was the crime of the ages. No greater crime could have been conceived. The crucifixion of Christ was the ultimate expression of man's hatred of God, an act of high-handed rebellion and outrage. Yet God turned the crucifixion into the means of His grace, the ultimate expression of His love for us. No greater manifestation of kindness can be imagined.

Once we were prodigals of the universe dwelling in the far country. We had spent our substance in riotous living and were in the grip of famine and want. Nobody cared. Our place was with the swine, and our daily bread was the husks that they ate. In our sin we were a disgrace to the One who had created us. We did not even have the good sense of the prodigal mentioned in the Lord's parable (Luke 15), for we did not know our way home. We groped in darkness and blindly longed for a God we did not know. But when we were yet a great way off, the Father saw us and had compassion on us. He ran and fell on our necks and kissed us. Now we who "were far off" are "made nigh by the blood of Christ."

b. The Body That Unites (2:14-18)

(1) Peace Procured for Us (2:14-16)

(a) The Old Barrier Abolished (2:14-15) "For he is our peace, who hath made both one, and hath broken down the middle wall of partition between us; Having abolished in his flesh the enmity, even the law of commandments contained in ordinances; for to make in himself of twain one new man, so making peace."

The enmity between Jew and Gentile was deep, acrimonious, ancient, and enduring. Jews regarded Gentiles as unclean scavenger dogs. Gentiles despised Jews as grasping, canting, religious hypocrites. Jewish ritual laws, especially the laws concerning clean and unclean food, made it virtually impossible for a conscientious Jew to have table fellowship with a Gentile, so social intercourse was practically forbidden. The commercial instincts of the Jews—developed in Babylon, practiced in Biblical times, and brought to a fine art in later ages—made the Jews moneylenders to the world. Gentiles were often obliged to borrow Jewish money, but that did not endear the Jews to them. The Gentiles used the Jews, but detested them.

So there was what Paul called a "middle wall of partition" between Jew and Gentile. Paul chose this phrase with care. In the temple at Jerusalem a stone palisade about 4-1/2 feet high warned Gentiles, on pain of death, to go no farther. They could enter the court of the Gentiles, but there they had to stop. The Jews fanatically defended the farther temple courts from Gentile intrusion. Indeed, Paul almost suffered death at the hands of a Jerusalem mob when the rumor circulated that he had taken some Gentiles beyond the wall (Acts 21:28-31). The physical "middle wall of partition" was not destroyed until the temple itself was destroyed.

Paul used that physical barrier as a type—a picture—of the great division in the ancient world between Jew and Gentile. Christ, Paul wrote, has broken down that barrier; in Him Jew and Gentile meet on common ground. We are all one in Christ. The cross has swept away the obstacles created by Jewish rituals and laws. Just as Jews and Gentiles united to crucify Christ, so Jews and Gentiles are now united in Christ and His church. The old barrier has been abolished.

(b) The New Bond Established (2:16) "And that he might reconcile both unto God in one body by the cross, having slain the enmity thereby."

The church is the body of Christ. In this body all believers are common members. There are no divisions based on racial origins, religious backgrounds, class distinctions, national boundaries, or color prejudices in the true church. All believers are equal members of this marvelous, mystical body. A new bond has been established.

This truth is seen only faintly now perhaps, because of human failings. But it is an eternal truth in the counsels of God and one that will be universally displayed when the church is finally seen as that "one new man" mentioned by Paul in Ephesians 2:15.

Glimpses of this unity can be seen even in the present imperfect state of the church. At one time I met regularly with a number of Christians—Britishers and Germans, Russians and Armenians, Jews and Arabs. Week after week we gathered around the Lord's table. We were all one in Christ. United in His church, we enjoyed harmony and peace even when out in the world our national groups warred and squabbled.

(2) Peace Proclaimed to Us (2:17-18)

(a) All Difference Gone (2:17) "And came and preached peace to you which were afar off, and to them that were nigh."

The Gentiles were afar off; the Jews were nigh. Yet both were equally lost. They were at war not only with each other but also with God. Then peace through the blood of Christ was proclaimed to both, and all differences were gone. In Romans 3:22-23 Paul wrote, "There is no difference: For all have sinned, and come short of the glory of God." The smug and surly elder brother was just as lost as the profligate prodigal. One was afar off, the other was nigh, but both were equally estranged from the father and needed to be reconciled. The differences between them were in the outward expressions of their pride, self-will, and rebellion; they both had the same inner need of forgiveness and grace.

The gospel reduces all people to the same level. All people are brought into the great equation of salvation through the same common denominator: repentance toward God and faith in the Lord Jesus Christ. The flood in Noah's day destroyed the people who stood on the highest mountains and those who cowered in the deepest valleys. All in the ark equally experienced God's mercy and salvation. The gospel teaches that all people who do not trust in Christ are equally lost—the distant Gentile and the nearby Jew.

(b) All Distance Gone (2:18) "For through him we both have access by one Spirit unto the Father."

Father, Son, and Holy Spirit unite to bring us back to God and give us access to the Father. The Jews of the Old Testament had acceptance by virtue of sacrifices, but they did not have access. They could not go into the holy of holies. Only the high priest had that kind of access, and then only once a year, under the most stringent of conditions, after the most elaborate of precautions, and for the briefest of moments.

When the Lord Jesus "through the eternal Spirit offered himself without spot to God" (Hebrews 9:14), God reached down and rent the temple veil. He thus rendered Judaism obsolete and at the same time opened up the way for all believers—Jews and Gentiles alike—to enter His presence. All distance is gone.

One day a little boy named Willie stood wistfully at the gates of Buckingham Palace. He longed to go in and see the king. Between him and the king, however, were iron gates, rigid protocol, armed soldiers, and watchful police. What he wanted was quite out of the question.

A policeman who was ordering the lad to leave suddenly stiffened and sprang to attention as a well-dressed, confident man approached. A brusque nod from the man and the policeman unlocked the gates and stood aside. "Come with me, sonny," said the man, taking the little boy's hand. "We're going in to see the king."

Into the palace they went. Inside were forty housemaids, fifty footmen (including one man who did nothing but wind clocks all day), and six hundred rooms. Willie and the man walked on and on—to the north wing, up stairs, along endless passages, to the king's corridor on the main floor, and into the master suite. (They were a quarter of a mile away from the kitchens!)

The man seemed to know the way and chatted about the rooms they passed: the magnificent ballroom that contained two majestic thrones on a raised dais; the stamp rooms that housed the world's most valuable collection; the Belgian suite with its forty-four rooms for the use of state visitors; the royal wardrobe; the music room; the dining room with a table as large as a skating rink; the dazzling green drawing room.

Finally they arrived in the king's presence, and the man spoke.

"Hello, Father. Here's a little boy who wants to meet you. Meet my friend Willie. Willie, this is the king." The little boy had taken the hand of Edward, prince of Wales, the king's son. Through him, Willie gained access to the king.

We too have taken the hand—the nail-printed hand—of the King's Son, the Prince of Peace. Through Him and Him alone, Jews and Gentiles alike have access by one Spirit to the Father.

c. The Building That Delights (2:19-22)

(1) The New Household (2:19) "Now therefore ye are no more strangers and foreigners, but fellowcitizens with the saints, and of the household of God."

In Ephesians 2:19-20 Paul used the illustrations of a fellowship, a family, and a foundation to explain the new relationship Gentiles now have with God through Christ.

The first illustration is that of a *fellowship*. Once the Gentiles were strangers and foreigners (sojourners). In Old Testament times if they resided among God's people, they were known as "strangers within the gates." Their status was that of tolerated aliens, unless they became proselytes. They did not enjoy citizenship and had no part in the divine covenants. No matter how good or godly such a sojourner might be, he was never known as a saint—although such men as Uriah the Hittite and Araunah the Jebusite are royally mentioned in the holy Scriptures.

For many years I have lived in the United States and enjoyed life among warmhearted, generous Americans. But as a Canadian citizen, my rights in the United States have been limited. I have been free to work, travel, own property, raise a family, and pay my share of taxes! But I have not been free to vote or have any say in government. For a long time I was required to register my whereabouts every year with the Department of Immigration, and at all times I have had to carry a card identifying me as a registered alien. In other words, I am constantly reminded that I am a stranger and a sojourner.

This is reminiscent of the situation of the Gentiles living amidst the Old Testament people of God. No matter who they were or what they did, no matter how good their intentions were or how exemplary their lives, the Gentiles were simply resident aliens. There was friendship with the Jews perhaps, but not true fellowship. How could there be when the Gentiles were uncircumcised strangers from the covenants and commonwealth of Israel?

But now, through Christ, Gentiles are fully integrated into the body politic of the true commonwealth. There is a new fellowship. Gentiles are fellow citizens with the saints. The Greek word translated "fellowcitizens" is *sumpolitēs*. *Sumpolitēs* comes from the word *politēs*, from which we derive our word "politics." *Sumpolitēs* means "a member of a city or state" and conveys the idea of belonging to a country. In Ephesians 2:19 the word implies full union, the possession of the same citizenship.

In Christ Gentiles enjoy a new citizenship. They are full citizens in the heavenly Jerusalem, and the seat of their government is in Heaven. Jews and Gentiles alike now share in the same fellowship. They are equal members of a new society, of another and better country, of a new and far more glorious commonwealth.

The second illustration is a *family*. Jews and Gentiles alike are now members of a new household, the household of God. No longer are Gentiles excluded from the family because of their birth. It was a rare privilege in Old Testament times to be born into a Hebrew family, to be a child of Abraham and an heir of the covenants of God. Now, by virtue of the new birth, both Jews and Gentiles become full-fledged members of God's family. They are Abraham's true spiritual descendants, heirs of the new covenant, children of the living God, members of His household, and brothers and sisters in the royal family of Heaven.

(2) The New Habitation (2:20-22)

(a) The Foundation of the Building (2:20) "And are built upon the foundation of the apostles and prophets, Jesus Christ himself being the chief corner stone."

The third illustration used to explain the new relationship Gentiles have with God is a *foundation*. Paul described the church as a glorious building that rests on a magnificent foundation: Christ and His apostles. The Holy Spirit says, "Other foundation can no man lay than that is laid, which is Jesus Christ" (1 Corinthians 3:11). Everything rests on Him. Without Him there would be no building. If we build on anything else but Christ, we build in vain, for we build on sand (Matthew 7:24-27).

Before their conversion the Gentiles were building on men's idle philosophies or on vain pagan religions. The Jews were building on burdensome rabbinical traditions. None of those foundations could last. They were sandy foundations, firm enough to stand for a while but inadequate when storm tides came. After accepting Christ, both Jews and Gentiles rested on the enduring foundation described in Ephesians 2:20.

The Holy Spirit identifies the apostles and prophets as being part of the foundation of which Christ is the chief cornerstone. They are included because the New Testament revelation was committed to them (John 14:25-26; 15:26-27; 16:12-13). It was the apostles who received the Holy Spirit's inspiration to declare New Testament truth. It was the apostles who received the Holy Spirit's illumination to disseminate New Testament truth. Thus in a sense the apostles and prophets of the New Testament were God's foundational gifts to the church. Their ministry ceased when the New Testament was written and published; their particular kind of work was no longer needed.

Christ is called the chief cornerstone because of its key position in the foundation. The cornerstone was hewn out first, and its corners, planes, and angles were all true. It was dropped into place last to bind all the other stones together and to ensure that all the foundation's lines were accurate. The cornerstone is called "the stone of testing." Likewise the doctrines of the church must line up squarely with what Christ revealed.

A Mormon once asked me which church I attended. I told him and he replied, "Does your church have apostles, prophets, evangelists, pastors, and teachers?"

I answered, "We have evangelists, pastors, and teachers, but we do not have apostles and prophets."

"How can your church be the true church," he said, "if it does not have all the gifts mentioned in Ephesians 4:11?"

"You are overlooking Ephesians 2:20 and Ephesians 3:5," I responded. "These Scriptures are as important as Ephesians 4:11, for they make it clear that the work of the apostles and prophets was to build the foundation of the church. When I build a house my first concern is to get a proper foundation laid, so I call in men who know how to do that. Once the foundation is in, I don't need them anymore. Instead I need carpenters, bricklayers, plumbers, electricians, roofers, and painters. It would be foolish to keep foundation men on the payroll once their job was done. The apostles and prophets completed their foundation-building job in the first century when they wrote the New Testament and then shared it with the world. The church no longer needs them."

"What would you say," he asked, "if I told you that God has raised up a new prophet for these latter days?"

"I should want to know what he prophesied," I replied, "because if it's in the Bible, I don't need it, and if it's not in the Bible, I don't want it."

"I am here," the man said, "to testify to you, sir, that God has raised up another prophet. His name is Joseph Smith, and the new revelation is the Book of Mormon."

"Well sir," I could only say, "based on Ephesians 2:20 and 3:5, Joseph Smith is a false prophet and the Book of Mormon is a book of lies."

The ultimate touchstone, the true cornerstone, is Christ Himself. Mormon doctrine concerning Him is from the evil one.

(b) The Framework of the Building (2:21) "In whom all the building fitly framed together groweth unto an holy temple in the Lord."

In this Epistle Paul compared the church to a body, a building, and a bride. Two of these metaphors stand in remarkable contrast. A healthy body is complete at birth; a building grows by addition.

When a normal baby is born, all his parts are already in place. His body will grow, but not by addition. David wrote, "In thy book all my members were written, which in continuance were fashioned, when as yet there was none of them" (Psalm 139:16). Likewise the church was complete in the purposes of God from the council chambers of eternity. Its growth as a body is directed toward maturity.

A building, on the other hand, starts from a plan and grows when parts are added a bit at a time until it is complete. This is the growth Paul had in mind in Ephesians 2:21. His dear friend Luke had described this kind of church growth in the progress reports in the book of Acts (Acts 2:41,47; 5:14; 6:1,7; 11:21; 14:1; 17:12,34; 18:8; 19:10).

It is fashionable in some church circles to decry numbers. "This is the day of small things," some say. Others say, "The Lord said, 'Fear not, little flock'" (Luke 12:32). This attitude is as wrong as the one that takes pride in large crowds and great numbers. Numbers in themselves can be misleading and they are no certain yardstick for measuring success in a ministry, but the church should experience steady growth. There should be an increase in numbers as well as growth in grace.

(c) The Function of the Building (2:22) "In whom ye also are builded together for an habitation of God through the Spirit."

In Old Testament times God chose to dwell among His people in material buildings: first in the tabernacle and later in the temple. The types of the temple are millennial; the types of the tabernacle are mystical. The one relates to Israel, the other to the church.

The tabernacle was built of fifty boards. Each board had been part of an acacia tree, the gnarled tree of the wilderness. After the tree was cut down—its old life terminated—the boards were fashioned. Each board was completely encased in gold so that the board itself was hidden forever. Each board stood on a socket of silver, shoulder to shoulder with its fellow board. The boards were held together by four visible bars and one invisible bar that ran through the heart of each board.

Today God dwells not in a material house, but in a spiritual one. Believers are "an habitation of God through the Spirit." Like the acacia trees, each believer was once firmly rooted in this desert world until the axe of conviction laid him low. Cut off from the old way of life, he is put "in Christ" and made to stand on redemptive ground, shoulder to shoulder with other believers. Four visible ties hold believers together: the apostles' doctrine, fellowship, breaking of bread, and prayer (Acts 2:42). One invisible bond unites us: the Holy Spirit, whose great work runs through the heart of each believer. Together we form the church, whose function is to be the habitation where God is pleased to dwell today.

The word translated "habitation" in Ephesians 2:22 occurs in only one other place in the New Testament. Describing the fall of commercial Babylon, the imperial city of the beast to be built on the banks of the Euphrates, John recorded the angel's words: "Babylon the great is fallen, is fallen, and is become the habitation of devils, and the hold of every foul spirit, and a cage of every unclean and hateful bird" (Revelation 18:2). Evil spirits will take up their abode in the haunted ruins of that cursed Vanity Fair of the beast's empire. In contrast, God resides on earth in His glorious church through His Spirit. Thank God that as long as He dwells on earth, the devil can never set up a permanent habitation here.

C. The Revelations of the Christian Life (3:1-21)

In Ephesians 3 Paul embarked on another of his famous digressions. He reminded his readers of the enlightenment, the ennoblement, and the enablement that they possess in Christ.

1. Our Enlightenment (3:1-9)

a. Paul as a Prisoner for the Truth (3:1) "For this cause I Paul, the prisoner of Jesus Christ for you Gentiles."

The stewardship of the revelations Paul received had been costly to him. These revelations are not to be taken lightly. Paul staked his life and liberty on them; he would die for these truths. He was a prisoner because he had dared to proclaim them. He was in chains because of the opposition of the Jews, but he considered himself a prisoner of Jesus Christ, not a prisoner of the Jews or Nero.

The Jews were infuriated when Paul taught that believing Gentiles were full members of God's family and the fellowship of saints. The Jews' national pride was stung. Even in the church many Jewish believers thought that Gentiles should become Jews in order to be Christians, or at least they should be regarded as second-class citizens in the kingdom. Paul's emancipating gospel annoyed many Jews, even within the church. They disliked his wholehearted acceptance of Gentiles into the church, free from all Jewish laws, traditions, and customs. They resented his vocal and tireless championship of the Gentile believers' cause. They felt threatened by his zealous, far-reaching efforts to bring more and more Gentiles into the church. The vast majority of unbelieving Jews regarded Paul with horror and considered him a dangerous heretic. Paul, however, did not criticize the Jews for opposing him. He knew where they were coming from; he had been there himself.

b. Paul as a Pioneer of the Truth (3:2-4)

(1) The Truth Entrusted to Him (3:2) "If ye have heard of the dispensation of the grace of God which is given me to you-ward."

The Greek word translated "dispensation" here comes from a word meaning "stewardship." God had entrusted Paul with great truths.

Paul was their custodian, their steward. He was under obligation to communicate them to others. He discharged this trust nobly through his preaching and writing.

Today we are living in an age—a dispensation—of grace, during which God deals with people on the basis of His grace. God's grace is reigning supremely. This age stands in contrast to the age of law that preceded it and the age of judgment that will follow it.

When we speak of an age of grace, we do not mean that God did not demonstrate His grace in other ages. Obviously He offered grace to men who were under the law; the entire ceremonial law illustrated God's grace. It is equally obvious that God will offer grace to men in the judgment age because millions will be saved during that period (Revelation 7). It is also evident that during our age of grace, God's law—that is, His moral law—still has a vital role (Romans 13:9) and at times God acts in judgment (Acts 5:1-11).

(2) The Truth Enlightening to Him (3:3-4)

(a) How It Was Communicated To Him (3:3a) "By revelation he made known unto me the mystery."

In Galatians 1:16-17 Paul told us that he did not receive his gospel from men; immediately after his conversion he "conferred not with flesh and blood," but sought out the vast silences of Sinai. There, alone with the Hebrew Scriptures and the Spirit of God, he thought through the Old Testament in the light of Calvary. He had to discard much of what he had been taught while studying to be a rabbi. He had been obsessed with the vain traditions of men, but the risen Lord now filled Paul's vision and colored all his concepts. The Holy Spirit came upon him and revealed new truths. He went into Arabia with Genesis, Isaiah, and the Psalms in his luggage, and he came back with Romans, Ephesians, and Thessalonians in his heart.

Paul did not have the enormous advantage of being Jesus' constant daily companion. He did not sit at His feet like Peter and John. The great truths of the New Testament that Paul so gloriously preached were given to him through God's direct revelation.

(b) How It Was Communicated By Him (3:3b-4) "As I wrote afore in few words, Whereby, when ye read, ye may understand my knowledge in the mystery of Christ."

Perhaps Paul was referring to a previous letter in which he had briefly mentioned the mystery (for instance, Romans 11:25; 16:25-26;

1 Corinthians 2:7; 15:51-52). Perhaps he was referring to earlier remarks in this same letter to the Ephesians (1:9-10). In any case, he communicated the great mystery, the great secret, in writing. It was far too important to be passed on simply by word of mouth. Because Paul communicated in writing, all of us can study the mystery and benefit from his reflections on the revelations given to him.

The revolutionary truths Paul wrote about were not his own spontaneous ideas. They were the product of divine inspiration and personal insight. The word translated "knowledge" in Ephesians 3:4 is *sunesis*, which refers to natural insight and reflective thought. Paul was one of the greatest intellectuals of all time, but mental ability alone did not conceive the mystery. God revealed it to him. On the other hand, divine illumination alone did not account for Paul's grasp of this new truth; he made the effort to think it through and write it down.

c.   Paul as a Partner in the Truth (3:5-6)

(1) How the Truth Was Concealed (3:5a) "Which in other ages was not made known unto the sons of men."

It was no secret, of course, that God intended to bless the Gentiles, just as He had blessed the Jews. His intentions were revealed in many Old Testament prophecies, including His first great promise to Abraham (Genesis 12:3). Paul quoted some of these prophecies in Romans 15:9-12, drawing on all three sections of the Hebrew Scriptures to emphasize his point. The promises to the Gentiles were often ignored by the Jews in their insular pride of religion and race.

It was no accident, surely, that the promised land was a bridge connecting Europe, Asia, and Africa, and that the great arterial highways of international commerce, communication, and conflict passed through it. God had always intended that His chosen people would become a spiritual blessing to all mankind—a truth that had too easily been forgotten.

Even in the deportations and dispersal, God intended for His chosen people to have a redemptive impact on other nations. The book of Acts makes it abundantly clear that Jewish communities around the world formed a natural springboard for global evangelism.

(2) How the Truth Was Revealed (3:5b-6)

(a) Its Custodians (3:5b) "It is now revealed unto his holy apostles and prophets by the Spirit."

In embryonic form, the great truths of the Epistles were first revealed to the disciples by the Lord. For instance, Jesus announced the truth about the universal church and the local church to the disciples (Matthew 16:16-19; 18:1-35). Jesus was also the first to teach the distinctive Pauline concept of being "in Christ" (John 15:1-8). The Lord promised that the Holy Spirit would superintend the writing of the Gospels (John 14:26), the Epistles (John 16:13), and the book of Revelation (John 16:13). But the Holy Spirit waited until after Pentecost to enlighten the apostles with the full measure of New Testament truth.

The apostles and the prophets—the custodians of this truth— had the foundational gifts necessary to produce and propagate the New Testament writings. Chief among these custodians was Paul. His giant intellect wholly yielded to the Holy Spirit became the human vehicle to discern and explain God's great mysterious truths.

(b) Its Contents (3:6) "That the Gentiles should be fellowheirs, and of the same body, and partakers of his promise in Christ by the gospel."

The new equality of the Gentiles was a bitter pill for most Jews to swallow. For centuries they had prided themselves on being God's chosen people. They had nurtured a growing contempt for Gentiles and wallowed in religious and racial snobbery. They had considered themselves to be God's favorites. Now all this superiority was shattered. It turned out that all along God had loved the Gentiles just as much as He had loved the Jews (witness the events in the book of Jonah, for instance). Now God was proving this truth in an astonishing way by bringing Jews and Gentiles together in a new body that ignored the special privileges the Jews had enjoyed for some thousand years. Gentiles were not going to be added to the existing corporate body of the Jewish people, the nation of Israel. There would be an entirely new body to which Jews and Gentiles would be added on equal terms.

Jews and Gentiles would share equally in the same *legacy*. They would be "fellowheirs." There would be no double portion for the Jews. Jews and Gentiles alike would receive the same blessing.

They would share equally in the same *life* too. There would be one body, its head being Christ and its members believers. Jews and Gentiles were all one in Him—all washed by His blood, all partakers of the same Spirit of life, and all equally dependent on Him and on one another.

Jews and Gentiles would also share equally in the same *light*. In

Christ, there were no longer any special promises to Jews, no revelations made to them alone. The full blaze of New Testament truth was the property of the church, not Israel.

It made no difference that Saul of Tarsus had been a Hebrew of the Hebrews, a trained rabbinical scholar, a tribal member of the nation of Israel, and a practicing and zealous Pharisee. In the church he was an equal partner with the Philippian jailor and the runaway slave Onesimus.

d.   Paul as a Propagator of the Truth (3:7-9)

(1) The Working of It (3:7) "Whereof I was made a minister, according to the gift of the grace of God given unto me by the effectual working of his power."

Paul realized that the revelations of truth he received were gifts of God's marvelous grace. That he had been chosen to be the steward of such far-reaching revelations never ceased to astonish Paul. His insights were certainly not generated by the strength of his own intellect. They were just one more evidence of God's mighty power working within him.

God's grace and power are at work today in members of the body of Christ. When a brother gifted as an evangelist speaks, the Holy Spirit works, people are convicted, souls are saved, and trails of blessing follow him everywhere.

A brother who is an able expositor can open up the wonders of the Word. Because he has received a gift of grace, God's people are blessed and enriched by his ministry through pulpit or pen. God's grace and power are at work in his life.

Another brother is a successful administrator. He knows how to organize and motivate people. Under his ministry the church grows. His abilities are a gift. God's grace and power are working within him.

A sister is a true "mother in Israel." Her home is a haven for her family and a lighthouse for her neighborhood. Her children rise up and call her blessed. All the little ones in the area know her and love her. She mothers them, listens to them, talks to them, laughs and cries with them, and leads them to Christ. Other women in the community consider her a true friend. Tradesmen sense God's presence when they deal with her. Her husband is blessed. Her church feels the impact of her prayers. God's grace and power are at work in her life too.

God's grace and power—His gift to us all—should be at work in all our lives.

(2) The Wonder of It (3:8a) "Unto me, who am less than the least
      of all saints, is this grace given."

With these words, Paul guarded against the natural tendency to
take pride in the extraordinary gifts God had given him, particularly
the apostolic gift that enabled him to be the custodian of divine
revelation and New Testament truth. He was, he said, less than the
least of all saints, and was awed that God had chosen him to receive
this gift.

We detect here a growing development of heartfelt, genuine
humility in Paul. In 1 Corinthians 15:9 he wrote that he was "the
least of the apostles, . . . not meet to be called an apostle" because
he had persecuted the church. In 1 Timothy 1:15 he called himself
the chief of sinners. He never forgot the wonder of being chosen to
be a custodian of divine truth.

At times Paul was driven to defend his apostleship because attacks
on him were really attacks on what he taught. He reluctantly but
resolutely declared, "I suppose I was not a whit behind the very
chiefest apostles . . . though I be rude [the Greek word rendered
rude can be freely translated *layman*] in speech . . . . in nothing am
I behind the very chiefest apostles, though I be nothing" (2
Corinthians 11:5-6; 12:11). But he even defended his apostleship
with as much self-depreciation as the occasion permitted.

(3) The Wealth of It (3:8b-9)

(a) Its Hidden Resources (3:8b) "That I should preach among the
      Gentiles the unsearchable riches of Christ."

The Greek word translated "unsearchable" here means
"untrackable" and suggests a labyrinth or maze. The wealth we have
in Christ is hidden treasure. We cannot track it down, but the story
of it has been told. Paul had a glimpse of it and vouched for the fact
that the Lord Jesus was rich (2 Corinthians 8:9).

A story about another kind of hidden treasure was told by
Alexandre Dumas in *The Count of Monte Cristo*. It was a standing joke
among prisoners in the dungeons of the Chateau D'If that the
learned abbe Faria was insane because he claimed to have knowledge of a fabulous hidden treasure. The abbe befriended Edmond
Dantes, a fellow prisoner. Faria educated him and adopted him as
his son. Dantes carefully avoided the subject of the treasure, not
wanting to awaken traces of his friend's former madness. But there
was no imbalance of mind in the abbe. As he was dying, the abbe put
the secret of the treasure into Dantes' hand.

In time Dantes escaped from the terrible prison and found the treasure in an underground grotto. It lay in an oaken coffer, bound with steel and closed with a lock and padlock. Hardly believing his good fortune, Dantes pried open the treasure chest, scarcely daring to breath lest the secret be a cruel hoax. But it was true! There before him lay the wealth of an empire: heaps of golden coins; stacked bars of gold; and an accumulation of diamonds, pearls, and rubies worth the ransom of a dozen kings. The treasure transformed the poor, victimized Dantes into the avenging Count of Monte Cristo.

We, the children of Adam's ruined race, also have been victimized. We have been born into a sin-cursed world; we are heirs to a fallen nature; we have been born in sin and shaped in iniquity. Our every prospect is blighted by the law of sin and death. But we have in our hands the secret of a hidden treasure, a treasure hidden in Christ. All spiritual wealth is vested in Him, and all that limitless wealth is ours. It transformed us when we became Christians from spiritual paupers into wealthy sons of God—joint-heirs with Jesus Christ. Now we can avenge ourselves on the prince of this world, on the lord of darkness, on evil spirits that rule the high places. We can use our new-found resources to live godly lives in Christ Jesus and introduce others to all that God has for those who believe in Him.

One thing is sure: We can never find that wealth apart from Christ. It is untrackable. Science, psychology, politics, social reform, education, or culture cannot lead us to that treasure. The spiritual treasure we need is found in Christ and in Him alone.

(b) Its Heavenly Resources (3:9) "To make all men see what is the fellowship of the mystery, which from the beginning of the world hath been hid in God, who created all things by Jesus Christ."

No wonder we cannot find this treasure on our own. It is in Heaven! It is hidden in Christ in God. God entrusted the news of this treasure to Paul to share with all men. He shared the news in his preaching and teaching, but he could only reach a small percentage of people. So under the Spirit's leading, he wrote down the good news that spiritual things hidden from the world's beginning are now universally available to mankind.

Perhaps his imprisonment in Rome made Paul realize the uncertainties of life, the absolute certainty of his eventual death, and the urgency of putting the good news into writing. Doubtless Paul realized that he was now writing under the Holy Spirit's direct inspiration, but he could scarcely have envisioned the results of penning a letter to a congregation of Gentile Christians. His letter would be treasured and duplicated countless times. Everyone would want a copy. The letter would find its way into the divine library. For centuries the letter would be read, memorized, quoted, discussed, and expounded. It would be translated and published and it would bear fruit in lands around the globe. And no wonder! The letter revealed a glorious secret about God's Son and the Gentile world.

Paul revealed a secret that God had kept to Himself. He had kept it hidden when He visited fallen man in Eden, when He talked with His friend Abraham, and when He gave the law to Moses. He told David, a man after His own heart, many things, but He did not tell him this secret. He spoke to Isaiah and Jeremiah, to Ezekiel and Daniel, but still He kept His secret. He did not tell the twelve minor prophets, and then He kept this burning secret for four more silent centuries.

Finally God sent His Son, who was involved in the secret. Jesus dropped hints of it here and there, but He did not give it away. The day of Pentecost came and the church was born. Peter preached, souls were saved, and the secret was out, but still men did not grasp it. So God saved Saul, shared the secret with him, and said, "You tell the world."

What a secret it was! God was going to create a church. He would baptize Jews and Gentiles into it, making no difference between them. That church would be the mystical body of Christ. He would raise it higher than angels. He would seat it with Himself in the heavenlies. It would share fully and forever all that Christ has. That church would be His crowning masterpiece. Creation itself, the showpiece of God's eternal power and godhead, would pale before the everlasting splendors of the church.

What a shout of joy there must have been when the secret was first unveiled in Heaven. Imagine Christ Himself, in a battle-scarred human body, sitting down at God's right hand, turning to His Father and saying, "Now, Father, let's send the Holy Spirit to bring home My Bride."

2.   Our Ennoblement (3:10-13)

a.   Our Triumph (3:10-12)

(1) The Manifold Wisdom of God (3:10) "To the intent that now unto the principalities and powers in heavenly places might be known by the church the manifold wisdom of God."

The Greek word that Paul used here to describe God's wisdom occurs nowhere else in the Bible. It means "infinitely diversified" or more poetically, "many-colored." From whichever way you view God's wisdom, new flashes of truth blaze forth. His wisdom is inexhaustible, as has been displayed in creation. The more we study medicine or astronomy or physics or microbiology, the more complex each facet of nature seems.

For instance, the ancient Greeks invented the word we translate "atom" to describe the ultimate, uncuttable, building blocks of the universe. In the late nineteenth century the discovery of radioactivity indicated that atoms themselves have internal structure. Work on cathode rays showed that within the atom are charged particles called electrons. Atoms, scientists realized, are much more complex than originally thought. Then they discovered that electrically positive protons and electrically neutral neutrons clump in the atom's nucleus. Whirling around this nucleus are negatively charged electrons. Scientists envisioned the atom as a miniature solar system, infinitely small and emptier than space. More discoveries followed, and the quantum theory was stated. Three families of subatomic particles have been named: gauge particles, quarks, and leptons. Indeed, the deeper physicists delve, the more elusive final answers seem to be. Such is God's wisdom demonstrated in creation—infinitely diversified and inexhaustible.

What is true of creation is true of redemption. The Bible, in which the plan of redemption is recorded, reveals the many-colored wisdom of God. We are constantly finding new depths in verses that have been familiar friends since we first met the Lord. God's infinite wisdom is now being displayed to principalities and powers in heavenly places.

It would seem that these principalities and powers are the hostile angels in the unseen world. They are the fallen ones who help Satan rule his planet and stand in stark contrast to the holy angels, known as thrones and dominions, who side with God and serve the redeemed. The principalities and powers are God's sworn enemies. They are the Christian's constant foes, with whom he has to do unremitting battle (Ephesians 6:12). These dark lords of the night are blinded by Satan and are destined to spend eternity in fires God has prepared especially for them. It is fitting that the futility of their schemes should be made plain through the church. In contrast to God's wisdom, Satan's "deep things" are exposed in the church as utter folly, the senseless plottings of a tormented and perverted mind. No wonder principalities and powers bitterly hate the church and those in its ranks.

(2) The Majestic Purpose of God (3:11) "According to the eternal purpose which he purposed in Christ Jesus our Lord."

God's plans, which center in the church, are part of His eternal purpose. He made His plans before time began, before the rustle of an angel's wing disturbed the silence of eternity. God was not surprised by Adam's sin or Lucifer's fall. God in His omniscient wisdom foresaw these tragic events that introduced such dimensions as sorrow, suffering, and shame into the universe. His answer was the cross of Christ, reared on a skull-shaped hill on a rebel planet in a remote corner of a galaxy. Through the cross He displayed His wisdom, love, and power as a means of redeeming fallen man and rebuking fallen angels.

How wonderful it is that God had us in mind before He created the stars. He wrote our names on His heart before He created the world, before the dust of the ages was concentrated in that one primeval atom, before the roar of creation's "big bang."

(3) The Marvelous Love of God (3:12) "In whom we have boldness and access with confidence by the faith of him."

We have full access to God's presence. We can draw near to Him and to His rainbow-circled, cherubim-guarded, highly exalted throne. We can come without pomp and ceremony, without formal and ritualistic preparations, without mediators of any sort. We can come directly to Him at any time, day or night, with the confidence of a son or daughter. No one on earth, in Heaven, or in Hell can bar our way. Such is God's love for us!

The Greek word translated "confidence" in Ephesians 3:12 means "confident assurance." One would not have this confident assurance if he entered a neighbor's house uninvited, opened the refrigerator, pulled up a chair to the table, and helped himself to supper. But one would have this confident assurance in his father's house because that is where he belongs and he knows he is welcome there.

The Greek word translated "boldness" here usually means "free speech," as in 2 Corinthians 3:12. The right of free speech is the privilege of every citizen in a democracy. But Paul had a higher meaning in mind. In the New Testament the word means every believer's right to come directly to God, having no other priest, mediator, or advocate than the Lord Jesus Christ. What arrogance for a religious system to interpose man-made functionaries between the child of God and his Father's smile. The only mediator needed is Christ; in other words the Christian has access "by the faith of him" (Ephesians 3:12).

Imagine showing up at the door of your father's house, only to find someone guarding the door. You say, "Excuse me please."

The guard asks, "Where do you think you are going?"

"I'm going in to see my father," you answer.

He says, "You can't do that! I'll take your message. You can only approach him through me."

"Get out of the way, mister," you say. "I'm his son. My father loves me. I sure don't need you or anyone else to come between us."

You should not allow a priest or a pretender to come between you and your Father in Heaven.

b.   Our Tribulations (3:13) "Wherefore I desire that ye faint not at my tribulations for you, which is your glory."

All of a sudden Paul came back down to earth. Did the rattle of his chain or the changing of the guard make him freshly aware of his physical circumstances? Had the soldier assigned to Paul impatiently jerked the manacles that made him almost as much a prisoner as his captive? Perhaps the soldier laughed out loud at the contrast between Paul's spiritual claims and his physical chains (if the soldier spoke Greek, he could understand every word that Paul dictated to his secretary).

Paul had been glorying in his limitless resources in Christ and his eternal prospects, while the harsh reality was that he was a prisoner anticipating a trial for treason before Nero. Not much of a future, one might think. Now Paul suddenly seemed to realize how other people might be viewing his situation. After all, he was in trouble only because he preached these glad tidings, and particularly because he preached them to the Gentiles. So he inserted a sentence to reassure his readers since they too might face tribulation for their faith in Christ. Some already had. Paul urged them not to be cast down on his account. He had long since learned to glory in tribulations (2 Corinthians 12:7-10).

Perhaps the best illustration of joy during difficult circumstances comes from *Uncle Tom's Cabin*. Poor Tom had been sold into the cruel hands of the bestial Simon Legree. Simon hated him, tormented him, thrashed him within an inch of his life, and threatened to tie him to a tree and roast him in a slow fire. But Tom remained unmoved by the threats. His soul was in the sky with the Savior. The storm clouds frowned, but Tom's eyes focused on the rainbow. He saw the great white throne, the white-robed throng, the crowns, the palms, and the harps. His ears were filled with seraph songs and the voice that sounded like the voice of many waters. He remained uncowed by Simon Legree and said, "Mas'r, I know ye can do dreadful things but, after ye've killed the body, there ain't no more ye can do. And oh! there's all eternity to come after that!"

Paul focused on the glories of Heaven as he faced trying circumstances on earth. Chains and beatings didn't really matter. He could endure the trials and tribulations of time because he knew that all eternity would follow.

3.   Our Enablement (3:14-21)

a.   The Secret of Our Enablement (3:14-15)

(1) It Is Related to Our Access to the Father (3:14) "For this cause I bow my knees unto the Father of our Lord Jesus Christ."

According to court etiquette in Paul's day, when someone approached the throne he bowed the knee. True, God is our Father, just as He is the Father of our Lord Jesus Christ. True, we are bidden to come boldly to Him. True, He loves us with an everlasting love. True, we have instant access to Him day or night. True, no request is too great or too small to be brought to Him. True, no earthly child in our culture goes down on his knees before his human father. But our Father is *God*. The Scriptures clearly teach that God should be approached with reverence and awe. Evidently Paul knelt when he prayed. This posture helped to remind him of the awesome majesty and nobility of the One he knew he could address as Father.

(2) It Is Related to Our Acceptance by the Father (3:15) "Of whom the whole family in heaven and earth is named."

The Greek word translated "family" here is *patria*, which in this case would be better translated "fatherhood." The link to the word "Father" *(pater)* in the preceding verse would be clearer. The sentence in verses 14-15 can be rendered, "I bow my knees to the Father from whom all fatherhood takes its name."

All fatherhood is derived from God the Father. He is the Father of fathers, the ultimate Father, the one whose fatherhood is the pattern for all fatherhood. All fatherhood should resemble His, for His fatherhood is perfect. The closer the resemblance, the more human fatherhood expresses fatherhood as God intended it to be.

Some of us have had fathers who distorted or destroyed the whole concept of fatherhood. Some of us have had very good fathers.

Some of us have never known our human fathers. Some of us are fathers ourselves and need to conform our fatherhood not to the writings of behavioral psychologists, but to the Father after whom all fatherhood is named.

In any case, all of us in God's family are eternally ennobled by the acceptance of our glorious Father on high. Whether our human fathers were good, bad, or indifferent, we can come to that perfect Father and revel in His marvelous fatherhood.

We have a faint illustration of what fatherhood is all about in Mark Twain's classic, *Tom Sawyer*. The two chief characters in this book are Tom and his sadly neglected friend, Huckleberry Finn. Tom had no father at all. He was raised by his Aunt Polly, a somewhat kindly, but exasperating guardian. Huck had a father, but he was a brute, a bully, and a drunkard who either totally neglected the boy or tyrannized him. At one point Huck was taken under the protective wing of the wealthy, well-meaning widow Douglas, who forced culture on the boy.

In contrast to Huck were the sons of the Welshman. They and their father acted with speedy efficiency when Tom brought the news that he and Huck had unearthed Injun Joe's savage plans to rob and mutilate the widow Douglas. How much better it would have been for Huck if that sturdy Welshman had adopted him. The boy needed fatherhood.

There are many youngsters like Huckleberry Finn in this world of broken homes and ruined marriages, and we can be sure that Satan himself is behind the present-day attacks on the home. The Biblical view of fatherhood needs to be restored as the model. Whether or not a person has a godly father, Christ has made the fatherhood of God available to anyone who comes to God through Him.

b.   The Sources of Our Enablement (3:16-19)

(1) It Is Channeled through the Invincible Spirit of God (3:16)
     "That he would grant you, according to the riches of his glory, to be strengthened with might by his Spirit in the inner man."

The first source of the believer's strength is the Holy Spirit in the inner man.

The governing principle in man does not reside in instinct, as it does in animals. It does not reside in the intellect either, for brilliant people are not always right. It does not reside in the emotions, for feelings often lead us astray. It does not reside in the will, for a strong-willed person can be a tyrant. It does not reside in the conscience, for a conscience can be weak, warped, or wrong. It goes deeper than that. The ruling principle in man resides in the spirit.

God created the human spirit to be the receptacle of the Holy Spirit. He says, "The spirit of man is the candle of the Lord" (Proverbs 20:27). Before the fall, the Holy Spirit was to fill the human spirit and thus control all man's thoughts, feelings, and decisions. The Holy Spirit was to rule his body so that his whole life would be the expression of God.

When man fell, the Holy Spirit vacated the human spirit and this controlling principle was lost. Man living in sin is not what God had in mind when He said, "Let us make man in our image, after our likeness" (Genesis 1:26). A new ruling principle resides in man's soul—sin. Now he is subject to the law of sin and death.

At conversion the human spirit is regenerated. The Holy Spirit returns and relights the candle. The believer can do what no unbeliever can do—live in fellowship and communion with God. He has the enablement of the Spirit in his inner man. Paul's great prayer for all believers was that they might be strengthened by the Holy Spirit because that is part of God's plan. His inexhaustible riches in glory are available to us so that we can exhibit them to a lost world.

(2) It Is Channeled through the Indwelling Son of God (3:17a)
    "That Christ may dwell in your hearts by faith."

Once in history a man lived here on earth who was God manifested in flesh, man inhabited by God, and man as God always intended man to be. For some thirty-three years He lived and moved and had His being among us. For about 12,600 days He walked and talked, laughed and cried, worked and played. He rubbed shoulders with people, experienced pain and pleasure, dealt with pressures, was tempted and tried, and lived with human limitations—all without sinning. He went about doing good. He performed miracles for others, but never for Himself. He could have commanded stones to become bread when He was hungry. After all, He changed water into wine and multiplied a little lad's lunch to feed a multitude. He could have come down from the cross, but He never did.

Satan put Him to the test to see if He would spoil God's redemptive plan by using His deity to override His humanity. Christ's public ministry began and ended on the same note of temptation. In the wilderness Satan taunted, "If thou be the Son of God, command that these stones be made bread" (Matthew 4:3). In other words,

"Use your deity to put an end to your suffering. Why be hungry as a man, when as God you can work a miracle?" At Golgotha passersby reviled Him: "If thou be the Son of God, come down from the cross" (Matthew 27:40). They were saying, "Use your deity to put an end to your human suffering." But Jesus had not come here to spare His life. He did more miracles than men could count, but only to benefit others.

So in His character, conduct, and conversation; as an infant, a child, a teenager, a young man, a man in the prime of life; at all times, in all places, under all circumstances; at home, at school, at work, at play, in the synagogue, on the highway; as a brother, as a friend, as a neighbor, as the babe of Bethlehem, as the child of Mary, as the carpenter of Nazareth, as the preacher from Galilee—Jesus lived life on human terms. He was never less than God and at the same time never more than man. He was content to live on our terms. Filled, anointed, led by the Holy Spirit, joyful in all things, and wholly yielded to the Father, He demonstrated what God had in mind when He created man. His sinless life was filled with love for God and love for other people.

This Jesus, said Paul, still lives. He not only lives in glory at the right hand of God; He also lives in us. Ephesians 3:17 says, "Christ may dwell in your hearts by faith" and can be rendered, "Christ may take up His abode in your hearts by faith."

Our hearts are His home. Our bodies are His temple. Just as He lived His human life in the power of the Holy Spirit and in constant communion and cooperation with the Father, so we are to live our lives in the power of the Holy Spirit and in constant communion and cooperation with Him. His purpose, to use Isaiah's expressive phrase, is thus to "prolong his days" (53:10). He does this by indwelling our lives (Colossians 1:27).

The genius of the gospel lies in the fact that Christianity is Christ. We can't imitate the life that Jesus lived. That is impossible, as most of us have discovered. We have tried and failed. Christianity is the living Christ taking up His abode in us and continuing to live His peerless life in our human bodies.

Christ makes Himself at home in you and me by faith. Faith is the operating principle. The *truth* of Christ's indwelling presence is beyond question. Colossians 1:27 says, "Christ in you, the hope of glory." The *transmission* of Christ's indwelling presence hinges on our faith—that is, our willingness to believe that His indwelling is a fact and to turn over the control of our lives. The enablement to be like Christ comes from Him. His life, not ours, produces in our character, conduct, and conversation what people will recognize as genuine Christianity. He will fill our lives with love for God and love for man.

(3) It Is Channeled through the Ineffable Salvation of God (3:17b-19a)

(a) God's Love Experienced (3:17b) "Rooted and grounded in love."

Most of us have a sentimental view of love. The Bible does not ignore the emotional side of love, but it usually emphasizes the volitional side. Love is not something we add to our Christian lives as time goes on. Love is the root and the foundation of Christian life. In Ephesians 3:17 Paul used two contrasting spheres to illustrate the importance of a right start: the world of the biologist and the world of the builder. A bulb grows and a building grows, but they grow in different ways. They have one thing in common, however. They both must have a right start.

We must be rooted in love. A plant will not grow unless it is rooted in the proper soil. Paul viewed love as the soil in which all Christian experience must grow. If our service for God lacks love, it is like sounding brass and tinkling cymbal (1 Corinthians 13:1). If our Christian lives are not rooted in love, they will wither and fade. Love, the soil of the soul, provides the nutrients necessary to sustain fragrant, fruitful Christian lives. God's everlasting love is what Jesus exhibited in His life and death, and if we are rooted in that love, His love will be reproduced in us.

We must also be grounded in love. The Greek word translated "grounded" in Ephesians 3:17, *themelioō*, relates to the foundation of a building. The Lord Jesus used the same word in His parable of the wise and foolish builders. Speaking of the man who built his house on the rock, Jesus said, "And the rain descended, and the floods came, and the winds blew, and beat upon that house; and it fell not: for it was *founded* upon a rock" (Matthew 7:25, italics added). No matter how great a Christian organization we build, no matter how efficient and seemingly successful we are, no matter how imposing a church we erect, if our efforts are not grounded in God's love, they will amount to nothing.

Some years after Paul wrote to the Ephesians, the Lord Jesus had to warn this same church:

I know thy works, and thy labour, and thy patience, and how thou canst not bear them which are evil: and thou hast tried them which say they are apostles, and are not, and hast found them liars: And hast borne, and hast patience, and for my name's sake hast laboured, and hast not fainted. Nevertheless I have somewhat against thee, because thou hast left thy first love. Remember . . . and repent . . . or else . . . (Revelation 2:2-5).

Love must be the basis of the life of a church; otherwise it cannot last. The church at Ephesus in John's day was insolvent. Its many works could be compared to spurious coins—coins that had never known the mint of love. Perhaps Paul sensed what would happen to the church at Ephesus and that is why he emphasized the need to base Christian life and church life on the foundation of love.

(b) God's Love Examined (3:18) "May be able to comprehend with all saints what is the breadth, and length, and depth, and height."

Paul challenged us to try to measure God's love to see if it can be expressed in finite terms. If we use length, we create a line. If we add breadth, we create a surface. If we add depth, we create a solid. But how can we add height? This fourth dimension defies understanding.

What in terms of physical reality is the difference between depth and height? If we have depth, we also have height; the two are just different directions within the same dimension. Height cannot be considered a fourth dimension unless it symbolizes a spiritual dimension. John only used three dimensions to describe the celestial city (Revelation 21:16). But Paul introduced a spiritual dimension to help us comprehend the love of God.

Let's examine the dimensions of God's love.

The length of God's love. How long is God's love? When did God *start* loving us? Was it when we first loved Him? Was it when we first responded to the Spirit's call? Was it when we were born? Was it when He created man and first saw us in Adam? Was it when He made the worlds and planned a planet to be our island home in space? Was it when He first decided to create us, knowing that if He acted in creation He would also have to act in redemption? When did God's love start? It never started! It has always existed. It is everlasting, as eternal as God is eternal.

When will God *stop* loving us? If we are disobedient, fall into sin, and bring shame and dishonor to the name of His Son, will He stop loving us then? What if we keep on sinning? What if we exceed the seventy times seven times (Matthew 18:21-22)? God will never stop loving us. He has not even stopped loving the people who are eternally lost. He loves them even though it is His holiness that predominates in their experience. The length of God's love stretches back beyond our farthest thought and forward on and on forever.

The breadth of God's love. How wide is God's love? It is wider than the sea, wider than the world, wider than the universe. When God demonstrated His love by becoming a man and living on earth, that love was not narrow, parochial, or prescribed by creed or custom. He loved the rich young ruler and the woman caught in adultery. He loved Nicodemus and Zaccheus the publican. He loved Judas who betrayed Him. He loved Caiaphas and Annas, the scheming political priests who judged Him during a trumped-up trial in the dead of night and who used cheap tricks to try to get Him to incriminate Himself. He loved Herod, who murdered John and mocked Him. He loved poor, weak, self-seeking Pilate, who was torn between justice and ambition. He loved Nero, Hitler, and Stalin. And wonder of wonders, He loves us too! His love is wide enough to embrace everyone.

The depth of God's love. How deep is God's love? Christ came down from the towering battlements of Heaven to the dark recesses of the tomb. He came from Heaven's glory to Galilee and was content to be raised in a despised provincial town and to be known as the carpenter's son. He tread the long and lonely road from Galilee to Gethsemane where He wept His heart out over the horror of our sin and the torment of the approaching cross. From Gethsemane He went to Gabbatha to be bullied, baited, falsely accused, scourged, and crowned with thorns in Pilate's judgment hall. Then He went from Gabbatha to Golgotha where He was nailed to a cross, hung up to die, and exposed as an object of derision. He plunged into the eerie darkness of that midday midnight when as the sin bearer He was abandoned by God and crushed beneath the weight of the world's sin. From Golgotha He went to the grave and on down into Hades itself. How deep is God's love?

Years ago sailors venturing into uncharted seas would let out a sounding line to locate the bottom. "No bottom with this line," the sailor might report to the bridge. Another length of line might be added. "Deeper than that, sir," the officer of the watch might report. The sailors might even attach all the line they had on board to the sounding weight. "Deeper than that" they might note in the log.

We too can let out our sounding lines into the depths of God's love. In the end we can only say, "It's deeper than that. No bottom with this line." Love took our Savior all the way from glory to the grave.

The height of God's love. How high is Christ's love? He has ascended to glory and is sitting at the right hand of the Father. In those heights Christ reigns in splendor and brightness beyond that of the noonday sun. He is adulated and adored, worshiped and praised, by the shining and sinless sons of light who throng around His throne.

Will Jesus forget us, now that He is on the throne of the universe with galaxies swirling around His feet and ten thousand times ten thousand angels hanging on His words and rushing to do His will? No!

Our thoughts go back to Joseph, unfairly imprisoned by the captain of pharaoh's guard on false charges brought against him by the man's own wife. He ministered to pharaoh's cupbearer, also in prison, and assured him that he need have no fears for he would soon be lifted up and exalted again. "When it is well with thee, think of me," said Joseph. The king's cupbearer was indeed restored to his high estate. "Yet," says the Holy Spirit with an economy of words that bespeak a prodigal pathos, "Yet did not the chief butler remember Joseph, but forgat him" (Genesis 40:23).

But Jesus will not forget us. We are already seated with Him in heavenly places. And He has promised, "I will come again . . . that where I am, there ye may be also" (John 14:3).

(c) God's Love Exhibited (3:19a) "To know the love of Christ, which passeth knowledge."

We can know Christ's love! Calvary love surpasses creature love.

A traveler in the African bush came to a place where a fire had recently burned. Beside his path he saw the charred embers of a nest, and on that nest the carcass of a mother hen. Idly he touched the remains with his foot and to his astonishment, out from under the heap ran some baby chicks. Mother love had caused that hen to give her life for her brood. But that was only creature love.

What can we say about Calvary love? What can we say about the love that is stronger than death? What can we say about the love that many waters cannot quench? What can we say about the love that will not let us go? What can we say about the love that suffers long and is kind?

Years ago in Britain D. L. Moody met a young man named Henry Morehouse. Fascinated by the great evangelist, Morehouse begged a favor. "Mr. Moody," he said, "if I come to Chicago, will you let me speak in your church?" Not thinking it likely that this youth would ever come to Chicago, Moody carelessly agreed.

Sometime later the young man knocked on Moody's door in

Chicago. "Hello, Mr. Moody. Remember me? I'm Henry Morehouse. I've come to speak in your church."

Reluctantly, Moody made the arrangements. "Never mind," he assured his deacons. "It will only be for one service. He can't do much harm in half an hour. In any case, I'll get up afterward and put things right."

That night Morehouse preached on John 3:16 and spoke of God's love with Holy Spirit power. Moody was deeply moved. The church leaders asked Morehouse to preach again and again. He preached every night for an entire week on John 3:16. Moody had never heard preaching so powerful. Indeed, Morehouse became known as the man who moved the man who moved the multitudes.

The last night came. Again the young visitor announced his usual text and said: "I have been trying to tell you how much God loves you. Suppose I could borrow Jacob's ladder and could climb that shining staircase until at last I stood on the sapphire pavements of the city of God. Suppose I were to seek out Gabriel the herald angel and were to say to him, 'Gabriel, you stand in the presence of God. Tell me, how much does God love the world?' I know exactly what he would say. He would say, 'Henry Morehouse, God so loved the world that He gave His only begotten Son that whosoever believeth in Him should not perish but have everlasting life. That's how much God loves the world.'"

We can know that love, but paradoxically it passes knowledge.

(4) It Is Channeled through the Infinite Sufficiency of God (3:19b)
     "That ye might be filled with all the fulness of God."

God Himself is the source of our enablement. We are to be progressively filled, right up to the measure of God's fullness. This truth is beyond all understanding. Yet Paul prayed that we might experience the fullness.

D. L. Moody did. He rarely spoke of his experience because it was too sacred, but it is recorded in his biography. He had been walking the streets of New York City, oblivious to the crowds and traffic, wrestling with God about a claim God was making on his life. Suddenly he gave in and felt an overwhelming sense of God's presence sweep over him like waves. He went to a friend's house, declined the offer of a meal, and asked for a room where he could be alone. Time passed. He was alone with God in a way he had never known before; he was filled with the fullness of God. At last Moody cried out to God to stay His hand, for he could take no more. After that experience his ministry was never the same. An anointing on him surpassed all that had gone before.

If ever there was One who was filled with all God's fullness, it was the man Christ Jesus. Of course, even when He lived on earth He never ceased to be God. But He accepted life on our terms, and as a man was always filled with God's fullness. There was never a time— as a babe, as a boy, as a man—when He was not filled with the Spirit. Jesus was not anointed for His ministry until John baptized Him in the Jordan and the Spirit came down on Him, but He was always filled with the Spirit. John 3:34 says, "God giveth not the Spirit by measure unto him."

What would God be like if He were a boy of twelve? To answer that question, we only have to look at a boy named Jesus who was filled with all God's fullness. What would God do if He were like us? If He were fiercely tempted, what would He do? To know the answer, we only have to look at the man Jesus, who was filled with God's fullness.

What would God do if He were confronted with all the sorrows of mankind? With this world's sick, poor, bereaved, and demon-possessed? With this world's prodigals? What would He do if He were confronted with religious error, with His nation's oppressors, or with a close friend who harbored treachery in his heart? What would He do if His family decided He was insane or going to extremes? What would He do with His money, with His extraordinary talents, and with His time? What would He do if He faced betrayal and injustice? What would He do if someone spit in His face? What would He do if He were forced to endure a painful, horrible, and lonely death? To answer these questions, we only need to look at the One who was filled with all the fullness of God. All we need to do is look at Jesus.

When Paul prayed that we might be filled with all of God's fullness, he was praying that in our character, in our conduct, and in our conversation, we might be like Jesus. What then, in human terms, was the secret of Jesus' life? Obedience! "Lo, I come," He said, "(in the volume of the book it is written of me,) to do thy will, O God" (Hebrews 10:7). He "became obedient unto death, even the death of the cross" (Philippians 2:8).

Imagine for a moment that we tiptoe into the garden of Gethsemane. We creep past Peter, James, and John, who already are asleep. We see Jesus staring aghast into the cup of suffering that our sins have filled. We see the sweat and blood on His brow. We hear Him say, "Father, if it be possible, let this cup pass from me:

nevertheless not as I will, but as thou wilt" (Matthew 26:39). In the garden we have learned the secret to being filled with the fullness of God; the secret is obedience.

c.   The Scope of Our Enablement (3:20-21)

(1) A Power Inexhaustible (3:20)

(a) Inexhaustible in Its Ability (3:20a) "Now unto him that is able to do exceeding abundantly above all that we ask or think."

God is able to do all that we *ask*. No man could do that, no matter how rich, powerful, or willing he might be. What are we asking for? Peace in the midst of storm? The salvation of a loved one? Help in an emergency? Guidance in a decision? Victory over sin? Blessing on a ministry? No matter what we might ask, God is able to do it.

God is able to do all that we ask or *think*. We all have thoughts that we never express. We have secret yearnings, hopes, ambitions, and dreams. We have longings that are so intangible we can barely put them into words—unspoken prayers for holiness, happiness, godliness, love, and fulfillment. God reads those thoughts. No matter what we long for, God is able to do it.

God is able to do *all* that we ask or think. He has not restricted us to one request. He is not small, parochial, or limited. He is pleased when our thoughts and prayers are commensurate with His omnipotence.

A man once did Alexander the Great a service, and Alexander told him to ask for any type of reward he wished. The man made such an enormous demand on the treasury that the imperial treasurer refused to pay it. The man appealed to Alexander, who said, "This man knows the greatness of Alexander and has asked accordingly. We are greatly honored. Grant his request."

God is able to do *above* all that we ask or think. He can take what we ask and enlarge it. He can take our thoughts and go beyond them. We can only see the here and now; He can see the then and there.

God did above all that Paul could ask or think for Ephesus, though his prayers were not answered the way he expected. Paul wanted to evangelize Asia Minor and Ephesus during his second missionary journey, but God kept on saying no. In Acts 16:6-9 Luke recorded:

> When they had gone throughout Phrygia and the region of Galatia, and were forbidden of the Holy Ghost to preach the word in Asia, After they were come to Mysia, they assayed to go

into Bithynia: but the Spirit suffered them not. And they passing by Mysia came down to Troas. And a vision appeared to Paul in the night; There stood a man of Macedonia, and prayed him, saying, Come over into Macedonia, and help us.

Although God knew that Paul desired to evangelize Asia Minor, He led Paul to Europe where he planted church after church and changed the history of the world. Only after his stint in Europe did God lead Paul back to Ephesus (Acts 18:19-21). Then during his third missionary journey, God enabled Paul to plant a great, flourishing church there (Acts 19:1-20). God did not veto Paul's thought; He simply improved it.

God is able to do *abundantly* above all that we ask or think. He doesn't just make minor improvements in our plans. He overrules them and gives them a magnificence worthy of Himself.

For example, Paul wanted to go to Rome. He wrote to the saints there about his desire to visit them and how often he had intended to come (Romans 1:10-13). But God always seemed to hinder him. Why? Because He was going to do abundantly above all that Paul could ask or think.

By hindering Paul, God caused him to write to the Romans, thus giving us Paul's doctrinal masterpiece. How impoverished the church would have been through the centuries if Paul had simply gone to Rome and had never written to the church there.

But that was not all God did. In the end He sent Paul to Rome— in chains! How could that be viewed as doing abundantly above all that Paul could ask or think? Surely Paul never asked to go to Rome as Nero's prisoner, accused of high treason and facing the possibility of a terrible death. But out of that imprisonment came the Epistles to the Ephesians, the Philippians, the Colossians, and Philemon—not to mention Paul's bold witness that reached into the palace and into the ranks of the powerful Praetorian Guard. Truly he could write, "I would ye should understand, brethren, that the things which happened unto me have fallen out rather unto the furtherance of the gospel" (Philippians 1:12).

God is able to do *exceeding* abundantly above all that we ask or think. Only eternity will reveal how marvelously God has answered all our prayers. (And we thought that He had ignored them!) He has some wonderful surprises waiting for us on the other side of the sea. God's infinite power is inexhaustible in its ability to enable us.

(b) Inexhaustible in Its Availability (3:20b) "According to the power that worketh in us."

The Greek word translated "power" here is *dunamis*. It means God's untrammeled, unequaled, unlimited power—the power that energized the galaxies. Yet God is so gentle we can barely see His power at work in our lives.

Think of the life-transforming power that took a cursing, cowardly fisherman named Peter and transformed him into the peerless preacher of Pentecost; of the power that took Saul of Tarsus, the arch-persecutor of the infant church, and turned him into the great apostle Paul; of the power that took the Lord's pharisaical and unbelieving brother James and made him a pillar of the church! That is the power "that worketh in us." When we get to Heaven we will meet myriads of people, all of whom will be able to tell of the working of that power in them. It is as gentle as the forming of a dew drop, as imperceptible as the growth of a tree, and as lasting as the throne of God.

(2) A Purpose Inescapable (3:21) "Unto him be glory in the church by Christ Jesus throughout all ages, world without end."

God does everything for His glory. That is a basic axiom of sound hermeneutics. That is an important key to understanding His ways and interpreting His Word. God's grace, God's government, and God's greatness may be other keys to understanding the Scriptures and God's ways with men and nations. But these keys only unlock certain doors. God's glory is the master key that unlocks all doors. God does everything for His glory, and Paul ended his magnificent doxology on this note.

God enables us because His supreme purpose is to bring glory to Himself. Our lives are to glorify God *personally*—"Unto him be glory." To glorify and worship a creature—no matter how splendid, powerful, and great that created being is—robs God of glory. All idolatry, however well-meaning, is high treason against God because it gives His glory to another.

Satan tempted Christ by offering Him a crown without a cross. Satan offered the kingdoms of this world with all their power and glory, but at a price. "All these things will I give thee, if thou wilt fall down and worship me" (Matthew 4:9; also see Luke 4:5-7). Jesus, refusing to give glory to anyone but God, instantly stabbed Satan with the Sword: "It is written, Thou shalt worship the Lord thy God, and him only shalt thou serve" (Matthew 4:10).

Our lives are also to glorify God *publicly*—"Unto him be glory in the church by Christ Jesus." In our public worship, in our gatherings as His people, in our corporate testimony, we are to glorify God. We are to display to the spirit hosts in the heavenlies and to all mankind on earth the person of Christ. He is the head of the body; we are its members.

Our lives are to glorify God *perpetually*—"throughout all ages, world without end." When we stop praising God, we defraud Him and demean ourselves. The hosts of Heaven who surround His throne are always praising Him. The chant of the cherubim is a ceaseless "Holy! Holy! Holy!"

The psalmist brought the Hebrew hymnbook to a resounding close with thirteen calls to praise the Lord. "Praise ye the Lord!" He began the last Psalm with that call and he ended it with that call. That Psalm is what we call "an envelope Psalm"—it ends the exact way it begins. It is what we would call today a "round"; that is, as soon as we come to the end of it we have really arrived back at the beginning, which means we go through it again—and again and again.

We are to praise Him perpetually. That will be our joy through the ages . . . down here, generation after generation . . . up there, as the eternal ages roll. Thus Paul completed another major section of this matchless letter. Left breathless and speechless, all we can say is "Praise the Lord!" Then in typical Pauline fashion, he rattled his chain and brought us back to earth again in Ephesians 4:1.

PART III

The Christian
and His Behavior

Ephesians 4:1 – 6:9

III. THE CHRISTIAN AND HIS BEHAVIOR (4:1–6:9)

A. In His Mystical Relationships (4:1-16)

1. The Greatness of the Mystical Body (4:1-6)

a. Its Uniqueness (4:1-3)

(1) It Is Undaunted (4:1a) "The prisoner of the Lord."

With these words Paul dignified his chains. He was not the prisoner of Nero. He was the prisoner of the Lord. A mere caesar could not arrest an apostle without God's permission. Paul was undaunted. Since he had to wear a chain, he wore it like a chain of office. If every move he made had to be accompanied by the rattle of fetters, he made each clank of iron a note in a melody of praise to God. He converted his prison into a palace. He considered himself shut up with God.

Since Paul could no longer roam the world in evangelistic zeal, he became a prayer warrior. Soldiers barred the way to this world, but no soldier could close the way to Heaven. Since Paul could not preach, he prayed. Since he could not plant churches, he upheld those who could at the throne of grace. Since he could not go to Spain, he prayed for Spain. He prayed for Timothy, Titus, Luke, and Aristarchus. He prayed for the saints at Jerusalem, Antioch, Philippi, Ephesus, and Rome. He prayed for the caesar, the senate, the Roman people, the world, and the soldier who shared his cell. God shut Paul up with his pen and his prayers, so Paul praised Him by writing letters and interceding at the throne.

(2) It Is Undivided (4:1b-3)

(a) Its Character (4:1b-2) "I . . . beseech you that ye walk worthy of the vocation wherewith ye are called, With all lowliness and meekness, with longsuffering, forbearing one another in love."

A Christian's character must be in keeping with his calling. And what a calling it is! Paul had to ransack his vocabulary to find words to describe what is ours in Christ in the heavenlies, and then he said that we are to walk worthy of that calling. We are going to be like

Christ for all eternity so we need to begin being like Him now. The place to begin is at home, at school, at work, at play, in the church, and in our community. We must begin with one another, with those whose lives are linked with ours.

The word *lowliness* refers to humility of mind. Thoughts of God's wisdom, love, and power should put an end to all our pride.

The word *meekness* challenges us to cultivate the spirit of the Lord Jesus (2 Corinthians 10:1). Meekness is not much admired among men because they too readily mistake it for weakness. But meekness is admired in Heaven. Only a strong person can display complete self-control and restraint in the face of extreme provocation. This kind of meekness is a fruit of the Spirit (Galatians 5:23).

Longsuffering is an expression of love. Paul said, "Charity [love] suffereth long, and is kind" (1 Corinthians 13:4). How impatient we can be when we don't get our own way or when someone does or says something to irritate us. Jesus never responded with impatience. He urged us to be forbearing, to put up with one another.

As members of the mystical body of Christ—with His Spirit indwelling us, with the Lord Himself as the head of that body, with Christ living His life in us and through us—how much like Him we should be!

(b) Its Curriculum (4:3) "Endeavouring to keep the unity of the Spirit in the bond of peace."

The Greek word translated "endeavouring" literally means "studying" (2 Timothy 2:15). We have to study to keep the mystical body undivided. We are in the school of God, where the chief subject in the curriculum is Christ. We are to study to be like Him; we are to apply our minds to the problems He sets before us. The problems are not merely academic. Often the problems are practical, like getting along in a Christlike way with other people—sometimes with difficult, defeated people we dislike.

In the school of God there are tests so we can evaluate our progress in becoming Christlike. We can evaluate whether Christ is being expressed in and through our bodies and the mystical body of Christ, for this is what the Christian life is all about.

b. Its Unity (4:4-6)

(1) Its Functional Unity (4:4a-b)

(a) The Diverse Life It Shows (4:4a) "One body."

We look at the church today and we see it torn and divided. In the words of hymnist S. J. Stone,

> . . . with a scornful wonder
> Men see her sore oppressed,
> By schisms rent asunder,
> By heresies distressed.

Men look at the church and see it divided into Catholic, Protestant, and Orthodox communions. They see state churches, countless nonconformist groups, and the endless splintering of the professing church into denominations, sects, and factions. They see liberals and fundamentalists, charismatics and conservatives. They see churches divided on doctrine, churches espousing opposite views on church government, churches bitterly divided on issues. And the confusion over all these divisions is aggravated by a multitude of heresies and cults all claiming to be Christian.

There is, however, only one church. Where man sees disunity, God sees unity. He sees a church comprised of men, women, boys, and girls who have trusted in Christ for salvation, who have been washed from their sins in His blood, and who have been born from above. They are all one in Christ—some living on earth, even more living in Heaven. Life, not light, unites the body of Christ. All who are saved and are members of that body share one life—the life of Christ. That is the unity of the church. The shared life of Christ may be expressed in diverse ways, but wherever a person belongs to the body, that life is there. It makes no difference whether the believer is young or old, gifted or retarded, wise or foolish, high church or low church, oriental or occidental, enlightened or confused, victorious or defeated. What matters is that the life of Christ is present.

(b) The Divine Life It Shares (4:4b) "One Spirit."

It is the Holy Spirit who imparts that divine life. His first work is to convict and enlighten. Then He regenerates, adds the new believers to the body, indwells, fills, seals, anoints.

Paul said, "If any man have not the Spirit of Christ, he is none of his" (Romans 8:9). The indwelling Holy Spirit distinguishes the genuine believer from someone who merely professes to be in the church. One has the Holy Spirit; the other does not. One has spiritual life; the other does not.

Those who share new life in Christ do so because of the indwelling Holy Spirit. True believers may be misinformed about Him or wholly ignorant of Him. They may grieve Him. They may sadly distort what He says about Himself and His work. They may go to all kinds of excess, but He patiently continues to indwell them. As for false professors, although the Holy Spirit does not indwell them, He does continue to strive with them.

There are many false spirits and because of this 1 John 4:1-2 warns us to "try the spirits." There is only *one* Holy Spirit, one Spirit who imparts the one life shared by all the members of the mystical body of Christ.

(2) Its Fundamental Unity (4:4c-5)

(a) Of Calling (4:4c) "One hope of your calling."

All believers have a common hope: the second coming of Christ. They may be doctrinally divided as to when He will come, but they believe He will come.

Postmillennialists think He will come when the leaven of the gospel has sufficiently permeated society and made the world morally and spiritually ready for His coming.

Amillennialists, who view the church as spiritual Israel, see all the millennial promises of the Old Testament as being spiritually fulfilled in the church. They believe that there will be no literal millennium; Christ's coming will usher in the eternal state.

Premillennialists take the Old Testament millennial prophecies literally. They refuse to allegorize the prophecies and explain them away, believing that Christ will set up a thousand-year reign on this planet, the former scene of His rejection.

Post-tribulationists believe that before Christ can come to reign, the church must go through the fires of the great tribulation and be purified.

Midtribulationists think that the rapture of the church will take place halfway through the last seven-year period of Gentile dominance so that true believers will be snatched away in the nick of time.

Pretribulationists view the coming tribulation period as a time when God will wrathfully judge Israel and the nations, and the church will escape altogether.

Partial-rapture theorists believe that only the watchful, ready portion of the church will be raptured. The rest will be left behind to be purged by persecution (a theory, really, of a ruptured church rather than a raptured church). And so it goes on.

As with all major Bible doctrines, the enemy has succeeded in making this glorious truth of our hope confusing and conflicting.

But the bottom line is, we all have one hope. Our calling is sure: Jesus is coming again. We agree on that because He said so (John 14:1-3). Satan wants us to squabble over the details; God keeps this ultimate, blessed hope before us.

(b) Of Confession (4:5) "One Lord, one faith, one baptism."

"One Lord." That is our way of saying, *"I'm saved."* This is the common confession of the redeemed. We may express the message in different ways, belong to different communities of faith, and hold to different convictions, but we have only one confession: Jesus is Lord.

Paul wrote, "If thou shalt confess with thy mouth the Lord Jesus, and shalt believe in thine heart that God hath raised him from the dead, thou shalt be saved" (Romans 10:9). The evidence of our salvation is the heartfelt confession of Jesus as Lord. This confession turns our lives over to Him and makes Him our center, sum, and circumference for salvation, sovereignty, and security. This is not the glib mouthing of words, for Christ Himself warned that not all who say "Lord, Lord" are His (Matthew 25:1-12). No, this confession is the heart response of those who want to know Him, love Him, trust Him, and obey Him. In this confession the mouth speaks "out of the abundance of the heart" (Matthew 12:34).

"One faith." That is our way of saying, *"I'm sure."* Jude 3 speaks of "the faith which was once delivered unto the saints." That is the faith Paul had in mind here—that great body of assuring truth that Luke called "the apostles' doctrine" (Acts 2:42), the foundation stone on which our certainty of salvation rests (Ephesians 2:20; 3:5).

There is only one faith. The bottom line of all Christian belief is Christ: Christ as He is revealed in the Scriptures; Christ as God the Son, eternal, uncreated, self-existing, omnipotent, omniscient, omnipresent, holy, loving, and true; Christ as the second person of the godhead, coequal with the Father and the Spirit, possessing all the attributes of deity, creator, and sustainer of all things, ineffably sublime; Christ as the Son of man, virgin-born, conceived of the Holy Ghost, immaculate, triumphant over sin's curse, victor over demons and disease and disaster and death; humble and holy, loving and lowly, patient and pure, glorious, gracious, and good.

Christ is the One foretold by the prophets; the One who fulfilled the law; the One who pleased God in His character, career, conduct, and conversation; the One who went about doing good, healed the sick, cast out demons, raised the dead, fed the multitudes, stilled the storm, walked the waves.

Christ is the One who was rejected, betrayed, falsely accused, crucified, and buried; the One who died for us to purge our sins; the One whose body defied the corruption of the grave; the One who rose from the dead and ascended on high; the One who sat down at God's right hand, sent the Holy Spirit, heads the church, and is coming again.

Christ is the essence of our one faith. Hallelujah! What a Savior!

"One baptism." That is our way of saying, *"I'm separated."* Despite arguments to the contrary, Paul had water baptism—not Spirit baptism—in mind here. If he had meant Spirit baptism, he would have linked it with "one Spirit" in Ephesians 4:4, not with "one Lord" in verse 5. Also we must remember that Paul did not address this Epistle to theologians, but to ordinary believers who would naturally think of their own water baptism when they read the unqualified words, "one baptism." In that day, there was only one baptism. The unscriptural idea of infant baptism had not been invented in apostolic times. Baptism of believers by immersion was the New Testament mode of baptism.

This one baptism effectively separated the believers from the world. In many instances it was the crucial test of a person's faith. It was the ultimate confession that could cost him his job, his family, his friends, and sometimes even his life. It still remains the test in some cultures. In Muslim lands, among some Jews, and even in some so-called Christian lands, believers can pay a high price for being baptized.

When performed publicly—in a river or at a seaside resort, for instance—baptism is still a daring confession of faith that announces loudly to a watching world that the believer has died with Christ, has been buried with Him, and is now raised with Him to live in newness of life.

(3) Its Family Unity (4:6) "One God and Father of all, who is above all, and through all, and in you all."

That God is our Father is essentially a New Testament truth. This truth was not entirely unknown to the Old Testament saints (Malachi 2:10), but it was Jesus who really taught us to call God *Father.* Christ's first recorded utterance reveals His glorious awareness of His wondrous relationship to God: "Wist ye not that I must be about my Father's business?" (Luke 2:49) His Father's business was not the work of a carpenter, but the work of the cross.

When Jesus responded to the disciples' request that He teach them to pray, He said, "After this manner therefore pray ye: Our

Father which art in heaven, Hallowed be thy name" (Matthew 6:9). In His parable of the prodigal son and the elder brother, Jesus used the word *father* twelve times. He died with that name on His lips and rose from the dead assuring His loved ones that His Father was their Father.

In His last recorded utterance on the way to His ascension, Jesus used the name again. "Wait," He said, "for the promise of the Father" (Acts 1:4). He then added that the *Father* had put the restoration of the kingdom to Israel into His own power (Acts 1:6-7). Then Jesus was gone! But the name still echoes on earth. It is the greatest of all the names for God. He had been known as a Shepherd, a Shield, a Rock, the Lord of hosts, the holy One of Israel—all the wondrous metaphors by which He revealed Himself to the sons of men. But what name can compare with *Father?*

Our Father is *absolute in His power.* As Paul wrote, there is "one God and Father of all, who is above all." No foe can daunt us. No fear can haunt us. No power in Heaven, earth, or Hell can triumph over Him. He is above all. He rules the galaxies, from earth to the uttermost star. No government on earth can overrule His decrees. He is above all, and He is our God and Father. Blessed be His name!

Our Father is *absorbed in His purpose:* "One God and Father of all, who is . . . through all." The Greek preposition translated "through" here is *dia.* In this context *dia* has the general sense of dividing a surface in two with an intersecting line. *Dia* includes the idea of proceeding from and passing on out. It denotes any cause by means of which an action passes to its accomplishment—the passing through whatever is interposed between the beginning and the end of such action. God is through all. In other words, "Known unto God are all his works from the beginning of the world" (Acts 15:18). God knows what He is doing, where He is going, and how He will accomplish His purposes.

Nowhere is this more evident than at Calvary. There God allowed the opposition of earth and Hell to unite against Him and have its diabolical way. The Greek, Latin, and Hebrew letters on Jesus' cross proclaimed not only His title—"Jesus of Nazareth the King of the Jews"—but also the world's united contempt (John 19:19). Greek reasoning, Roman rule, and Hebrew religion joined to endorse the crucifixion of God's King. Hell triumphed! Satan won! God had sent His only Son. Now He had no more heralds to send. As in the parable, the people said, "This is the heir; come, let us kill him, and the inheritance shall be ours" (Mark 12:7). For a little while, it looked as though God was checkmated by men on earth and by plots of the pit. But not so! God was simply on His way through.

The dark hill of Calvary was not the end of the journey. God was "proceeding from." He was intersecting time, drawing a line through the ages. He was dividing the human race in two: saved and lost, believing and unbelieving, reprobate and regenerate. He allowed men to bury His Son in the tomb. He allowed Jesus' body to lie there while He finished drawing that line. Then, having "proceeded from," He "passed on out." Jesus came out of that tomb, ascended into Heaven, took His place at God's right hand in glory, and began the countdown to Armageddon. Our Father is absorbed in His purpose.

Our Father is also *abiding in His presence:* "One God and Father of all, who is . . . in you all." *En,* the preposition translated "in" here, denotes "being or remaining within, with the primary idea of rest and continuance" *(The Companion Bible).* We are familiar with the concepts of the Holy Spirit indwelling the believer (1 Corinthians 3:16) and the Lord Jesus indwelling the believer (John 15:4). Here we learn that the Father also indwells the believer. The thought is beyond all thought! God the Father, God the Son, and God the Holy Spirit are all at home in our hearts.

2.   The Gifts of the Mystical Body (4:7-13)

a.   Grace to Accompany Gifts (4:7) "But unto every one of us is given grace according to the measure of the gift of Christ."

Paul taught us how the body of Christ functions and grows. The Lord has provided everything that the body needs: grace so that its members can function in harmony one with another; and gifts so that the body can live and grow through the ordinary lives of men.

"Grace" was one of Paul's favorite words. The Greek word translated "grace," *charis,* occurs 156 times in the New Testament. No less than 110 of these occurrences are in Paul's Epistles. *Charis* always conveys the idea of free, undeserved favor. Once we understand that God's free and undeserved favor has given us any gifts we have, we will be more diligent in developing and using those gifts and more humble in enjoying them.

Gifts without grace can be harsh, abrasive, and presumptuous in their effect on others, and tend to create egotism and self-complacency in ourselves. Gifts without grace produce pride, friction, and carnality—a truth all too evident in Paul's letter to the Corinthians. The more gifts we have, the more grace we need. That is why Paul spoke of grace being "according to the measure of the gift."

The Lord Himself has bestowed on us any gifts that we have. As James M. Gray's hymn puts it:

> Naught have I gotten but what I received;
> Grace hath bestowed it since I have believed.

Moreover, all gifts are given so that we can manifest to the world and to one another the marvelous traits and abilities of the Lord Jesus.

b.   Gifts to Accompany Grace (4:8-13)

(1) The Gifts Assured (4:8-10)

(a) The Old Testament Promise (4:8) "Wherefore he saith, When he ascended up on high, he led captivity captive, and gave gifts unto men."

Gifts without grace are undesirable, but so is grace without gifts. The church needs both gifts and grace.

The gifts bestowed by the Lord on His church came at Pentecost in fulfillment of the promise in Psalm 68:18. Interestingly, the Jews used this Psalm in connection with Pentecostal celebrations in the synagogue.

When Paul wrote Ephesians 4:8, he had in mind a picture of a victorious king who has overthrown his foes. He is ascending the mountains, entering triumphantly into his city. He is laden with the spoils of war and bestows lavish gifts on his cheering people. He has freed the hostages held by the enemy and has ravished the enemy's domains. The freed captives are special recipients of his princely gifts.

We can see the parallel. Jesus triumphed in battle over sin and Satan. He carried the war into the enemy's domains and led forth from the lower regions a multitude of captives ("he led captivity captive"). Then Jesus took His place on high and "gave gifts unto men." He bestowed liberal, magnificent gifts on His own.

Paul saw in all this a fulfillment of Psalm 68:18, which he quoted in Ephesians 4:8 with a slight alteration. (We find many amended quotations in the New Testament. The Holy Spirit, the Author of both the Old and New Testaments, certainly had the latitude to use His own material in whatever manner suited Him and to bring out shades of meaning He had in mind from the beginning.) The Jews saw in Psalm 68:18 a reference to Moses' ascent of mount Sinai to receive the law, which he then gave to Israel. They associated the giving of the law with Pentecost. Whatever truth there might have been in this use of the passage, Paul lifted everything to higher ground.

(b) The New Testament Proof (4:9-10) "Now that he ascended what is it but that he also descended first into the lower parts of the earth? He that descended is the same also that ascended up far above all heavens, that he might fill all things."

At His birth, the Lord Jesus descended from Heaven's heights to a Bethlehem barn. At his death, He descended into Hades. There He preached to "the spirits in prison" (1 Peter 3:18-20), presumably the disembodied spirits of all those who had died in previous ages. At that time Hades seems to have been divided into two realms, each separated from the other by an impassable gulf (Luke 16:19-31). In one realm were the spirits of the wicked dead, already in torment though not yet in Hell *(Gehenna)*. In the other realm were the spirits of the blessed dead. (The second realm was called *paradise* by Jesus when He was speaking to the dying thief and *Abraham's bosom* by the Jews in their commentaries.)

Jesus went to these captives in Hades with a proclamation. He proclaimed His everlasting triumph over sin, Satan, death, and the grave. To those in the dark realm, it was a message of eternal despair. During their lifetimes they had rejected Him by rejecting the light God had graciously given them. Now they were without God, without Christ, and without hope. One man in their ranks represented them all—the thief who while dying had cursed Christ and blasphemed His claims. With what horror-filled eyes he must now have looked on the One he had so rashly scorned but a few hours before.

To those in paradise the Lord's message was full of unspeakable joy and glory. How the prophets must have rejoiced at the fulfillment of their often misunderstood and barely comprehended prophecies! How Abraham, David, and all the others must have shouted for joy! One man in their ranks represented them all—the thief who died calling on Christ to remember him in His kingdom. Now he was alive forevermore. With what wonder-filled eyes he must have looked on the One in whom he had so boldly believed a few hours earlier.

After proclaiming His triumph to those in Hades, the Lord arose in triumph, bringing the souls of the blessed dead with Him. Many of them were united with their bodies and shared in His resurrection as the first fruits of the second harvest. Paradise was thus emptied, and we are not told more about this beyond the intimation here in Ephesians that when the Lord ascended, He took with Him the captives He had delivered from the nether regions. Now all who die in Christ go to be with Him, "which is far better" (Philippians 1:23).

(2)   The Gifts Assigned (4:11-13)

(a)   The Nature of Them (4:11) "And he gave some, apostles; and some, prophets; and some, evangelists; and some, pastors and teachers."

The gifts listed here are different from most of those mentioned in 1 Corinthians 12. There, for the most part, the gifts are bestowed on believers. Here, gifted believers are bestowed on the church. In 1 Corinthians the gifts are viewed primarily from the standpoint of the local church. In Ephesians they are viewed from the standpoint of the universal church, the whole body. The five gifts listed in Ephesians 4:11 can be summarized in this way:

1. Those gifted to deal with *situations*
   a. Those equipped to *guide* the infant church in ways it ought to go (apostles)
   b. Those equipped to *guard* the infant church in what it ought to know (prophets)
2. Those gifted to deal with *sinners* (evangelists)
3. Those gifted to deal with *saints*
   a. Those called to *tend* the flock of God (pastors)
   b. Those called to *teach* the flock of God (teachers)

The gifts of apostles and prophets were foundational (Ephesians 2:20) and unique to the early church. We have missionaries (sent ones) and preachers today, but we do not have apostles and prophets. Those gifts were temporary and transitional, intended to help the church become established according to the Holy Spirit's plans.

There were primary apostles and secondary apostles. The primary apostles were called and commissioned by the Lord Jesus as His sent ones. Paul was such an apostle, although he had been "born out of due time" (1 Corinthians 15:8). Primary apostles were men who had seen the Lord, who had been with Him from the beginning, and who were eyewitnesses of His resurrection. They were given the task of imparting New Testament truth to the church by direct inspiration of the Holy Spirit. Secondary apostles—men like Barnabas, Timothy, and Silvanus—were intimately linked with the primary apostles.

The prophets spoke by direct illumination of the Holy Spirit. Their work was essential too. Their task was to disseminate New Testament truth before the completion and distribution of the New Testament. The Spirit of God empowered the prophets to impart truths (already revealed to the apostles) to local congregations. Occasionally the prophets foretold things to come. Usually, like their Old Testament counterparts, they were "forthtellers" rather than foretellers. They "forthtold" truth already revealed by the Holy Spirit but not yet in general circulation.

The gifts of apostles and prophets died out with the end of the first century and the completion of the New Testament canon of Scripture.

Evangelists are always needed. The evangelist, a man especially gifted by the Spirit of God to win souls, is the church's salesman, so to speak. All believers can be soul-winners, but not all believers can be evangelists. When the evangelist comes to town, sinners turn to Christ in significant numbers. A person either has or does not have the gift of the evangelist. If the person has the gift of the evangelist, something happens when he preaches: people come to Christ. If he does not have the gift, the response to his message is likely to be sparse. Nobody can produce fruit like the evangelist. His message and methods may be shallower than those of the pastors and teachers, but he gets the souls because God has given him the gift. A person who does not have this gift should not fret, but thank God some people do have it.

The pastor is simply a shepherd, as the name of the gift implies. He loves the Lord's people and has a heart for the flock. He cares for the weak, the sick, and those who are going astray. He counsels the young, cares for the needy, and comforts the bereaved. He does these tasks supremely well because he has the shepherd's heart and the pastoral gift.

The teacher expounds the Bible's great truths: its sublime doctrines; its underlying principles; and the broad scope of its history, theology, purpose, and impact. He compares spiritual things with spiritual (1 Corinthians 2:13), shows God's ways with men down through the ages, and communicates God's stirring plans for the future. The teacher develops consistent hermeneutics and discerns a unifying principle broad enough to explain all of God's revealed ways.[1] He teaches others how to divide the Word of truth (2 Timothy 2:15) and opens their eyes to the wonders of Scripture.

(b) The Need for Them (4:12-13)

i.   The Purpose Involved (4:12) "For the perfecting of the saints, for the work of the ministry, for the edifying of the body of Christ."

If we delete the comma after the word *saints,* we receive the full force of this statement: "For the perfecting of the saints for the work of the ministry." The word translated "perfecting" *(katartismos)* only occurs here. Its verb form, however, occurs in many places in Scripture and is translated in a variety of ways in the New Testament. For instance, it is used of mending nets in Matthew 4:21. In Matthew 21:16 Jesus used the word in His response to the chief priests and scribes who objected when people hailed Him with their hosannas: "Have ye never read, Out of the mouth of babes and sucklings thou hast perfected praise?" The word is used in Hebrews 10:5 to describe the incarnation of the Word: "A body hast thou *prepared* me" (italics added). This is a reference to the unique creative act involved in the virgin birth; God brought into being a perfect vehicle through which the incarnate Word of God could fully express God's thoughts, likeness, and ways to men. The thought, then, behind the word *katartismos* is that of making something fully ready, of perfectly equipping someone, of fully preparing something. The proper use of the gifts is to bring the body of Christ to its full potential.

The universal gifts that God has given to the church are intended to build up the local church and the universal church. The Holy Spirit does not intend that those with these gifts should monopolize the ministry. Gifted people should help equip others to carry out the work of winning people to Christ, shepherding the flock, and teaching God's Word.

ii.   The Period Involved (4:13) "Till we all come in the unity of the faith, and of the knowledge of the Son of God, unto a perfect man, unto the measure of the stature of the fulness of Christ."

The Holy Spirit wants us to achieve the stature of Christ. What a goal! The same Greek word translated "stature" here is used to describe Zacchaeus, who was "little of stature" (Luke 19:3). It can also be translated "age," as in the account of the man born blind whom Jesus healed and whose parents were interrogated by the authorities. His parents answered, "He is of age; ask him" (John 9:21). In effect they said, "He has grown up." The Holy Spirit wants us to grow up until we display, here on earth, something of Christ's stature and maturity.

This ultimate goal will not be realized until the rapture when all the individual members of the body of Christ will be glorified together with the head. In the meantime, we should not expect the church universal to display this glorious unity and maturity. Denominational differences, doctrinal conflicts, dispositional clashes, and other issues constantly divide the church. However, the goal is certainly achievable within the fellowship of any local church.

If an individual believer is to mature fully, he needs the fellowship of other believers. The idea of an arm or a leg developing in isolation from other members of the body is ludicrous. No one can attain full spiritual maturity apart from the give-and-take of a local church fellowship. The New Testament does not mention freelance evangelists, independent missionaries, itinerant Bible teachers, or other Christians who have no local fellowship and are responsible to no one but themselves.

3.   The Growth of the Mystical Body (4:14-16)

a.   Growth Diabolically Inhibited (4:14) "That we henceforth be
      no more children, tossed to and fro, and carried about with
      every wind of doctrine, by the sleight of men, and cunning
      craftiness, whereby they lie in wait to deceive."

This verse is full of interesting words. The word translated "children," for instance, is derived from a word that literally means "one not old enough to speak"—in other words, a small infant. A child who is not yet old enough to speak is helpless. He is picked up and put down at the will and whim of others. He has no vocabulary with which to express his wishes. The gifts to the church are designed to get us past the highly vulnerable stage of infancy in our Christian lives.

A new convert soon manifests evidence of spiritual life, but his opinions and ideas are unformed and largely inarticulate. His theology embraces little beyond the bare fact of his salvation. Most likely his views on the Holy Spirit, prophecy, or the church are what he has picked up uncritically from others. He is vulnerable and needs the ministry of gifted men to protect him.

The spiritual infant has no doctrinal stability. He is "tossed to and fro." (The Greek word translated "tossed to and fro" literally means "surging like the sea.") His opinions are constantly changing. He has not yet mastered principles of hermeneutics and applied them to the Scriptures. He has not yet, through exegesis of the Bible, formed convictions of his own regarding bedrock truths. Thus a spiritual babe will often enthusiastically espouse one viewpoint for a while, then discard it and adopt another. His viewpoints are fluctuating and might even be out of harmony with the Scriptures.

The expression translated "carried about" means "borne hither and thither." In Mark 6:55 the sick were "carried about." In other words, Paul was painting a picture in Ephesians 4:14 of a person who is helpless in the hands of others.

So in verse 14 Paul gave us three vivid illustrations of the vulnerability and doctrinal peril of those who have not yet matured in the faith. He took us into the nursery, out to sea, and into the hospital.

But Paul was not finished. He used some more word pictures to illustrate how some people take advantage of the spiritual immaturity of some believers. People who are not well established in the Word are easily swayed. They are carried about from one teacher to another "with every wind of doctrine." This weakness is bad enough when the teachers are all saved people, but it can be deadly when false teachers come. They were coming to Colossae, which was not too far from Ephesus. In Acts 20:29 Paul warned the Ephesian elders to watch out for "grievous wolves" who would come in, "not sparing the flock."

Paul had a gambling scene in mind as he continued to illustrate how some people take advantage of the spiritually immature. The word translated "sleight" in Ephesians 4:14 literally means "a cube" and refers to dice. The word metaphorically signifies slyness or trickery. Satan and his teachers play tricks with the truth. For example, cultists are adept at supporting their heretical teaching with a verse of Scripture that is taken out of context or slightly twisted. Someone even quoted John 3:7—"Ye must be born again"— to support his belief in reincarnation!

Paul spoke of the "cunning craftiness" of false teachers. The word translated "craftiness" in Ephesians 4:14 could also be translated "subtlety." Paul used the same word in 2 Corinthians 11:3: "The serpent beguiled Eve through his subtilty." Eve was no match for the devil. But she had God's Word and all she needed to say when Satan tempted her was, "Thus saith the Lord!" Her failure to adhere faithfully to God's Word led to her downfall. God did not expect her to argue with the enemy or dialogue with him. God did expect her to adhere faithfully to the plain, literal sense of His Word.

The same word is used to describe the Lord's enemies when they tried to trip Him up by questioning the lawfulness of paying tribute to Caesar. Luke said, "He perceived their craftiness" (Luke 20:23).

Those who take advantage of the spiritually immature "lie in wait to deceive." The clause, "Whereby they lie in wait to deceive" (Ephesians 4:14), is a translation of a group of Greek words including *pros* ("with a view to"), *planē* ("deceive"), and *methodeia* (which refers to Satan's strategies, wiles, schemes, methods, and cunning devices). *Planē* signifies "wandering" and is the root of our word "planet." At Colossae false teachers were lying in wait to lead people astray. *The Companion Bible* points out that the association of *methodeia* with Satan in 6:11 shows that the deceitful schemes in 4:14 are of the devil, and not merely error. What was craftily and methodically being taught in Colossae—and what is being taught in the cults today—is not just error. It is calculated deception that emanates from the father of lies.

The growth of the body of Christ, then, was being diabolically inhibited in Paul's day. Satan was attacking the church with all his craft and power. No wonder the church needed apostles, prophets, evangelists, pastors, and teachers!

Satan threw everything he had at the early church. In the providence of God, he used every trick of his trade during the first century. Satan has no new tricks for us—only variations of tricks already played. He is bankrupt of ideas. In the apostolic age every wile of Satan was met and answered by the apostles and prophets, and the New Testament furnishes us with all we need to combat Satanic error and delusion. We can thank God for that. Satan overplayed his hand in his desperate attempt to stop the infant church. He shot his bolt. He has been fully unmasked and can only trade now on people's ignorance of God's Word.

b.   Growth Divinely Inherent (4:15-16)

(1) The Law of Love (4:15a) "Speaking the truth in love, may grow up into him in all things."

We can go to two extremes. We can speak the truth but not in love, in which case we are being *ungracious*. Truth spoken in that spirit often offends and does little good because it alienates the people we are seeking to win. Or we can speak in love and suppress the truth, in which case we are being *unfaithful*. People who do not want to hurt someone's feelings may say nothing and allow a sinful situation to continue. They suffer in silence. True love, however, will always speak at the right time, with the right words, in the right spirit, and using the right approach.

Paul spoke the truth in love to the Ephesians. He got down to very practical issues later in chapter 4. He talked about lying, anger, stealing, unclean conversation, and marital relationships, but no one took offense because earlier he made so many warm and positive comments. None of the Ephesian Christians thought that Paul was being harsh or unkind. They all knew that he loved them. We can accept the truth from someone with whom we share mutual love. As Solomon said, "Faithful are the wounds of a friend" (Proverbs 27:6).

(2) The Law of Life (4:15b-16)

(a) The Head Controls (4:15b-16a) We "may grow up into him in all things, which is the head, even Christ: From whom the whole body fitly joined together and compacted by that which every joint supplieth, according to the effectual working in the measure of every part, maketh increase of the body."

Paul returned to one of his favorite illustrations: the church is compared to a body, of which Christ is the head. In other passages Paul developed the theme of the interdependence of the members of the body and our mutual suffering and joy. Here the theme is our mutual development. We are to grow up as individuals and as a body.

Nothing is more wonderful than the way a body grows. Light, warmth, nourishment, exercise, and protection contribute to the fascinating process of growth to maturity. Likewise Christ gave various gifts to His church to stimulate growth. The growth of His body may not be continuous (time-lapse photography developed by Moody Institute of Science shows that in plants there is a period of growth followed by a period of rest), but the process continues until maturity is reached.

Not all parts of a body grow at the same speed or to the same size. The measure of our individual spiritual growth is Christ. How much like Him have we become? To what extent is His glorious life being reproduced in us, the members of His body?

Paul was anxious that the church at Ephesus and all who would ultimately read this circular letter might grow spiritually. He did not want contentment with mere fundamentalism to stunt growth at Ephesus. He did not want intellectualism to stunt it at Colossae. He did not want materialism to stunt it at Laodicea. "Look at Christ," Paul was saying. "Look at Him; live like Him; be like Him."

(b) The Heart Consoles (4:16b) "Unto the edifying of itself in love."

For the second time in two verses Paul mentioned love. Why? Love is the most important ingredient in spiritual life and growth.

> Love never faileth.
> Love is pure gold.
> Love is what Jesus
> Came to unfold.

Paul's emphasis on love in this letter was inspired. By the time the apostle John wrote to the church at Ephesus, the Lord had to write "Ichabod" over its door (1 Samuel 4:21). Revelation 2:2-4 says in effect: "I know all about you—how you are standing up for the truth and how you are standing up in the task. I know how busy you are and how doctrinally sound you are, but I have something against you. You don't love Me anymore." Poor insolvent Ephesus! Love for the Lord was lacking and without that, everything else was spurious. The Lord took such a serious view of this lack of love that He threatened to remove the church altogether unless the believers there repented.

---

1. See *Bible Explorer's Guide.*

B. In His Moral Relationships (4:17–5:21)

1.   A Complete Deliverance (4:17-24)

a.   A New Life (4:17-21)

(1) The Sinner's Condition (4:17-19)

(a) His Intellect Darkened (4:17-18)
"This I say therefore, and testify in the Lord, that ye henceforth walk not as other Gentiles walk, in the vanity of their mind, Having the understanding darkened, being alienated from the life of God through the ignorance that is in them, because of the blindness of their heart."

The behavior of a believer is to be radically different from that of the unconverted. Paul reminded his readers of the blindness of lost people. Certainly no enlightened Christian should let such ignorant people influence what he believes or how he behaves.

What a collection of words and phrases Paul used to describe the heathen and humanistic thought of his day! Never were his words more graphically illustrated than in our day. People who are outside of Christ simply cannot think straight on moral and spiritual issues. They may articulate the issues, but they leave out the spiritual dimensions because they are blind to them. Therefore they cannot come to any true conclusions. In Ephesians 4:17-18 we hear echoes of Paul's terrible indictment of fallen mankind in Romans 1.

The lost walk in the "vanity of their mind." The Greek word translated "vanity" in Ephesians 4:17 is *mataiotēs*. It occurs only two other places in the New Testament. Paul used *mataiotēs* in Romans 8:20 to describe the disappointing misery of the world of nature as a result of the curse: "The creature was made subject to vanity." Nature, red in tooth and claw and groaning in a minor key, is far removed from the pristine bliss of Eden. Then Peter used *mataiotēs* to describe the language of apostates. Although they are "wells without water, clouds that are carried with a tempest; to whom the mist of darkness is reserved for ever . . . they speak great swelling words of vanity" (2 Peter 2:17-18).

Man's thinking, alienated from God, is vanity. He thinks up all kinds of false religions and philosophies, and boasts of how right he is. Yet his notions are empty and dangerous.

The understanding of the lost is "darkened." Paul told the Corinthians, "The god of this world hath blinded the minds of them which believe not, lest the light of the glorious gospel of Christ, who is the image of God, should shine unto them" (2 Corinthians 4:4).

The nonsense some men believe shows how darkened their understanding is. Christian Scientists, for instance, believe that death is not real and that pain is an error of the mortal mind. Mormons believe that they can become gods. Hindus believe that, depending on how we behave in this life, we might come back as a cow, a cuckoo, or a cockroach. The scientific community embraces the theory of evolution. The humanist thinks that man is essentially good and quite able to cope with moral problems. In practice, humanism licenses lawlessness and lust.

Lost people proclaim lies as truth, immorality as morality, high-sounding nonsense as science, and philosophical speculations as religion. Their lack of understanding results from "being alienated from the life of God." The opposite of life is death. Men without God are spiritually dead. No wonder they are unable to think straight in matters of faith and morals.

Man was created to be inhabited by God. God intended for the human spirit to be inhabited by the Holy Spirit. The indwelling Holy Spirit was to enlighten the intellect, ennoble the emotions, and energize the will. Thus the life of man would express, in human terms, the life of God. The fall ruined all that. Sin entered and the Holy Spirit left. Without the life of the indwelling Holy Spirit, the natural man is spiritually dead, "alienated from the life of God."

The genius of the gospel is that when we accept Christ as Savior, we are cleansed by His blood and regenerated by His Spirit. The Holy Spirit takes up residence in the human spirit, making it possible for the saved person to have fellowship with God, cooperate with the Holy Spirit, and begin to live the kind of life God intended man to live—a life governed by the Spirit of God. Before a person receives Christ, he is adrift on life's stormy seas without a compass, rudder, or anchor. He is subject to every wind of error that may blow into his life.

The understanding of unsaved people is darkened because they are cut off from the life of God as a result of indwelling ignorance that is caused by deep-seated, inner blindness. What a vicious circle. The darkness is self-perpetuating. The lost move from darkness to darkness in darkness.

No wonder Christians should not walk as "Gentiles walk." We must never copy the beliefs, thought patterns, convictions, and codes of conduct of unsaved people. Even the most brilliant of them are blind leaders of the blind. Einstein never wanted to believe in God. Marx was an atheist. Darwin jettisoned the faith of his youth. Freud hated Christianity. Nietzsche hated God. Nearly all the well-known philosophers leave God out of their reckoning.

(b) His Inclinations Depraved (4:19) "Who being past feeling have given themselves over unto lasciviousness, to work all uncleanness with greediness."

The next step downward from willful blindness and wicked beliefs is wanton behavior, a theme Paul developed in Romans 1. In Ephesians 4:19 Paul wrote that people gave themselves up. In Romans 1:24, emphasizing the other side of the story, Paul wrote that God gave them up.

Occurring only in Ephesians 4:19, the Greek word *apalgeō* is translated "past feeling." Those who are past feeling have lost their sense of pain. The sense of pain is vitally important to a healthy body. A person with no sense of pain might accidentally put his hand into the fire and not know it until his hand is badly burned. Many of the terrible wounds that lepers suffer are the result of insensitivity to pain caused by their disease.

People who embrace wicked philosophies soon lose their sensitivity to evil and put their precepts into practice. They give themselves up to lasciviousness (also see Mark 7:22) in order "to work all uncleanness with greediness."

The word translated "work" in Ephesians 4:19, *ergasia,* describes a regular, gainful occupation. This word is used to describe how the slave owners used the demon-possessed girl they had in their power (Acts 16:16,19). *Ergasia* is also used in the passage about Demetrius and the silversmiths of Ephesus who "brought no small gain" to themselves by making shrines of the pagan goddess Diana; their wealth was threatened by the conversion of many Ephesians to Christ (Acts 19:24-27). (Incidentally, these confrontations with the slave owners and the silversmiths are the only two occasions recorded in the book of Acts when Gentiles instigated persecution against Paul.) The word is also found in Luke 12:58 where the Lord denounces the blind leaders of Israel: "When thou goest with thine adversary to the magistrate, as thou art in the way, give *diligence* that thou mayest be delivered from him" (Luke 12:58, italics added). Here *ergasia* means "work hard, take pains, do your best."

So in Ephesians 4:19 Paul was saying that those who are past feeling work hard at their vileness. They hope to gain from it and many do. People who run prostitution rings, sell drugs, and enslave people in hellish lusts are so greedy for gain that they disregard the effect their work has on others. Likewise, those who write, print, and sell pornography and glorify sodomy and other kinds of perverted sex are greedy beyond description.

(2) The Saint's Conversion (4:20-21)

(a) The Change (4:20) "But ye have not so learned Christ."

In another flash of genius Paul did not link Christian belief and behavior to a creed or code. He linked them to Christ. He did not link them to a precept or principle, but to a person.

Christianity is Christ. All we have to do is place ungodly philosophies and practices alongside Him and we can see at once how false and filthy they are. When we think of Christ, we think of the sermon on the mount, of His priceless parables, of the Lord's prayer. We think of One who went about doing good, who was humble and holy, loving and lowly, patient and pure, selfless and kind.

If we think of Christ, we reread Ephesians 4:18-19 with a growing sense of horror and shame. Could the contrast be greater? And to think that millions of people choose darkness rather than light! They would rather have lust and corruption than the living Christ. Given the choice, the crowd still cries, "Barabbas!"

"But ye have not so learned Christ," Paul reminded us in Ephesians 4:20. Life with Christ is a life of victory over the mental darkness and moral depravity of the lost. The Lord Jesus clarifies our thoughts, cleanses our lives, indwells our hearts, quickens our consciences, and stiffens our resolve.

(b) The Challenge (4:21) "If so be that ye have heard him, and have been taught by him, as the truth is in Jesus."

We always need to be cautious of the "ifs" in the New Testament. Here the word *ei* followed by the indicative mood means that the hypothesis is assumed to be fact. The classic use of this form of the word "if" is in 1 Corinthians 15:17 where Paul wrote, "And if Christ be not raised, your faith is vain; ye are yet in your sins." The "if" casts no doubt on the fact that Christ has been raised.

Paul used a similar form of argument in Ephesians 4:21. There is no doubt that these Ephesian Christians had heard of Christ. Even the most elementary knowledge of Christ would be enough to provide a contrast between the lifestyle He exemplified and expounded and the lifestyle espoused by the pagans among whom the Ephesian Christians lived. The truth is in Christ Jesus. The way of lust and license is false; it ends in disease, defilement, demoralization, and death. Paul made it clear that a new life is fundamental to being a Christian.

During World War II, I lived in a much-bombed industrial town in south Wales. When a bomb damaged a store or commercial enterprise, the dogged proprietor would most likely clear away the worst of the rubble, board up broken windows, clear a space for the merchandise, and put up a sign that read, "Business as usual." Such a sign said a lot about the commendable determination of the stricken shopkeeper to keep going, but such a sign would be most inappropriate for a Christian life. We are not to conduct "business as usual." We are to conduct business "under new management."

b.   A New Look (4:22-24)

(1) What Must Be Put Off (4:22-23)

(a) The Old Disposition (4:22a) "Put off concerning the former conversation."

The Greek word *anastrophē* occurs thirteen times in the New Testament and is always translated "conversation" in the King James text. The English word "conversation" has undergone a drastic change of meaning since the days of King James. The true meaning of *anastrophē* in today's English is "manner of life." Paul was saying that the believer is to put off his former manner of life through deliberate choice and determined action. The old disposition to sin must be "put off," or as some scholars render it, "put away." The believer has a new disposition because he is indwelt by the Holy Spirit. The Holy Spirit brings the disposition of the Lord Jesus into his life.

What a marvelous disposition He exhibited! He was never unkind or selfish. He never lost His temper, never had to apologize, never was rude or impatient. He was loving and thoughtful of other people. We search the Gospels in vain for any flaw in His character. Because our sinful disposition is quite incompatible with our Savior's disposition, we must take off the old disposition. We each have a new suit of clothes, so to speak, and so we take off our old sin-stained clothes once and for all. We are not to try to wear the new clothes over the old. We are to take off the old clothes and put them away.

Years ago in Vancouver I saw these words on a sign in the window of a dry cleaning establishment: "If your clothes aren't becoming to you, they should be coming to us." That was a clever slogan, but it does not express Paul's message. He was not telling us to send our old garments of sin to the cleaners and then wear them again. They are not becoming to us at all. They must be put away forever. God has something better for us—something new.

Sometimes the cleaner pins a little note on a garment: "Sorry. This stain will not come out." God knows that a person cannot eradicate the deep stains that sin has left on his character. It is hopeless for him to try. God has a much better solution. He tells him to take off and put away the habits of his old nature once and for all.

(b) The Old Desires (4:22b) "Put off . . . the old man, which is corrupt according to the deceitful lusts."

The "old man" is best described by Scofield as "the man of old," the man the Christian used to be. He was born with the incorrigible nature that God has put to death in the death of Christ (Romans 6:6).

Paul described this Adamic nature as being "corrupt according to the deceitful lusts." The old man has deceitful desires that produce corruption in him just as putrefaction produces corruption in a corpse. There is nothing attractive about a decaying carcass; it fills us with horror and disgust. Its corruption is most offensive. Nobody would want to share life with a corpse.

No wonder Paul urged us to put off the old decaying man. The fact that we need any urging at all shows how deceitful the old nature is. We still feel some fatal attraction, even though the desires of the Adamic nature lead to the grave's corruption, vileness, and horror.

(c) The Old Direction (4:23) "Be renewed in the spirit of your mind."

Many of our problems have to do with the way we have been trained to think. The human mind is brilliant. It can unravel many mysteries of the universe, find ways to split atoms, unravel DNA, and weigh stars. But without God it cannot think properly about matters of faith and morals.

Satan always attacks the mind. Ever since our first parents ate of the tree of the knowledge of good and evil, the human mind has been vulnerable because it has a natural bent toward evil thoughts.

It is attracted by sin. It is blind to spiritual truth, unless it has the Holy Spirit's illumination.

The regenerating work of the Holy Spirit brings the mind of Christ into the human personality. The Holy Spirit gives a new direction to the thought life of a Christian. His carnal mind wants him to continue in the old direction, but he must deliberately put it off. There are some books he is not to read, some shows he is not to watch, some conversations he is not to have, some stories he is not to tell. He puts off such evil, and he is renewed in the spirit of his mind.

(2) What Must Be Put On (4:24) "Put on the new man, which after God is created in righteousness and true holiness."

The "old man" is the Adamic nature; the "new man" is the new nature, the nature of Christ. Just as we inherited Adam's fallen nature by natural birth, we inherit Christ's nature by the new birth. Righteousness and true holiness marked the nature of the Lord Jesus, and as we deliberately "put on" the new nature, righteousness and holiness will be seen in our lives. People will recognize us for what we are. Christlike Christians display the life and loveliness of the Lord Jesus; carnal Christians still wear the rags of the "old man."

2.   A Converted Disposition (4:25-26)

a.   A Transformed Tongue (4:25) "Putting away lying, speak every man truth with his neighbour: for we are members one of another."

Complete deliverance from the old nature is expressed in a converted disposition—including a transformed tongue, which James said no man can tame. In Ephesians 4:25 Paul moved from principles of the faith to the practice of the faith. He started spelling things out, giving specific examples of what happens when we put off the old nature and put on the new nature.

It seems incredible that Paul should have had to tell Christians not to lie. Yet we are all surprised sometimes at "the hidden things of darkness" that lurk in our souls (1 Corinthians 4:5). How easy it is in an unguarded moment when someone asks an awkward question to take refuge in a lie. But a lie on the lips of a Christian instantly grieves the Holy Spirit, who describes Himself as "the Spirit of truth" (John 15:26). Nothing short of confession and an application of the blood of Christ can erase that sin. We are to discard all falsehood.

God is truth, unchanged and unchanging. The lie is the idiom of Satan's language. Lies are the evil one's common currency of speech. He, above all else, is "the father of lies" (John 8:44).

Zechariah wrote, "Speak ye every man the truth to his neighbour" (Zechariah 8:16). (Paul was quoting him in Ephesians 4:25.) Zechariah was a postexilic prophet. One of his great burdens was to urge the restored Jewish remnant not to repeat the sins that had made their exile necessary. Throughout chapter 8, Zechariah reiterated the phrase, "Thus saith the Lord of hosts," as the Lord contrasted His former acts of government and His present acts of grace. One of the fundamentals for staying in the land, the Lord said, was to speak the truth. How significant and sad that centuries later the Jewish people ended up hiring false witnesses against the Lord. They paid for this sin when they were exiled again for nearly two thousand years.

Paul picked up Zechariah's warning and addressed it to Christian believers. But there are some fundamental differences between the restored Jewish remnant and Christian believers. For instance, we are not in the land; we are in the Lord. Our position is not in Canaan; our position is in Christ. We are not concerned with a place; we are concerned with the person of Christ. Israel could lose its position—and it did; we cannot lose our position in Christ.

We have something Israel did not have. Israel had the divine statute, but we have the Holy Spirit! If Israel needed to put away lying, how much more should we. All deceit grieves the Holy Spirit and consequently leaves us bereft of joy, peace, and power.

There is something particularly deceitful about lying to a fellow member of the body of Christ, but all lying is destructive. We are to have a transformed tongue, one that speaks the truth in love.

b.   A Transformed Temper (4:26) "Be ye angry, and sin not: let not the sun go down upon your wrath."

The Greek *orgizō*, translated here as "Be ye angry," is imperative; it is a positive command. There is nothing wrong with being angry for a righteous cause. Anger can be wholesome. There are times when we should be angry. Anger can be kindled by the fire of Hell or by the fire from the altar of God. Anger kindled by the old man is always sinful, destructive, and devilish. Anger kindled by the Holy Spirit at the sight of some injustice, some great depravity, or some monstrous iniquity, is intended to give those who are engaging in the sinful activity reason to fear. The person who cannot get angry at the seduction of an innocent girl, at the corrupting of a child, at those who practice and propagate perversion and pornography, must either be spineless or wholly without moral conviction.

Jesus was angry when He drove the moneychangers out of the temple. A beautiful children's hymn written long ago embodies a lovely prayer, but begins with a wholly false concept of the Lord Jesus:

> Gentle Jesus, meek and mild,
> Look upon a little child,
> Pity my simplicity,
> Suffer me to come to thee.
> (Charles Wesley)

Is Jesus gentle? Yes. Is Jesus meek? Yes, indeed. Is Jesus *mild*? A thousand times NO! Surely Charles Wesley used that word only because he could think of no other word to rhyme with *child*.

Jesus was anything but mild, bland, soft, and passive. There was nothing mild about Him when He denounced the scribes and Pharisees for their hypocrisy and called them a "generation of vipers" (Matthew 3:7). There was nothing mild about Him when, whip in hand, He strode into the temple (Matthew 21:12-13). Jesus was angry, but he did not sin. He also wept over the Christ-rejecting city of Jerusalem and its people in view of its impending doom (Luke 19:40-44; Matthew 23:34-39).

The Greek word translated "sin" in Ephesians 4:26 is *hamartanō*, which literally means "to miss the mark." Paul was saying, "Be angry, but don't miss the mark. Control your anger." The apostle was quoting from Psalm 4:4, which in the Septuagint version reads, "Tremble and sin not." Concentrated anger is powerful enough to produce trembling.

We should note carefully how Ephesians 4:26 is positioned in the text. Its neighbor is the tongue (4:25) because it is all too easy for us to say wrong things when we are angry. Its other neighbor is the devil (4:27), because Satan is swift to take advantage of powerful emotions.

We should also note that the Holy Spirit added this caution to Ephesians 4:26: "Let not the sun go down upon your wrath." The word translated "wrath," *parorgismos*, communicates the idea of provocation. If you have to be angry—if the cause is righteous, the provocation severe—then let the storm burst but make sure the expression of your anger is not promiscuous or prolonged. Let calm follow the storm and be sure that your fellowship with God is not broken. Do not let the day end without quieting your spirit and making sure you have not grieved the Holy Spirit. You must not nurse anger. A converted disposition includes a transformed temper.

3.   A Conquered Devil (4:27) "Neither give place to the devil."

The author of the bad behavior described in Ephesians 4:17-19,22,25 is unmasked in verse 27. It is the devil. The mother of all sin is lust, and the father of sin is the devil. James said that when lust has conceived, it brings forth death (James 1:15). Sin did not begin on earth; it began in Heaven. Sin did not begin in the human heart but in the soul of Lucifer, the highest anointed cherub in glory. Sin was already hoary with antiquity before the fallen Lucifer introduced it into this planet.

Satan does not like people. He hates us with a hatred that beggars description. His sole interest in Adam's race is to deceive us, degrade us, distress us, and then destroy us. Since man was made in the image and likeness of God, the more Satan can deface that image, distort it, and turn it into a mere caricature, the more his distorted soul is satisfied. He constantly opposes us, even more so when we have been born again and the image of God has been restored in us.

Regenerated believers are no longer the devil's dupes; they are his deadly enemies. He fears as well as hates us. From the moment of our salvation right down to the gates of death, he keeps up the pressure of his opposition. But we must not give in. Paul said, "Neither give place to the devil." It is not that the devil is afraid of us personally. Rather, he is desperately afraid of the Holy Spirit who indwells us. Satan never knows when we will enter into all that is available to us—when we will become filled with the Spirit and triumphantly wage battle in his realm. Paul expected that we *will* live triumphant lives. We are not to give place, ground, or opportunity to the devil.

Note where Ephesians 4:27 finds its home in the text. Its immediate neighbors are temper (4:26) and theft (4:28). The devil lurks between anger and dishonesty, waiting to exploit them to ruin our testimonies and dishonor the Lord's name.

4.   A Conspicuous Difference (4:28-29)

a.   In Conduct (4:28) "Let him that stole steal no more: but rather let him labour, working with his hands the thing which is good, that he may have to give to him that needeth."

What greater proof of a changed heart and life could there be than for a former thief to seek honest employment, become concerned about those unable to work, and give of his own wages to alleviate the problems of the poor? The idea that a Christian can continue stealing is ludicrous.

One reason for the low ethical standards all too common among professing Christians today is that some leaders no longer preach repentance as a prerequisite to regeneration. They foster an "easy believism" that makes no moral demands on the conscience of the new convert. Yet the very word *conversion* implies a change of belief and behavior. It seems incredible that the Holy Spirit should have to spell it out: "Now that you're saved, don't steal. Go to work." But there it is in Ephesians 4:28. It is a sad commentary on our moral decay that the Bible must be so specific about what should be an obvious fact.

The verse also tells the former thief to work with his hands. There is nothing dishonorable about manual labor, although our society tends to esteem white-collar workers more. When Jesus came, He forever glorified manual labor by becoming a village carpenter. Paul was not ashamed to ply his trade of tentmaking when funds were low. He not only covered his own expenses, but also helped supply the material needs of fellow laborers. Among the Jews it was common practice for all men to learn a trade, even if they intended to become rabbis and teachers. Indeed, more often than not, the local rabbi was expected to earn his living.

b.   In Conversation (4:29) "Let no corrupt communication proceed out of your mouth, but that which is good to the use of edifying, that it may minister grace unto the hearers."

Paul went back to the fountainhead: if the heart is right, character will be right, conduct will be right, and conversation will be right. No corrupt communication will flow out.

The Greek word translated "corrupt" here literally means "bad, rotten, putrid." The word is used to describe decaying animal or vegetable matter. Corrupt language, unbecoming in any person, is unthinkable in a Christian. Nothing will destroy a testimony more swiftly.

Think of Peter's words when Jesus was on trial. The people who gathered around the fire in the courtyard of the high priest's house accused Peter of being a disciple. They said, "Surely thou also art one of them; for thy speech bewrayeth thee" (Matthew 26:73). The comment was astute, but when Peter began to curse and to swear, his accusers held their peace. They had been skeptical of his denials, but now they were convinced he was telling the truth. No follower of the Lord Jesus would curse and swear.

The conversation of Christians should be edifying and directed toward the spiritual welfare of others. Our speech should be marked by grace. Yet rare is the dinner table where conversation promotes godliness. Our guests should leave more edified, uplifted, and ennobled than they were when they came. Surely we should cultivate the habit of wholesome and enriching conversation.

One wonders if some of the parents who weep over erring sons and daughters sowed seeds of disinterest in godliness at the family table. Perhaps the conversation at dinner consisted of gossip and criticism of the fellowship, leaders, decisions, and spiritual temperature of the church. A constant diet of dissecting the message, depreciating the messenger, and constantly undermining what is sacred and spiritual, cannot fail to leave its mark. Let us determine before God that henceforth we will allow no corrupting comments in our homes. Rather, let us direct all our conversation toward positive ends.

5. A Christlike Demeanor (4:30-32)

a. An Ungrieved Holy Spirit (4:30)

(1) Who He Is (4:30a) "Grieve not the holy Spirit of God."

The Holy Spirit can be *resisted* (Acts 7:51). Resisting the Spirit is a sin of the unsaved, especially those who have had many opportunities to hear and heed the gospel. This sin is not dispensational, like blaspheming the Holy Spirit (Matthew 12:31). Only people who saw Jesus perform mighty miracles and attributed them to Satan, could blaspheme the Holy Spirit. People in all ages can resist the Holy Spirit. In Noah's day, for instance, God warned, "My spirit shall not always strive with man" (Genesis 6:3).

The Holy Spirit can be *quenched* (1 Thessalonians 5:19). Quenching the Spirit is a sin of the church. Paul warned the infant Thessalonian church about this sin right after he taught them about the rapture. His warning was part of his closing, pithy remarks to that church.

Many local churches today are going nowhere, winning no one, making no impact, losing numbers, and moving in ever-smaller

circles because they have quenched the Holy Spirit. Their fellowship is undisciplined, inconsiderate, quarrelsome, prayerless, unhappy, unthankful, critical of the preacher, and slack on matters of
faith and morals, and as a result the Spirit is quenched. (See the
context of 1 Thessalonians 5:19.) The members often try to solve
these problems by firing the preacher, streamlining the machinery,
livening up the music, buying more advertising, getting on the
radio and television, or imitating the methods of "successful"
churches. But none of these tactics will work. The results, if any, will
be disappointing. Instead of genuine conversions, there will be false
professions because "that which is born of the flesh is flesh; and that
which is born of the Spirit is spirit" (John 3:6). There will be
conversions without repentance, programs without power, and
religion without the Holy Spirit.

The Holy Spirit can be *grieved* (Ephesians 4:30). This is a sin of
the individual believer. The word "grieve" is a love word. You cannot
grieve someone who does not love you. You might annoy, upset,
infuriate, or disappoint him, but you cannot grieve him. You can
only grieve someone who loves you. You can grieve the Holy Spirit.

The word translated "grieve" in Ephesians 4:30 is in the active
voice and means "to cause pain or sorrow." We grieve the Holy Spirit
(we cause Him pain) by doing and saying things that are contrary
to His character. In the Bible the Spirit of God reveals Himself as the
Holy Spirit. Because He is holy, the kind of ungoverned behavior
that Paul described in the context of this verse must cause Him
indescribable pain and sorrow. We are commanded not to grieve
Him because of who He is—the Holy Spirit.

(2) What He Does (4:30b) "Whereby ye are sealed unto the day of
    redemption."

Paul had already told the Ephesians that the seal of the Holy
Spirit is the earnest of our inheritance (Ephesians 1:13-14). A seal
indicated ownership and possession.

One of the Holy Spirit's ministries is to keep us safe and secure
from the wiles of the devil, the weaknesses of the flesh, and the
wickedness of the world until we are "saved to sin no more"[1]—until
"the day of redemption." That glorious day is coming when the sons
of God will come into their own (Romans 8:19), when the saints of
God will be displayed to the universe as the exhibit of God's
marvelous grace (2 Thessalonians 1:10). We must not make the
Holy Spirit's work harder. We must not grieve Him by refusing to
cooperate with Him in His maturing, molding work in our lives.

b.   An Ungrudging Human Spirit (4:31-32)

(1)   Things to Be Discarded (4:31) "Let all bitterness, and wrath, and anger, and clamour, and evil speaking, be put away from you, with all malice."

This is a typical Pauline list. What an ugly accumulation of human characteristics! They sour our lives, scald our brethren, stain our characters, spoil our testimonies, and sadden the Holy Spirit.

Nothing could be more grieving to the Holy Spirit than a bitter, resentful spirit. Bitterness soured the soul of Simon Magus (Acts 8:23) when Philip preached Christ in Samaria, and showed that Simon's profession of faith was utterly false.

The Greek word translated "anger" in Ephesians 4:31 is the same word used for legitimate anger in verse 26. Anger is listed as an evil that grieves the Holy Spirit because it can easily get out of control. "Wrath" is a translation of a different Greek word that means "a violent outbreak of anger." Wrath boils up and subsides again just as swiftly, but leaves behind all kinds of scars. That kind of anger grieves the Holy Spirit of grace.

The word translated "evil speaking" is *blasphēmia*, from which we derive our word "blasphemy." *Blasphēmia* refers to slanderous, injurious talk and to railing (1 Timothy 6:4). The word is used to describe the mockery of the multitudes who reviled Christ when He was on the cross (Mark 15:29).

"Malice" is a translation of *kakia*, the usual Greek word for depravity, which denotes a vicious disposition. This kind of disposition, so contrary to the Spirit of Christ, undermines character, grieves the Holy Spirit, and produces the crop of noxious weeds listed in Ephesians 4:31. These characteristics have no place in the life of a child of the King. They are to be put away.

(2)   Things to Be Displayed (4:32) "Be ye kind one to another, tenderhearted, forgiving one another, even as God for Christ's sake hath forgiven you."

Here Paul emphasized the positive. He told us we must display spiritual graces instead of soul-destroying grudges. How can we do less? We must forgive others, for the sake of the Lord Jesus Christ, just as God has forgiven us for what we did to Him, for the sake of the Lord Jesus Christ.

Wuest translated the beginning of this verse as, "And be becoming kind." We might not be able to achieve the kind of total revolution of inner disposition demanded by the Holy Spirit all at once. God is reasonable. He knows our frame. He makes allowance for us to learn and practice, even though we already have the indwelling Holy Spirit to provide the energizing power needed for change. But God does demand that here and now—right away—we start putting away the old nature and putting on the new.

6.   A Categorical Demand (5:1-7)

a.   Love Is to Be Enthroned (5:1-2)

(1) The Exhortation (5:1) "Be ye therefore followers of God, as dear children."

The new birth places us in a new family where we are God's beloved children. The family of God is the idea of the family raised to the superlative. The world knows nothing about this kind of bond. The world has lodges and fraternities, but it cannot weld people together in families. The family is God's idea. Satan hates the family and has designed and put into operation many forces that can destroy the family.

In the family of God we are to be followers of God. The Greek word translated "followers" here can also be translated "imitators." Just as children in a human family often imitate their parents, so in God's family we are to imitate God. He is our model. Since God is love, we must imitate Him and express love to those in the family of faith and to the lost world outside.

A friend of mind copastors a large church. Thousands attend its services and participate in its ministries. Every Sunday the aisles are filled with people coming forward for salvation, rededication, and church membership. Years ago I asked him what the secret of success was. He replied, "Our people love God, our people love each other, and our people love the lost." No wonder people flock to that church.

In writing to the successful church at Ephesus, Paul reminded the Christians there that love is to be enthroned and exhorted them to imitate God.

(2) The Example (5:2) "Walk in love, as Christ also hath loved us, and hath given himself for us an offering and a sacrifice to God for a sweetsmelling savour."

Paul generally used the word *walk* to describe a person's outward life, the life that other people see. The word depicts progress in the Christian life because the Christian life never stands still. It is a life of movement. As Christians, we are either moving forward or sliding backward. We are becoming more like Christ or we are slipping back into our old ways.

We must keep Calvary before us and make Calvary love the goal toward which we walk. The Lord Jesus is the supreme example of love. At Calvary He expressed His love for us and His love for God.

Jesus said, "Greater love hath no man than this, that a man lay down his life for his friends" (John 15:13). Paul added, "God commendeth his love toward us, in that, while we were yet sinners, Christ died for us" (Romans 5:8). The love that took the Son of God from the heights of Heaven and the throne of the universe to that cross of shame and woe, on a skull-shaped hill called Calvary, to die on our behalf is "more than tongue can tell."[2]

Calvary expressed the Lord's love for His Father too. There was a burnt-offering aspect to the cross (Leviticus 1). In Old Testament times the burnt offering was the highest expression of love for God. Its unique feature was that it was all for God. The burnt offering was one of the three sweet-savor offerings, and there were different grades of burnt offerings ranging from a turtledove to a full-grown bullock. The size of the offering indicated the measure of one's appreciation and love.

When the offering was a turtledove or a pigeon, the priest helped, thus indicating that while the expression of appreciation and love was acceptable and pleasing to God, it was so feeble that a more mature believer needed to help make it known. When the offering was a bullock, the offerer was still considered unable to comprehend all that Calvary meant. But a full-grown bullock represented a mature, virile appreciation and love for God.

All of the full-grown bullock was burnt on the altar except the skin. The skin was given to the priest. Here again the symbolism is significant. The priest represents the fulltime minister of the gospel, the person whose whole life is given to the ministry. Sacred themes occupy his thoughts daily and continually, while secular matters play a minimum part in his life. Reserving the skin for the priest was God's Old Testament way of saying that not even the most consecrated believer can fully understand the devotion of Christ to His Father as expressed in offering Himself on the cross; he cannot get beyond the surface. Yet the goal of our lives is still to love as Christ loved.

b.   Lust Is to Be Dethroned (5:3-7)

(1) God's Demands Are Not to Be Underestimated (5:3-5)

(a) The Principle Is Underlined (5:3-4)

i.   The Holy Spirit States His Antipathy to Lust (5:3-4a)

a.   Immorality in Our Walk (5:3) "Fornication, and all uncleanness, or covetousness, let it not be once named among you, as becometh saints."

The expression translated "not be once named" can be rendered "not be even named." In other words, such sins are unthinkable for a child of God.

In Romans 1:24 Paul linked uncleanness with dishonoring the body through carnal sin. In Paul's day, as in ours, sexual promiscuity was taken for granted. Everybody indulged in it; it was an acceptable lifestyle. Many of Paul's heathen converts had been brought up in a permissive atmosphere where it was common for a man to keep a mistress, frequent houses of ill repute, gratify his lusts in casual liaisons, or accept a partner without bothering with the formality of marriage. These practices were considered natural, not immoral. Yet the Holy Spirit says that such behavior must not even be mentioned in Christian circles. They are the antithesis of genuine Christianity. Moreover, covetousness itself—the root sin from which sexual sins are often the fruit—must be banished from our accepted moral code.

Our society may be tolerant of these sins. Governments may pass laws legitimizing behavior that a generation ago would have brought a prison sentence. The Holy Spirit, however, will not tolerate such immorality. The conduct of a Christian is controlled not by a heathen society, but by the Holy Spirit.

b.   Impurity in Our Talk (5:4a) "Neither filthiness, nor foolish talking, nor jesting, which are not convenient [befitting]."

Just as offensive to the Holy Spirit and just as destructive of spiritual life as immorality in our walk is impurity in our talk.

"Filthiness" comes from the word *aischrotēs,* which signifies something shameful or obscene. A Christian should not tell dirty jokes or talk about things that make other people blush. In our day, open talk about intimate matters is acceptable. Nothing is sacred. The language of the gutter is freely used in books and broadcasts. Vulgar talk that would have been considered pornography a generation ago is now hard to avoid. The tendency is for us Christians to lower our standards also. The world is always trying to pour us into its mold, but the Holy Spirit brings us back to the gold standard of

Christlike behavior; He takes us away from the worthless paper currency of the world's immoral ways.

"Foolish talking" is silly talk. The original Greek is rendered "buffoonery" in the lexicons. "Clowning" would be the more modern word. The trouble with flippant talk is that it degenerates into worse talk. After a serious meeting we often allow Satan to snatch away the seed by foolish talking. Often when a person is facing eternal issues, someone will inject a flippant word and the moment of decision disappears. Flippancy in conversation can become a habit with some people and it is almost impossible to have a serious conversation with them. They turn everything into a joke or a pun.

"Jesting" is ribaldry. This word is used in classical writings to describe cultured insolence. Although some people think it is clever to make cutting remarks, the Holy Spirit expresses His personal antipathy to such ego-building, hurtful words. They are not to be used by God's people.

ii.   The Holy Spirit States His Antidote to Lust (5:4b) "But rather giving of thanks."

Since we have to talk about something, let us elevate our conversation to a higher plane. Let us use our tongues to express gratitude to God for all that He has done for us and use our conversational skills to encourage others to think seriously about spiritual things.

(b) The Penalty Is Underlined (5:5) "No whoremonger, nor unclean person, nor covetous man, who is an idolater, hath any inheritance in the kingdom of Christ and of God."

Paul bluntly wrote that a person who is guilty of non-Christian practices cannot expect to have any share in the kingdom of God. These practices prove that he is not in the kingdom of God; they betray the presence of an unregenerated heart. Jesus told Nicodemus, "Except a man be born again, he cannot see the kingdom of God" (John 3:3).

A cheap form of Christianity is in circulation today. It is not really Christianity at all, just a popular counterfeit. People make professions of faith that entail no repentance, no genuine conversion, no regeneration by the Holy Spirit, and no dynamic new life in Christ. Such people can be deceived into thinking that they are Christians, but they see no need—and feel no impulse from an indwelling Holy Spirit—to give up sinful practices or resist them. It is "business as usual," the same old dirty business as before. Such people are as lost as they were before they went through the meaningless motions of professing to believe, being baptized, and joining local churches. Their penalty is devastating. Hell awaits them. Their lives reveal that their professions of faith were only lies.

Let us make sure we understand that lust is to be dethroned. God's demands are not to be underestimated.

(2) God's Demands Are Not to Be Undermined (5:6-7)

(a) We Are to Recognize Deception (5:6) "Let no man deceive you with vain words: for because of these things cometh the wrath of God upon the children of disobedience."

Paul challenged the notion that people can be saved and still habitually commit the gross and grievous sins he was denouncing. He contradicted the notion that the penalty for such sins in the lives of Christians is simply exclusion from the coming millennial kingdom. There may indeed be millennial loss for negligent Christians, but people who indulge in the vices Paul was describing are not Christians.

"Let no man deceive you," says the Holy Spirit. Those whose teaching undermines God's absolutes in the realm of personal morality are speaking vain words. The word translated "vain" in Ephesians 5:6 literally means "hollow, empty." Teaching that lacks substance and divine authority is deceptive.

We know that people who practice immorality are not Christians because the Holy Spirit calls them "children of disobedience." The expression is also used in Ephesians 2:2 to describe lost people.

In Romans 1:18-32 Paul wrote that the wrath of God is to be poured out on the ungodly. God's parental discipline will assuredly visit His own children who fall into moral sin, as David discovered. But His wrath is reserved for the unsaved who sin habitually. God will not pour out His wrath on those whom He has saved from wrath (1 Thessalonians 5:9).

(b) We Are to Repudiate Deception (5:7) "Be not ye therefore partakers with them."

No true child of God can compromise when tempted to take part in immoral behavior. God demands that we make a clean break with the ungodly lifestyle of our unregenerate days. Such a deliberate break with our past sins is proof that we not only profess Christianity, but we also possess Christ.

7.   A Convicting Distinction (5:8-14)

a.   Where Light Radiates (5:8-10)

(1) It Brings a Change of Character (5:8) "Ye were sometimes darkness, but now are ye light in the Lord: walk as children of light."

As children of God we cannot be partners in immorality because
there can be no fellowship between light and darkness. Light drives
out the darkness. Light refuses to coexist with darkness. Biblical
morality is always a matter of black or white, light or darkness, truth or
falsehood, good or bad, right or wrong. There are no shades of gray.

Paul recognized that once we walked in darkness. Some allowance perhaps can be made for the unsaved, but we are now children
of light and there is no excuse for us to live immoral lives. Professing
Christians who live immoral lives prove by their behavior that their
professions of faith were spurious.

When I was conducting meetings in a small town in Iowa some
time ago, the brother who took me back and forth to the airport
shared his testimony with me. His story was that he attended an
evangelistic service and although he did not understand what was
happening to him, the Holy Spirit convicted him of sin. A few days
later the pastor and the evangelist visited him, and his conviction
grew. That night he and his girlfriend returned to the services being
held at the church; he was drawn there by the new stirrings of God
in his soul. When the invitation was given, he turned to his girlfriend
and said, "I'm going forward. What about you? I've got to get this
matter settled."

The girl, who had been raised a Catholic, had come into contact
with the gospel some months before. She had asked him at the time,
"What does it mean when they say you have to be saved?"

His answer had been definite: "Don't let it worry you. That's just
their idea. There's nothing to it." But now he knew there was something to it after all. "I'm going forward," he said. "What about you?"

"I'm coming too," she answered.

That night they both accepted Christ. They now had a new
problem because they were living together as man and wife although they were not married. No one said anything to them about
their situation, but the Holy Spirit did. They knew that they could
no longer live in sin. For the time being they decided not to break
up their living arrangement, but to use separate bedrooms. For a
while they struggled with the complications of their situation.

"I began to devour the Bible," he told me, "looking for some light
on what we were doing. I was soon convinced that we could not go

on living as we were." They sought pastoral counseling, and within a week they were properly married in the sight of God and man.

When they were still in the darkness of their unregenerate state, they found it easy to come to terms with living in sin. But once they were saved, the indwelling Holy Spirit made such accommodation impossible. As children of light they knew instinctively from the inward voice of the Holy Spirit that living in sin was wholly incompatible with living for God.

(2) It Brings a Change of Conduct (5:9) "The fruit of the Spirit is in all goodness and righteousness and truth."

The phrase translated "fruit of the Spirit" here is sometimes translated "fruit of light." Paul repeatedly emphasized light and the word "light" occurs five times in Ephesians 5:8-14. First John 1:5 tells us that "God is light, and in him is no darkness at all."

If we are "children of light" (Ephesians 5:8), we will display the characteristics of light. If we are children of God, we will display the character of God. That character will be evident to our fellow men through our conduct. God always acts according to His character. He is good, He is righteous, and He is true. Our conduct as Christians will reflect these moral qualities of goodness, righteousness, and truth. We will not habitually be bad, wrong, or false. The conduct of a Christian is the best evidence of his new birth and the best testimony to the unsaved of the regenerating power inherent in his new birth.

The English evangelist Tom Rees told a story about a man who was saved in one of his meetings. The new convert had been a terrible drunkard and a domestic tyrant. His craving for drink had reduced his family to abject poverty. Although he had a roaring, godless camaraderie with his workmates and drinking buddies, he abused his wife and neglected his home.

Then he met Christ. He immediately gave up alcohol. He became a loving husband, a good provider, and a tender father. His home showed evidence of the transformation the new birth had wrought. Food appeared on the table, his wife and children were warmly clothed, and new comforts were added to the home from time to time.

His drinking companions did not like the change. They missed the vile oaths, dirty stories, and ribald songs. They found themselves confronted by a stranger—a man who went to church, sang hymns, read his Bible, gave his testimony, worked hard, and refused to drink with them or waste time on the job. During his lunch hour this transformed man sat alone rather than listen to the filthy conversations of his former friends. He would read his Bible, and the sight of the Bible infuriated his workmates. They began to persecute him. They attacked the Bible and ridiculed him for being foolish enough to believe it.

One of them tackled him with a Scripture passage that is a favorite of those who drink. "Hey Bob," he said, "how about that place in the Bible where Jesus was in somebody's house and turned water into wine? That's a pretty tall story, wouldn't you say? You don't believe *that*, do you?"

The converted drunkard had not been saved very long. He was not a skilled apologist, but his answer was classic. He said, "Fred, I don't know anything about that. I can't say if Christ turned water into wine in that house, but I know that He has changed beer into furniture in my house."

Where light radiates, it brings a change of character and a change of conduct.

(3) It Brings a Change of Criterion (5:10) "Proving what is acceptable unto the Lord."

Is this behavior acceptable to the Lord? That question is the criterion for judging conduct. The criterion is not personal preference, and whether or not the world approves does not matter. The Christian judges conduct according to whether or not the Lord approves it.

It is not difficult to discover what is good, right, and true. All we have to do is stand for a few minutes alongside the Lord Jesus. We only have to read about how He lived, what He did, and what He permitted to be part of His life. From His first breath in the cradle to His last breath on the cross, He spent His life under the smile and approval of His Father in Heaven.

We complicate the problem of judging behavior by considering shades of gray. Nowadays psychology tempts us to make excuses, shift blame, explain away guilt, and wrap up unacceptable behavior in high-sounding phrases. But there are no shades of gray for the Christian whose supernatural life enables him to choose conduct pleasing to the Lord.

The Christian is equipped with this supernatural life by the supernatural experience called the new birth. He is empowered to live this supernatural life by the supernatural indwelling and filling of the Holy Spirit. He is supernaturally added to a fellowship of other supernaturally transformed individuals, who are joined together in a supernatural body known as the church. The church, which was supernaturally injected into history on the day of Pentecost, will be just as supernaturally ejected out of history at the

rapture. The believer becomes a member of this mystical, supernatural body of Christ by yet another supernatural work of the Holy
Spirit known as the baptism of the Spirit. There is nothing natural
about being a Christian! His new life in Christ is supernatural from
start to finish. It's just as supernatural as the birth, life, miracles,
teaching, character, death, burial, resurrection, ascension, en-
thronement, and second coming of the Lord Jesus Christ.

The criterion for judging what is to be permitted in our lives is
whether or not the conduct is acceptable to the Lord. That standard
settles all the issues. It sweeps away all the befuddling, pettifogging
compromises and excuses. When Christ is brought into the picture,
the choices are clear.

b.   What Light Repudiates (5:11-12)

(1) What Is Done in Darkness Is Not Something with Which We
    Can Compromise (5:11) "Have no fellowship with the unfruitful
    works of darkness, but rather reprove them."

Instead of showing a spirit of genial tolerance toward the works
of darkness, we are to take a firm stand against them. The Greek
word translated "reprove" means "convict." The classic New Testament example of reproof is the account of John the Baptist when he
reproved King Herod for stealing Herodias, his brother Philip's
wife, and for "all the evils which Herod had done" (Luke 3:19).

This particular Herod was Antipas, who ruled for forty-three
years over Galilee and Perea, regions where both John and Jesus
ministered. Antipas possessed all the vices of his terrible father,
Herod the Great, and none of his father's better qualities. Antipas
is described as covetous, greedy, self-indulgent, utterly dissipated,
and suspicious. He possessed the cunning of a fox; in the East such
craftiness was usually considered good statesmanship.

Philip was the best of the sons of Herod the Great—the best of a
bad lot. At one time it seemed as if Philip would be sole heir to his
father's domains. The old tyrant changed his will, however, leaving
Philip wealthy but bereft of position and power.

This turn of events did not sit well with Philip's unscrupulous and
vicious wife. Herodias had married her half uncle Philip when his
prospects were bright. So it little suited her pride and ambition that
her husband would not sit on a throne.

Then Herod Antipas came to visit his half brother Philip in
Jerusalem. At once Herodias saw her chance and began a sordid
affair with Antipas. The pair agreed that when he came back from
Rome, he would get rid of his wife and marry Herodias. Their

adulterous marriage followed, and Antipas did not have to look far for trouble. Herodias became his curse and ruin.

John the Baptist boldly and publicly denounced Herod Antipas for what he had done. This rugged prophet refused to compromise with the unfruitful works of darkness. Safety dictated silence, but John spoke out. He reproved Herod for stealing his brother's wife and accused him of breaking God's law. For this firm stand, John earned the implacable hatred of Herodias, who schemed for ten months to bring about his death. In the end she succeeded in the terrible manner described in the Gospels.

Regardless of the consequences, we cannot compromise with what is done in darkness.

(2) What Is Done in Darkness Is Not Something about Which We Can Converse (5:12) "It is a shame even to speak of those things which are done of them in secret."

This is the day of talk shows on radio and television. Nothing is sacred. All aspects of sex are explored and aired with a blatant frankness that falls discordantly on sensitive ears. No matter how offensive the subject, the stations continue to spill it all out. People tell even the most intimate details and discuss them over the air waves.

Worse yet, shameful perversions are treated as a theme of entertainment, with the same brazen, pandering publicity. If they are not careful, Christians can be caught up in this so-called openness. The Holy Spirit, however, says that we should avoid talking about such evils. If we do talk about them, we are to speak against them. Certainly we are not to make such shameful topics the subject of casual conversation. The base and bestial practices of wicked people are not fit topics for the children of God to discuss glibly.

The word translated "shame" here is translated "filthy" in Titus 1:11. This word can also be translated as "deformed" or "ugly." It is used in Ephesians 5:12 to underline behavior that is indecent and offensive to modesty and purity. People who practice such behavior are shameful, and so are those who talk about them.

c.   Why Light Regenerates (5:13-14)

(1) The Work of the Spirit (5:13) "All things that are reproved are made manifest by the light: for whatsoever doth make manifest is light."

The word translated "reproved" here, *elenchō*, means "to convict, to bring in a verdict of guilty." The Lord Jesus used this same word to describe the convicting work of the Holy Spirit in the human heart: "When he is come, he will reprove the world of sin, and of righteousness, and of judgment" (John 16:8).

The Holy Spirit brings secret works of darkness into the light. Most of us have at one time or another turned over a stone or a log and recoiled at the ugly creatures that make darkness their home and scurry away in terror when exposed to the light. It is a terrible fact that we all harbor sins in the dark recesses of our souls. They live and flourish there, multiplying and reveling in being unseen. But once we let the light shine in, once we let the Holy Spirit do His convicting work in our hearts, the hidden works of darkness will be exposed.

The book of Job tells us how this saint of God faced calamity, criticism, and conviction. We see him first in Satan's hands, overwhelmed by disaster and yet retaining his integrity and faith in God. We see him next in men's hands, being accused and scornfully criticized. His response to them was angry self-defense; in his last speech (Job 29–31) he referred to himself by personal pronoun no less than 195 times. Finally we see Job in God's hands, abhorring himself. The man who had argued vehemently to justify himself when faced with criticism—and who in so doing exposed all the hidden and unsuspected bitterness, sarcasm, pride, anger, and self-righteousness of his soul—was repenting in dust and ashes.

Only the Holy Spirit can expose our sins to the light. When He does, we can see them for what they are—ugly beyond words.

(2) The Work of the Savior (5:14) "Wherefore he saith, Awake thou that sleepest, and arise from the dead, and Christ shall give thee light."

Light and life go together. Life craves light and cannot in its higher forms exist without light.

The phrase "shall give thee light" (another rendering would be "shall shine upon thee") comes from the Greek word *epiphauō*, which occurs only here. It was a word used to describe the rising of the sun. In Ephesians 5:14 *epiphauō* means that Christ will "shine upon" the believer. The whole verse is a paraphrase of Isaiah 60:1-2.

The Christian has new light and new life. The new light chases away the darkness in which he once groveled. The new life replaces the deadness that once possessed him and held him in corruption and uncleanness. Just as Lazarus, coming forth from the death and darkness of the tomb, was glad to be relieved of his vile graveclothes, so the new Christian throws off with horror the conduct and conversation that characterized him before he came to Christ.

Imagine a surgeon wanting to keep on the gloves that he wore while performing an autopsy on a decaying corpse! Obviously the doctor would want to get rid of the contaminated gloves and scrub his hands in antiseptics. Likewise, the idea of a Christian still wanting to walk and talk as he did before he came to know the Savior is incongruous.

8.   A Conscious Decision (5:15-17)

a.   Concerning Time (5:15-16)

(1) We Are to Be Wise concerning Our Ways (5:15) "Walk circumspectly, not as fools, but as wise."

The Greek word translated "circumspectly," *akribōs*, is one of ten synonyms in the Greek New Testament for the idea of being perfect. This verse could be translated, "Walk carefully or precisely, exactly, assiduously."

In some European countries, property is often protected by a high wall, the top of which is covered with embedded broken glass to discourage intruders who might try to climb over it. One can sometimes see a cat walking along the top of such a wall. The cat walks circumspectly, carefully, precisely, and assiduously. It picks up one paw and carefully places it where there is no glass. When that paw is in place, the cat reaches forward tentatively and gingerly with the next one.

We are to walk circumspectly during our relatively few years on earth. We are to be testimonies to the Lord Jesus Christ.

(2) We Are to Be Wise concerning Our Days (5:16) "Redeeming the time, because the days are evil."

The Greek word translated "evil" is *ponēros,* from which we derive our word "pornographic." We live in a pornographic society. Pornography is becoming increasingly difficult to avoid, especially during our spare time. Some of the books we are given to read plant impure thoughts in our minds. At strategic locations magazines wait to be picked up so their stories and photographs can pollute our minds. And television is the worst pornographer of all.

Once impure thoughts plant themselves like evil seeds in the receptive soil of our souls, they are difficult to eradicate. They grow like poisonous, prolific weeds. Their deadly fruit is temptation and sin.

The way to keep our thoughts pure, of course, is not to allow this world to plant vileness in our minds in the first place. Some contamination cannot be avoided, but much could be avoided if we simply decided to redeem the time. To "redeem the time" means to "buy up the time." We could avoid many traps if we were to buy up our spare time when the temptations of pornography are strongest. We must convert our spare time into another kind of time: time when we study the Bible; time when we turn our thoughts toward the throne of God in prayer; time when we pick up a good book, go for a walk, do some gardening, or visit someone in the hospital; time when we do what we have sinfully neglected because we were "too busy."

b. Concerning Truth (5:17) "Wherefore be ye not unwise, but understanding what the will of the Lord is."

Failure to do what the Holy Spirit says is the height of folly. The Greek word translated "unwise" here is *aphrōn;* it can also be translated "senseless." Surely it is the height of stupidity to have in one's hand the very Word of the living God—inbreathed by the omniscient, all-wise Creator of the universe—and neglect to read it, study it, memorize it, and obey it! The angels must look at our foolishness in astonishment. We spend years going to college to study medicine, physics, chemistry, business management, engineering, and history. We invest time and money to sit at the feet of those we consider to be learned. We buy their books, attend their lectures, apply our minds to master what they have to say. But we neglect our Bibles. What folly! What an exposure of our warped sense of values!

There is no wiser, no more knowledgeable being in the universe than the Author of the Bible. There is no more patient teacher than the Holy Spirit. There is no greater book than the Bible. There is no greater privilege this side of Heaven than to have a copy of the inspired Word of God. Yet we often let it gather dust.

Refer the average professing Christian to the book of Habakkuk, for example, and he will probably have to turn to the index or flip pages in order to find it. Ask him to name the covenants—what they contain and where they are found—and he cannot do it. Ask him the difference between the sin offering and the trespass offering, and you are speaking to him in a foreign language. Ask which Mary sat at Jesus' feet and he might know, but ask which Herod murdered the apostle James and he will likely be unable to answer.

Ask when Paul wrote Romans or why he wrote 2 Corinthians. Ask whether Isaiah and Jeremiah were acquainted with one another or why David wrote Psalm 24. Ask the significance of the feast of weeks or who reigned when Amos preached. Ask in what ways Daniel filled in the details of the silent centuries between the books of Malachi and Matthew. Ask him to name the twelve apostles or the seven churches of Asia to whom John sent letters. Ask when Jesus was transfigured. Ask him to name the "I Am" sayings of Jesus. Ask him to quote Psalm 23 or give the reference for "Jesus wept." Ask him to name three of David's soldiers or the differences between the beliefs of the Pharisees and the Sadducees. You will be appalled at his abysmal ignorance.

The average church-attending, professing Christian knows little about the one Book in all the world that should mean the most to him and about which he should know the most. That same person may know who starred in *Gone with the Wind,* the score of yesterday's football game, or the Dow Jones industrial average.

No wonder the Holy Spirit says, "Don't be senseless, but understand what the will of the Lord is." The will of the Lord is found in the Word of God. To know the will of God, we must know the Word of God. We must make a conscious decision to study the Bible as much as, if not more than, any other subject.

9. A Captivating Discovery (5:18-21)

a. How to Be Filled with the Spirit (5:18) "And be not drunk with wine, wherein is excess; but be filled with the Spirit."

The Holy Spirit draws a deliberate parallel—one we would not dare to draw had He not drawn it for us first—between a man filled with wine and a man filled with the Holy Spirit. Since He has given us the illustration, we can examine it closely and see what it implies.

Most of us have seen an intoxicated person. First he deliberately chooses to drink intoxicating spirits. Then he drinks more and more until he is drunk. At this point his behavior changes. I have known men who were timid when they were sober, but who became belligerent and pugnacious when they were drunk; men who were hard as nails when sober, but sentimental and tearful when drunk; men who were congenial and friendly when sober, but morose and surly when drunk. I have seen drink turn a moral man into an immoral man and make a filthy-minded man sing hymns learned at his mother's knee or argue about religion. Drink turns a man into another kind of person. It distorts his conduct and degrades his conversation.

Drink temporarily transforms a person's personality, but there is no such thing as permanent intoxication. The man who is drunk on Saturday night is sober on Sunday morning. If he wants to remain intoxicated, he needs another filling. Of course over the long run, drunkenness deteriorates and destroys a person's character.

Being intoxicated illustrates—in reverse—being filled with the Spirit. To be filled with the Holy Spirit is a deliberate choice. In Ephesians 5:18 Paul said, "Be filled." Most of the Holy Spirit's ministries to believers are once-for-all, sovereign acts of God. The indwelling, the baptism, the sealing, the earnest, and the gift of the Spirit are in no way dependent on us. They are wrought in us by the Holy Spirit at the time of our conversion; they are irreversible and irrevocable. The filling of the Holy Spirit, however, is different. It is conditional because it depends on our cooperation with the indwelling Spirit of God.

When a Christian is filled with the Spirit, he is transformed into another kind of person. He exhibits the loveliness of Christ and the fruits of the Spirit. It is evident in his walk and in his talk that something has happened. People take knowledge of him that he has been with Jesus.

The Holy Spirit's filling is not permanent. Paul used the present continuous tense: "Be ye being filled with the Spirit." A person can be filled with the Holy Spirit one moment and grieve the Holy Spirit the next. When he grieves the Spirit, he needs to confess his sin, claim cleansing in the blood of Christ, and seek a fresh filling.

Stephen Olford used an equilateral triangle to illustrate the process of a continuous filling. The base of the triangle can be labeled "The Lordship of Christ." We determine by God's grace that Jesus is to be Lord—

> Lord of every thought and action
> Lord to send and Lord to stay
> Lord in speaking, writing, giving,
> Lord in all things to obey,
> Lord of all there is of me,
> Now and for Eternity.
> (E. H. Swinstead)

One side of the triangle can be labeled "The Word of God." (The same phenomena associated in Ephesians 5:19 with being filled with the Spirit are associated in Colossians 3:16 with being filled with God's Word.) The remaining side of the triangle can be labeled "The Spirit of God."

With this simple figure in mind, note what happens. As we begin to read the Word of God, the Spirit of God brings some divine truth to our attention: a promise to claim, a sin to confess and avoid, a command to obey. Because we have established the basic premise that Jesus is Lord and made that the foundation of all our behavior, our immediate response is to obey. We yield on whatever issue in the Word of God the Spirit of God has brought to our attention. As we yield, He fills us and we receive the power to turn that teaching into practical reality. As this process continues, the Holy Spirit enlarges our horizons, increases our capacity, deepens our spirituality, and enables us to grow in grace and increase our knowledge of God.

Sin or self can short-circuit this process. A person can be filled with the Spirit one moment and be filled with self or fall into sin the next. Peter's experience just prior to ascending the mount of transfiguration is an example. At the time he was not indwelt and filled by the Holy Spirit, but his experience illustrates how swiftly a change from spirituality to carnality can take place (Matthew 16:13-23). The Lord asked His disciples who people thought He was. The disciples replied that people were ranking Him with John the Baptist, Elijah, Jeremiah, the prophets—the greatest men of the past and present. That answer was not good enough, so the Lord asked the disciples, "Whom say ye that I am?"

Instantly Peter replied, "Thou art the Christ, the Son of the living God."

Jesus responded, "Blessed art thou, Simon Barjona: for flesh and blood hath not revealed it unto thee, but my Father which is in heaven." Jesus then began to talk to the disciples about the cross.

Peter was aghast. "Be it far from thee, Lord," he blurted out.

Jesus turned on him. "Get thee behind me, Satan," He said. "Thou art an offence unto me: for thou savourest not the things that be of God, but those that be of men." Peter was a channel for the Holy Spirit one moment and was speaking in the flesh the next. Such is human nature.

That is why Paul wrote, "Be ye being filled." When we lose the *infilling* of the Spirit, we need a fresh filling. The way back is the way of the cross, the cross Peter so vehemently rejected. We must come back in repentance and with confession to the gracious Spirit of God, beg His pardon for having grieved Him, ask for cleansing, and receive a fresh filling. (We should note that in this age no believer loses the *indwelling* of the Spirit.)

When the truth about the filling of the Holy Spirit is first revealed to us, there is a crisis. We have to choose whether or not to yield to the Spirit. The crisis sometimes coincides with conversion, but more often comes later. Often we spend time in a spiritual wilderness first, and God has to bring us, like Israel of old, to the Jordan for a fresh, more mature comprehension of our spiritual death, burial, and resurrection with Christ.

In the Old Testament, the children of Israel symbolically entered into an experience of death, burial, and resurrection at the Red Sea. In the strength of that experience, they could have gone directly into Canaan. Their unbelief at Kadesh-barnea, however, led to forty years of wilderness life. They had to have a fresh experience of the truth of death, burial, and resurrection at the Jordan before they could enter into victorious living in Canaan.

At the time of his conversion a Christian could enter into the truth of Romans 12:1 and present his body as "a living sacrifice, holy, acceptable unto God, which is [his] reasonable service." However, months—even years—of worldliness, carnality, and defeat often intervene before he has a new experience with God that opens up the way to a Spirit-filled life. That crisis experience, be it early or late in his Christian pilgrimage, is the moment of surrender and yielding that is taught in Romans 6.

Once the lordship of Christ is established, there is a process of a continuous filling as described in the above illustration of the triangle. But what happens when, in the ongoing process of fullness and failure, the Christian discovers unsuspected areas in his life that have never been yielded? Does he have to start all over again? Must he present to the Holy Spirit, one by one, the members of his body and the various areas of his life? Perhaps the following illustration will help answer these questions.

An avid collector of old books is visiting a home. Browsing through his host's bookshelves he notices a battered old book. The cover is frayed, the casing is cracked, the pages are loose—some are even missing—but his collector's eyes gleam. He says to his host, "How long have you had this book, my friend?"

The host glances at it. "That old thing!" he says. "I don't know. It's of no use to me. I was going to throw it away. My wife picked it up off the floor behind the chair there the other day. It must have fallen off the shelf. I think it used to belong to my father. You can have it if you like. Pay for it? Dear me, no. Take it." The guest gratefully accepts the book, lamenting only to himself that some of its pages are missing.

Several days later the collector visits his friend again. "Oh by the way," the host says, "remember that old book I gave you? Well, I moved the chair yesterday, and guess what? I found more pages. If you give me the book back, we can start all over. I will give you the book again, including these missing pages."

Wouldn't that be an odd thing to say? It is not necessary to start all over again each time another missing page is found. The original owner only has to say, "Remember that book I gave you? I found a few more pages. I'm sorry they were missing. Here, they belong to you."

This illustration of the battered book can help us understand the filling of the Spirit of God. When the Holy Spirit shows someone an area of disobedience in his life, something not yet surrendered, there is no need for him to go back and start all over again. All he needs to do is say, "Gracious Holy Spirit, here is an area where I have been holding back what belongs to You. I meant for You to have all of me when I first surrendered to You. Please take this area of my life too."

So the message of Ephesians 5:18 is "Be ye being filled." It is the filling of the Spirit that enables us to do all that the Spirit of God demands of us in the previous verses and all that will be required in the verses that follow.

b.   How to Be Thrilled in the Spirit (5:19-20)

(1) Joyful Acclamation in Song (5:19) "Speaking to yourselves [to one another] in psalms and hymns and spiritual songs, singing and making melody in your heart to the Lord."

When Christians are filled with the Spirit, there will be joyful ministry. Our hearts will overflow with music and song in public worship. The second fruit of the Spirit, after all, is joy. The Christian faith is a happy, joyful, singing faith, which is one reason why we have so many hymnbooks.

Several explanations, most of them rooted in the practices of the early church, can be given for the three categories of music that Paul listed here. What do these categories suggest to us today?

"Psalms" suggest what we might call *Scriptural* music—the singing of the Psalms themselves, for instance, or other portions of Scripture. Attempts have been made to fit tunes to the actual words of Scripture, but without the rhythm and rhyme we normally associate with western-style music, the songs are often stilted and awkward. The *Psalms of David in Metre*, which are used in the Church of Scotland, are perhaps better for singing. Many of these are remarkably true to the Biblical text. They lend themselves to our kind of singing because they can be sung to well-known tunes. Probably the best-known example is the lovely rendering of Psalm 23, which we so often sing to the haunting tune of "Crimond" that Jessie S. Irvine composed a little more than a century ago.

> The Lord's my shepherd, I'll not want;
> He makes me down to lie
> In pastures green; He leadeth me
> The quiet waters by.

"Hymns" suggest what we could call *spiritual* music—classical compositions that form the backbone of our better hymnbooks. These great hymns are clearly Biblical in content and have stood the test of time.

Each generation produces music; many hymns have a brief day, but some always survive. For instance, hymns of Martin Luther, Charles Wesley, and Isaac Watts will be sung as long as the church remains on earth; some hymns born out of the Moody-Sankey revivals have won their place in the ranks of the immortals. Our own day has its contributions too.

"Spiritual songs" suggest what we might classify as *soulful* music, including choruses, lighter compositions, and popular Christian ballads. A few survive for a generation or two, but most die as quickly as they are born. They serve a purpose, however, if they lift our hearts and souls to God in joyful adoration. They can put a new spring in our steps or give us words to express our aspirations to know God better. They can help us express our resolve to love God more, grieve Him less, and serve Him better.

Hymnbooks are an excellent means of teaching and reinforcing truth. Wise indeed are the parents who teach their children to learn and love good Christian music and the great, doctrinal hymns of the church. How often the words of a hymn leap to the mind of a preacher as the best way to communicate a truth.

Not only will joyful ministry emanate from our Spirit-filled lives in public worship; there will also be joyful music in private worship. Overflowing with music and song, we will sing and make melody in our hearts to the Lord.

(2) Joyful Acceptance of Wrong (5:20) "Giving thanks always for all things unto God and the Father in the name of our Lord Jesus Christ."

All things? Are we to give thanks when things go wrong? When injustice comes? When death or sickness enters? When a loved one goes astray? Can we still sing when times are hard?

Paul could. We only have to picture him and his dear friend Silas in the Philippian jail to see what it means to be filled with the Spirit. Their backs were torn, their limbs were cramped by the stocks, and their future was uncertain, yet they were singing! That prison cell was so shaken that its doors burst open; the other prisoners were so spellbound they could not budge. The jailer himself was so moved that his first words were, "What must I do to be saved?" (Acts 16:30)

One reason the church today is so weak is that it has forgotten how to sing. Often we make Christianity dull and dreary, a drudgery rather than a delight. No wonder the world reacts as did the man who was offered a tract by a sour-faced Christian. The man looked at the Christian's face and said, "No thanks. I've enough trouble of my own." Let us get back our joy in the Lord.

c.   How to Be Drilled by the Spirit (5:21) "Submitting yourselves
       one to another in the fear of God."

This verse summarizes the practical implications of being filled with the Spirit, and it introduces the next major section of the letter. The next section deals with human relationships and reviews our various roles and positions in life. The key to each relationship is submission, the kind of submission the Son yielded to the Father when He lived on earth as a man. That kind of submission, so often contrary to human nature, is an evidence of the filling of the Spirit. The Holy Spirit will drill us in submission by the pressure of human relationships. It may take time, but eventually we learn that the path of submission is best; we learn to fall in line with the will of the Holy Spirit.

All of life and society should swing around the pole of obedience to divinely ordained authority. Sin entered the world through one man's disobedience; our salvation was wrought through another's obedience unto death, "even the death of the cross" (Philippians 2:8).

Looking back over the section of the Epistle that concludes with Ephesians 5:21, we see that yielding ourselves to the Holy Spirit is the key to all our *moral* relationships. Looking ahead to the sections following Ephesians 5:21, we see that yielding ourselves to the Holy Spirit is also the key to all *marital* relationships and to all *material* relationships.

---

1. William Cowper, "There Is a Fountain."
2. J. E. Hall, "More Than Tongue Can Tell."

C. In His Marital Relationships (5:22–6:4)

1. As a Partner (5:22-33)

a. Some Priorities of the Marriage Relationship (5:22-29)

(1) The Wife: Loyalty Revealed in Surrender (5:22-24)

(a) The Exhortation (5:22) "Wives, submit yourselves unto your own husbands, as unto the Lord."

This verse, taken out of context, has caused many husbands to repress their wives and many wives to be resentful and rebellious. Standing alone, this verse seems arbitrary and unfair. But it does not stand alone. No verse of Scripture stands alone. This verse is preceded by the command that we submit ourselves one to another in the fear of God. What a pity that preachers so often ignore this context when beginning a series of messages on husband-wife relationships. The context includes not only the Holy Spirit's instruction for mutual submission, but also His teaching about the Holy Spirit's infilling—the blessed oil that makes the machinery of marriage run smoothly.

Two words dominate the Biblical teaching in Ephesians 5:22-29: *submission* and *love*.

The Greek word translated "husband" in Ephesians 5:22 is *anēr*. *Anēr* is one of the words translated "man" in the New Testament. Paul was telling the wife to submit herself to her own man. The thought that comes to mind at once is that the husband is to be just that—a man. *Anēr*, which never refers to the female sex, is used here like an honorable title.

The wife is required by the Holy Spirit to submit to her man—her husband—"as unto the Lord." That perspective lifts this command to a higher, holier, and more heavenly plane. What woman in all the world who has met and fallen in love with Jesus would not willingly do anything for Him? Never in the Gospels do we find a woman treating Him badly, speaking against Him, or doing anything to harm Him. The women of the New Testament loved and honored Jesus. He was so manly, so honorable, so attractive, so thoughtful, and so kind. It is the men in the Gospels who opposed Him, not the women.

(b) The Example (5:23) "The husband is the head of the wife, even as Christ is the head of the church: and he is the saviour of the body."

God has ordained a hierarchal structure throughout the universe. First Corinthians 11:3 reveals that God has established the principle of hierarchal structure in all of life's relationships: "The head of every man is Christ; and the head of the woman is the man; and the head of Christ is God." A hierarchy is discernible also in the unseen spirit world. We read about principalities and powers, the rulers of this world's darkness, and wicked spirits in high places. We read about Satan as the prince of the power of the air who presides over all these fallen demonic forces. There are also hints of a hierarchy in the ranks of the unfallen angels—thrones and dominions, angels and archangels, cherubim and seraphim.

Indeed, order is the unifying factor in all of God's creation. Sin introduced disorder and chaos into the universe. Sin began on earth when Satan challenged our first parents to defy God's authority.

God's order in human relationships goes back to the garden of Eden. God created the man first, investing in Adam the position of headship. God created the woman second, giving Eve a subordinate (but not subservient) position in relation to the man. Adam was made to be ruled from his head; Eve was made to be ruled from her heart. But Satan persuaded Adam and Eve to change roles. Eve took the lead and the place of headship. Satan cleverly aimed the temptation at Eve's *mind* and engaged her in an intellectual discussion on whether or not she should do something that God had expressly forbidden. The result was that she was deceived. When Adam approached, Satan withdrew and allowed Eve to tempt him, thus aiming the temptation at Adam's *emotions*. The Bible says that Adam was not deceived; he disobeyed.

In the new creation, God reestablishes the original order. Man is to be the head, under Christ; the woman is to acknowledge the headship of the man. This sounds strange and chauvinistic to today's "emancipated" woman, but it is God's order for society nevertheless. We can ignore God's order only at great risk to the home, the community, the nation at large, and the individuals involved. Nothing is more unsightly than to see a woman developing dominant masculine traits or a man exhibiting marked feminine traits.

In the Christian home God's order is to be firmly established. The governing principle is not merely God's order in creation. Everything is lifted to a higher plane. Christ, rather than creation, is set before us as the model. Ephesians 5:23 says, "The husband is the head of the wife, even as Christ is the head of the church: and he is the saviour of the body." ("Body" refers to the church, His mystical body.) The analogy is deliberate. The church owes its obedience to its head—to Christ. The wife owes her obedience to her husband, who is to mirror the Lord Jesus to her through his behavior. Just as Christ is the Savior—the deliverer and defender of the church—so the husband is to be the protector of his wife, who is one flesh with him.

(c) The Expectation (5:24) "As the church is subject unto Christ, so let the wives be to their own husbands in every thing."

We are to consider the marital relationship on this lofty plane. The relationship between Christ and His church is unique. Nearly all of the brides mentioned in the Bible illustrate this relationship. We can see it clearly in the stories of Jacob and Rachel, Boaz and Ruth, and David and Abigail. We can see it too in the progressive stories of Adam and Eve, Isaac and Rebekah, and Joseph and Asenath. Taken together, these last three marriages are pictures of the church's past, the church's present, and the church's prospects.

The story of Adam and Eve illustrates the past and shows how the church was formed. Adam was put to sleep in the will of God. Then God opened his side and took from him what was needed to form his bride. This scene is reminiscent of Calvary, where the Lord Jesus entered into the sleep of death in the will of God. Jesus' side was opened and out gushed water and blood, the elements that made possible the creation of the church—His bride.

The story of Isaac and Rebekah illustrates the present. Their love story typifies the work of the Father and the Spirit in finding the bride for the Son. In Genesis 22 Isaac went to mount Moriah as a willing sacrifice, obedient unto death. But in Genesis 24 he was a passive observer, waiting with his father for the coming of the bride. All the action was in the hands of the unnamed servant whom Abraham sent to seek, invite, persuade, and bring the responsive bride to his son. In this present age the Son's work is finished and He sits on His Father's throne. The Holy Spirit is the active One. He is here to seek out a bride—the church—for the Father's beloved Son, who is waiting at His right hand in glory.

The story of Joseph and Asenath illustrates the prospects of the church (Genesis 41:45). Asenath was taken from obscurity and elevated to share the lofty position occupied by Joseph at the right hand of pharaoh. In the same way, our past is blotted out and our destiny is to sit with Christ on His throne and share His glory for all eternity.

The point here is that since the brides of the Bible are obviously intended to typify the unique relationship between Christ and His church, the marriage of every believer should do the same. Every married Christian couple should be an illustration to the world of the relationship that exists between Christ and His church.

In Ephesians Paul discussed the whole concept of marriage in the Lord on this high level. The marriage relationship is unique and as sacred as the relationship between Christ and His church. This perspective should end all carnal quibbling over who is responsible to do what. All marriages are to function like Christ and His church. All marital decisions are to be made on the spiritual plane.

(2) The Husband: Love Revealed in Sacrifice (5:25-29)

(a) The Exhortation (5:25a) "Husbands, love your wives."

The Holy Spirit's word translated "love" here is *agapaō*, the highest kind of love—spontaneous love, love irrespective of rights. The word carries the idea of "making much of a person." When a wife knows that her husband loves her with this highest kind of love—love irrespective of rights, love that makes so much of her— she feels no resentment over her responsibility to render loyal submission to him.

"Husbands, love your wives" is a command. We tend to think of love primarily in terms of emotions. That is natural because we are most conscious of love in the realm of emotions. God, however, relates love to the will rather than to emotions. He commands us to love. He commands us to love Him: "Thou shalt love the Lord thy God with all thy heart, and with all thy soul, and with all thy mind, and with all thy strength" (Mark 12:30). He commands us to love our neighbors as we love ourselves. He commands us to love one another. That is because God is love. Love is the greatest revelation of God. "God commendeth his love toward us, in that, while we were yet sinners, Christ died for us" (Romans 5:8).

Obviously if love can be commanded, it does not belong solely to the realm of emotions. The emotions we associate with falling in love sometimes fluctuate. Sometimes they fade away altogether. Emotions need to be cultivated. The word *agapē* refers to love as a principle. The New Testament reserves another word, *phileō*, for love as a feeling. *Phileō* is distinct from love as a fact and is associated instead with the ideas of kissing and fondness. *Agapē*, not *phileō*, is always used to describe man's love for God. God does not tell us to be fond of Him; He commands us to love *(agapaō)* Him.

Phileō, however, is sometimes used to describe God's love for us. God is fond of us! John used *phileō* in describing the Lord's love for Lazarus (John 11:3,36). The Lord not only loved Lazarus; He was very fond of him. In John 11:5, however, where Lazarus's sisters are included in the Lord's love, *agapaō* is used to place the Lord's relationship with Martha and Mary on a more spiritual plane. *Agapē*, the cause and ground for *phileō*, places love on the highest plane—beyond the reach of momentary emotions—where the spirit rules both soul and body.

(b) The Example (5:25b-27)

i.   Love That Travails (5:25b) "Christ also loved the church, and gave himself for it."

Such was the love of the Lord Jesus that He "gave himself" (literally, "gave up Himself") for His beloved. He died that she might live. "Greater love hath no man than this, that a man lay down his life for his friends" (John 15:13).

Any woman would find it easier to defer to a husband she knew would die for her than to a husband she felt might sacrifice her to his fears, lusts, or ambition. The husband is to make sure that his love for his wife is of such a quality that, come what may, she will reign so supremely in his heart that no sacrifice would seem too great for him to make for her. He must keep before him the example of Jesus and His great love for His church.

One might hesitate, perhaps, before using Samson as an example. Yet, despite his glaring imperfections, Samson was a striking type of Christ in his determination to take a Gentile bride. His parents could not understand why he would want a Gentile bride, a pagan woman. But Samson's heart was already engaged. (Besides, God's plans were involved.)

The day came when Samson went to meet the woman his heart so greatly desired. On his way he met a roaring lion. But Samson was strong and filled with the Spirit. (There are more references to the Holy Spirit in connection with Samson in the book of Judges than all the other judges combined.) Samson was not worried about a mere lion, however fierce. He tore that lion apart with his bare hands and went on to claim his bride. That she proved unworthy of him only adds to the sad parallel. She allowed fear and family pressure to turn her away from him. Samson's subsequent vengeance on those who dared to interfere with his beloved wife also adds to the parallel.

One can imagine Samson alone with his bride. For the first time she sees the marks on his body from his battle with the lion. "Oh Samson," she might have said, "those are terrible marks! Why are you so marred?"

And Samson may have replied, "These, my beloved, are the tokens of my love. I was willing to die for you."

On a greater and grander scale, Christ demonstrated love for His church. Husbands are to have love like Christ's for their wives.

ii. Love That Transforms (5:26-27) "That he might sanctify and cleanse it with the washing of water by the word, That he might present it to himself a glorious church, not having spot, or wrinkle, or any such thing; but that it should be holy and without blemish."

Paul's eloquence began to soar above time and sense. In Ephesians 5:26-27 husbands, wives, and the ordinary and orderly arrangements of a human home are left behind. All we see here are Christ and His church. We see love that finds us in our sins, love that regenerates, love that transforms, love that enables, and love that ennobles. We see love that is not content with leaving us as it found us; it is actively at work making us beautiful beyond description.

All too often we only see the spots, blemishes, faults, and failings of God's people. We major on the negatives. We see that the church is weak and divided. We do not yet see the church as Christ sees it, as He has always seen it. He sees it as perfect and complete, glorious, bright as the morning, fairer than day, lovely as the flowers of paradise, sweeter than the dawn. He sees the church as it will be when His transforming work is done. He sees it without spot or wrinkle. Without spot—beyond the reach of temptation. Without wrinkle—beyond the reach of time. Christ sees the church as holy and without blemish. He sees it as the mirror image of Himself.

This is not hyperbole. This is reality. Because Christ gave Himself for the church, He is now able to "sanctify and cleanse it with the washing of water by the word." This washing of course has nothing to do with baptismal regeneration. We are saved by the *blood* of Christ, not by the *water* of baptism.

The Greek word translated here as "washing," *loutron*, is only used one other place in the New Testament: Titus 3:5, which refers to "the washing of regeneration." *Loutron* primarily means "a vessel for washing," and seems to refer to the Old Testament laver.

The priest, when he approached God, came first to the brazen altar where an animal was sacrificed and its blood shed. This ritual symbolized the *radical* cleansing for sin, which is the basis of our salvation. Sin is so deep a stain that it can only be washed away in the blood of the Lord Jesus.

Having been to the altar, the priest proceeded toward the tabernacle where God sat enthroned in holiness behind the veil. Coming to the laver, which was made of mirrors, he saw that although he was only a few steps away from the holy place, he was already defiled by contact with this world. He did not need a new sacrifice at this point; he needed to be washed in water to remove the revealed defilement. He needed *recurrent* cleansing.

The blood of Christ secures our regeneration; the water of the Word acts like the laver. Like the mirrors of the Old Testament laver, the Word of God *reveals* to us the defilements we have picked up just by walking through this evil world. The Word of God—also a cleansing agent—*removes* the defilement. Psalm 119:9 says, "Wherewithal shall a young man cleanse his way? by taking heed thereto according to thy word."

The Lord has traveled on earth. He knows what this world is like. We are not yet in His world, in the glory land. He is patient with us. He works with us so that one day we will be seen in all of His glory and perfection. His love travails and transforms; it is the divine model for the husband's role in marriage.

(c) The Expectation (5:28-29)

i.   The Self Motive (5:28-29a) "So ought men to love their wives as their own bodies. He that loveth his wife loveth himself. For no man ever yet hated his own flesh; but nourisheth and cherisheth it."

Paul's explanation moved from the bride to the body and from the body to the bride. His train of thought went from a man and his wife to Christ and His church, from the church as a bride to the church as a body. The roots of his illustrations are as deep as the origin of the human race.

It all began in the garden of Eden. A man was put to sleep in the will of God. His body was opened and a bone was removed from his side. God used that bone to build a body—a bride. The body and the bride are two distinct concepts, yet strangely and mysteriously bound together. When God presented the bride to Adam, He said, "They shall be one flesh" (Genesis 2:24).

On the foundation of Genesis 2:24, Paul built his doctrine of marriage. In marriage two people become one. Marriage is much more than physical union. It is psychological and spiritual union, which is why all violations of the sacred marital relationship are totally damaging to personality and why all casual, unblessed liaisons earn God's judgment and bring inevitable retribution.

Paul was concerned in Ephesians 5:28-29, however, with the husband's duty to love his wife. He particularly emphasized the husband's duty to love his wife as much as he loves his own body.

The "self motive" is here. Most well-adjusted people love themselves. Love of self, of course, can be a very bad thing, especially when it expresses itself in selfishness. There is, however, a normal and wholesome love of one's self that, though it must be kept in its proper place, is not sinful. The believer's motivation goes far beyond mere selfishness; it is based on the essence of what God planned marriage to be. In marriage two persons become one person. After God married Adam and Eve, He "called *their* name Adam" (Genesis 5:2, italics added). They were two people with one name. This precedent is followed today when a bride gives up her family name and takes her husband's family name. In a sense, she loses her identity in his.

A man is to love his wife in the tender, caring way he loves his own body. A man instinctively provides for the comfort of his body. Using plain common sense, he protects his body from harm, heeds its signals, and desires its well-being. When a man becomes over-tired, famished, or gnawed by a toothache, he will do whatever he can to solve the problem.

Life is too uncomfortable when we ignore bodily demands, so we usually waste little time responding to them. For better or for worse, we are wedded to our bodies. They can make life blissful or tormenting. We cannot ignore our bodies, but self-indulgence can be as harmful as neglect. In between stoic harshness and epicurean self-indulgence is the happy medium where most of us live. The sane and sensible thing to do is to nourish our bodies and cherish them.

Just as a man must take care of his body, a husband must see to his wife's comfort. He must protect her from harm, desire her well-being, and pay close attention to the signals that she sends. She can, after all, make his life blissful or tormenting. He needs to help her develop her potential, nourish her, and cherish her. These are the sensible things to do if he wants to live in peace and comfort. Paul, however, did not end his injunction to husbands on the level of selfish motivation.

ii. The Supreme Motive (5:29b) "Even as the Lord the church."

The Lord views the church as His bride; it is His body. He loves it, nourishes it, and cherishes it. It is precious to Him. Nothing on earth or in Heaven compares with it. He died to redeem it. He watches over it. His Holy Spirit is here to guide it and gladden it. At the Father's right hand, Christ is importunate on the church's behalf. He anticipates with delight the coming day when the church will be complete, when it will be like Him forever, when it will reign with Him over God's vast empires in space. As far as the Lord is concerned, nothing is too good for His beloved. The church is the love of His life, the center of His thoughts, and the object of His purposes.

A man should view his wife in the same way. He should not use his wife's faults and weaknesses as reasons for neglecting her or for failing to give her the love and attention he vowed to her. Does not the Lord see many imperfections in His church? Of course He does. But with love and patience, kindness and forbearance, He ministers to His church. He knows that the day will come when the church will be perfect, glorious, and all that He meant it to be.

Love covers a multitude of sins (1 Peter 4:8). The kind of love described in 1 Corinthians 13 is divine. Such love is a fruit of the Spirit and is possible only through a filling of the Holy Spirit. Every husband should take a weekly tour of that chapter and apply each of its clauses to himself and his attitude toward his wife.

b.   Some Principles of the Marriage Relationship (5:30-33)

(1) The Concept (5:30-32)

(a) A Man and Christ's Body (5:30) "We are members of his body, of his flesh, and of his bones."

Having reviewed the priorities of the marriage relationship, Paul turned to the principles of the marriage relationship.

In Christian marriage, the model never to be forgotten is the Lord Jesus. A believer is a member of His body. No more intimate relationship could be imagined than the organic relationship that exists between one member of a physical body and another member. Each member of a body shares the same life, is controlled by the same spirit, is washed by the same blood, and is ruled by the same brain. The idea of a leg, an arm, or an eye existing independently is ludicrous.

Because we are members of Christ's body, the high and holy standard of Christian marriage is reachable; the standard is not just a lofty ideal. The link between each believer and Christ may be mystical, but it is certainly not mythical. Ephesians 5:30 says, "We are members of his body." Christ's life is our life. His love is our love. His Spirit energizes our spirits. His blood cleanses all.

When Paul wrote that husbands are to love their wives "as the Lord the church," he was not being idealistic. He is being intensely practical. Because we are members of His body, our lack of love is replaced by His boundless love. Our little tributaries of love soon dry up, but the ocean tides of His immeasurable love come in and overflow the banks of the narrow channels of our love.

The husband is not to resolve: "I will love my wife as Christ loved the church. I will do my best to imitate Christ." The result would only be an imitation. The Holy Spirit is telling every Christian husband to draw on the fact that he is a member of Christ's own body—"of his flesh, and of his bones," as the King James version adds. A mystical but real, organic relationship exists between the believer and Christ, making it possible for a man to love his wife as Christ loved the church.

If this relationship between Christ and us did not exist, then Paul's whole idea of marriage was just a noble dream. But this relationship is not merely a glorious concept. It is a down-to-earth, hard-fact reality. It is the principle on which all else rests. Our organic oneness with Christ certainly exists. We have God's Word for that. Any breakdowns are on our side, not His.

The key to making the principles of the marriage relationship work is faith. Our problem is that we only half believe them. The principles, however, remain the same. We are members of His body. And, of course, this principle applies to the wife in her role, in the same way it applies to the husband in his role.

(b) A Man and Christ's Bride (5:31-32) "For this cause shall a man leave his father and mother, and shall be joined unto his wife, and they two shall be one flesh. This is a great mystery: but I speak concerning Christ and the church."

On the one side, a Christian husband is mystically linked with the body of Christ. On the other side, he is maritally linked with his wife. Now Christ's life and love flow through him to her, completing the circuit. Of course the Christian wife is also directly linked with Christ and His love flows through her too. Faith throws the switch that allows the power to flow and the results to show.

Paul's teaching on marriage, like the Lord's teaching in Mark 10:2-12, is based on Genesis 2:23-24. Marriage was God's idea. Its purpose was to make paradise complete—to bring Heaven down to earth. In instituting marriage, God had eternity's values in view and the ultimate reality of Christ and His church in mind. Sin, however, has dimmed the bright ideal. Even when we know the truth that is found in Christ, our chronic unbelief often hinders us from seeing the truth work in our lives. The fact remains, though, that God intends the Christian home to be an outpost of Heaven in a sin-cursed world. The home is to be a place where family, friends, visitors, and neighbors can come, see, and sense the wonders of God's mysterious purposes at work.

It is no accident that the first and second times that love is mentioned in the Bible occur when and where they do.[1] The first mention of love is *the love of the father for the son* in Genesis 22. Abraham loved Isaac, yet God demanded that he take his only begotten son to mount Moriah and enact Calvary there. "Take now thy son, thine only son Isaac, whom thou lovest, and get thee into the land of Moriah; and offer him there for a burnt offering upon one of the mountains which I will tell thee of" (22:2). The spiritual significance of this illumines all of a past eternity.

The second mention of love is *the love of the son for his bride* in Genesis 24. "Isaac brought her into his mother Sarah's tent, and took Rebekah, and she became his wife; and he loved her" (24:67). The spiritual significance of the marriage of Isaac and Rebekah illumines all of the endless ages yet unborn.[2]

There are hidden depths in Christian marriage that are linked with God's eternal purposes. Paul gave us glimpses, and a comprehensive study of Old Testament brides will reveal more. Some of those brides teach us truth regarding Christ and His church; others (such as Abraham and Sarah, Abraham and Katurah, and Hosea and Gomer) teach us truth regarding Jehovah and Israel.

(2) The Conclusion (5:33) "Nevertheless let every one of you in particular so love his wife even as himself; and the wife see that she reverence her husband."

Paul brought his discussion of the Christian as a partner to a close by restating the principles of the marriage relationship in practical terms. Considering marriage as analogous to the mystical relationship between Christ and the church is interesting and inspiring. But we must bring the discussion "down to earth." After all, the husband-wife relationship is a practical matter, subject to immense stresses and strains.

If we forget all the ideals and mysticism, we must remember this: Husbands are to love their wives just as much and in the same way as they love themselves. No summary could be shorter, simpler, or plainer. Nearly all domestic friction and unhappiness would cease if husbands observed this basic principle. A wife would be unlikely to resist a husband who loved her as he loved himself. (If the husband goes on to love her as Christ loves the church, so much the better.)

Paul had a parting word for the wife too: Reverence your husband. The wife is to put her husband on a pedestal, make much of him, admire him, speak well of him, and defer to him.

In this age of feminism it is common for women to reject God's counsel on this issue. Someone may say, "Ah, but you don't know my husband." Well, God knows him, and God says that he is to be reverenced as a husband.

Someone else may object, "My husband is weak, foolish, and undeserving of my respect. How can I reverence him?" Paul would answer, "By being filled with the Spirit; by counting on your mystical union with Christ in the oneness of the body; and by realizing that in reverencing your husband you are fulfilling God's will and enabling the Holy Spirit to make you more like Jesus and show the world the loveliness of Christ through you."

Alexander Whyte said in his book on Bible characters that when Paul wrote his parting word to the wife, he had one eye on Rebekah. If we read the full Genesis account of Isaac and Rebekah, we discover practical lessons as well as interesting typology. On the practical level, Isaac and Rebekah's marriage deteriorated. A number of factors contributed to the deterioration.

In the first place, Isaac was placid, quiet, and submissive. Not a fighter, he was far more disposed to give in than to stand up for himself. Rebekah, by contrast, was resolute, clear-thinking, and practical. She was a doer who had married a dreamer. Then too, Isaac let Rebekah down when he played the coward for his own safety (Genesis 26:6-9). That would be hard to forgive and, humanly speaking, impossible to forget. Worst of all, as time went on Isaac cultivated another first love: good food. He loved Esau because he brought him venison. Once he had loved Rebekah; now he loved himself.

All of these factors turned Rebekah into a disgruntled wife. She ceased to reverence her husband. The original romance faded and disappeared. The harsh reality of daily life led her to go her own way, assert her dominant personality, and cultivate favoritism. A domestic tragedy of terrible proportions resulted. Egged on by his mother,

Jacob lied, cheated, and deceived Isaac. Esau threatened to kill Jacob. Jacob had to leave home hurriedly, and Rebekah never saw her favorite son again. Isaac belatedly took the spiritual lead when it was almost too late.

For a wife to reverence her husband may be difficult; not to do so will be disastrous. The command does not mean that the wife has to submit to bullying or endorse her husband's foolish decisions. It does mean that instead of tearing him down, she must build him up. It does mean that she must respect the God-ordained, husband-wife role in marriage, conceding that God knows best and could overrule.

A capable, strong-willed woman who is married to an incompetent, passive man certainly has a problem, but it is not too difficult a problem for God to solve. If she will seek the Holy Spirit's filling, if in the power of His enablement she will reverence her husband, build him up, and help him where he is weak and she is strong, her husband will develop the masculine qualities that command her reverence. If she refuses to reverence her husband, she will dominate him and cause him to become resentful. Or she could cause him to develop feminine characteristics that are most unlovely in a man, while she develops masculine characteristics that are most unlovely in a woman.

2. As a Parent (6:1-4)

a. The Child's Simple Task (6:1-3)

(1) The Principle (6:1) "Children obey your parents in the Lord: for this is right."

This verse summarizes the whole duty of a child, manward and godward. His sole duty is to learn to obey authority, and his parents are to be his only voice of authority. Later on, parental authority will compete with the school's authority, the government's authority, and possibly an employer's authority.

We are born rebels. Each of us raises the voice of selfishness and rebellion at an early age. We need to learn to obey. Children who learn to defy parental authority will go on to defy other authority and will often grow up to defy divine authority.

There exists of course the sad possibility that parental authority might be arbitrary. Yet God's rule still applies. A child owes obedience to his parents. The larger issues must be left with God, the ultimate source of all authority. He can sovereignly overrule in the end the misuse of parental authority.[3]

Children raised in Christian homes have an awesome privilege. Many children are born into homes where God is hated and atheism holds sway. Others are raised to bow to idols and false gods. Others grow up in cruel environments. Of all the millions of children born every year, relatively few are born into Christian homes. We have no idea how the selection is made, but it has incredible advantages.

Children raised in homes where God is known, where Christ is loved, where the Bible is read and believed, and where the Holy Spirit is honored have great opportunities. From their earliest days, these privileged infants are taught to say the saving name of Jesus, are taught to say childish prayers, are taken to Sunday school, are told Bible stories, are encouraged to memorize the living Word of God, and—above all—are taught the way of salvation through Jesus Christ. While others born the same day are being raised, in China for example, to chant the Communist International, to scoff at the idea of God, to revere Marx and Lenin, and to believe in dialectical materialism, children in Christian homes are being taught John 3:16. While others are being taught to worship Krishna, bow before idols, believe in reincarnation as the secret of life and nothingness as its ultimate and most blissful goal, children in Christian homes are being taught to sing,

> Jesus loves me! this I know,
> For the Bible tells me so.
> (Anna B. Warner)

Children raised in Christian homes also have an awesome responsibility. A child who rebels against parental authority in a Christian home earns God's displeasure. For him to obey is right. Anything else is terribly and criminally wrong. The whole duty of a child in a Christian home is to obey Mom and Dad. That is God's supreme command to that child.

One could think of instances where a godless parent might demand that a child do things that are morally wrong and contrary to the laws of God and man. Paul was not requiring that children obey orders contrary to the laws of God. He had the Christian home primarily in mind.

We get just one glimpse of Jesus between His birth and His baptism. We see Him when He was twelve years old, already in complete control of the knowledge that He was the Son of God. Yet we read that He went down to Nazareth with Joseph and Mary "and was subject unto them" (Luke 2:51). What a lesson in obedience! To think of Him—the Lord of life and glory, the Creator of the universe, the One who was the express image of God, the One whom angels worshiped—being in willing subjection to a village carpenter and his wife!

(2) The Precept (6:2) "Honour thy father and mother; which is the first commandment with promise."

The Decalogue—the ten commandments found in Exodus 20—is the essence of the law. It is the heart and core of divine legislation; the other six hundred commandments are expansions and expositions of it. The Decalogue divides man's duty into two categories: his duty to God and his duty to man. The commandment concerning children, quoted by Paul in Ephesians 6:2, is the fifth commandment. Because it deals with human relationships, it is often included with the last five commandments, thus dividing the Decalogue into four statements that summarize man's duty to God and six that summarize man's duty to man.

This division, however, is artificial. When the Lord Jesus summarizes the Decalogue in two statements, He gives us the true division. He says, "Thou shalt love the Lord thy God with all thy heart, and with all thy soul, and with all thy mind, and with all thy strength. . . . Thou shalt love thy neighbour as thyself" (Mark 12:30-31). When we review the Decalogue, we see that this division was inherent in the law. The first five commandments are tied together by the phrase "the Lord thy God," the remaining five by the phrase "thou shalt not." This division links the command to honor thy father and thy mother with the commandments that address man's duty to God.

The distinction is important, for the fifth commandment puts the parents in the place of God over their young children. And for the rest of their lives, the children are to render honor to their mothers and fathers as the human authors of their being—as those who loved them, protected them, taught them, and sacrificed for them.

Failure to honor one's parents is an insult to the God who chose them. Rebellion against parents is high-handed rebellion against God. All sin is rebellion against God, but by grouping the fifth commandment with those that address our duties to God, the Holy Spirit makes it clear that defiance of parental authority is also sin against God Himself. (Under the Mosaic law a son who persisted in rebellion against parental authority was guaranteed a short life. He was to be publicly accused and stoned to death.)

God, however, does not want children to honor their parents

because of a threat, so he appended a promise to the fifth commandment. Paul reminded his readers of that promise when he added this to Ephesians 6:2: "Which is the first commandment with promise." That promise is the subject of the next verse.

(3) The Promise (6:3) "That it may be well with thee, and thou mayest live long on the earth."

A child who grows up to love, honor, and obey his mother and father lays the foundation for a happier, more stable, and more successful life than does a child who is rude, disrespectful, self-willed, and rebellious. A stormy path lies ahead for a disobedient child. He will drift into bad company, resent all rule and authority, and in many cases end up on the wrong side of the law. Contemporary society has produced a bumper crop of young people who are determined to "do their own thing." Many of them are enmeshed in the drug and sex scene, and are filled with restlessness and rage.

b.   The Father's Sublime Trust (6:4)

(1) A Word about Methods (6:4a) "Fathers, provoke not your children to wrath."

The Bible is a balanced book. God does not command children to obey their parents without giving an injunction to parents. Fathers (or parents, as the Greek word *pateres* can be translated) are not to provoke their children to wrath by being unreasonable in their demands, outrageous in their punishments, or inconsistent in their examples, rules, and controls.

My father often referred to children as "the little people." It was a quaint expression, yet a profoundly wise one. Children are people. They are not mindless objects to be bossed and bullied; they are people who have thoughts, feelings, hopes, fears, likes, and dislikes. As children grow older, winds of change blow over their developing bodies, minds, and personalities; life becomes more complex and decisions more significant. But children are people and must be respected as people. Because they are little people, they need constant supervision, counsel, and limits. They are growing up in a confusing world, and they encounter people whose values are quite different from those of their parents.

Parents need to study their children. The growing-up process takes every child through various phases of development. A parent ought to know about these phases and recognize when a child enters each stage.

No two children are alike. Some are strong-willed; others are passive. Some are clever; others are slow. Some are adventurous; others are timid. Some are bold; others are shy. Wise parents will study their children and make allowances. Many books on parenting are available today, but not all of them are equally good because much modern psychology leaves God out entirely. The best textbook of all remains the Bible, especially the book of Proverbs. Wise parents know the Bible, study its case histories of parents, and ponder its stories of boys and girls.

Every child needs to have a solid moral foundation on which all other Biblical instruction can be built. Parents should lay this foundation early. They should encourage their children to memorize the ten commandments, segments of the sermon on the mount, and many other Scripture passages. Psalm 119:11 says, "Thy word have I hid in mine heart, that I might not sin against thee." Parents should also teach their children to know, love, and sing good hymns and choruses with a message. In later years those ingrained truths will come back. The Holy Spirit will be able to draw on this material when confronting the boy, girl, man, or woman with the issues of time and eternity.

(2) A Word about Motives (6:4b) "Bring them up in the nurture [discipline] and admonition [instruction] of the Lord."

Spiritual education of children was a strong emphasis of Old Testament law. Israel was to keep the feast of the Passover, for instance, so children would ask, "What is meant by this feast?" Parents were required to put Bible verses on the doorposts of their homes. Children leaving the shelter of home would be confronted by those verses and would carry the haunting memory of some Word from God into their outside activities. Returning home, the children would again be faced with the verses on the doorposts. The verses would cause the children to think afresh, in the light of God's Word, of where they had been and what they had been doing and saying.

Christian parents have no greater responsibility in life than to make sure that their children are raised in the fear of God, in the knowledge of God, in the knowledge of the gospel, in reverence for God's Word, and in the presence of the Lord Jesus.

Television, that great thief of time and worldly molder of character, needs to be banished or put under severe restraint. In its place, parents must substitute good books, wholesome music, and Christian education—all bathed in godly example and fervent prayer for each child's early conversion and lifelong consecration to the will of God.

Parents neglect these responsibilities to their peril. They will pay a high price indeed if they ignore Ephesians 6:4 and fail to heed this admonition from the Lord.

---

1. See Phillips, *Exploring Genesis* (Neptune, NJ: Loizeaux, 1980).
2. See *Exploring Genesis* for a more detailed discussion of the wondrous way Genesis 22–24 foreshadows God's purpose with His earthly people (the Jews) and His heavenly people (the church).
3. It may well be in this day of much child abuse that God's will would be for an abused child to be placed in a foster home; probably the preference would be the home of a near relative. In Bible times the extended family was much more common than it is today, at least in western society.

D. In His Material Relationships (6:5-9)

1. Men and Their Masters (6:5-8)

a. The Human Master's Claims (6:5-6a)

(1) Be Obedient (6:5a) "Servants, be obedient to them that are your masters according to the flesh."

The Greek word translated "servants" here is usually translated "slave." Slavery was the blight of the age in Roman times. Vast numbers of people—including many members of the early Gentile church—were bought and sold like cattle. These slaves had no civil rights and were subject to the whims of their masters—for better or for worse. They were considered pieces of property of varying value. In danger of the scourge, the cross, or worse, they were held in the iron grip of relentless laws. The slave revolt led by Spartacus only reinforced the resolve of slave owners to keep their whips in hand.

Many slaves were highly skilled. Some were highly educated. Some enjoyed, within limits set by entrenched customs, the friendship of their masters. But all slaves lived with the peril of a change of ownership hanging over their heads. The death of a benevolent master, or his displeasure, could bring a swift change of circumstances.

Often slaves harbored deep resentments. The Holy Spirit, however, told the enslaved Christians to accept their lot in life. The time had not yet come when the shackles could be removed. As slaves they had one supreme social duty: to obey their masters.

Happily the days of slavery are gone from most of the world. Men are no longer bought and sold like so many pieces of furniture. In the workaday world, however, men sell their talents and their time, and the same principles of servanthood apply.

When we accept employment we put our skills at the disposal of our employers for so many hours a day. We expect certain remuneration for performing certain functions. To that extent, our time and talents are not our own. We have bargained them away. Thus our employers have every right to expect that we will be industrious, conscientious, and cooperative.

We live in an age of labor strife, but the Holy Spirit does not make exceptions for us. As Christians we are to be different from other people in the marketplace. We are to be obedient, cheerful, and loyal servants. We are to be the most willing and diligent people on the payroll. We are to do our best and be dutiful, polite, and dependable. That is the law of Christ. Joseph followed this law when he worked for Potipher, when he was in prison, and when he moved into the palace. God expects the same of us. Others may waste their employer's time. Others may perform their tasks in a slovenly way. Others may criticize and complain. But we Christians are to obey our masters. It is God's command.

(2) Be Subservient (6:5b) "With fear and trembling, in singleness of your heart, as unto Christ."

Subservience is not a quality we admire. Obedience yes, but not subservience. We should not have to stand in fear and trembling before anyone but God. The subservience demanded in Ephesians 6:5 is absolute yieldedness to Christ. The Christian employee must be afraid—not afraid of his superiors in the marketplace, but afraid of disobeying his Lord. If he does not show wholehearted respect to his employer, he is disobeying the Lord.

The word *singleness* in Ephesians 6:5 means wholehearted dedication to the task at hand, the determination to give it all diligence and expedition. That kind of dedication sounds like nonsense to many employees today. Today slacking on the job is considered clever, and unions will fight for a man's right to remain on the job no matter how insolent, incompetent, or indifferent he may be. He may be lazy, lie, show up late for work, and disaffect the other workers, but the union will champion him. The union has taken away his fear of man. Often he never did have any fear of God.

I was with friends in a fine restaurant in England some years ago. The waiter first asked if we wanted drinks. We declined, and thereafter we were subjected to the most insolent and careless service I have ever experienced in a restaurant. The waiter was barely civil. He practically threw things on the table and took our orders with sneering contempt. We all noticed his behavior. I said to my brother-in-law, "Should we not complain to the management?"

He replied, "It would do no good. They could not fire him. The union is too strong for that, and the labor laws here are all on his side."

A Christian employee cannot afford to project an image like that waiter. He is to be on the job for Jesus. He should do his work as though the Lord Himself were doing it. He is the only Bible some people will read. He may not fear his boss. He may find it difficult to like his boss and even more difficult to respect him. But ultimately he is not serving his boss. He is serving the Lord, and he should certainly serve Him with singleness of heart.

(3) Be Diligent (6:6a) "Not with eyeservice, as menpleasers."

We are not to do our best only when we are being watched, only when we are looking for human approval, or only when the boss is around. We should disprove that old English proverb: "When the cat's away, the mice will play." The slave was not to do his best only because he was afraid of being whipped, and we should not do good work only because we are afraid of being demoted or fired.

The Christian employee is to be diligent. He is not to call in sick when he is healthy. He is not to waste his boss's time in idle conversation or conduct personal business when he should be working. He is not to drag his feet, pad his break times, arrive late, leave early, or demand that two people do a job he could do alone. Those are the world's ways, not the Christian's.

b.   The Heavenly Master's Claims (6:6b-8)

(1) The Higher Plane (6:6b-7) "As the servants of Christ, doing the will of God from the heart; With good will doing service, as to the Lord, and not to men."

The Lord is always present. We serve Him, not men. All service is on a higher plane for believers. We are in God's will when we do "secular" work, just as much as when we do "sacred" work. The Holy Spirit in Ephesians 6:6-7 abolishes the distinction between those of us in secular employment and those of us in fulltime Christian service. All of us are in the ministry. All of us are in fulltime service— the plumber as much as the preacher, the economist as much as the evangelist, the policeman as much as the pastor, and the miner as much as the missionary.

All these vocations are in God's will, and God's will must be done from the heart. We can serve God out of a sense of *discipline*. Discipline says, "I have to"; it is motivation from a will that has been *compelled*. We can serve God out of a sense of *duty*. Duty says, "I ought to"; it is motivation from a mind that has been *convinced*. Or we can serve God out of a sense of *devotion*. Devotion says, "I want to"; it is motivation from a heart that has been *captured*.

God's will for every employee is that he serve his human master with all his heart—with wholehearted commitment to his employer's gain and advantage. His commitment should be like Joseph's when he served Potipher. The Christian employee should give the kind of selfless service the slave girl gave to Naaman's wife.

When we Christians serve our human masters, we are serving the One who loved us enough to die for us and who gave us an example of service. Mark 10:45 reads, "The Son of man came not to be ministered unto, but to minister, and to give his life a ransom for many." That kind of service took Jesus all the way to Calvary.

(2) The Heavenly Plan (6:8) "Knowing that whatsoever good thing any man doeth, the same shall he receive of the Lord, whether he be bond or free."

What a prospect! We may never receive recognition, reward, promotion, or praise down here, but we will receive it in Heaven. The Lord's payday is not at the end of the week; it is at the end of our lives. Sometimes God rewards us along the way, but these encouragements are only tokens of what is to come. Payday is at the judgment seat of Christ. Our efforts will seem worthwhile when we hear the Lord say, "Well done, thou good and faithful servant" (Matthew 25:21).

In the millennial kingdom we will rule cities, counties, provinces, countries, and continents. In eternity we might well manage worlds and galaxies in God's vast, new empires in space. We are in training for tasks of great honor in eternity as we handle mundane details down here. We may be experiencing scorn and disappointment now, but we will be crowned with glory and honor then.

2. Masters and Their Men (6:9)

a. A Word about Mutual Responsibility (6:9a) "Masters, do the same things."

Just as the master (the employer) is purring with satisfaction at the demands God puts on his slaves (his employees), the Holy Spirit turns all this heavy artillery on him. "You too," He says. "Do the same things. This is a two-way street. You have obligations and responsibilities too."

The employer expects a fair day's work; he must give a fair day's pay. The employer wants the employee to be diligent and promote the best interests of the company; the employer must be diligent and promote the welfare of the employee. Trade unions would never have formed if Ephesians 6:5-9 had been the cornerstone of all employee-management relations.

Trade unions grew out of the "dark Satanic mills" of newly industrialized Europe. The Victorians had their qualms, but largely ignored them in the interests of big business and moneymaking. The invention of joint-stock corporations made it possible for people to grow rich without pangs of conscience. A corporation with limited liability, owned by shareholders scattered up and down the countryside, had no conscience.

Friedrich Engels, seeking material for his book on the proletariat of south Lancashire, described the standing pools of refuse and sickening filth that poisoned the atmosphere of the densely populated valley of the Medlock. He wrote:

> A horde of ragged women and children swarm about, as filthy as the swine that thrive upon the garbage heaps and in the puddles. . . . The race that lives in these ruinous cottages behind broken windows mended with oilskin, sprung doors and rotten doorposts, or in dark wet cellars in measureless filth and stench . . . must really have reached the lowest stage of humanity.

Engels justifiably asked how people who were compelled to live in such pigsties and who were dependent for their water supply on a pestilential stream could live natural lives and bring up children to be anything but savages. What kind of posterity, Engels asked, was England breeding in its feverish search for wealth? The economists of his day gave him no answers. Instead, disease answered. Asiatic cholera in 1831 and typhus in 1837 and 1843 marched out of their strongholds in the industrial towns, defied every effort to halt their spread, and threatened to devastate the entire country.

There were other warnings too. A sullen, savage, and ever-increasing working class was turning against the rest of the nation's traditions and taboos. Smoldering resentment and discontent were building. Class hatred was growing. Marx and Engels began urging workers to unite. Revolution was in the air. Ever-expanding multitudes felt that this world was nothing but a dingy prison. Rebellion, rancor, and indignation were taking root. In such a soil, orators of social revolution and agitators could thrive.

The world's answer to this sick society was communism. God's answer is Christ.

b.   A Word about Managerial Restraint (6:9b-c)

(1) The Abuse of Power (6:9b) "Forbearing threatening."

The use of the whip hand to keep subordinates in line has been the problem with power from the beginning. Love, not force or fear, is the best way to encourage people to work. Force and fear, the weapons most often used by masters and employers, are counter-productive in the end because they breed resentment and rage.

Employers do have the right to use their authority to get things done. There is a legitimate use of power. All society is based on that premise. As long as sin reigns on this earth, laws must be enforced. An employee can be punished or dismissed if his behavior warrants such action. But God forbids browbeating and bullying.

Power has a tendency to erode character. Lord Acton said it well: "Power tends to corrupt, and absolute power corrupts absolutely." Those in power need to watch themselves and be careful not to abuse their power. Giving orders to people feeds the ego and inflates pride. Power is a heady draught. Power intoxicates and calls for more until people with power begin to want power for power's sake.

The almost unlimited power of slave owners led to fearful abuses. The tyranny of the Nazi concentration camps and the horrors of totalitarian governments also warn of where abuse of power leads.

Paul told us to refrain from threatening. It is contrary to Christian character and violates the law of Christ.

(2) The Abuse of Position (6:9c) "Knowing that your Master also is in heaven; neither is there respect of persons with him."

God is not impressed with a person's position, but He is keenly interested in what the person does in that position.

There will be abuses of position. Injustices will be done. But there is One who is watching. The Lord has His eye on what is happening, and He has His own way of squaring accounts—sometimes down here, certainly in Heaven. The day is coming when He will right wrongs and review all lives. Master or slave, it will make no difference then.

According to Ephesians 6:9, God will have the last word, and with this verse Paul ended another segment of his letter. He had one more major matter to discuss: the intrusion of the unseen world into the affairs of earth. The last segment of the letter warns Christians to beware of the dark influence that evil spirits exert.

PART IV

The Christian
and His Battles

Ephesians 6:10-20

IV. THE CHRISTIAN AND HIS BATTLES (6:10-20)

A. Assessing the Enemy (6:10-17)

1. A Word of Encouragement (6:10) "Finally, my brethren, be strong in the Lord, and in the power of his might."

As soon as Paul was saved, he threw himself wholeheartedly into the battle. Luke used the word *endunamoo* to describe Paul's activities as a new believer: "Saul increased the more in *strength,* and confounded the Jews which dwelt at Damascus, proving that this is very Christ" (Acts 9:22, italics added). Paul used the passive form of *endunamoo* when he told us to "be strong."

People who have been Christians a long time are not always strong Christians. Some remain weak in faith throughout their lives. And new Christians are not necessarily weak Christians. They may be uninformed Christians for a while, but they do not have to be weak. Being strong in the Lord has nothing to do with how long we have been saved. Our strength is derived from God, not from ourselves. We are to be strong "in the power of his might." We are to be strong in His mighty power, as in Ephesians 1:19 where Paul was referring to the mighty strength that God exhibited when He raised Christ from the dead. God makes that strength available to us.

Paul's introductory reminder to be strong was important because he was about to hurl us into battle against a mighty, tireless, and implacable foe. We must never underestimate the enemy. God doesn't.

2. A Word of Enlightenment (6:11)

a. Our Protection (6:11a) "Put on the whole armour of God."

As Paul wrote this he was chained to a Roman soldier. He had been in the company of soldiers, centurions, and tribunes for years, so he knew all about armor. No doubt his familiarity with Roman armor gave him the idea of using the imagery of Christian armor.

Roman armor was designed to protect the soldier's body from the enemy's weapons. Christian armor is designed to protect the soul. God does not throw us unprotected into the battle against Satan's empire. God has provided all that we need for complete protection of mind, heart, soul, spirit, conscience, and will. But we must put that armor on piece by piece—deliberately, thoughtfully, and intelligently.

b.   Our Protagonist (6:11b) "That ye may be able to stand against the wiles of the devil."

The evil one has many names in Scripture, the most common being *devil* and *Satan* (Revelation 20:2). As the devil, he is the *accuser*—the one who constantly assails us before God. As Satan, he is the *adversary*—the one who opposes God and constantly seeks to prevent us from entering into our birthright as children of God.

The evil one is a defeated foe, as Paul emphasized in Colossians 2:15. We stand, in Christ, on the victory side of the cross. The evil one may rage and roar, but he is powerless before a child of God who is arrayed in the armor of God, filled with the Spirit of God, and strong in the power of His might.

The Greek word translated "wiles" in Ephesians 6:11 is *methodeia*. Paul had already used the word *methodeia* in 4:14 (translated "wiles" in Revised Version). There he told the Ephesians not to be children, not to be swayed by every wind of doctrine and the craftiness of deceitful men. Satan's wiles can be seen in the deceptive strategies of the cultists who have been taught by that old liar, the devil. *Methodeia* only occurs in these two places in the New Testament.

The devil is full of evil tricks. We cannot possibly know them all, but God does. We cannot possibly guard against them all, nor can we overcome them in our own power. But God can. We are predisposed by our fallen nature to listen to Satan's lies. Through deceit he gained a foothold against the human race in the first place (Genesis 3).

The fall of the human race hinged on two pivots: deception and disobedience. Eve was deceived; Adam was disobedient. Satan is unremitting in his efforts to take full advantage of those two beachheads he has established, and with tragic success. Most of the world lies in his lap. We who have been saved are on guard against the enemy, but he still does everything in his power to deceive us and make us disobedient. So God commands us to put on the armor He has provided so that we can stand against Satan's wiles.

3.   A Word of Enablement (6:12-17)

a.   The Arena (6:12)

(1) This Is Not an Ordinary Battle (6:12a) "We wrestle not against flesh and blood."

Our enemies are not people. We must see beyond people. Satan may use people to persecute us, lie to us, cheat us, hurt us, or even kill us. But our real enemy lurks in the shadows of the unseen world, moving people as pawns on the chessboard of time. As long as we see people as enemies and wrestle against them, we will spend our strength in vain. Certainly we see wicked people, hear the evil things they say, and feel the hurts they inflict on us. People are involved, but they are not the real problem. This is not an ordinary battle. We are in a greater arena than the one we can see.

(2) This Is Now an Occult Battle (6:12b-e)

(a) We Wrestle Satan's Crowned Dignities (6:12b) "Against principalities."

Paul listed four distinct Satanic orders against whom we wrestle in our spiritual warfare: principalities, powers, the rulers of this world's darkness, and wicked spirits in high places.

Hosts of spirit beings reside in the unseen world. We cannot see them unless they choose to be seen. In the beginning they were all good and glorious. They came from God's hand, took their place around God's throne, and sang His praises. There were ranks upon ranks of angels and archangels, cherubim and seraphim. At the head of them all—the highest of all created intelligences, the supreme creature in the ranks of the angel throng—was Lucifer, son of the morning, the anointed cherub.

When Lucifer fell, the heavenly hosts divided. Many sons of light fell with Lucifer and were also cast out of Heaven. Satan is now their lord. He is given many impressive titles in the Bible, for although he is a fallen fiend, he is still powerful. Satan is called the god of this world, the prince of this world, and the prince of the power of the air. It was he who deceived Eve and used her to bring about Adam's downfall. Satan was thus able to seize the kingdom of this world to ruin it and to rule it in defiance of the living God.

The Bible does not tell us all we might like to know about the spirit world, but we do know that there are ranks in the angelic orders of Heaven who did not fall. Several angels are specifically named in Scripture. Gabriel, for instance, stands in God's presence and often appears as the herald angel. Michael the archangel is a warrior. He is the field marshal of the armies of Heaven, the defender of the nation of Israel, the one who will ultimately be God's agent to cast Satan down from the heavenlies where he roams today.

Paul mentioned thrones, dominions, principalities, and powers in Colossians 1:16. At Calvary Christ "spoiled" the principalities and powers (Colossians 2:15), which are linked in Ephesians 6:12 with Satan's fallen hosts. The thrones and dominions would seem to be unfallen angels ranking high in the hierarchy of Heaven. In Revelation 4–5 we have a hint as to who "thrones" are. There they are called "elders." They sit in the presence of God and respond to His dealings with men in wonder and worship. Scripture gives no hint as to the place of those called "dominions."

There are also ranks in Satan's spirit realm. At the head of his countless minions are the principalities—princes who share with Satan the power that he wields over other fallen angels, over evil spirits, and over this world. The word Paul used to describe these beings is *archē*, which literally means "beginning" and can be translated "chief ruler" or "magistrate." So principalities are high-ranking, governing authorities who are under Satan's control.

We learn from Daniel 10 that Satan places spirit princes over various kingdoms of men on earth. We read of "the prince of Grecia" and also of "the prince of Persia." The prince of Persia alone was powerful enough to hinder the herald angel and keep him from fulfilling his commission for three weeks. Such crowned dignities of Satan wield enormous power, but they are defeated foes for the Christian. We wrestle against them in prayer and Christian service. They strongly resent any challenge to their terrible hold on the kingdoms of men.

(b)   We Wrestle Satan's Conquering Deputies (6:12c) "Against powers."

The Greek word translated "powers" is *exousia*. It is the usual word for delegated authority, for the liberty and right to exert power.

Satan is powerful, diabolically clever, and tireless, but he is not God. He is a created being and has none of the attributes of deity. He is full of knowledge and cunning, but he is not omniscient. He does not know everything and he makes mistakes. One mistake was to attack Adam and Eve. His biggest mistake was to organize and motivate the crucifixion of Christ.

Satan has enormous power, beyond anything we can conceive. He can give people the ability to perform miracles, for instance, but he is not all-powerful. He is not omnipotent. He can be thwarted and overruled by the power of God.

> Satan trembles when he sees
> The weakest saint upon his knees.
> (William Cowper)

Christ's resurrection is a crowning example of Satan's power being broken.

Satan can move swiftly with the ease and freedom of a spirit unencumbered by a physical body. He can be here one moment, a million miles away the next, but he is not omnipresent. He cannot be everywhere at once. He can only be in one place at a time. We learn in Revelation 2:13 that Satan has a dwelling; that is, he has a throne on earth. In John's day, it was at Pergamos. The very idea of a seat or throne is associated with a single locality. We do not know where Satan has his throne on earth today, but the fact that he has one proclaims the companion truth that he is not omnipresent.

Satan seeks to compensate for his lack of omniscience, omnipotence, and omnipresence by efficiently organizing the countless clever beings who share power with him in the spirit world. Some of these beings are actually called "powers." They wield authority delegated to them by Satan. They gather information, influence events, implement Satan's schemes, inflict woe and bondage on the human race, and laugh at man's blindness in refusing to believe that such evil beings exist.

Modern man is in much the same plight as seventeenth-century man. In 1665 London was in the grip of the great plague. People were dying by the thousands—faster than they could be buried. Corpses were stacked like cordwood outside stricken houses and were carted away to hastily-dug pits on the outskirts of the city. Business came to a halt. Court disbanded. People fled London, taking the disease with them.

Nobody knew the cause of the plague. The most common notion was that the air caused it, so people sealed up their homes to keep contaminated air outside. They burned noxious material in their fireplaces to help drive out the deadly air. They buried their noses in flowers. Out of ignorance, they disregarded the most basic rules of sanitation and hygiene. Open sewers ran down the streets. Rats and vermin multiplied, and their fleas spread the plague. But people were unable to see any link between the unsanitary conditions and the spread of the plague.

If someone were to go back to 1665 and say that the plague was spread by bacteria, the people would not pay attention to him. They would not believe there could be germs so small that they could not be seen with the naked eye or that millions of germs could be found in a drop of ditch water. People knew nothing about germs or viruses. They would have laughed scornfully at anyone who tried to explain the real source of their troubles. Since germs could not be seen, smelled, touched, heard, or tasted, no one suspected that they could have caused the plague.

Likewise, most people today do not believe in evil spirits. Some may be interested in the occult, fascinated with ghosts and witches, and drawn toward what the more erudite call parapsychology. But most scorn the idea that Satan has organized and launched a diabolical plot against the human race. They scoff at the idea that evil spirits, ruthless in their hatred of mankind, are dedicated to keeping people in bondage, sin, and shame.

Why can we not halt the drug trade that is destroying countless lives and damning souls? Why has it been so hard to pass stiff laws against drunk driving? Why has sodomy become acceptable? Why is pornography such big business? Why can we not stamp out child abuse and the legalized slaughter of the unborn in abortion clinics? Why did the horrors of the Nazi prison camps, the Spanish Inquisition, and the Gulag Archipelago take place? Why can we not stop war or ban the deployment of apocalyptic weapons?

The Bible makes the answer clear: the human race is being manipulated by vast numbers of evil spirits who have great power. They encourage lust, greed, hate, fear, selfishness, and pride. People talk about making contact with extraterrestrial beings and speculate as to whether or not intelligent life exists elsewhere. But the human race has already been invaded from outer space and is held in bondage by awesome powers. People in general do not know that; they refuse to believe it when told; and they do not realize they have no hope apart from the gospel of the Lord Jesus Christ.

(c) We Wrestle Satan's Capable Deceivers (6:12d) "Against the rulers of the darkness of this world."

The Greek word *kosmokratōr* only occurs here in Scripture and means "world rulers." The beings that the Holy Spirit is exposing in this phrase are "the world rulers of this darkness."

Satan's master plan for holding the world in subjection can be summed up in a single word: deception. He keeps people in a state of spiritual, philosophical, religious, political, social, and personal blindness. He has invented every false religion and is behind every false philosophy, every false ideology, and every false theory. He keeps people in a state of darkness, and he has a legion of evil spirits whose supreme task is to fasten false ideologies like iron shackles on the souls of men.

Think of the outrageous beliefs that otherwise intelligent people hold in the name of religion. Think of the millions of people who are enslaved in various forms of idolatry. Think of the countless cults that caricature the gospel. Think of the deceptive philosophies such as communism, evolution, and humanism, which control multitudes of people. Where do all these false ideologies come from? Why are they so attractive? How can they recruit people and hold them in fanatical devotion? How can they multiply their adherents? Think of the fanaticism of Islam, the tireless zeal of the Mormons, the world goals the communists pursued, and the spread of soul-destroying, family-destroying, and society-destroying humanism.

Behind all these ideologies is more than the persuasive power of clever leaders. Behind them all are Satan's capable deceivers—the rulers of this world's darkness. Their supreme task is to blind people to the gospel.

Man's natural blindness to his lost condition and to the saving power of the gospel is so great that it takes the fulltime presence of the Holy Spirit to make it possible for any converts to be won at all.

Satan is the unsuspected god of this world. He is not afraid of us, but he is desperately afraid of the Holy Spirit. That is why we can only wage our warfare "in the power of his might" (Ephesians 6:10).

(d) We Wrestle Satan's Countless Demons (6:12e) "Against spiritual wickedness in high places."

We fight against spiritual hosts of wickedness, against wicked spirits in the heavenlies. The unseen world is swarming with demons. One poor man in Jesus' day was in bondage to a legion of them (some six thousand men comprised a Roman legion) and was beyond all human help (Mark 5:1-17). When Jesus came to earth there was an extraordinary outburst of demonic activity. There will be another outburst when the antichrist reigns. (That outburst of demon activity seems to have already begun.)

Satan has countless hordes of demons at his disposal. The word Paul used to describe these demonic hordes is *ponēria*, translated "wickedness" in the King James version of Ephesians 6:12. The decadence and depravity of our age are demon-inspired. Demons seem to be obsessed with holding people enslaved to their senses—to sexual and sensual sins. Perversion, pornography, and permissiveness are encouraged, promoted, and aided by evil spirits whose goal it is to befoul and destroy the human race.

There is considerable speculation about where demons originated. Some theologians think that they are the disembodied spirits of a pre-Adamic race. Craving to be embodied, they possess people and drive them to commit vile sins. The incident of the man possessed by a legion of demons lends credence to this view. When Jesus ordered the demons to come out of the man, those foul and fierce spirits pleaded to be allowed to enter a herd of swine. The swine instantly ran down a steep place into the sea and drowned. They preferred death to demon possession.

We are engaged in a battle with the occult. The moment we try to pray or attempt to do anything for God, these unseen but potent and organized hordes of Satan oppose us.

b.   The Armor (6:13-17)

(1)   A Demand (6:13) "Take unto you the whole armour of God, that ye may be able to withstand in the evil day, and having done all, to stand."

The least we can do is stand. We can take our stand for God, as Martin Luther did when he announced that he was going to the fateful confrontation with Rome at Worms. When facing all the power of earth and Hell, he said: "On this I take my stand. I can do no other. God help me."

We are living in "the evil day." Paul had already reminded the Ephesians that "the days are evil" (Ephesians 5:16). The days were evil then; they are evil today. We are to withstand this evil and, having done all that is possible, we are still to stand. We are to give no ground to Satan.

Perhaps the best commentary on this subject is 2 Samuel 23 where David's mighty men are listed. This review comes at the end of David's reign, just before Solomon's glorious kingdom was established. Chapter 23 is a mirror of the endtimes when at the judgment seat the Lord will review our lives prior to setting up His millennial kingdom. First and foremost in the list of David's men is Adino the Eznite "that sat in the seat, chief among the captains" (23:8). One wonders what Joab thought of that. Abishai and Asahel, brothers of Joab, were also listed, but not Joab. Love and loyalty to the king was the ultimate test, and Joab failed in both of these areas.

Similarly we look in vain for Ahithophel. His son Eliam is listed, but Ahithophel, for all his one-time professed loyalty to David, proved himself a traitor.

Nor do we find the name of Jonathan. He loved David and was loyal up to a point. But in the end he loved this present evil world and died rendering loyalty to the wrong king. He let family come between himself and David.

Much could be said about Adino, true to David in the place of danger. He faced eight hundred men. Much could be said of Eleazar who stood for God in the face of desertion. How revealing is the Holy Spirit's comment that after Eleazar's great victory "the people returned after him only to spoil" (2 Samuel 23:10).

Note what is said of Shammah, who stood for God in the place of discouragement. One might expect to see valor blaze forth in defense of a strategic pass, bridge, or gate. Shammah, however, saw value in "a piece of ground full of lentiles." He stood against the Philistines and fought over that ground. Look at how the Holy Spirit records his victory: "The people fled from the Philistines. But he stood . . . and the Lord wrought a great victory" (2 Samuel 23:11-12).

Like Shammah, we are to stand firm against the enemy. We are to stand fast against the manipulation of human life and society by principalities, powers, rulers of this world's darkness, and wicked spirits in high places. They are all the more dangerous because they are invisible.

Taking a stand may mean doing what some have already done— rolling up their sleeves and becoming active in the messy fight against perversion, pornography, abortion, drugs, alcohol, vice, error, and organized crime. Thank God for such men. Pray for them. Support them. They are fighting against the unseen spirit powers who exploit fallen human nature, fan human passions, inflame human lusts, and encourage human errors. God demands that we too "withstand in the evil day, and having done all, to stand."

(2) A Description (6:14-17)

(a) Provisions for Our Security in the Battle (6:14-17a)

i.   Protection for What We Sow (6:14a) "Stand therefore, having your loins girt about with truth."

The Roman soldier's belt or girdle held in place the armor that protected the lower part of his body—the seat of vital organs and the organs of life-creating force. We need truth's protection at the source of spiritual procreative power so that Satan cannot tamper with what we sow. Truth is vital.

We must be sure that the seed we sow is the truth of God. Often we say, "Thus saith the Lord," when we do not communicate His truth. We just express our own opinions, or we misrepresent truth because of our failure to understand it. How often have we heard well-meaning preachers proclaim erroneous teachings with all their hearts? Such men seek to persuade people to do this or experience that, but they are teaching error. Preachers and Bible teachers need to have their loins girt about with truth. They must master the principles of hermeneutics, study the Scriptures in depth, know the mind of the Lord, and be filled with the Spirit of truth. Otherwise, they may teach as God's truth what is not God's truth at all.

We all must be careful with what we sow because "that which is born of the flesh is flesh" (John 3:6). Nowhere is Satan more active than where we sow. That is why truth is the first piece of armor we must put on. The devil is the father of lies; deception is his business. He wants us to sow error sugar-coated with truth. We must be absolutely sure before God that we are wearing the truth, the whole truth, and nothing but the truth. We must not preach opinions; we must preach God's truth. We must sow His truth. Sincerity is not enough; we must also be right.

ii.   Protection for What We Show (6:14b) "The breastplate of righteousness."

The Roman soldier's breastplate protected his upper vital organs, particularly the lungs and heart. Proverbs 4:23 urges us to protect our hearts: "Keep thy heart with all diligence; for out of it are the issues of life." Matthew 15:18-19 says: "Those things which proceed out of the mouth come forth from the heart; and they defile the man. For out of the heart proceed evil thoughts, murders, adulteries, fornications, thefts, false witness, blasphemies." Satan tries to corrupt the hearts of believers so that they will display ugly passions instead of the love of Christ. Righteousness must be the guardian of our hearts.

The Greek word translated "righteousness" in Ephesians 6:14, *dikaiosune*, occurs ninety-two times in the New Testament (including thirty times in the book of Romans). Paul's first use of *dikaiosune* in Romans is instructive. He told us in Romans 1 that he was not ashamed of the gospel of Christ, for "therein is the righteousness of God revealed" (1:17). The theme of Romans is righteousness. Paul spoke of righteousness *revealed* (1:17), righteousness *required* (1:18; 3:10-16), righteousness *received* (4:5), and righteousness *reproduced* (6:12-23).

The Epistle to the Romans teaches us that God is righteous—He always does what is right. He does what He does because He is who He is. He does what is right because it is impossible for Him to do anything wrong. He makes no mistakes. He is not swayed by fear or favor.

Just as God does what He does because of who He is, we do what we do because of who we are. Since we are sinners by birth, by nature, by practice, and by choice, we do what is unrighteous and wrong. Sin has tainted even our most noble thoughts, our most generous deeds, and our highest aspirations.

The genius of the gospel is that God does not ask us to imitate His righteousness, for no human being could possibly do that. Instead God gives us His righteous nature by means of regeneration. He gives us His Holy Spirit to live within us and to reproduce Christ's righteousness in us and through us. Christians are to show the righteousness of God to the world. The world is waiting to see men and women behaving like Jesus.

Satan attacks the heart, so we need this breastplate. The righteousness of Christ is glorious armor for us to wear in a world of sin. When people look at us, what should catch their eyes first is the gleaming glory of Christ's righteousness. Satan has already assailed the righteousness of Christ with all the resources at his disposal and found it impenetrable. It will protect our hearts—the innermost springs of our beings—from all the unrighteousness so evident in this fallen world.

iii.   Protection for Where We Go (6:15) "Your feet shod with the preparation of the gospel of peace."

We should be prepared to go, but there are some places where Christians must not go. There are some doors we must never darken unless we are encased in God's armor and our feet are protected by the gospel of peace. We should only go to these places when we are sent to save. The temptations are too great otherwise.

Everywhere we do go, we should be soldiers of the King, ambassadors for Christ. We have our marching orders in Matthew 28:19-20:

> Go ye therefore, and teach all nations, baptizing them in the name of the Father, and of the Son, and of the Holy Ghost: Teaching them to observe all things whatsoever I have commanded you: and, lo, I am with you alway, even unto the end of the world.

Millions of people still do not have even a text or two of Scripture. Lost men and women everywhere are held in the iron grip of Satan and his hosts. Surely there is someone to whom we can go with the gospel.

The oft-forgotten word in Ephesians 6:15 is *preparation*. We need to be prepared. Usually we shrink back from Christian service because we are not prepared. We should make an effort to master Scripture and learn the skills of soulwinning. Jesus spent over three years training the twelve apostles. Paul invariably had an entourage of young men he was training to become evangelists, pastors, teachers, missionaries, church planters, and soul-winners.

A man does not become a craftsman overnight. He has to learn the secrets of the trade and how to use the tools of the trade. He has to learn to read blueprints, measure accurately, and cut and join precisely. Likewise, one does not become a great Bible expositor overnight. One does not master principles of hermeneutics and homiletics in a day. One does not grasp the scope of Scripture in a week or two. Each of us needs to serve an apprenticeship, attend God's school, learn by doing, and be attentive to the Holy Spirit.

We must be prepared, and then we must be prepared to go. Where? Wherever God sends us—home or abroad. He may send us to our own family, neighbors, and friends. He may send us to a high-profile ministry or to some kind of service behind the scenes. He may send us to a delightful ministry or a dangerous ministry. Wherever God sends, we must go with our feet shod with the preparation of the gospel of peace.

iv.   Protection for What We Do (6:16) "Above all, taking the shield of faith, wherewith ye shall be able to quench all the fiery darts of the wicked."

Paul had often seen the shields Roman soldiers carried into war. The shields were made so that a row of soldiers could lock shield to shield, forming a wall of iron. Such a wall would be difficult, if not impossible, for a foe to penetrate. Each individual shield was big enough to cover the soldier's whole body. Darts and arrows hurled at the soldier hit the shield and fell harmlessly to the ground.

The wicked one (for that is the force of the words "the wicked" in Ephesians 6:16) throws many fiery darts. He has been studying human nature ever since man was created. Satan helped forge fallen human nature. He is a master psychologist. One person he assails with lusts of the flesh. He has a whole arsenal of darts that can set the senses aflame. Another person he assails with lusts of the eye; someone else with the pride of life. The lust of appetite, the love of applause, and the lure of ambition are among the host of darts Satan uses to kindle fierce fires in our souls. He knows our weaknesses and strengths. He sends his legions of evil spirits to titillate our senses, inflame our desires, corrupt our souls, weaken our wills, deceive our minds, deaden our consciences, and distort God's truth.

Satan has a thousand wiles and he never gives up. If you success-fully resist him now, he will come again later. Perhaps he will tempt you with something in a book or on television, a clever remark by a college professor, or a friend's snub or sneer. Perhaps he will arouse a sleeping lust or put an utterly lewd or corrupt thought in your mind. Perhaps he will entice you with a brilliant and seemingly flawless philosophy. (Everyone should read C. S. Lewis' classic on temptation, *The Screwtape Letters,* and his brilliant passage on temp-tation in *Perelandra.*)

We will never be out of range of Satan's fiery darts, but they can be quenched and rendered harmless by the shield of faith (literally, the faith). Satan's fiery darts cannot penetrate the shield of deter-mined, living, dynamic faith in God. That is why Satan designed the original temptation in Eden to persuade our first parents that God was not to be trusted.

The first temptation in the garden of Eden questioned *the goodness of God.* "Yea, hath God said, Ye shall not eat of every tree of the garden?" (Genesis 3:1) The implication was that the limitation was unkind; God was unkind in refusing to allow man to have something that he wanted.

The second temptation questioned *the government of God.* "Ye shall not surely die" (Genesis 3:4). Satan planted the idea that disobedi-ence to God was not really a serious matter, that it would not have the adverse result that God had said it would.

The third temptation questioned *the goals of God.* "God doth know that in the day ye eat thereof, then your eyes shall be opened, and ye shall be as gods, knowing good and evil" (Genesis 3:5). This most terrible slander of all suggested that God was selfish and jealous, that He was deliberately refusing to allow man to attain full maturity.

In this struggle in the garden of Eden, Eve threw away the only weapon she had: the Word of God. The result? She was deceived, lost her faith in God, and was pierced by Satan's fiery darts. Adam followed her into sin. His sin was more deliberate—downright disobedience—but its root was the same unbelief. He saw his beloved wife in her fallen condition and, instead of trusting God to work out her salvation, he deliberately followed her into sin. He too questioned the goodness of God, the government of God, and the goals of God.

Satan presented the same temptations to the Lord Jesus—the second man, the last Adam—in the wilderness. Satan said, "If thou be the Son of God, command that these stones be made bread"

(Matthew 4:3). The Lord had been on a forty-day fast, so He was desperately hungry. Satan was suggesting that God the Father was withholding an entitlement from Jesus and that He should take matters into His own hands and use the power inherent in His sonship to change His God-given circumstances. Satan was challenging the *goodness of God.*

The second temptation followed the same pattern. Having taken the Lord to a pinnacle of the temple, Satan urged, "Cast thyself down: for it is written, He shall give his angels charge concerning thee" (Matthew 4:6). Satan tempted Jesus to question and challenge *the government of God.* Satan was saying, "Cast Yourself down. You will not die. God would not let that happen to You. To put God to the test is no serious matter."

The third temptation, in keeping with the others, challenged *the goals of God.* Satan showed the Lord all the kingdoms of the world and offered them to Him—on Satanic terms. Satan was slanderously insinuating that God was jealous and selfishly keeping Jesus from kingdoms that were rightfully His.

The shield of faith rebuffed Satan at every point and quenched his fiery darts. To each tempting suggestion, Jesus replied with a verse of Scripture. He simply fell back on the Word of God and thereby demonstrated His unequivocal faith in God.

Our faith in God should be so alive and robust that we never question the circumstances in which we find ourselves, the limitations He has placed on us, or His right to dictate the terms of our lives. We never question the goodness of God. We never doubt His government. Because of our faith we shrink from sin because it offends Him, grieves His heart, and inevitably brings into our lives the consequences He says it will. We never question God's goals either. If He has not yet brought us into the kingdom, we believe that one day He will. The place, the process, and the time period are all in His purposes. Such faith effectively quenches Satan's darts.

v.   Protection for What We Know (6:17a) "The helmet of salvation."

Soldiers wore helmets because a blow to the head could be fatal. The head is the site of a person's intellectual powers, the faculty that sets him apart from the beasts—in his origin, his development, and his potential. Only a human being can think and express thoughts in an organized, verbal, and articulate way. Only a human being can state his thoughts in terms of music or mathematics, physics or philosophy, anthropology or astronomy. The head has to be protected at all costs.

God gives us a helmet to protect our thoughts from Satanic influence and interference. Satan usually goes after the mind. Paul told his friends at Corinth that "the god of this world hath blinded the minds of them which believe not" (2 Corinthians 4:4). The protection God gives us from Satan's deceptions, denials, and distortions is the helmet of salvation. Without this protection, our thinking—brilliant as it may be—is open to the damning influence of Satan's rulers of darkness.

Apart from God's salvation, man cannot reach correct conclusions about psychological, social, philosophical, and spiritual phenomena. He can orbit spacecraft and journey to the moon. He can split atoms and tinker with the genetic code. But sin impairs his thinking about his relationship to God and his fellows. His first sin separated him from God. His second sin separated him from man. Satan tries to ensure that he is kept in bondage and blindness in both relationships.

Satan's lies are diabolically clever. Under the influence of demonic insinuation and suggestion, man deliberately sets aside divine revelation in favor of human reasoning. Satan's deceptions appeal to the unregenerate mind. They seem to make lots of sense and they appeal to human pride. To the unsaved, the theory of evolution is more plausible than the story of creation. Communism used to seem much more practical than Christianity (especially Christianity as distorted and disseminated by Satan's dupes). A creed demanding works seems more logical than the cross. Humanism is more attractive than holiness. Psychology seems more reasonable than salvation. Satan never gives up his attacks on thought processes.

Satan would like to undermine our belief in the Bible as the inspired, inerrant, and infallible Word of God. He would like to distort our doctrines so that we base our beliefs on erroneous or inadequate hermeneutical processes. He would like us to think wrong thoughts about God the Father, the Holy Spirit, and the Lord Jesus. He would like us to be mistaken about the plan of salvation and the daily practice of Christianity. He would like us to espouse cultish absurdities. He would like us to dilute God's demands that we be like Jesus—that we be holy, loving, joyous, peaceful, patient, kind, and self-controlled. He would like us to emphasize service at the expense of worship. He would like us to be occupied with the cares of this world and the deceitfulness of riches so that we lose sight of the world to come. He would like us to lower our standards and allow the world to pour us into its mold, or go to the other extreme and mistake isolation for separation. Satan has ten thousand wiles—all aimed at influencing what we think.

God's protection for us against all these attacks on the mind is the helmet of salvation. God's salvation must encompass what we think. Paul's Epistle to the Romans gives the most complete exposition of that salvation, so Romans is one book we should master—that is, we should put it on. Actually we need to explore the whole Bible, so that our understanding of the salvation God has provided for us will be comprehensive.

As we put on the helmet of salvation and learn to appreciate its worth, we will use it to test all our thoughts. For instance, the thought that a certain movie would be good to watch or a certain book would be good to read may enter your mind. Before you translate that thought into action, you will test it with the helmet of salvation. Would watching that movie or reading that book be consistent with living a holy life, with becoming more like Jesus? Would the philosophies and ideas presented win the approval of God? We have to see or read some things in order to be stirred to holy indignation and wrath. We need to hear some arguments so that we can study them and refute them. But these subjects must be allowed to occupy our minds only with the Holy Spirit's approval.

We must always remember that the mind is Satan's domain. He goes after the mind to influence our thoughts, words, and deeds. God goes deeper; He goes after the heart. Because our minds are vulnerable, they must be protected by God's salvation. The more we wear the helmet of salvation, the more we will think about the things of God, fill our minds and memories with God's Word, and dwell on the enormous cost of our salvation and its ramifications in our lives. Therefore, the more we wear the helmet, the more we will be protected against Satan's lures and lies.

(b) Provisions for Our Success in the Battle (6:17b) "The sword of the Spirit, which is the word of God."

So far each piece of armor that the Holy Spirit has named has been for defense, not offense. Now He names the Sword that enables us to attack the enemy. Napoleon once said, "The best form of defense is attack." Neither principalities, nor powers, nor the rulers of the world's darkness, nor wicked spirits in high places, nor Satan himself, can withstand the Sword of the Spirit, which is the Word of God. The powers of earth and Hell have no defense against it.

God's Word is like a sword. Hebrews 4:12 says that it is "quick [living], and powerful, and sharper than any twoedged sword, piercing even to the dividing asunder of soul and spirit, and of the joints and marrow, and is a discerner of the thoughts and intents of the heart."

The best answer to secular humanism is the Word of God. The best answer to dialectical materialism is the Word of God. The best answer to behavioral psychology, liberal theology, cults, and false religions is the Word of God.

Because the Word of God is the Sword of the *Spirit*, it cuts through all Satan's ranks, deceptions, and devices. The devil is no match for the Holy Spirit. God's Word is the breath of God. It is the Holy Spirit's creation and partakes of His life. It is alive with His authority.

We should wield the Sword of the Spirit when we pray because it will cut through Satan's hindering hosts. We should quote it when we preach because our power does not lie in words of man's wisdom, but in words the Holy Spirit supplies. We should use the Sword of the Spirit when we face our problems, our circumstances, our needs, our temptations.

The same "almighty word / Chaos and darkness heard, / And took their flight" in the dawn of creation.[1] The word of God spoke worlds into being. The word of God rang from the lips of Jesus in magnificent authority when He cast out evil spirits, cleansed loathsome lepers, and raised the dead. The Word of God is God-breathed. The same breath made man a living soul and quickens his spirit.

Are you downhearted? The prophet said, "Thy words were found, and I did eat them; and thy word was unto me the joy and rejoicing of mine heart" (Jeremiah 15:16). Are you perplexed? The psalmist said, "Thy word is a lamp unto my feet, and a light unto my path" (Psalm 119:105). Are you tempted? The Holy Spirit says, "Wherewithal shall a young man cleanse his way? by taking heed thereto according to thy word" (Psalm 119:9). Are you in trying circumstances? Jesus quoted Deuteronomy 8:3 to the devil when He was famished with hunger: "Man shall not live by bread alone, but by every word . . . of God" (Matthew 4:4). Do you find it hard to pray? Ephesians 6:17 says, "Take . . . the sword of the Spirit, which is the word of God."

Our armor is complete. We are ready to wage war, and the next verse tells us how.

---

1. Quotation is from a hymn by John Marriott.

B. Assailing the Enemy (6:18-20)

1. Warring (6:18a) "Praying always with all prayer and supplication in the Spirit."

T he Greek word translated "prayer" here is *proseuche*. This word is restricted in the New Testament to mean prayer to God, and it takes cognizance of God's power and sufficiency. *Proseuche* also gives prominence to the devotional side of prayer. No wonder Satan feels threatened whenever a believer prays. It is not the weak and stammering believer he fears, nor the wandering and inadequate prayer he makes. The fact that a child of God is appealing to the almighty Father is what causes Satan to fear.

Satan does not fear eloquence in prayer either. He does not fear perseverance. (Quite often prayer is the most spasmodic and disjointed of our activities.) He does not fear our understanding of the way prayer works. No, he fears the simple fact that a needy child of God is at the mighty throne of God. Satan harnesses all his minions to bar the way to the throne of God. But no demon, no angel-prince, no fallen angel can face the Spirit's flaming Sword. The Word of God clears the way to the throne of God for the child of God.

When we pray we enter three realms. First we enter *the hidden place* where we are alone with God. It may be a bedroom, a barn, a cathedral, or a car. It can be a busy street or a bus seat. The place doesn't matter, as long as we can withdraw from the restless world around us and lift our hearts to God. Jesus recommended a "closet"—a quiet place (Matthew 6:6). He often sought mountain solitudes, a garden, or the wilderness. In the hidden place, all else is shut out and we are shut in with God.

The second realm is *the heavenly place,* the sphere mentioned in Ephesians where our blessings and battles are. In the "heavenlies" evil spirits swarm to hinder, harass, distract, and discourage. This is where we need the whole armor of God. This is where we need the Spirit's mighty Sword. This is where prayer is a battle.

In prayer we battle wandering thoughts. My prayer for Aunt Susie reminds me of her cat. Thoughts of the cat remind me that Jim said there was a mouse in his office. That reminds me to get a mousetrap at the hardware store. The hardware store reminds me of the camera shop next-door and the roll of film I took in to be developed, and so on. Several minutes later I realize that I haven't been praying; I have been daydreaming. The enemy has been busy.

We also battle wicked thoughts when we pray. These come unbidden with startling suddenness. I think of a phrase from a book I should never have read, a scene from a movie I should never have watched, a voice from the past saying foul words or blaspheming. The enemy has been busy again. From the subconscious mind he dredges up filth that is lying stagnant and rotten on the ocean floor of the soul.

We battle worldly thoughts too. Our prayers focus on material things—the need to pass next week's exam, the urgent need for a raise in pay or a better job, the need for healing. It's not wrong to pray for material things, but we should not be preoccupied with them. When other tactics fail, the enemy tries to hinder our prayers by calling our attention to the concerns of time and sense. Paul's prayers barely touch on such concerns. "Give us this day our daily bread" (Matthew 6:11) is the only line in the Lord's prayer that is not otherworldly.

What can we do to win the battle? We can try praying aloud. We can try using more of God's Word in prayer. We can recognize the source of these distractions and put the enemy to rout with the Sword of the Spirit.

The third realm is *the holy place.* At last we find ourselves inside the veil. As Cleland B. McAfee put it:

> There is a place of quiet rest,
> Near to the heart of God,
> A place where sin cannot molest,
> Near to the heart of God.

There we engage in what Paul called in Ephesians 6:18 "all prayer"—prayer in all its aspects. We are absorbed in confession, adoration, petition, intercession, thanksgiving, and praise. Paul specifically mentioned the aspect of supplication. The Greek word translated "supplication" is *deesis,* which suggests a petition for a specific personal need. Such a petition would be made with the awareness of God's ability to supply that need.

There is nothing wrong with supplicating the throne for our needs, especially our spiritual needs (although "all prayer" has a much broader scope). We must not be superficially pious and ignore our needs. God's truth is wonderfully balanced. Often God allows us to have needs so that we will be moved to pray about them.

All prayer and supplication, to be effective, must be "in the Spirit." Otherwise we will not really be praying; we will merely be saying prayers. Prayer is the most purely spiritual exercise in which we can engage. Praying in the Spirit does not mean going into a trance or speaking an ecstatic utterance. The Holy Spirit does not overpower our mental faculties. He directs, but He does not dominate. He never acts despotically. "The spirits of the prophets are subject to the prophets" (1 Corinthians 14:32).

The direction of the Holy Spirit is the ultimate solution to wandering, wicked, and worldly thoughts. He gently inclines our thoughts through channels He has in mind. He brings to our minds those passages of Scripture that are most appropriate to the moment. He brings to us the gentle assurance that our prayers are heard and that He controls all the factors of space and time that are involved in the answers to our prayers.

Meeting up with the Holy Spirit, the ranks of the enemy melt away as smoke dissipates in the wind. They flee in terror, for they are desperately afraid of the Holy Spirit of God.

2.   Watching (6:18b) "Watching thereunto with all perseverance and supplication for all saints."

The Greek word *agrupneō,* translated "watching" here, literally means "lying sleepless." Many of us know firsthand what that's like. The Lord used the same word when He spoke of His coming: "Take ye heed, watch and pray: for ye know not when the time is" (Mark 13:33). In His discourse on the endtimes Jesus said, "Watch ye therefore, and pray always, that ye may be accounted worthy to escape all these things that shall come to pass" (Luke 21:36). *Agrupneō* is also used to describe the work of an elder: "Obey them that have the rule over you, and submit yourselves: for they watch for your souls, as they that must give account" (Hebrews 13:17).

We are to "lie sleepless," watching and praying. Watching sights the enemy; praying fights the enemy. Spiritual warfare is serious business. The enemy is real. He seeks to harm us and our loved ones. He wants to destroy our testimonies and hinder the work of God. We take the battle all too lightly. We would do well to have some sleepless nights over the state of our country, the woes of the world, the condition of our churches, the needs of family and friends, and our own spiritual lives.

Paul told us to persevere in our watching. We give up too soon, but Satan never gives up. He is tireless, persistent, resourceful, and desperate to delay his doom as long as possible and do as much damage as he can in the meantime. When God sends sleepless nights, let us pray. Let us seize insomnia as a gift from God so that "with all perseverance and supplication for all saints" we can turn the quiet night hours into golden moments of communion with God.

3.   Witnessing (6:19-20)

a.   Sharing in a Brother's Opportunity (6:19) "And for me, that utterance may be given unto me, that I may open my mouth boldly, to make known the mystery of the gospel."

This is an example of how to employ supplication as a means of smiting the enemy. We can offer supplication for brothers near or far away. Prayer *annihilates distance.* Paul was under arrest in Rome and his readers were scattered throughout Asia Minor, but prayer takes no account of distance.

Prayer *annihilates dread.* Paul was chained to a guard, charged with treason, and expecting to be arraigned before Nero. Yet the prayers of God's people could help him overcome his fears and cautiousness and enable him to speak boldly.

Prayer *annihilates difficulty.* There are inherent difficulties in communicating the "mystery" of the gospel. Paul wanted to proclaim this mystery, and man's dullness of hearing and his inability to comprehend had to be overcome. That, Paul knew, was the work of the Holy Spirit, but before the Spirit of God could do His work, the human messenger needed his mind to be flooded with divine light and his tongue to be touched with God's eloquence. Paul also needed hearers whose ears and hearts had been made receptive. These needs could be met through prayer.

Paul realized that his situation in Rome was a golden opportunity. He could win members of the imperial guard to Christ and make converts in caesar's household. Possibly he would have the privilege of witnessing to Nero and members of the Roman court. There were Christians and churches all over Rome that he could encourage to be bold by being bold himself.

Paul asked his brothers in Christ to share in his opportunities by means of prayer. Their prayers could strengthen his spirit and batter the unseen enemy. Their prayers could smite the foe, render him powerless to hinder the witness, and break his hold on the minds, hearts, wills, and consciences of those Paul was seeking to win for Christ. His brothers could share in Paul's witnessing, even though some of them were hundreds of miles away. Distance, a purely human factor, means nothing to God.

b.   Sharing in a Brother's Opposition (6:20) "I am an ambassador in bonds: that therein I may speak boldly, as I ought to speak."

One of the most important officials in the Roman world was the imperial legate. As one of the emperor's personal representatives, a legate lived in an outpost of the empire and enforced imperial policy. He was directly accountable to the emperor, and lesser officials were responsible to the legate. He was an ambassador. The word translated "ambassador" in Ephesians 6:20 is *presbeuō*, which means "the emperor's legate."

Paul was Christ's legate. As Christ's ambassador Paul had already magnificently represented the throne of Heaven in province after province and city after city throughout the empire. In Athens, Antioch, Paphos, Philippi, Corinth, and Crete, God had used Paul to shake Satan's kingdom to its very foundations. Now Satan had him in chains, but Paul was dauntless. He was still Christ's ambassador; Satan could not change that. Paul was an ambassador in bonds.

Every time Paul moved his arm, his chain rattled, making him aware of the enemy's opposition. Through prayer his fellow believers could help him face that opposition to the gospel. They could help bear his chains. They could lighten his load and buoy up his spirits.

We do not understand how prayer works. How a brother praying for me in southern California can lift my spirits as I minister in northern Canada is beyond my understanding. How my prayers in Chicago can bring a fresh surge of victory to a believer in China, I cannot say. You and I only know that when God considers all the aspects of a situation and all the forces that govern the universe, prayer is one of the key factors He takes into account. We know prayer works because God says it does.

PART V

Conclusion

Ephesians 6:21-24

V. CONCLUSION (6:21-24)

A. Paul's Fellow Worker (6:21-22)

1. His Titles (6:21a) "That ye also may know my affairs, and how I do, Tychicus, a beloved brother and faithful minister in the Lord."

Intelligent prayer is based on information. It is hard to pray in the abstract. Tychicus brought information about Paul to the Christians at Ephesus who were praying for him.

Tychicus is mentioned in the companion letter to the Colossians. He was a native of Asia Minor (Acts 20:4) and possibly of Ephesus. He and Onesimus carried the Epistle to the Ephesians, the Epistle to the Colossians, and possibly a letter to the Laodiceans (Colossians 4:16) to the churches of Asia. Tychicus was one of the men chosen to accompany Paul when he took a financial gift from the Gentile churches to Jerusalem. On occasion Paul used Tychicus as a messenger (2 Timothy 4:12; Titus 3:12).

Paul called Tychicus "a beloved brother." The family of God makes brothers and sisters of all who love the Lord. Some become *beloved* brothers, often nearer to us than our natural siblings. Tychicus had the privilege of being a beloved brother to the great apostle Paul.

Tychicus was also a "faithful minister." The word translated "minister" in Ephesians 6:21, *diakonos,* means "an active servant." Tychicus was willing to devote himself to the service of God; he was a helper to Paul and an active worker for the cause of Christ. Paul had chains on his arms; Tychicus had them on his heart. His sole ambition was to be useful in relieving Paul's restrictions and furthering the kingdom of God. People like Tychicus are invaluable in the Lord's work. *A beloved brother* and *a faithful minister* are titles of nobility in the kingdom of God. We should covet them for ourselves.

2. His Task (6:21b-22)

(a) To Minister Tidings to Them (6:21b-22a) "Shall make known to you all things: Whom I have sent unto you for the same purpose, that ye might know our affairs."

Tychicus would bring information about Paul's health, for instance. Paul was not a well man. He had not completely recovered from the ill-treatment and maulings he had suffered in championing the cause of Christ.

There would also be information about Paul's finances. Paul had no regular income as far as we know. He lived by faith. God's people helped him. Although Paul never mentioned his financial needs, he did say on one occasion that he had learned how to have plenty and how to do without.

The Christians at Ephesus were probably wondering whether Paul had prospects of a speedy or late trial. Tychicus would be able to bring the saints up to date on the details of Paul's approaching legal battle. The mills of justice were evidently moving slowly.

Tychicus would also report on Paul's psychological condition. In Scripture Paul nearly always appears as a victorious Christian, on top of his circumstances. But 2 Corinthians implies that he experienced depression too.

There would be stories about soldiers won to Christ, news of Paul's latest Epistles, a description of the house where Paul lived, the remarkable account of a vital Christian ministry being carried on despite chains, tales of visitors coming to Rome from all over the world. Tychicus would have to relay all this information. It would be grist for the mill of prayer.

(b) To Minister Tenderness to Them (6:22b) "That he might comfort your hearts."

Paul did not forget for a moment the tender love of so many in the Ephesian church. He remembered his last farewell to the Ephesian elders at Miletus when "they all wept sore, and fell on Paul's neck, and kissed him, Sorrowing most of all for the words which he spake, that they should see his face no more" (Acts 20:37-38). Tychicus would bring them comforting news because Paul was optimistic about the outcome of his impending trial.

Paul had a feeling that his work was not yet done, and he had ambitious plans to evangelize the rest of the world, starting with Spain. Beyond Spain were Huns, Goths, and Vandals to be reached with the gospel. Yonder too were the islands of Britain. Even if his optimism were unfounded and he should be executed, Paul was anticipating a triumphant exodus. He was not afraid of death.

Although Paul was separated from the Ephesians by miles and circumstances, he harnessed himself in the whole armor of God and sallied forth to do battle on their behalf daily. He loved them all. The proof was a letter ablaze with the love that many waters cannot quench—an Epistle for them that was God-breathed and deathless as God's throne.

B.   Paul's Final Word (6:23-24) "Peace be to the brethren, and love with faith, from God the Father and the Lord Jesus Christ. Grace be with all them that love our Lord Jesus Christ in sincerity. Amen."

Peace—the Hebrew salutation. *Grace*—the Gentile salutation. *Love with faith*—the Christian salutation.

Peace! Grace! Love! Faith! These words will ring on the chimes of time until at last earth's shores recede and we stand amid the scenes of glory and lay our armor down . . . until grace gives way to glory . . . until faith gives way to sight . . . until love's vast ocean fills all horizons and bathes our souls in bliss.

"Peace be to the brethren." In this world we are in a battle. Satan's dogs of war will bark at our heels and hound us right down to the river. But we are not at war with the brethren. We may not agree with some of our brothers and sisters in Christ. We may dislike and dispute some of their doctrines, but we are not at war with them. If we are, we are fighting the wrong battle.

"Love with faith." Love is the source and faith is the force. Love reaches down; faith reaches up. Love is the alpha and omega, the beginning and the end; faith lies in between. Love reaches out the hand of God; faith takes hold of it. Love provides all we need; faith appropriates it.

"Grace." Thus Paul began this letter (Ephesians 1:2). Thus he ended it. It is God's unmerited, unlimited favor that shines upon us all the time along all the way. It is grace that set our feet on the highway to Heaven. It is grace that keeps us company all the journey through. It is grace that will see us safely home at last.

Peace, love, faith, and grace come from God the Father and the Lord Jesus Christ, who are coeternal and coequal. How wonderful that God, in the supreme and crowning revelation of Himself, is a Father. Here Paul did not emphasize God as Judge, though He is a Judge; nor did he emphasize God as the Creator, though He is the Creator; nor did he emphasize God as a holy God, though He is holy beyond all we could imagine. Instead, he emphasized that wonderful word *Father!* God is the Father, made known to us as such by the Son, *"the* Lord Jesus Christ" (Ephesians 6:23, italics added), who is *"our* Lord Jesus Christ" (6:24, italics added).

Paul added a safeguard to his benediction. Our love for Christ is not to be sentimental. It is wrong to use sentimental terms of endearment such as "dear Jesus" when addressing our Lord. In His title *Lord Jesus Christ*, the human name *Jesus* is flanked by titles of dignity and power. He is Master and Mediator, Lord and Christ. Paul emphasized the dignity of the title in his last word: "Grace be with all them that love our Lord Jesus Christ in *sincerity*" (italics added). Sincerity, not sentiment, should characterize our love.

The word translated "sincerity" in Ephesians 6:24 is *aphtharsia,* which literally means "without corruption." Our love should be incorruptible. It should be a deathless unfading love that takes on the nature of immortality (see 1 Corinthians 15:42). With his final word, Paul left us face to face with our Lord Jesus Christ, contemplating a love relationship that reaches into eternity.

Exploring

PHILIPPIANS

CONTENTS

PREFACE

As I walked through the wilderness of this world," said John Bunyan, "I lighted on a certain place where was a Den, and laid me down in that place to sleep: and, as I slept, I dreamed a dream. I dreamed, and behold, I saw a man clothed with rags, standing in a certain place, with his face from his own house, a book in his hand, and a great burden on his back..."

The den was Bedford jail, in which Bunyan was imprisoned for twelve years for preaching the gospel. In that jail he wrote *Pilgrim's Progress*, which for centuries was a bestseller, second only to the Bible. The book was published in 1678 and by the end of the nineteenth century had been printed in 112 languages and dialects. About the writing of *Pilgrim's Progress* Bunyan said:

> When at the first I took my pen in hand,
> Thus for to write, I did not understand
> That I at all should make a little book.
>
> . . . .
>
> Thus I set pen to paper with delight,
> And quickly had my thoughts in black and white.
> For having now my method by the end,
> Still as I pull'd, it came; and so I penn'd
> It down.

The apostle Paul also walked through the wilderness of this world and was put in prison for preaching the gospel. There he too took his pen in hand and the inspiration flowed ("As I pull'd, it came"). The apostle's words, however, came not by the inspiration of an idea but by the inspiration of the Holy Spirit.

As he wrote, Paul was thinking of his dear friends at Philippi. They had sent him a gift which he gratefully acknowledged. Irrepressible joy, a fruit of the Spirit, flooded his soul and poured over each page.

As we read the exultant stanzas of the Epistle to the Philippians, we might think that Paul was in a palace, not in prison. He mentioned his chains again and again, but we do not hear them clanging dismally. We hear them chiming like Christmas bells. The apostle had converted his chains, just as he had converted some of his guards. His chains had been transformed into the bonds of Christ and were therefore tokens of that "good, and acceptable, and perfect, will of God," which had long been his delight (Romans 12:2).

Come then and let us explore these prison pages together and learn from Paul how to be "more than conquerors through him that loved us" (Romans 8:37).

INTRODUCTION

P hilippi was a Macedonian hill town overlooking the coastal plain and the bay at Neapolis. The old Thracian settlement had been fortified by Philip II of Macedonia (father of Alexander the Great) to commemorate the addition of a new province to his kingdom and to protect the frontier against the Thracian highlanders.

The plains of Philippi were famous in Paul's day as the site where the armies of Antony and Octavian (who later became the emperor Augustus) had met and mastered the armies of Cassius and Brutus, the conspirators who had assassinated Julius Caesar. There the Roman republic breathed its last gasp and gave way to the age of the caesars about 42 B.C.

Augustus made Philippi a Roman colony, one of those bastions of the Roman way of life that were scattered across the empire. Like the Roman roads, the colonies were part of the system of fortifications securing the empire against insurgents and invaders. All of the colonies bore the unmistakable stamp of Rome.

Paul arrived in Philippi fresh from Troas where he had just seen a vision of a man from Macedonia urging him to "come over...and help us" (Acts 16:9). Paul's thoughts had at once turned to Europe's wretched paganism. None of the gods of Greek mythology, Rome's pantheon, Asiatic cults, or Egyptian superstition was worthy of man's serious thought, let alone his worship. Their stories were often cloaked in impressive imagery and, especially among the Greeks, garbed in the beauty of poetry and art, but the gods of paganism were demons. They "left man powerless against his passions, and only amused him while they helped him to be unholy."[1] Paul was sure that he had received an unequivocal call from God. The apostle's momentous vision was one of those mysterious turning points of history; the future of mankind was changed forever.

From Troas to Neapolis, the port of Philippi, was 125 miles.

Paul—accompanied by Silas, Timothy, and Luke—had made the journey in two days, with an overnight stop at the harbor of Samothrace. When Paul stepped ashore at Neapolis, the East was behind him and the West was before him. The triumphs of his past fifteen years were great enough, to be sure, but they were nothing compared to his prospects. Behind Paul lay the Orient with its commercial wealth, great cities, libraries, renowned temples—and decay. Before him lay Athens, feasting on the glories of its past, and Rome, the dynamic ruler of the world.

Nine miles from the port was the town of Philippi, which Luke (some think with local pride as a native of the place) called a "chief city" (Acts 16:12). The missionaries journeyed there on foot and were treated to a tremendous view of mountain, sea, and plain. The Via Egnatia ran straight from Neapolis to mount Symbolum, rounded the west side of the hill, headed straight to Philippi, and ran the length of the forum to the center of the town.

An acropolis, the old city climbed a hill. Its streets were steep, its houses old, its temples visible for miles. The colony of Augustus, spread out on the flat land at the foot of the hill, was very Roman, very proud, and very full of Roman soldiers and retired veterans. By the time Paul arrived in town, the grandchildren of the soldiers who had helped Octavian win the mastery of the world were middle-aged.

At every turn the missionaries were confronted with Rome: Roman houses, Roman officials, Roman soldiers, Roman togas, Roman speech, Roman merchants. There were few Asians and they were found only among the slaves, artisans, and poorer store-keepers. Together with the Greek population, the Asians belonged, for the most part, to depressed areas of the city. Military towns did not attract Jews until they became commercial centers, so there were hardly any Hebrews and hence no synagogue in Philippi.

Paul's experiences in Philippi are recorded in Acts 16. First he met a small group of devout women meeting by the river for prayer on the sabbath.[2] He told them the story of Jesus and met with instant success. His most prominent convert was Lydia, who apparently was not a Jewess but a "God-fearer." She was a native of Thyatira in western Asia Minor, a city famous for its purple-dyeing. Lydia, who sold the purple fabrics in Philippi, seems to have been wealthy. She put her home at the disposal of Paul and his colleagues for the duration of their stay.

Paul next encountered a demon-possessed slave girl whose

owners made merchandise of her dreadful affliction and "psychic" abilities. Paul set the poor woman free from demon-possession and thus infuriated her owners. They saw their gains vanish and lost no time in stirring up the city against Paul and Silas. It was not difficult to foment the latent antisemitism always so near the surface in Gentile society. The hated missionaries were dragged before the magistrates. Faced with an angry mob, the authorities made short work of the case. Paul and Silas were beaten, thrust into stocks in the inner prison, and left in that cramping and painful position to reflect on this first public European reaction to the gospel.

The missionaries' reaction was to sing! Then came the earthquake, the liberation of all the awe-struck prisoners, their stunned inaction, the jailer's conclusion that they had fled, his attempted suicide, his astonishment upon discovering that all was well, his midnight conversion, and his subsequent kind treatment of Paul and Silas.

The next morning word came from the authorities that the missionaries could be released, but for the sake of the new converts Paul put fear into the hearts of their unjust judges by announcing his and Silas's Roman citizenship and by challenging the magistrates to come and make amends. The magistrates pleaded with Paul and Silas to leave town, but the missionaries were in no hurry to go. They went first to the house of Lydia and had a farewell meeting with the believers. Then leaving Luke behind to do follow-up work and organize the church, the apostle and Silas and Timothy departed for further European conquests. The first western citadel had been taken by storm.

When Paul wrote to the Philippians, he was a prisoner awaiting trial in Rome. The purpose of the letter was to thank his friends for their financial support and to ask some of them to put aside their quarrels. It seems that when he wrote he was expecting his case to come up before the tribunal to which he had appealed. Perhaps by this time his confinement was stricter than before, but it did not hamper Paul's victorious style of Christian living. The keynote of his letter is joy. Come what may, he was on the winning side! His prayer was that all God's people might catch the vision of a triumphant life in Christ.

COMPLETE OUTLINE OF THE EPISTLE TO
THE PHILIPPIANS

I. Paul's Triumphant Experiences (1:1-30)

A. The Prisoner and His Pen (1:1-8)
1. Paul Was Thinking of the Philippians (1:1-2)
   a. Ecclesiastically (1:1)
      (1) Who the Letter Was From (1:1a-c)
         (a) Paul's Firm Signature (1:1a)
         (b) Paul's Fellow Servant (1:1b)
         (c) Paul's Formal Status (1:1c)
      (2) Who the Letter Was For (1:1d-f)
         (a) The Philippian Saints (1:1d)
         (b) The Philippian Shepherds (1:1e)
         (c) The Philippian Servants (1:1f)
   b. Evangelistically (1:2)
      (1) The Greeting (1:2a)
      (2) The Godhead (1:2b)
2. Paul Was Thankful for the Philippians (1:3-8)
   a. For Their Fellowship in the Gospel (1:3-5)
      (1) How He Ministered to Them (1:3-4)
         (a) Remembering Them Personally (1:3)
         (b) Remembering Them Prayerfully (1:4)
            i. With Persistence (1:4a)
            ii. With Petitions (1:4b)
            iii. With Pleasure (1:4c)
      (2) How They Ministered to Him (1:5)
   b. For Their Faithfulness in the Gospel (1:6)
      (1) The Work Had Been Commenced in Them (1:6a)
      (2) The Work Would Be Completed in Them (1:6b)
   c. For Their Fearlessness in the Gospel (1:7)
      They were not afraid of:
      (1) His Chains (1:7a)
      (2) His Charge (1:7b)

d. For Their Friendship in the Gospel (1:8)
  (1) Love's Outpouring (1:8a)
  (2) Love's Objectives (1:8b)

B. The Prisoner and His Prayers (1:9-11)
He wanted the Philippians to be:
1. Superlative in Their Devotion to Christ (1:9)
  a. Love Without Limit (1:9a)
  b. Love Within Limits (1:9b)
2. Sound in Their Doctrine of Christ (1:10a)
3. Sincere in Their Demonstration of Christ (1:10b-11)
  a. In Experience (1:10b)
  b. In Expectation (1:10c)
  c. In Expression (1:11)

C. The Prisoner and His Purpose (1:12-18)
1. Paul Related How the Gospel Was Spreading (1:12-18a)
  a. By Means of His Bonds (1:12-13)
    (1) His Chains Were Divinely Planned (1:12)
    (2) His Chains Were Distinctly Productive (1:13)
  b. By Means of His Brethren (1:14-18a)
    (1) A New Climate (1:14)
      (a) The Number of Those Now Witnessing (1:14a)
      (b) The Nature of Those Now Witnessing (1:14b)
    (2) A Notable Contrast (1:15-18a)
      (a) Paul Discerned the Difference (1:15)
      (b) Paul Discussed the Difference (1:16-17)
      (c) Paul Dismissed the Difference (1:18a)
2. Paul Rejoiced That the Gospel Was Spreading (1:18b)

D. The Prisoner and His Prospects (1:19-26)
1. He Faced Them Prayerfully (1:19)
  a. The Buoyancy of His Optimism (1:19a)
  b. The Basis of His Optimism (1:19b)
2. He Faced Them Positively (1:20-21)
  a. His Determination (1:20)
  b. His Discernment (1:21)
    (1) About This Life (1:21a)
    (2) About That Life (1:21b)
3. He Faced Them Preparedly (1:22-23)

The blessedness of:
a. A Fruit-bearing Life Down Here (1:22)
b. A Far Better Life Up There (1:23)
4. He Faced Them Practically (1:24-26)
   a. His Assessment (1:24)
   b. His Assurance (1:25-26)
     (1) Looking at the Realities (1:25a)
     (2) Looking at the Reasons (1:25b-26)

E. The Prisoner and His Pulpit (1:27-30)
He urged the Philippians to be:
1. Unyielding in the Battle (1:27a)
2. Undivided in the Battle (1:27b)
3. Unafraid in the Battle (1:28-30)
   a. Paul's Exhortation (1:28-29)
     (1) The Opposition They Faced (1:28a)
     (2) The Opportunity They Faced (1:28b-29)
       (a) Of Being Different (1:28b)
       (b) Of Being Disciples (1:29)
   b. Paul's Example (1:30)
     (1) In the Past (1:30a)
     (2) In the Present (1:30b)

II. Paul's Tremendous Examples (2:1-30)

A. Christ: Triumph in Sacrifice (2:1-18)
1. Paul's Approach to the Example of Christ (2:1-4)
   a. His Distress (2:1-2a)
     (1) The Basis of His Appeal (2:1)
       (a) The Supreme Basis
       (b) The Supernatural Basis
       (c) The Supporting Basis
     (2) The Burden of His Appeal (2:2a)
   b. Their Discord (2:2b-4)
     (1) The Need for Likemindedness (2:2b)
       (a) In What They Thought
       (b) In What They Wrought
       (c) In What They Sought
     (2) The Need for Lowliness (2:3)
       (a) The Cause of Their Discords (2:3a)

    (b) The Truth Verbalized (2:16)
        i. As Part of the New Life (2:16a)
        ii. As Proof of the New Life (2:16b)
  c. Transformation in Our Concepts (2:17-18)
    (1) Paul's Example (2:17)
    (2) Paul's Exclamation (2:18)

B. Timothy: Triumph in Service (2:19-24)
  1. An Example of True Service (2:19-20)
    a. Timothy's Commission (2:19)
    b. Timothy's Commendation (2:20)
  2. An Example of Total Service (2:21)
    a. The Rarity of This Example (2:21a)
    b. The Rebuke of This Example (2:21b)
  3. An Example of Tested Service (2:22-24)
    a. Why Paul Was Sending Timothy (2:22)
      (1) The Philippians Knew Paul's Love for Timothy
         (2:22a)
      (2) The Philippians Knew Timothy's Loyalty to Paul
         (2:22b)
    b. When Paul Was Sending Timothy (2:23-24)
      (1) His Anticipation of Definite News Soon (2:23)
      (2) His Anticipation of Dramatic News Soon (2:24)

C. Epaphroditus: Triumph in Sickness (2:25-30)
  1. His Ministry (2:25)
    a. Sent to the Philippians by Paul (2:25a)
      (1) What Paul Thought of Him
      (2) What Paul Wrought with Him
        (a) Paul's Fellow Servant
        (b) Paul's Fellow Soldier
    b. Sent by the Philippians to Paul (2:25b)
      (1) How He Was Sent
      (2) How He Had Served
  2. His Malady (2:26-27)
    a. The Selflessness of His Suffering (2:26)
    b. The Seriousness of His Sickness (2:27)
  3. His Memory (2:28-30)
    a. What Paul Required of These Believers (2:28-29)
      (1) Rejoice (2:28)
      (2) Receive (2:29a)

(3) Reward (2:29b)
  b. What Paul Remembered of This Brother (2:30)
    (1) His Commitment (2:30a)
    (2) His Companionship (2:30b)

III Paul's Typical Exhortations (3:1–4:23)

A. You Cannot Defraud a Man Who Knows the Power of Proper Theology (3:1-21)
  1. The Christian and His Beliefs (3:1-3)
    a. The Dimensions of the Christian Life (3:1)
      (1) Singing Fervently (3:1a)
      (2) Standing Firmly (3:1b)
    b. The Dangers of the Christian Life (3:2)
      (1) The Character of the Deceiver (3:2a)
      (2) The Conduct of the Deceiver (3:2b)
      (3) The Claims of the Deceiver (3:2c)
    c. The Distinctives of the Christian Life (3:3)
      (1) Exposing the Form (3:3a)
      (2) Expressing the Faith (3:3b)
      (3) Excluding the Flesh (3:3c)
  2. The Christian and His Behavior (3:4-14)
    a. Paul's Past Glory (3:4-6)
      (1) What Once He Had (3:4)
      (2) What Once He Hailed (3:5-6)
        (a) His Status as a Pure Jew (3:5a-b)
          i. He Was a Jew by Religion (3:5a)
          ii. He Was a Jew by Race (3:5b)
            a. The National Claim: Stock of Israel
            b. The Tribal Claim: Tribe of Benjamin
            c. The Parental Claim: Hebrew of Hebrews
        (b) His Stature as a Practicing Jew (3:5c-6)
          i. He Was a Fundamentalist Jew (3:5c)
          ii. He Was a Fanatical Jew (3:6a)
          iii. He Was a Fastidious Jew (3:6b)
    b. Paul's Present Gains (3:7-11)
      (1) What He Discounted (3:7-8)
      He wrote off all his:
      (a) Human Religion (3:7)

        (b) Human Resources (3:8)
           i. How He Valued What He Found in Christ (3:8a)
           ii. How He Valued What He Forsook for Christ (3:8b)
    (2) What He Desired (3:9-11)
        (a) A Complete Appreciation of Salvation Truth (3:9)
           i. A Position to Enjoy (3:9a)
           ii. A Possession to Enjoy (3:9b-c)
              a. Discarding a False Righteousness (3:9b)
              b. Discovering a Flawless Righteousness (3:9c)
        (b) A Complete Appropriation of Sanctification Truth (3:10-11)
           i. The Personal Gain (3:10a)
           ii. The Progressive Gain (3:10b-d)
              a. Christ's Resurrection Power (3:10b)
              b. Christ's Rejected Position (3:10c)
              c. Christ's Redemptive Passion (3:10d)
           iii. The Prospective Gain (3:11)
  c. Paul's Projected Goals (3:12-14)
    (1) Assessing His Situation (3:12)
        (a) Realistically (3:12a)
        (b) Resolutely (3:12b)
    (2) Adjusting His Sights (3:13-14)
        (a) A Full Stop (3:13a)
        (b) A Fresh Start (3:13b-14)
           i. The Plan (3:13b)
           ii. The Prize (3:14)
3. The Christian and His Brethren (3:15-19)
  a. Faithful Brethren (3:15-17)
    (1) An Exhortation (3:15-16)
        (a) Our Standing (3:15a)
        (b) Our State (3:15b)
        (c) Our Steps (3:16)
    (2) An Example (3:17)
        (a) Paul's First Example (3:17a)
        (b) Paul's Further Examples (3:17b)
  b. False Brethren (3:18-19)
    (1) Their Number (3:18)

(a) Paul's Warning about Them (3:18a)
(b) Paul's Weeping about Them (3:18b)
(2) Their Nature (3:19)
(a) Their Doom (3:19a)
(b) Their Desires (3:19b-d)
    i. Their God (3:19b)
    ii. Their Glory (3:19c)
    iii. Their Goal (3:19d)
4. The Christian and His Birthright (3:20-21)
  a. Our Position (3:20)
    (1) Our Beloved Homeland (3:20a)
    (2) Our Blessed Hope (3:20b)
  b. Our Prospect (3:21)
    (1) A Glorified Body (3:21a)
    (2) A Guaranteed Belief (3:21b)

B. You Cannot Defile a Man Who Knows the Power of Positive Thinking (4:1-9)
1. Thinking about One's Spiritual Life (4:1-5)
  a. Paul's Positive Thoughts about the Philippians (4:1-2)
    (1) His Pleasure As He Thought How Dear They Were (4:1)
    (2) His Plea As He Thought How Divided They Were (4:2)
  b. Paul's Positive Thoughts about His Partners (4:3-5)
    He wanted them to be:
    (1) Helpful (4:3)
    (2) Happy (4:4)
    (3) Holy (4:5)
2. Thinking about One's Secular Life (4:6)
  a. Our Worries (4:6a)
  b. Our Wants (4:6b)
3. Thinking about One's Secret Life (4:7-9)
  a. What Paul Shared with the Philippians (4:7-8)
    (1) The Secret of a Guarded Thought Life (4:7)
    (2) The Secret of a Guided Thought Life (4:8)
      (a) The Choices (4:8a)
        i. Thoughts That Promote Inner Character
        a. Excluding That Which Is False
        b. Extolling That Which Is Fine
        c. Exalting That Which Is Fair

          ii. Thoughts That Promote Inner Cleanliness
           a. Excluding That Which Besmirches
           b. Extolling That Which Beautifies
           c. Exalting That Which Builds
        (b) The Challenge (4:8b)
    b. What Paul Showed to the Philippians (4:9)
        (1) By Verbal Example (4:9a)
        (2) By Visual Example (4:9b)

C. You Cannot Defeat a Man Who Knows the Power of Perpetual Thanksgiving (4:10-23)
  1. The Experiences Connected with This Kind of Life (4:10-13)
    a. Knowing How to Wait (4:10)
    Paul acknowledged:
        (1) The Final Coming of the Philippians' Gift (4:10a)
        (2) The Faithful Character of the Philippians' Giving (4:10b)
    b. Knowing How to Want (4:11-13)
        (1) What Paul Denied (4:11a)
        (2) What Paul Declared (4:11b-13)
          (a) The Serenity of Contentment (4:11b-12)
             i. The Apprehension of the Lesson (4:11b)
             ii. The Application of the Lesson (4:12)
                a. No Matter Why (4:12a)
                b. No Matter Where (4:12b)
                c. No Matter What (4:12c)
          (b) The Secret of Contentment (4:13)
  2. The Exercises Connected with This Kind of Life (4:14-23)
    a. Personal Needs (4:14-20)
        (1) Explanation (4:14-16)
          (a) The Reason for Paul's Past Financial Need (4:14-15a)
          (b) The Relief of Paul's Present Financial Need (4:15b-16)
             i. The Lacking Concern of the Churches (4:15b)
             ii. The Loving Concern of Their Church (4:15c-16)
        (2) Exhortation (4:17)
        (3) Exultation (4:18)

PART I

Paul's Triumphant Experiences

Philippians 1:1-30

I. Paul's Triumphant Experiences (1:1-30)

A. The Prisoner and His Pen (1:1-8)

1. Paul Was Thinking of the Philippians (1:1-2)

a. Ecclesiastically (1:1)

(1) Who the Letter Was From (1:1a-c)

(a) Paul's Firm Signature (1:1a) "Paul."

As was customary in those days, Paul began his letter to the Philippians with his signature. What memories that name would evoke! Lydia and her dependents would think of that unusual sabbath prayer meeting by the riverside (Acts 16:13-15). Only Lydia and some other devout women had been present. The other women were Jewish perhaps, and Lydia herself was a God-fearing Gentile from across the Hellespont. They had been singing a Psalm or reciting a passage of Scripture when four men arrived. Luke (whom they possibly knew) no doubt made the introductions and then Paul began to talk. He had good news: the Messiah had come!

Lydia would remember the scene so well: Paul's enthusiasm, his compelling assurance, his Biblical erudition, his earnest appeal. Then and there she gave her heart to the Savior! She would remember welcoming Paul and his friends to her home and delighting in their conversation in the garden and around the table at mealtime. The Bible came alive. The story of Paul's life, conversion, and ministry amazed her.

The name of Paul would thrill the poor slave girl he set free from a bondage worse than death (Acts 16:16-18). Her enslavement to a consortium of masters who made merchandise of her had not been so hateful as her enslavement to evil spirits. The memory of demon-possession caused her very soul to shudder. But Paul cast out the demon in the name of Jesus!

The Roman jailer would smile happily at his wife and children when he heard the name of Paul. This keeper of the prison had never before known a man to sing after being thrashed by the lictors and placed in an excruciating position in the stocks! The jailer would remember that not one prisoner fled when the earth-quake opened the prison doors (Acts 16:23-34). What a command Paul had over men!

When the letter to the Philippians was opened and the signature was read, the whole church must have leaned forward expectantly. Here was a priceless piece of parchment—a letter from the great apostle himself.

(b) Paul's Fellow Servant (1:1b) "And Timotheus."

Timothy's name too would bring back memories. Half Jew, half Gentile, wholly Christian—devoted, eager Timothy was willing to run Paul's errands, arrange for meetings, and care for details in order to lighten the apostle's load. He was no Paul, but Timothy had drunk deeply of Paul's cup and was able to minister the Word acceptably and help organize the local church. When Paul and Silas and Timothy left Philippi, the Philippians must have missed him almost as much as they missed Paul. Yes, Timothy was a worthy companion for the great apostle!

(c) Paul's Formal Status (1:1c) "The servants of Jesus Christ."

When writing to the Philippians Paul felt no need to state his apostleship. In this rare Epistle there was no doctrinal error to correct as in Galatians, and no gross carnality to rebuke as in 1 Co-rinthians. Paul was no stranger to the church at Philippi, as he was to the church at Rome when he wrote to them. He was not breaking new theological ground. He was not stating one of the mysteries, as he did in his letter to the Ephesians. He was not imparting a pressing apostolic commission as in 1 Timothy. Paul was writing to supportive friends. True, there were some family squabbles in Philippi, but he felt no need to invoke apostolic authority to deal with them. He was sure that a word to the wise would be sufficient.

So Paul introduced himself and his dear friend Timothy as servants of Jesus Christ. The word translated "servant," *doulos*, is used by Paul thirty times in his Epistles. Its literal meaning is "slave or bondservant." The apostle took the humble place, the lowest place. He was the Lord's property, entirely at His disposal. Paul was a man whose will had been mastered, whose heart was engaged, and whose mind was enslaved to Jesus Christ.

The order of the words "Jesus Christ" implies "Jesus, who humbled Himself but is now exalted and glorified." Paul followed in His Master's footsteps; he took the lowly station of a servant. By so doing, Paul doubtless hoped to encourage the squabblers in the Philippian church to take the humble place also: to apologize to each other and put things right.

(2) Who the Letter Was For (1:1d-f)

(a) The Philippian Saints (1:1d) "To all the saints in Christ Jesus which are at Philippi."

The word translated "saints" literally means "holy or separated ones." It is one of those universal descriptive titles common in the New Testament for all those who belong to the family of God. The New Testament never refers to a special class set apart as holier than others. God divides the human race into two classes: sinners and saints. Saints are simply saved sinners.

The title of saint, however, is one of great import. It reminds us of what we are *positionally* through the finished work of Christ, and it reminds us of what God expects us to be *practically* as people set apart for himself.

Paul identified Timothy and himself as servants of "Jesus Christ" and addressed the Philippians as saints in "Christ Jesus." The converse order of the names "Christ Jesus" suggests "the exalted One who once humbled Himself." We too are exalted ones set apart for God and destined for the throne (Revelation 3:21). But the knowledge of what we still are practically should keep us from pride in our position. It is all too evident that the work of the Holy Spirit in our hearts is unfinished. His work—to bring our imperfect state into line with our perfect standing—often proceeds slowly. The completion will be instantaneous at the rapture when we come face to face with Jesus. Then "we shall be like him; for we shall see him as he is" (1 John 3:2).

(b) The Philippian Shepherds (1:1e) "With the bishops."

The word translated "bishops" here is *episkopos*. It is translated "overseers" in Acts 20:28 where it has direct reference to shepherding: "Take heed therefore unto yourselves, and to all the flock, over the which the Holy Ghost hath made you overseers, to feed the church of God, which he hath purchased with his own blood." Since the same people addressed in 20:28 are called elders in 20:17, we conclude that elders and bishops are one and the same. The word translated "elders" in 20:17 is *presbuteros* (presbyters).

The idea of a bishop presiding over a number of churches is foreign to the New Testament. In apostolic times each local church in healthy condition had a number of bishops—that is, elders—responsible for the spiritual welfare of the group, as is evident in the plural "bishops" in Philippians 1:1. Paul greeted the bishops as a separate group within the church, but gave them no primacy over the other saints. Modern ecclesiastical and hierarchical structures came later in church history and are an extra-Biblical development.

(c) The Philippian Servants (1:1f) "And deacons."

The word translated "deacons," *diakonos*, occurs twenty-two times in Paul's Epistles and refers to a servant, especially as seen in action. It is generally accepted that the office of deacon differed from the office of bishop in that the deacons took care of the more secular affairs of the local church and the bishops (or elders) took care of the more spiritual aspects. Philippians 1:1 is the only place where these two offices are mentioned together.

The function of deacons probably grew out of the incident in Acts 6, although the word *diakonos* is not used there. The pressures of the more mundane side of local church government had been increasing and the apostles were finding themselves reduced more and more to administrative roles, so they proposed that the Jerusalem church look for seven men to whom the more secular tasks could be delegated. The qualifications were basic; the seven were to be "men of honest report, full of the Holy Ghost and wisdom" (6:3). And the church chose men who were "full of faith and of the Holy Ghost" (6:5).

Two of the seven soon outgrew their humble role: Stephen became the first *martyr* of the church and Philip became its first foreign *missionary*. Stephen and Philip are illustrations of Paul's words in 1 Timothy 3:13: "They that have used [served in] the office of a deacon well purchase to themselves a good degree, and great boldness in the faith which is in Christ Jesus."

While Paul was thinking of the Philippians ecclesiastically—as saints, bishops, and deacons—he was also thinking of them evangelistically.

b.   Evangelistically (1:2)

(1) The Greeting (1:2a) "Grace be unto you, and peace."

Paul breathed his blessing on the congregation. His usual greeting to a church had added significance in this letter because of the squabble between two prominent women in the Philippian church. Their ungracious conduct was disturbing the peace and it would take grace to restore the peace. Where there is grace there can be no *commencement* of hostilities. Where there is peace there can be no *continuation* of hostilities. Grace means that war is impossible; peace means that the war is over. Contention only flourishes in the absence of grace and peace.

We can liken Paul's opening blessing to the torch shaped like a horn of plenty wielded by the Ghost of Christmas Present in Charles Dickens' *A Christmas Carol.* Everywhere the ghost went he sprinkled some mysterious substance from that horn on the people and at once a sense of goodwill and hearty fellowship descended. Scowls turned to smiles, and anger to apologies. It is good to know that such a miraculous "substance" does indeed exist. Its ingredients are grace and peace.

(2) The Godhead (1:2b) "From God our Father, and from the Lord Jesus Christ."

We arrive at the heart of Paul's greeting and at the heart of the gospel. Grace and peace are imparted jointly by God the Father and the Lord Jesus Christ. That is the good news, the evangel, the glorious distinctive that sets the Christian message apart from all human philosophies and manmade religions.

At the heart of the gospel is the revelation of God as Father—as *our* Father. The concept of God as a father was revolutionary for Jew and Gentile alike. Zeus, the pagan thunderer of Olympus, was a lustful, vengeful god; the gods of Syria and the Orient were carnal and cruel; the gods of Egypt were a strange conglomerate of sun and serpent, cows and crocodiles, cats and dogs, beetles and birds, all held together by a few strands of magic and mythology. Some of the pagan religions did conceive of God as a mother, but God as a father—good, loving, gracious, holy, parental, and intimate—was a thought beyond all thought.

And the Jews had only occasional glimpses of "God our Father." They knew Him as Elohim, Jehovah, and Adonai, and here and there a daring prophet made tentative mention of Father. The true and living God of the Old Testament was warm and personal, especially as revealed in His compound names,[1] but He was rarely spoken of as Father. The theology of His fatherhood was hardly developed at all. Only in the gospel is the fatherhood of God brought into the full light of day.

As for the sonship of the Lord Jesus Christ—that glorious truth is especially ours. We who live on this side of the cross have the revelation of One who is coeternal and coequal with the Father, a person who is one with the Father in essence and attributes, One who jointly with the Father is able to impart divine grace and peace to human hearts.

2.   Paul Was Thankful for the Philippians (1:3-8)

a.   For Their Fellowship in the Gospel (1:3-5)

(1) How He Ministered to Them (1:3-4)

(a) Remembering Them Personally (1:3) "I thank my God upon every remembrance of you."

The word translated "thank" here is first used in the New Testament in connection with the feeding of the four thousand: the Lord Jesus "took the seven loaves and the fishes, and *gave thanks*" (Matthew 15:36, italics added). The word is used in the same way in the story of Paul on board the storm-tossed ship: "He took bread, and *gave thanks*" (Acts 27:35, italics added). Paul was as thankful for the Philippians as he was for his daily bread. Every time he thought of them his heart rose to God in gratitude.

How many people there are for whom we should be thankful!

When I was young I was drafted into the army and shipped overseas to Palestine. In that distant land I found a home away from home. A young Arab Christian and his mother and sisters became my brother, my mother, my sisters. I thank God on every remembrance of them.

When I first came from Britain to Canada, a Christian man and his wife opened their home to me, treated me more like a son than a boarder, and introduced me to a larger circle of Christian friends including the young woman who later became my wife. I thank God on every remembrance of them.

The list goes on and on. It is a profitable exercise from time to time to recall the names and faces of those who have helped us in our journey through life. Remembering people who have blessed us is an effective antidote to criticizing and complaining. Doubtless Paul mentioned his practice of giving thanks with the hope that others would follow his example.

(b) Remembering Them Prayerfully (1:4) "Always in every prayer of mine for you all making request with joy."

"Always"—Paul remembered the Philippians in prayer with *persistence*. When we think of our own sporadic, fitful, intermittent prayer life, how Paul rebukes us!

Paul told the Romans he prayed unceasingly for them (Romans 1:9). He told the Corinthians he was always thanking God for them (1 Corinthians 1:4). He told the Ephesians he never stopped thanking God for them (Ephesians 1:16). He told the Colossians he was always praying for them (Colossians 1:3). He told the Thessalonians he was always making mention of them in his prayers (1 Thessalonians 1:2) and he was thanking God for them all the time (2 Thessalonians 1:3). He told Timothy he prayed for him day and night (2 Timothy 1:3). He told Philemon he made mention of him always in his prayers (Philemon 4).

Satan might be permitted to prevent Paul from doing many things dear to his heart. Paul the prisoner could not pioneer new countries and continents with the gospel; he could not visit the many churches he had founded; he could not confront the Jews in their synagogues or the Athenians on Mars hill; he could not preach with passion and persuasion from the pulpit; he could not lead teams of young men in itinerant evangelism and church planting. But Satan could not keep Paul from praying! And Paul, locked up in prison and besieging the throne of grace day and night, was far more dangerous to Satan than a free and active Paul cumbered about with much serving (Luke 10:40).

"Making request"—Paul remembered the Philippians in prayer with *petitions*. He made requests to God when he came before the throne on their behalf. As he thought of Philippi, he remembered the uproar in the city over his preaching. He had put the fear of caesar into the magistrates, but now that he was gone, persecution against the Philippian Christians might be renewed. So he presented to God a petition for their protection. News had reached Paul about a conflict between two of the sisters in the assembly, so he prayed for their peace. He had made no attempt to evangelize the busy little seaport of Neapolis. The Philippians should take the gospel there—so he prayed for their progress. They were generous in supporting the Lord's work with their money, so he prayed for their prosperity. Paul most certainly offered specific petitions. One cannot visualize him indulging in vague wishes that God would bless this, that, or the other.

"With joy"—Paul remembered his Philippian friends in prayer with *pleasure*. Joy is one of the keynotes of this letter. Paul could not pray for everyone with joy. His ministry was often watered with tears for those who spurned the gospel, for those who came so close but turned away, for those who were won to Christ but were overcome by the lies of the devil, the lure of the world, and the lusts of the flesh. The memory of his friends at Philippi, however, filled him with joy. They were the first fruits of Europe, the "wave sheaf" (Leviticus 23:9-11) of a mighty harvest that would be reaped on the continent during the next two millennia.

(2) How They Ministered to Him (1:5) "For your fellowship in the gospel from the first day until now."

The Philippians had stood by Paul, supported him, and followed him with their prayers. They had become his partners in the gospel. They had done for him what Jonathan had done for David—"strengthened his hand in God" (1 Samuel 23:16). They had let him know: "We are with you, Paul, all the way. You can count on us." They had proved their friendship in a practical way with their financial support. The Philippians had ministered to him.

We sometimes forget that Paul was a man of flesh and blood, "subject to like passions as we are" (James 5:17). His nerves were not made of steel. He was susceptible to temptation. He knew what it was like to be attacked by Satan with fits of spiritual depression and discouragement. If he did not give way to temptation, it was because he appropriated the laws of victorious Christian living, not because he was made of a different kind of clay. The pressures he faced were just as real, the problems just as great as (if not greater than) ours. When we think of Paul singing in that Philippian jail, we forget that his back was bruised, bleeding, and on fire with pain and his limbs were painfully cramped in the stocks. He was as appreciative as anyone else would be when the jailer released him, washed his stripes, rubbed in soothing ointment, gave him a meal, and showed him practical kindness.

Paul smiled as he thought back on his fellowship with his Philippian converts. "From the first day" Lydia had opened her home to him, "from the first day" the jailer had opened his home to him, they had been his faithful friends.

His fellowship with Lydia and the jailer and all the other Christians at Philippi had continued ever since. It was just as prompt, just as practical, and just as priceless now as at the beginning. Their concern pursued him to Thessalonica, Berea, Athens, and Corinth.

b.   For Their Faithfulness in the Gospel (1:6)

(1) The Work Had Been Commenced in Them (1:6a) "Being confident of this very thing, that he which hath begun a good work in you..."

The word translated "begun" is *enarchomai*. The only other place it occurs in the New Testament is Galatians 3:3: "Are ye so foolish? having begun in the Spirit, are ye now made perfect by the flesh?" The word translated "confident" is *pepoitha*, used in the sense of "I have persuaded myself" or "I trust." At Calvary the mocking chief priests used the word in the same way when hurling their insults at the dying Savior: "He trusted in God; let him deliver him now" (Matthew 27:43). In other words they were saying, "He persuaded Himself that God would keep Him."

Paul had no trouble persuading himself that God had begun a good work in the Philippians. The apostle could see plenty of proof that they were soundly saved. Their outward good works were evidence of the inward good work begun in their hearts by the

Holy Spirit. Their good works had not resulted in salvation (an impossibility), but their good works had resulted from salvation (an imperative).

The good work of God begins in us when the Holy Spirit takes up permanent residence in our hearts. He brings with Him the life of God: eternal, immaculate, spiritual life. We are immediately aware of this new life by a fresh consciousness of the old life (Romans 7). The world becomes aware of this new life when love breaks through: love for God, love for God's people, love for lost people, love out-flowing as a result of life infilling.

(2) The Work Would Be Completed in Them (1:6b) "He...will perform it until the day of Jesus Christ."

The Bible distinguishes between various days. We are living in man's *day*. In 1 Corinthians 4:3 the words translated "man's judgment" literally mean "man's day," the day in which man is exalting himself and judging while God remains silent.

The day of Christ[2] is the day when Christ will come and receive His church to Himself by way of the rapture[3] and we will appear at His judgment seat.[4]

The day of the Lord is mentioned sixteen times in the Old Testament. The first mention is in Isaiah 2:12, which refers to God judging the nations, dealing with idolatry and human pride, and shaking the earth. The day of the Lord is mentioned four times in the New Testament (1 Thessalonians 5:2 within a larger passage dealing with the day of Christ; 2 Peter 3:10; Revelation 1:10; and 2 Thessalonians 2:2 where the correct rendering is "the day of the Lord"). The day of the Lord embraces the coming period of judgment and the millennial age, and concludes with the cataclysmic dissolution of the universe.

The day of God (2 Peter 3:12; 1 Corinthians 15:24-28) is the eternal state beyond all the events of time when God is "all in all."

In Philippians 1:6 Paul's eye was on the day of Christ, the day He is looking forward to with the keenest anticipation, the day when His blood-bought bride will be caught away to be forever with Himself. The apostle was sure that the Holy Spirit would "perform" (complete) the work He had begun in the Philippians so they would be ready for the review of all believers' lives at the judgment seat of Christ.

The word translated "perform" is *epiteleō,* meaning "to finish, to bring through to an end." The Lord used the word when responding to the Pharisees who said, "Get thee out, and depart hence: for Herod will kill thee." He said, "Go ye, and tell that fox, Behold, I cast out devils, and I do cures to day and to morrow, and the third day I shall be *perfected* [come to an end of my work]" (Luke 13:31-32, italics added; also see John 19:30).

The Holy Spirit never loses sight of the end of His work. His work will not end until He has made us just like Jesus. He will continue working until He has made us presentable enough to pass with praise through the final test of the judgment seat and fit to be introduced in glory as the helpmeet of the glorious Man who sits at God's right hand. We may fail along the way, and indeed we often do; but He never does.

c.   For Their Fearlessness in the Gospel (1:7)

(1) They Were Not Afraid of His Chains (1:7a) "Even as it is meet for me to think this of you all, because I have you in my heart; inasmuch as both in my bonds..."

Paul had good grounds for his confidence in his Philippian friends. He was not just being optimistic; he was basing his assurance on solid evidence. For example they were not afraid of his bonds.

It was no light thing to be charged with proclaiming the advent of a kingdom other than Rome and a king greater than the caesar. Anyone who showed friendship and sympathy for such an insurrectionist might soon share his chains and his cross. The Philippians paid no heed to their danger. They boldly stood by Paul. They were brave indeed, for the caesars were not known to be tolerant toward those suspected of acts of treason, and the imperial spies and secret police were everywhere.

The bold stand of the Philippians can be likened to the stand taken by those who sheltered Jews during the Nazi reign of terror in Europe. Misfortune and persecution soon weed out one's fair-weather friends.

The Philippians had Paul in their hearts, and he had them in his heart as well—and that is probably the secret of Paul's astonishing prayer life. Whom do we pray for most? Those we love the most. Which prayer list most readily stirs us to pray? The one we have in our hearts.

(2) They Were Not Afraid of His Charge (1:7b) "In the defence and
   confirmation of the gospel, ye all are partakers of my grace."

The word translated "defence" is *apologia*, from which we derive
our English words "apology" and "apologetics." *Apologia* is first used
in the New Testament in Acts 22:1, where Paul began to defend
himself after the riot in the temple in Jerusalem. "Men, brethren,
and fathers," said Paul, "hear ye my defence." Following this
introduction, he presented his personal testimony to the saving
power of the Lord Jesus Christ. Now in Rome, Paul had every
intention, when his case came to trial, of seizing the occasion as an
opportunity to make the glorious gospel of the Lord Jesus known
to the highest tribunal in the land.

The word translated "confirmation" is *bebaiōsis,* a legal term
signifying a guarantee. The only other place the word is used in the
New Testament is Hebrews 6:16: "An oath for confirmation [as a
guarantee] is...an end of all strife." Paul's purpose in life was to
confront people with the unconditional guarantee of eternal life
through Jesus Christ—the glorious divine confirmation of pardon,
peace, power, a new life in Christ, a home in Heaven, and a place
in the family of God.

The Philippians were Paul's partners in his defense. They were
partakers of his grace. The same things that motivated Paul,
motivated them. The issues that swung in the balance affected
them as well. They knew the pragmatic importance of Paul's case
receiving a favorable hearing, and they knew the verdict could go
either way. Persecution or protection for the church of God was at
stake. The Philippians stood solidly with Paul. Perhaps the fact that
these citizens of a Roman colony were convinced of the rightness
of Paul's cause might carry some weight in high places. If so, well
and good; if not, the apostle's Philippian friends were prepared for
the consequence. Paul had already shown them the Christian way
to take public beatings, injustice, prison, and mob hate.

d.   For Their Friendship in the Gospel (1:8) "For God is my record,
   how greatly I long after you all in the bowels of Jesus Christ."

Throughout the New Testament, except in Acts 1:18, the word
splanchna ("bowels") is used as a metaphor for one's deepest inner
affections. We all know what it is like to be separated from those we
love. For a time perhaps the novelty of different surroundings

occupies the traveler's mind; the interest of new friends and acquaintances fills the emotional gap. But then the longing sets in and his thoughts and yearnings go out to his distant family, to friends of long standing, to those whose lives have been interwoven with his.

Paul was separated from people he loved and the coming of Epaphroditus with news from Philippi awakened the desire in Paul's heart to see all his dear friends again. He longed for the warmth and welcome of Lydia's home, for the hearty embrace of the jailer, and the loving attention of the jailer's children. For a moment his bonds seemed heavier than ever. If he had been free to follow his heart he would have said, "Timothy, pack the bags. We're going to Philippi." A wave of nostalgia swept over his soul. "Greatly I long after you," he wrote.

Paul was not indulging in self-pity or mere sentiment. His longings went much deeper. The wellsprings of Paul's emotions were in Christ. His heart beat in rhythm with the heart of Jesus. And he claimed God was his witness.

B. The Prisoner and His Prayers (1:9-11)

1. He Wanted the Philippians to Be Superlative in Their Devotion to Christ (1:9)

a. Love Without Limit (1:9a) "And this I pray, that your love may abound yet more and more."

Love is the most remarkable thing in the universe and the greatest fact is that "God is love" (1 John 4:8). No more sublime words have ever been penned outside the pages of God's own beloved Book than Anna B. Warner's simple couplet:

> Jesus loves me! this I know,
> For the Bible tells me so.

The greatest passage ever written on love is 1 Corinthians 13. This portion of Scripture is like a lofty cathedral transept—wondrous, awesome, bathed in tinted lights and shades—with every line and word designed to lift our thoughts higher and higher and fill our hearts with noble desires, dreams, and determinations.

The world's libraries contain volume after volume—fact and fiction, cold critique and warm biography—telling of love. It is the most fascinating subject on earth, the all-absorbing theme in Heaven.

Love will drive people to extraordinary lengths. It will make them do things nothing else can. Consider, for instance, what Jan de Hartog's heroine Betsy did.

De Hartog's story, set in the Dutch East Indies amid terrifying jungles and untamed wilds, is a calculated study in contrasts between Betsy and the hero, Dr. Brits-Jansen. Big, bossy, brave, the doctor strides through the story like a giant. His passion is leprosy: what it is, what it does, where it lurks, whom it attacks. Nobody knows more about the disease than he. He can diagnose it in a flash. With tireless zeal he wages war against leprosy in the aseptic hospital and in the pagan villages. The powers that be have armed him with warrants. His job is to stamp out the disease and he is authorized to isolate and quarantine the victims and burn their villages. And so he does the best he can. Following Brits-Jansen's adventures with breathless interest, we are attracted and outraged by the force of his formidable personality.

Betsy is a Salvation Army missionary who with her saintly husband runs a leper colony. She was saved from a life of wickedness, a life to which she had abandoned herself with the same reckless determination that Brits-Jansen gives to his leprosy crusade. Now she is out in the bush surrounded by suffering lepers in various stages of the dreadful, disfiguring, and contagious disease.

The difference between Betsy and Brits-Jansen is soon seen. His goal is to eliminate leprosy and no measures are too harsh. Her aim is to love the poor unhappy lepers more and more. Betsy lives with them, works with them, cares for them, comforts them, weeps with them. At last she becomes just like them—a leper. She dies a long, lingering death, beatified in the hearts of all who know her.

Betsy is just a character in a story, but the world has known many real-life missionaries who have done in fact what she did in fiction. They have learned to love more and more, giving up the comforts of home, the warmth of family and friends, the security of well-paying jobs, and the prospects of advancement, achievement, and renown in order to bury themselves with some jungle tribe or to work in some city slum.

Paul prayed that the Philippians would love without limit, that their love would abound more and more. He had received ample proof of their love for him, but there was a whole world of lost people to be loved. The men who had owned that poor demonic slave girl needed to be loved. The city magistrates who had unjustly beaten Paul and Silas needed to be loved. The Philippians had neighbors, friends, workmates, acquaintances, relatives, and other brothers in Christ who needed to be loved with the love of Christ.

b.   Love Within Limits (1:9b) "In knowledge and in all judgment."

Love is not to be mistaken for lust, nor does love operate without law. Love knows its limits, knows where to draw the line. While we can love all men, we do not love all that they do.

Love is to be universal but it is not to be gullible. Paul makes that clear by using the words *epignōsis* and *aisthēsis* in Philippians 1:9. *Epignōsis,* translated "knowledge," means "precise knowledge, knowledge acquired by further experience, the result of learning or perceiving." *Aisthēsis,* translated "judgment," also means "perception." *Aisthēsis* occurs only in this verse in Scripture. The margin of some Bibles renders the word "sense" and the Revised Standard Version translates it "discernment." A parent who loves his child "in knowledge and in all judgment" will not indulge his every wish and will not withhold rebuke and discipline.

Nobody ever loved us as God loves us; Calvary is the witness of that. But God's love—vast, eternal, boundless—never violates His holiness, never operates in conflict with His omniscient wisdom, and never ignores His own righteous laws. The fact that God is love and longs for all men to be saved and share His home in Heaven does not mean that there is no Hell. And the fact that Hell exists does not mean that God stops loving those who are there. Sin breaks God's laws and it also breaks His heart.

Love is not cold and calculating because it stays within the limits of sense. Love is always warm and giving. Love finds a way to work for the good of those brought within its wide embrace.

2. He Wanted the Philippians to Be Sound in Their Doctrine of Christ (1:10a) "That ye may approve things that are excellent [things that differ]."

The word translated "approve," *dokimazō,* literally means "to assay, examine, test" and it is used in reference to testing metals for purity. Paul's idea is that we should carefully examine things and approve them only if they pass the test.

We are to examine *things that differ* to see if they pass the test. Matters of doctrine are among the things that differ. Paul was aware, for example, of doctrinal differences in the church at Colossae. He recognized serious cultic errors in that church and exposed them in his letter to the believers there. Paul's Epistle to the Colossians was written about the same time as his Epistle to the Philippians.

Today cultists have their "Christs," but they are to be distinguished from our Lord Jesus Christ. We can—we must—love people whose doctrines differ from ours; but the fact that we love the people does not mean that we approve of what they believe, say, or do.

Paul's statement in Philippians 1:10 challenges us to recognize things that differ. The apostle wants us to discriminate not just between good and bad, right and wrong, true and false; he also wants us to discriminate between the good and the best.

My father used to say, "The good is the enemy of the best." He had very little formal education. He was raised in a small village where the schoolmaster only took his pupils through the basics of reading, writing, and arithmetic, but in spite of that handicap my father went on to become an acknowledged master in his chosen field and an outstanding expositor of the Bible. Many nights he would read and study until the early hours of the morning to fill his mind with relevant information about a particular Bible passage or character. If he was preparing for a conference, the space around his bed would be piled with heavy commentaries. Rarely did he do any light reading. All through the years of economic depression he struggled to keep his business afloat, provide for his family—and buy books. Our house was full of books, and nothing but the best books!

I would say to any young man contemplating the ministry and beginning to build his library, "Go for the best." I always look at the libraries in the homes I visit. All too often I see shelves lined with books that look impressive but are of little or no value. I see sets that have been eulogized in advertising copy, marketed at discount prices—and bought at the expense of something better. It is a pity that not only money but also time is spent on such books.

Many of these books are doctrinally unsound, espousing positions that are more harmful than helpful even to those who are mature enough to sense that something is wrong. Unless an idea is instantly recognized as a weed, it is planted in the mind and remains there as a potential danger. If a book is not doctrinally sound and the reader is not theologically astute, he can be sidetracked for years by a wrong idea.

When I was first beginning to take an interest in eschatology, someone gave me a book that suggested that Paul's last trump in 1 Corinthians 15 and 1 Thessalonians 4 (the rapture chapter) was the same as John's last trump (the last of the seven in the series) in the Apocalypse. I spent months considering that wrong idea and it was not until much later that I saw through its theological fallacy. The theory sounded right but proved inadequate to account for all the facts. I wasted many valuable hours of study time pursuing a phantom.

3.   He Wanted the Philippians to Be Sincere in Their Demonstration of Christ (1:10b-11)

a.   In Experience (1:10b) "That ye may be sincere and without offence."

The word translated "sincere" means "to be tested by the sunlight" or "to be unalloyed" or "of unmixed substance." In this verse Paul was dealing with two possibilities: it is possible to be wrong but sincere; it is also possible to be right but insincere. A person who is wrong but sincere is deceived; a person who is right but insincere is playing games.

First Paul warned against being wrong but sincere. Being sincere is not sufficient; we must also be right. People often say, "It doesn't matter what you believe as long as you are sincere," but they apply that fallacy only to religion. They would not be foolish enough to apply that philosophy to anything else, but they are more than foolish when they apply it to the one area of life that determines their eternal destiny.

Suppose a man went to the medicine cabinet, found what he sincerely thought was the aspirin bottle, and swallowed two of the tablets. They were the same size, shape, and color as aspirins, but they were actually deadly poison. Would the man's sincerity save him? Of course not. Being sincere is not enough; we must also be right.

The Bereans won the Holy Spirit's commendation because when they heard an apostle preach, they put his words to the test. They "searched the scriptures daily, whether those things were so" (Acts 17:11). They wanted to be right as well as sincere in their beliefs.

In Philippians 1:10 Paul also warned against being right but insincere. A hypocrite knows the truth and professes the truth, but does not practice it. When "tested by the sunlight" his insincerity will be revealed.

In Paul's day if an unscrupulous sculptor carved too deeply into the marble, he would put wax in the cut to hide his mistake. Since the wax looked like marble, the craftsman could deceive his customer until the statue was "tested by sunlight." The hot Mediterranean sun would soon melt the wax and the customer would discover (too late to get his money back) that his statue was not "of unmixed substance." So wise customers learned to write "without wax" into their contracts to purchase marble sculptures. They demanded that the workmanship be sincere.

We are to be "without wax." We are to live without offense, without stumbling. If we want to walk without stumbling, we must pay attention to where we are going, where we put our feet. Inattention will cause us to stumble even when the path before us looks smooth and plain because we are living in a world that has been deliberately booby-trapped by Satan. We are journeying through a minefield in which Satan has laid his snares. The only safety is in walking where Jesus walked, planting our feet in His footsteps. He walked through this world and He never stumbled. He knows the right way.

Peter's path was perilous indeed that night he boasted he would never betray his Lord. Before long he stumbled right into one of Satan's snares. Amid wrong company Peter warmed himself at the world's fire, and soon he denied his Lord and confirmed his lies with oaths and curses. The fall was terrible, but the Lord went out of His way to pick Peter up and set him on the right path again— a sadder and wiser man. Who of us has not stumbled and does not need Paul's warning?

b.   In Expectation (1:10c) "Till the day of Christ."

The day of Christ refers to the day of the rapture. Right after our translation to Heaven we will be summoned before the judgment seat of Christ. There everything will be "tested by sunlight" indeed. Paul wanted the Philippians (and us) to keep that day of judgment in mind. He didn't want any wood, hay, or stubble mixed in with the gold, silver, and precious stones of their (or our) Christian experience (1 Corinthians 3:12). Rapture will be followed by review, and review by rebuke and reward.

Appearing before the judgment seat of Christ is serious business. True, it is not like the great white throne judgment when condemnation will be followed by the terrors of a lost eternity. True, the question of our eternal salvation will not be raised on the day of Christ, for that issue was settled once and for all at Calvary. True, the Lord will find something in every believer's life that He will be able to commend—"Then shall every man have praise of God" (1 Corinthians 4:5). But the fact remains that the judgment seat of Christ is a *judgment* seat. Some will be saved "so as by fire" (1 Corinthians 3:15). They will see their wasted lives, unable to stand the fierceness of the testing flame, go up in smoke.

The Bible does not portray the judgment seat of Christ in a gala atmosphere. That day will be a time of searching, followed by consequences of millennial character. Not all will reign with Christ. A selfish, defeated, worldly, carnal Christian is living in a fool's paradise if he thinks he is going to emerge from judgment wearing a crown of glory and honor as though he had lived like the apostle Paul.

c.   In Expression (1:11) "Being filled with the fruits of right-
     eousness, which are by Jesus Christ, unto the glory and praise
     of God."

The fruit of righteousness is a good life. The word *righteousness* itself refers to doing what is right. Today people ask, "Is this course of action expedient? Is it popular? Does it make me feel good?" The Christian must ask, "Is it right?"

A Christian who is filled with the fruits of righteousness is good and does good. What Dean Alford calls "the whole purified habit of the regenerate and justified man"[5] is thrown, on the scales of life, on the side of goodness, uprightness, integrity, and decency.

Ordinary people often live comparatively good lives on the purely human level. Non-Christians may pay their bills, give to charity, perform neighborly acts, crusade for causes, uphold their beliefs, help each other, honor their commitments, abide by the law, and even go to church. Yet there is a vast difference between the morality of a decent but unregenerate individual and the goodness of a child of God. The difference lies in *means* and *motive*.

The superiority of Christian goodness is not a matter of degree but of kind. A Christian's righteousness exceeds that of the scribes and Pharisees (Matthew 5:20) not in terms of quantity but in terms of quality. The goodness that is the hallmark of true Christianity differs in *means* from the goodness of the unregenerate man. Paul made the difference obvious when he said that the fruits of righteousness "are by Jesus Christ."

The good man of this world is only relatively good; his goodness is often spoiled by a poor attitude, by incompleteness, or by some other inhibiting factor. The goodness of Jesus was absolute. It never varied; it never failed to come through; it was never ostentatious; it was never found wanting; it was never put on. Peter, who spent years in the intimate company of Jesus and observed Him under all conditions and in all circumstances, summed up His life in these words: He "went about doing good" (Acts 10:38). God Himself, viewing the life of Christ from the standpoint of absolute perfection, declared, "I am well pleased" (Matthew 17:5).

The genius of the Christian gospel lies in the fact that this same Jesus, by His Holy Spirit, through the miracle of regeneration, now lives in every believer. The *means* of our goodness is not our own effort to copy His life, but His living in us. The absolute goodness of the Lord Jesus is quite unattainable by a Christian apart from the supernatural. Christian goodness is the result of a Spirit-filled life—a life that is available to all of us in Christ, but seldom appropriated.

The goodness that is the hallmark of true Christianity differs in *motive* from the goodness of the unregenerate man. The goodness of the Christian is "unto the glory and praise of God." The Christian does good works not to earn his salvation, not to accumulate merit with God, not to win the applause and approval of men, not just to follow his conscience. His motivation is the glory and praise of God. That, after all, was the testimony of the Lord Jesus: "I do always those things that please him" (John 8:29). The Lord Jesus could say to His Father, "I have glorified thee on the earth" (John 17:4). Likewise, God's name is glorified when Christians do things that reflect His character. His name is defamed when those who profess to be saved do things that are unethical, immoral, inconsiderate, or unkind.

Thus Philippians 1:9-11 gives us insight into Paul's prayers for his brothers and sisters in Christ. He converted his cell into a cloister. When he prayed, his prison walls were alive with the sound of his supplications. He took the throne of grace by storm that God's people might be superlative in their devotion to Christ, sound in their doctrine of Christ, and sincere in their demonstration of Christ.

C. The Prisoner and His Purpose (1:12-18)

1. Paul Related How the Gospel Was Spreading (1:12-18a)

a. By Means of His Bonds (1:12-13)

(1) His Chains Were Divinely Planned (1:12) "But I would ye should understand, brethren, that the things which happened unto me have fallen out rather unto the furtherance of the gospel."

Paul had one supreme purpose in life and that was to spread the gospel. Nothing else mattered. After his vision of the Lord from Heaven on the Damascus road, all else took second place to the man with the nail prints in his hands. God in Christ had invaded time, and only the truths that related to Him were important in this life. Salvation from sin, a home in Heaven, union with Christ, life in a new dimension, and life driven by a new dynamic were the glorious realities that everybody needed to know. Paul's sole goal in life was to make Christ known.

Paul knew that Christ, now seated at the right hand of the Majesty on high, was in full control. All the factors of time and space were in His hands. Nothing happened by chance. All the varied threads of circumstance were being woven by Him into a pattern that would result in His eternal praise.

> Not till each loom is silent,
>   And the shuttles cease to fly,
> Shall God reveal the pattern
>   And explain the reason why
>
> The dark threads were as needful
>   In the weaver's skillful hand
> As the threads of gold and silver
>   For the pattern which He planned.[6]

Paul was a prisoner in chains. His liberty ended where the chains ended. He had been used to the widest freedom. He had been driven by an overwhelming compulsion to travel to earth's remotest bounds to make Christ known, and he had been astonishingly successful.

Years ago he had made plans to take Rome by storm. In all the fullness of the blessing of Christ, he would go there and lead the church to new and glorious victories. Roman roads would throb to the beat of marching men—armies of young men marching out of Rome to take the gospel to the globe. Paul would fire up his soldiers by filling them with new knowledge, new enthusiasm, new courage, and new vision.

People from all over the world would flock down those same highways to visit Paul at Rome. It was the strategic center, the most important city in the world. Paul would turn the city into such a center of evangelism, missions, and Bible teaching that when people thought of Rome, they would not think of caesar; they would think of Christ. The apostle would visit all the synagogues and reap a new harvest from among the Jews. He would preach in the forum. He would visit every house in Rome. He would stir up the saints, galvanize the church, win souls, inspire Christians, take the city and thence the world for the Lord from Heaven.

Paul had planned to go on from Rome to Spain, Gaul, the frontier lands along the Rhine, and lands where Huns and Goths and Vandals sat in pagan darkness. The islands of Britannia also beckoned. His plans for evangelism had been as wide as the world.

But Paul was in chains. A lesser man would have questioned God's ways, fretted over his enforced inaction, and perhaps become embittered. Not Paul! He knew his chains were divinely planned and God made no mistakes; he knew God had not lost control. Paul viewed his chains as a challenge. If he could not go, he would write and he would pray. People could come to him. He would still rule from Rome in the affections of God's people and have an impact on God's plans and purposes in this world. Though his palace was a prison, his throne a wooden stool, and his scepter an iron chain, Paul would have power greater than any caesar's.

(2) His Chains Were Distinctly Productive (1:13) "My bonds in Christ are manifest [open to sight] in all the palace, and in all other places."

Praitoriōn, the word translated "palace" here, has several meanings. In Matthew 27:27 it is translated "common hall" and in John 18:28 "judgment hall." In Jerusalem the word was used to refer to the magnificent palace built by Herod the Great; it seems that the Roman procurators took over this palace whenever they came to Rome on public business. In Philippians 1:13 *praitoriōn* probably refers to the headquarters built by Tiberius for the powerful and prestigious praetorian guard or more likely to the guard itself.

When Paul arrived in Rome, he was turned over to the custody of the praetorian prefect, the commander of this elite guard. Daily the apostle was chained to soldiers from this influential force of some nine thousand men. We can picture Paul making friends with his jailers—we can see him winning many of them to Christ and leaving an indelible impression on others. Thus his bonds did indeed further the gospel.

How else could Paul have been able to witness personally to these proud members of the emperor's bodyguard? Would they have listened to a Jewish missionary if as an ordinary visitor to Rome he had tried to approach them? Would they have flocked to his meetings? Not likely! But for months on end, for long hours at a time, the guards were forced into his company. They fell under the spell of his personal courtesy and charm as they watched him under the most trying circumstances, listened to him pray, heard him dictate letters, and attended his conferences with groups and individuals who thronged to the jail from all parts of the city and the world. Thus the gospel permeated this elite guard and we can imagine opinions of Paul and his message being bandied about in many a lively discussion in the barrack rooms.

News of the spread of the gospel to the praetorian guard must have delighted the old army men in the church at Philippi! But the witness extended beyond the guards. A wide circle of people in Rome, including members of the palace staff ("Caesar's household," Philippians 4:22) were won to Christ. By the time Nero turned on the Christian community in A.D. 64 (less than five years after Paul wrote this letter) Tacitus could bear witness to the fact that there were a vast multitude of converts in the capital.

b.   By Means of His Brethren (1:14-18a)

(1) A New Climate (1:14)

(a) The Number of Those Now Witnessing (1:14a) "And many of
the brethren in the Lord, waxing confident by my bonds..."

Enthusiasm begets enthusiasm; zeal inspires zeal. Paul's tireless commitment to the cause of Christ motivated others to get
going with the gospel. People need a leader. They need an
inspiring example, someone who will get out front and set the
pace.

One of the secrets of the success of the dynamic Israeli army is its
leaders. Anyone who is not a commando or a paratrooper does not
qualify to be one of its officers. The Israelis have removed the word
forward from their military vocabulary and replaced it with the
words *follow me.* Leaders who are willing to take the first step have
helped make this army, in spite of its many handicaps, a power to
be reckoned with in the Middle East.

Paul was the kind of man who said, "Follow me!" He was a born
leader, always out in front. Ever before him was the beckoning Lord
from Heaven. Paul's followers caught the vision when they saw his
single-minded, wholehearted, irrepressible, irresistible passion for
the glory of the Lord Jesus, the souls of lost people, and the welfare
and advancement of the church of God.

The Roman Christians saw Paul in his bonds fearlessly witnessing for Christ, and they caught fire. If Paul could win so many souls
for Christ while he was chained to a Roman soldier and restricted
to the four walls of a hired house, they who were free surely ought
to be able to work for God.

The Romans reread the letter Paul had written to them from
Corinth some years ago. *"I am debtor,"* he had said, "both to the
Greeks, and to the Barbarians; both to the wise, and to the unwise.
So, as much as in me is, *I am ready* to preach the gospel to you that
are at Rome also. For *I am not ashamed* of the gospel of Christ: for
it is the power of God unto salvation to every one that believeth; to
the Jew first, and also to the Greek" (Romans 1:14-16). Rereading
Paul's Epistle in the light of his example, the Romans caught fire
afresh. The principles, problems, and practice of the gospel that
form the warp and woof of his most important letter blazed with
new light and meaning.

Paul's boldness in his bonds, his transparent sincerity, his tireless
efforts, and his infectious enthusiasm dissolved the caution of his
Roman brethren and rekindled their commitment.

(b) The Nature of Those Now Witnessing (1:14b) "Many...are much more bold to speak the word without fear."

Some people are naturally timid. Some have inferiority complexes and are ruled by shrinking, retiring dispositions. They find it hard to witness for Christ. In fact they find it hard to strike up a conversation about anything, especially with strangers. Other people are bold, pushy, gregarious, and unabashed. Still others are willing enough to witness but are cautious because of the possibility of persecution. Paul's example can put new backbone into all types of people.

God always has people like Paul around to motivate others. George Verwer is one of them. Some years ago George invited me to participate in an Operation Mobilization conference in a suburb of Brussels. Boldness in witnessing was the keynote. Any natural reticence was inundated by a wave of zeal, planning, and example. The participants came together not only to study the Word; we also went into the city to give out tracts and knock on doors. One day about a thousand of us were to take the train into Brussels for an afternoon of door-to-door witnessing. So down to the local station we went and strung ourselves out all along the platform to await the arrival of the next train. When several trains thundered past without stopping, George ordered, "Everybody pray!" Hundreds of young people knelt down on the platform and began to pray loud and clear. The next train stopped!

I observed George providing the same kind of leadership in London. Then on the way home I stopped at the Operation Mobilization center in Richmond. Things were jogging along at a respectable pace. People were busy and routine work was getting done. Then George appeared on the scene and everything shifted into high gear. "Has anyone been out on the streets lately?" he demanded. Nobody had, so instantly a street meeting was organized. Every available person was marched to the nearest strategic street corner. Hymns were sung and this one and that one were put forward to give a testimony or say a few words. There was no escape. The plea of shyness was not even considered. Then we were armed with tracts and sent out two by two up and down the streets. We were to accost people and invite them to a meeting. George planned to preach in a large tearoom he had commandeered and he wanted an audience. The place was full before we were through.

Some souls were saved and many others were challenged. I particularly remember one fellow. It was the height of the hippie craze and this young man was a typical specimen: dirty clothes, long unkempt beard, straggling locks of uncombed hair, unwashed body, sin-stained soul. In cultured accents he argued with George about the reality of Christianity. George said to him, "Come with me and I'll prove to you that Christianity is real. I'm leaving tomorrow for India. You can travel at my expense and be my guest. If you live alongside me, listen to me, and watch me, I'll prove to you that Jesus Christ can save souls and cleanse hearts and lives." That kind of reality was not what this particular hippie wanted, but no one could stand on the sidelines when George Verwer was around. He made it clear that every believer belongs in the game, not in the stands.

Paul had the same explosive quality. People drew confidence from the sight of him carrying on with his evangelistic efforts in spite of his chains. Paul was unafraid of the Roman authorities, unintimidated by the charges lodged against him, and completely uninhibited by the presence of a soldier who might also be a spy.

(2) A Notable Contrast (1:15-18a)

(a) Paul Discerned the Difference (1:15) "Some indeed preach Christ even of envy and strife; and some also of good will."

The word translated "good will" here is *eudokia,* which was used by the angelic hosts in heralding the Savior's birth: "Glory to God in the highest, and on earth peace, good will *[eudokia]* toward men" (Luke 2:14). Jesus used the word in Luke 12:32: "It is your Father's good pleasure to give you the kingdom." Paul used *eudokia* to describe his own passion for the salvation of the Jews: "Brethren, my heart's desire *[eudokia]* and prayer to God for Israel is, that they might be saved" (Romans 10:1). To preach the gospel out of good will, then, is to preach it out of a sincere desire for the well-being of others. Philippians 1:15 refers not only to the desire to see men saved, but also to the desire to encourage and bless Paul's heart.

But not all preachers were motivated by such desires. Some were preaching Christ out of envy. They were jealous of Paul—envious of his success and resentful of his influence in the Roman church, which someone else had founded.

Some were preaching out of strife. The word translated "strife" means "factious rivalry." Nowadays we sometimes refer to denominational rivalry as strife.

It is amazing how much envy and rivalry there is among fulltime leaders in the Lord's work. When Billy Graham was preparing for his first Harringay crusade in London, many British pastors, evangelists, and evangelical leaders were invited to a meeting held to give them the opportunity to assess the young American preacher. In attendance was a well-known Christian leader whose city-wide evangelistic crusades had been quite successful. He rose and put a question to the man he evidently looked upon as a rival. "Mr. Graham," he said in his cultured accent, "tell me, do your converts stand?" Billy Graham refused to be drawn into an argument. Calling the man by name he said, "Tell me, brother, do yours?"

It is astonishing how quick we are to run down someone else's work, especially if it seems to be a little bigger or better than our own. Some people almost choke on any word of praise for another's ministry—especially if it is being carried on in a different denomination or organization, or uses methods different from or more successful than their own. Too many men have the spirit of "the old prophet" of Bethel (1 Kings 13) rather than the spirit of John the Baptist (John 3:26-30).

(b) Paul Discussed the Difference (1:16-17) "The one preach Christ of contention, not sincerely, supposing to add affliction to my bonds: But the other of love, knowing that I am set for the defence of the gospel."

Those who were preaching from an insincere motive were hoping to add affliction to Paul's bonds. The words translated "not sincerely" here carry the idea of a precious metal mixed with a base alloy—these preachers were mixing the pure gold of the gospel with the alloy of their jealousy. The word "affliction" alludes to the painful friction of a prisoner's chains against his ankles and wrists—these preachers were hoping their success would irritate Paul. They hoped that thoughts of their freedom (compared to his incarceration) would gall him. It is hard to imagine how anyone could be so mean-spirited, but there are people who take pleasure in other people's reverses.

How little Paul's rivals knew him! He was much bigger than they were. He ignored them—or perhaps it would be more correct to say that he prayed for them. He took his pleasure from those who hoped to encourage him by helping him spread the gospel. If Paul had his small-minded foes, he had his greathearted friends as well.

(c) Paul Dismissed the Difference (1:18a) "What then? notwithstanding, every way, whether in pretence, or in truth, Christ is preached."

The contentious crowd were not preaching a false gospel. Paul would not have taken any pleasure in doctrinal error. But since they were preaching the truth, they were delighting Paul instead of discouraging him. He could not applaud their motives—God would have to attend to those—but he could and did rejoice that the gospel was going forth.

There are people preaching the gospel today whose motives are suspect. Some of them seem to be building empires for themselves as they spend inordinate amounts of time pleading for money and then spend large portions of that money on questionable things. Other people draw their circle of fellowship so wide that they raise serious doubts as to whether they have any real convictions at all beyond the bare facts of the gospel. But the gospel is being preached. God's Word is being proclaimed, however uncertainly and unworthily. We can thank God for that anyway, and we can pray for these people.

God will bless His Word as He pleases. He is still sovereign and the Holy Spirit is still Lord of the harvest. "The wind bloweth where it listeth," said Jesus, "and thou hearest the sound thereof, but canst not tell whence it cometh, and whither it goeth: so is every one that is born of the Spirit" (John 3:8).

We would not have dreamed of using a man like Balaam—a psychic—to convey a divine message, but God used him. We would never have called Caiaphas a prophet, but God did. Remembering Jonah's miserable unforgiving spirit, his bitterness, and his narrow-minded prejudice, we would not have blessed his preaching, but God gave His blessing. We would never have blessed another Psalm of David after he committed adultery and murdered the woman's husband, but God did.

2. Paul Rejoiced That the Gospel Was Spreading (1:18b) "I therein do rejoice, yea, and will rejoice."

Paul magnanimously overlooked the mean spirit of jealous men and rejoiced that the gospel was being preached. He was irrepressible. No one could get him down. He was a man with a single passion: it was the gospel that mattered. He focused his attention on the preaching, not on the preachers. When anyone exalted Christ and won souls, he could only say, "Hallelujah!"

D. The Prisoner and His Prospects (1:19-26)

1.   He Faced Them Prayerfully (1:19)

a.   The Buoyancy of His Optimism (1:19a) "I know that this shall
     turn to my salvation."

We cannot be sure what Paul meant here by "salvation." The word seems to refer to his desire that his stand for Christ might be vindicated and that he might be delivered from bringing any disgrace on the gospel, especially in his approaching trial. His example, courage, and testimony had encouraged others to take a forthright stand for the gospel, and now he did not want to let them down by compromising or misrepresenting the gospel in any way when he went to court. Perhaps Paul was quoting Job 13:16, which in the Septuagint version reads, "This shall end in my salvation." Job was trying to vindicate his integrity and Paul wanted his integrity vindicated too.

Using the word *oida*, Paul said, "I know." *Oida* refers to intuitive, absolute knowledge, the knowledge of settled conviction. He was unwavering, though his prospects were uncertain. The trial would be full of potential pitfalls, especially if the case came before suspicious and evil Nero. Yet Paul buoyantly and optimistically expected the best. Come what may, God would deliver him from bringing discredit on that gospel which he had encouraged others to proclaim.

b.   The Basis of His Optimism (1:19b) "Through your prayer, and
     the supply of the Spirit of Jesus Christ."

Paul was too wise to rely on his own resolve and his own resources. He based his optimism on the fact that friends were praying for him. God's throne was under siege as the people of God sent up a barrage of prayer for him and, indeed, for the whole cause of Christ at this critical time.

The apostle was relying on "the supply of the Spirit." (The word translated "supply" is used only here and in Ephesians 4:16 in the Scriptures.) The Holy Spirit would see him through. God would give him the right words to say. Paul could think back to times when the Holy Spirit had thus ministered to him: when he spoke to the Jewish mob in the temple court (Acts 22); when he defended himself before Felix (Acts 24); and when he spoke again before Agrippa (Acts 26). Words had flowed—not words of man's wisdom but words the Holy Ghost supplied (1 Corinthians 2:13).

Well-meaning people often say to friends undergoing trial, "Everything's going to be all right." That variety of optimism is vague and unsatisfactory. Paul's optimism was based on the solid and substantial spiritual realities of prayer and the Holy Spirit.

2. He Faced Them Positively (1:20-21)

a. His Determination (1:20) "According to my earnest expectation and my hope, that in nothing I shall be ashamed, but that with all boldness, as always, so now also Christ shall be magnified in my body, whether it be by life, or by death."

The logo of one missionary organization is a picture of an ox with a plow on one side and an altar on the other. Underneath the picture are the words, "Ready for either." That was Paul's motto. He had already faced the future. He could be exonerated or he could be executed. The scales could swing either way. His goal could be accomplished "by life, or by death."

In the final reckoning all Paul cared about was magnifying the Lord Jesus Christ. He wanted to be an instrument in God's hands for that purpose. The word translated "magnified" in Philippians 1:20 means "to make great or to enlarge." Ordinary views of Christ were too small. Christ was big enough to fill the universe, but to most people He was remote and far away. Paul wanted to be a telescope to bring Him closer to their consciousness so they could see Him in all His glory and grace. Paul wanted to be a microscope to enlarge their vision of Christ—to make the various facets of His magnificent life manifest so that people could study Him in detail.

Paul's goal was a noble, daring ambition. By life or by death Paul wanted to reflect the Lord Jesus so that a thoughtless world would be forced to observe Him. Paul wanted to reflect Jesus by living the way Jesus lived, by doing what Jesus did, by saying what Jesus said, by reacting the way Jesus reacted, by thinking the way Jesus thought, and by dying the way Jesus died.

Paul wanted to be motivated by what motivated Jesus. The Lord Jesus had one supreme goal in life: to show men the Father. Jesus was God manifested in flesh; every line of deity was reproduced in His humanity. Every word He spoke was His Father's word; every action He performed was His Father's action. As man He put Himself wholly at the disposal of His Father so that His Father might think, love, act, and speak through Him. By life and by death the Lord Jesus on earth magnified His Father in Heaven. Jesus could say, "This is how God feels. This is how God thinks." As a result our four Gospels give us a perfect portrayal of God—manifest, magnified, brought to the place where we can see Him and understand Him. "We beheld his glory," said John of Jesus, "the glory as of the only begotten of the Father, full of grace and truth" (John 1:14).

Paul had one supreme goal in life: to show men the Lord Jesus. He wanted every line of the lovely life of the Lord Jesus to be reproduced in his life. He wanted to be able to say to his jailers, to his converts, to those who hated him, to those who loved him, to those who were closest to him, to those who met him in passing, "This is what Jesus is like." In his earthly body, by life and by death, Paul wanted to magnify Jesus in Heaven. He wanted to give men, women, boys, and girls a perfect portrayal of Jesus. He wanted to bring Jesus so close to others, to make him so large, that they could not help but see Him.

Paul was not just indulging in wishful thinking, for the Lord Jesus indwelt him, as He indwells us. Thus Paul could face even the bleakest future with confidence. In a sense he was actually looking forward to his trial. He had no intention of being ashamed. The word translated "ashamed" in Philippians 1:20 refers to the feeling that accompanies a dishonorable deed, the feeling that deters us from bad conduct through fear of shame. Paul said, "In nothing I shall be ashamed."

Far from expecting to play the coward before Nero, Paul intended to be bold. A bold person speaks what he thinks; he is fearlessly candid. Anyone answering to Nero—surrounded as he was by sycophants, and inflated as he was by his own ego (he actually imagined himself to be God)—needed to be fearlessly candid. It would take a bold man indeed to tell Nero the truth as it is in Christ Jesus. Paul intended to be that man. In fact he was eagerly looking forward to the opportunity.

Anticipating his trial, Paul spoke of his "earnest expectation." This expression, which means "to look with outstretched hand," is used in only one other place in the New Testament (Romans 8:19). J. B. Phillips translated the expression in Romans 8:19 as "on tiptoe" ("The whole creation is on tiptoe to see the wonderful sight of the sons of God coming into their own"[7]). Paul was on tiptoe to witness to Nero. The apostle expected to magnify the Lord Jesus before that wretched man and his corrupt court. It did not matter to Paul that he would likely pay for his candor with his life. In that case Christ would be magnified in his death.

b.   His Discernment (1:21)

(1) About This Life (1:21a) "For to me to live is Christ."

Everybody lives for something or someone. Many people, if they were being honest, would sum up their goals in this life with such statements as these: "For to me to live is pleasure"; "For to me to live is wealth"; or "For to me to live is position or power or prestige." All such goals fall short of Paul's target. Man's chief aim should be to glorify God and to enjoy Him forever. After a wild life of pleasure Augustine confessed, "Oh God, Thou hast made us for Thyself and our souls are restless until they find their rest in Thee."

Those who live for pleasure are in the end filled with regrets. Lord Byron, the pampered darling of English society, lived for pleasure. In a poem about growing old (written when he was thirty) he said, "I have squandered my whole summer while 'twas May.... I have spent my life, both interest and principle." When he was thirty-six he wrote:

> My days are in the yellow leaf;
> The flowers and fruits of love are gone;
> The worm, the canker, and the grief
> Are mine alone.

Robbie Burns wrote in "Tam O'Shanter":

> Pleasures are like poppies spread,
> You seize the flow'r, its bloom is shed;
> Or like the snow falls in the river,
> A moment white—then melts for ever.

Benjamin Disraeli (Lord Beaconsfield), one of Britain's greatest empire-building statesmen, said, "Youth is a blunder; manhood a struggle; old age a regret."

To avoid such bitter regrets we should follow Paul's example as we set our goal. The shining seraphim tell us what life's true goal should be. These holy ones, who dwell in the eternal sunshine of the presence of God, tune their harps and summon all the resources of unclouded intellect, deep and unsullied passion, and vast volitional powers to sound forth the praise of Him who sits on the throne. They sing, "Thou art worthy, O Lord, to receive glory and honour and power: for thou hast created all things, and for thy pleasure they are and were created" (Revelation 4:11).

We have been created to bring joy to the heart of God. Any lesser goal in life can never bring a sense of fulfillment and satisfaction. In giving pleasure to the Lord, we fulfill the deepest and most basic needs of our own lives. We would be wise to join Paul in affirming, "For to me to live is Christ."

(2) About That Life (1:21b) "To die is gain."

When my grandfather lay dying he said to my father, "There's nothing to dying, Leonard. It's the living that matters." A wise statement. We cannot die the death of the righteous unless we live the life of the righteous. Paul could say, "To die is gain," because he could also say, "To me to live is Christ."

In the Old Testament we meet a wicked old soothsayer named Balaam. He agreed to curse God's people for cold cash. When he discovered that he could not curse those whom God had blessed, he devised another way to earn the wages of unrighteousness. "My lord," he said to the king of Moab, "You cannot curse them, so corrupt them" (see Revelation 2:14). Balaam's diabolical counsel was all too successful. He and his royal master had the sinful satisfaction of seeing God's judgment fall on the Israelites they detested. In the course of his unavailing attempts to curse God's people Balaam had said, "Let me die the death of the righteous, and let my last end be like his!" (Numbers 23:10) It was mere sentiment and he later died under Joshua's avenging sword.

The Bible repeatedly warns that death is not the end. Hebrews 9:27 says, "It is appointed unto men once to die, but after this the judgment." The horror of the great white throne judgment awaits the lost. For them death is not gain, but unutterable eternal loss.

They have lived without Christ; they will die without Christ. Believers will face the judgment seat of Christ, where their works will be tested by fire. Some Christians will see gold, silver, and precious stones emerge from the flames. Others will see their works go up in smoke as wood, hay, and stubble; the Holy Spirit says they will be saved, but they will suffer loss.

Life and death are tied together. Since the purpose of Paul's life was to magnify Christ, he could face his prospects positively. No foe could daunt him; no fear could haunt him. Christ, not Nero, filled his vision.

3.   He Faced Them Preparedly (1:22-23)

a.   The Blessedness of a Fruit-bearing Life Down Here (1:22) "If I live in the flesh, this is the fruit of my labour: yet what I shall choose I wot not."

Paul was not dealing with the question of whether or not he was going to live. He was dealing with the question of whether or not he was going to "live in the flesh." Nero could kill the body, but he had no power over life itself.

The old-fashioned English word "wot" in Philippians 1:22 is a translation of *gnōrizō*, which occurs about two dozen times in the New Testament. The original word is sometimes translated "declare" or "make known" (as in Philippians 4:6). Paul said, "What I shall choose I wot not." He was making no active choice, voicing no personal desire about whether he would live or die in the flesh. He was completely at God's disposal. Paul had an interest, of course, in which way the decision might go, but he himself would do nothing to sway the balance. He would not seek martyrdom by enraging Nero with defiance and rash statements. On the other hand, Paul would not buy his life and freedom at the cost of cowardice and compromise.

If he were to be set free, he would go on living for Christ. *If I am to go on living down here,* Paul thought, *it will simply mean that much more work for Jesus and that much more reward by and by.* The apostle expressed these thoughts in his letter as follows: "If I live in the flesh, this is the fruit of my labour."

Paul was in a race. He had his eye on the finish line where Christ was waiting to congratulate him. Paul was running with all his might, and more so now that he was within sight of his goal. He was prepared for either a fruit-bearing life down here or a far better life up there.

b. The Blessedness of a Far Better Life Up There (1:23) "I am in a strait [I am being pressed] betwixt two, having a desire to depart, and to be with Christ; which is far better."

Paul was caught between two glorious alternatives. "I am held in suspense on both sides" is Handley Moule's rendering of the apostle's words. He was under pressure from both sides. His personal desire, however, was to depart and be with Christ. Paul was not looking on death as an escape. He was simply stating what to him was an obvious fact: what awaits the believer on the other side is so glorious, so full of joy unspeakable, and so rich a fulfillment of all the yearnings and longings of the human heart, that there really is no comparison between that life and this one.

Paul had a desire to depart. *Epithumia,* the word translated "desire" in Philippians 1:23, is translated "lust" thirty-one times in the New Testament. Paul was lusting to go to Heaven! He knew what it was like because he had already been there and he wanted to go back. He told his friends at Corinth that he did not know if he had been in or out of the body at the time of his visit. The place was so solid, so real, so substantial, he could have been in his body at a physical location. Yet he could have been there as a disembodied spirit—the whole experience was so completely beyond anything he had previously known in his body on earth. He did not know whether he had been physically transported (like Philip in Acts 8:39) or his spirit had been caught away, but he did know he had been to paradise (2 Corinthians 12:1-5) and had heard unspeakable words. *Arrētos,* the word translated "unspeakable," really means "untranslatable." What Paul had heard could not be expressed; it was a secret not to be spoken.

That experience created in him a new lust, a holy lust, a heavenly lust. Paul was lusting to go to Heaven so much that God had to keep him in balance by giving him what he called "a thorn in the flesh, the messenger of Satan to buffet me" (2 Corinthians 12:7). J. B. Phillips's rendering reads, "I was given a stabbing pain—one of Satan's angels—to plague me and effectually stop any conceit."[8] Handley Moule's translation says, "There was given me, as the allotment of my Lord, a splinter for to pierce the flesh." Paul was given a stabbing physical affliction and the trying, constant torment of an attendant messenger-angel of Satan. The affliction, both physical and spiritual, was so severe that Paul prayed three times for it to be removed.

Clearly Paul was caught away to paradise, the home of the blessed dead and of the Lord Himself (Luke 23:43). What he experienced there of glory—of final holiness and bliss, of life's ultimate secrets—was beyond the capacity of human language to describe. But Paul did say that he was lusting to go back there.

Yes, Paul had a desire to depart. The word translated "depart" is *analuō*. The only other place the verb *analuō* occurs in the Scriptures is Luke 12:36, which speaks of the Lord's "return" from the wedding. The noun form is used in 2 Timothy 4:6 where Paul, at the end of his pilgrimage, spoke of his "departure." The Greeks used the word in reference to a ship weighing anchor. When Paul wrote to Timothy, the apostle was anticipating immediate martyrdom and he was eagerly looking forward to setting sail at last for his eternal home.

To Paul, to go to be with Christ was the achievement of the highest possible bliss. To be with Christ was "far better." The original text is stronger; it says "far, far better."

Paul was prepared to face his prospects. He was ready to go or stay, as the Lord willed.

4. He Faced Them Practically (1:24-26)

a. His Assessment (1:24) "Nevertheless to abide in the flesh is more needful for you."

Brought back down to earth again, perhaps by a sudden twinge from his fleshly thorn, Paul took a fresh look at his situation. So much work was still to be done. Untold millions were still untold. The churches in Galatia, Asia, Macedonia, Achaia, and Rome had great needs. Legalism troubled the Galatian churches. Childishness troubled the church at Corinth. Gnostic heresy was raising its head at Colossae.

Paul's beloved friends at Philippi who were still going on for God needed him. Persecution might break out. They would need him to inspire them by his example and encourage them with his letters and visits. He pulled out his prayer list. Name after name, place after place, and page after page reminded him that he was still needed on this earth. Even if he had to stay in prison, he could minister to his brothers and sisters in Christ.

Paul reluctantly turned his thoughts from the land of harps and halos to a world of grime and guilt. His chain rattled on the floor as he moved his hand, and the harsh reality of this life intruded on the holy reality of that other world.

He longed to go but he was willing to stay. For now he was needed here. He would have an endless eternity to enjoy the bliss of the world beyond the sky. He could spare a few more passing years of time to get a little more done—to win more souls, to snatch more brands from the burning. The world was on fire. Now was no time to think of leaving the scene. He would stay—not for himself, but for everyone else. Paul put his desire on one side of the scales and his duty on the other, and settled on the side of duty.

b.   His Assurance (1:25-26)

(1) Looking at the Realities (1:25a) "Having this confidence, I know that I shall abide and continue with you all."

Feeling confident that he was more needed here for the time being, Paul had the inner assurance that he was not going to die yet. Nero, of uncertain temper, vile lusts, and ungovernable passions, might well be the human arbiter of his case, but he sat on a human throne. Paul had just come back from a spiritual excursion to a land where stood a higher throne. Nero had no power over him except as it was given from above.

Paul had the silent witness of the Spirit that it was more needful for him to remain in the flesh, so he confidently reassured his dear Philippian friends. "I know I will remain side by side with you all," he said in effect. His place at the oar was not going to be empty. He was going to stay a little longer and pull alongside them. He was going to stand in line with them and pass along buckets of water to the fire.

"I know," Paul said, using the Greek word meaning "know something intuitively." His knowledge was subjective, but he had no doubt about its validity. The Holy Spirit, it would seem, gave him this assurance as he wrote.

(2) Looking at the Reasons (1:25b-26) "For your furtherance and joy of faith; That your rejoicing may be more abundant in Jesus Christ for me by my coming to you again."

Paul's reason for being willing to stay was his desire to help the believers forward in their Christian living. He wanted to find increasing joy in their faith. He wanted them too to be able to exult in Christ when they saw in him living proof of what God can do in and through a man who trusts Him all the way.

Paul faced his prospects as one "married" to Another, even to Him who is risen from the dead. He was united to Christ for better or for worse, for richer or for poorer, in sickness or in health, in freedom or in prison, for life down here or life over there. Out of that union must come fruit unto God in Paul's life and in the lives of others.

E. The Prisoner and His Pulpit (1:27-30)

P aul urged the Philippians to be unyielding, undivided, and unafraid in the battle against the enemies of Christ.

1.   Unyielding in the Battle (1:27a) "Only let your conversation be as it becometh the gospel of Christ."

The meaning of the English word *conversation* has changed since the translation of the King James Bible. The word translated "conversation" here means "citizenship" or "manner of life." In this verse the word can be rendered "citizen-life" or "life as citizens."

The Philippian Christians were citizens of two worlds. They were citizens of the Roman world and they were citizens of the world that ruled Paul's desires. The two worlds were at war. The Christians' heavenly citizenship had to take priority over their human citizenship, as the powers that be soon came to understand. The caesars could not tolerate this priority even though the Christians' heavenly citizenship made them better human citizens, better neighbors, better workers, better soldiers, better teachers, better parents, better children. At the height of the Neronic and other persecutions, the line between the two worlds was so clearly drawn that Christians refused to offer even a merely symbolic pinch of salt on a pagan altar.

In a Roman colony like Philippi, the issues would be clear even before formal persecution broke out. The church at Philippi had been born amid harassment. There Paul had been beaten and imprisoned and there too he had been forced to make one of his rare appeals to his own Roman citizenship. His heavenly citizenship did not annul his human citizenship. Although he was not *of* the world, he was yet *in* the world.

The line is clearly drawn in many countries today, as those who live in communist, Hindu, and Islamic lands know only too well. The line is drawn, although not always so distinctly, in all lands. In

our society the pagan world often wears a friendly mask, but it is still
the enemy and we cannot settle for compromise. We must determine not to allow the issues to be blurred.

> Nay world, I turn away,
>   Though thou seem fair and good,
> That friendly, outstretched hand of thine,
>   Is stained with Jesus' blood.[9]

So Paul exhorted the people of God to be unyielding to the
enemy. He wanted their manner of life to be "as it becometh the
gospel of Christ."

2. Undivided in the Battle (1:27b) "That whether I come and see
    you, or else be absent, I may hear of your affairs, that ye stand
    fast in one spirit, with one mind striving together for the faith
    of the gospel."

This is the first intimation that there was discord in the Philippian
church. Later on Paul bluntly named names. Here he urged
believers in general to strive for unity in the Spirit. The things that
unite us are far more important than any personality clashes that
may divide us. Satan's strategy has always been to divide and
conquer.

The story is told of a man who had several sons who were always
squabbling. Their disunity was hurting the family business on
which they all depended for their livelihood. The father called his
sons together and handed a thin bamboo cane to the strongest of
them. "Snap that cane," the old man said. Thinking his father had
taken leave of his senses, the young man complied. The old man
tied two thin bamboo canes together. "Snap these," he said. Again
the young man had no difficulty. The father kept adding more and
more canes to the bundle. Soon the son was sweating and straining
to snap them and before long he found the task completely beyond
his strength. Singly or in small bundles the canes could be snapped
easily, but united the canes had more strength than the young man
had. The object lesson needed no comment.

Paul's concern was that the saints at Philippi unite in the task of
getting the gospel out. Whether he talked to them in person or
received news about them from afar, he wanted to hear that they
were standing fast, united in a common cause, battling with a single

mind for the faith of the gospel. There were too many real adversaries, too many golden opportunities, and too much to be done for Christ, for Christians to split the church over nonessentials.

In Paul's words there is perhaps an echo of the Lord's words recorded in John 13:35: "By this shall all men know that ye are my disciples, if ye have love one to another."

3.   Unafraid in the Battle (1:28-30)

a.   Paul's Exhortation (1:28-29)

(1) The Opposition They Faced (1:28a) "In nothing terrified by your adversaries: which is to them an evident token of perdition."

"Don't be scared out of your determination to live out your heavenly citizenship by anything your enemies might try to do to you," Paul was saying. "Their opposition to you is their own condemnation. Your calm collective courage in the face of danger and persecution is a sure token to your enemies of the perdition that awaits them."

Paul's call to courage in the face of danger has been heeded down through the centuries by millions of believers whose exploits have earned them mention on the honor roll of Heaven. *Foxe's Book of Martyrs,* although out of vogue now, is still a tribute to the often supernatural bravery of God's people in the face of terrifying ordeals. Nowhere has man's inhumanity to man been more dreadfully displayed than in the persecution of believers. In lands where freedom reigns, Christians do not have to fear police brutality, but in other lands they are still being tortured and tormented for their faith.

Our fathers were brought up on doses of John Foxe's classic, complete with harrowing illustrations. Now we hear of horrors inflicted on Jews, Christians, and political prisoners by the totalitarian regimes of our time. The twentieth century has put out of its mind—because it can no longer cope with the enormity of the statistics involved—the numbers of people who have been murdered, martyred, and maimed. Added to the accounts of Nazi death camps are stories from the Gulag Archipelago, Mao Tse-tung's China, Viet Nam, Cambodia, Rwanda, and the former Yugoslavia. Such stories are so commonplace that we have become hardened to them. They stir up passing exclamations of protest; then they are forgotten and new horrors take their place.

It has been said that more people have died for Christ in the twentieth century than in all the other centuries of the Christian era combined. We could dwell on our danger, but it is better to heed Paul's exhortation not to be afraid of our enemies.

(2) The Opportunity They Faced (1:28b-29)

(a) Of Being Different (1:28b) "But to you of salvation, and that of God."

To the enemies of the gospel, the bravery of believers was a witness to the coming perdition of the persecutors. To the faithful, the bravery of believers was a witness to the genuine and victorious salvation of the persecuted.

The bravery of the victims and their spirit of love and forgiveness turned the blood of the martyrs into the seed of the church. Nonbelievers had been known to die bravely, hurling defiance and vindictiveness into the faces of their executioners. The bravery of the Christians was different. They died with hymns on their lips, forgiveness in their hearts, and the light of Heaven on their faces. As he wrote, Paul could still remember how the face of Stephen had haunted him until he too made peace with God through the Lord Jesus Christ.

(b) Of Being Disciples (1:29) "Unto you it is given in the behalf of Christ, not only to believe on him, but also to suffer for his sake."

But why does God allow persecution to arise? Why is God silent while His people are being tormented? Why do the righteous suffer? Why do the wicked triumph? Paul's answer to all these questions is Christ.

God was silent while Christ shed tears in Gethsemane and while He endured torment on the cross. Out of the darkness came Emmanuel's orphan cry, "My God, my God, why hast thou forsaken me?" (Matthew 27:46) Yet out of Christ's agony came a salvation that was to be offered to all mankind.

Paul looked at suffering for the cause of Christ as a boon. The apostle discounted privation, pain, and prisons; he discounted persecution in the arena, on the cross, by the sword, and at the stake. He was saying to the Philippian disciples that some favored members of the body of Christ were being offered a privilege: they could "suffer for his sake." They could win a martyr's crown. To Paul that possibility was not a prospect to be avoided at all costs; it was a privilege to be embraced. Suffering for Christ's sake was a gift of God, a gift not given to everyone. "Unto you it is given," said Paul, as though some great advantage were being sovereignly bestowed by God.

Perhaps Paul had in mind the last beatitudes from the sermon on the mount: "Blessed [happy] are they which are persecuted for righteousness' sake: for theirs is the kingdom of heaven. Blessed are ye, when men shall revile you, and persecute you, and shall say all manner of evil against you falsely, for my sake. Rejoice, and be exceeding glad: for great is your reward in heaven: for so persecuted they the prophets which were before you" (Matthew 5:10-12).

Christians should feel honored when they are chosen to suffer with Christ, for their reward in Heaven will be commensurate with their sacrifice. If believers share in Christ's cross, they will share in His crown.

b. Paul's Example (1:30) "Having the same conflict which ye saw in me, and now hear to be in me."

Someone reading this commentary might justly ask, "Well, what about you? What have you suffered for Christ?" I would have to confess, "Very little." The reader might then ask me, "Would you be able to stand torture and a painful martyrdom?" I don't know. I trust I would be faithful unto death; I would certainly want to be. Doubtless God would give the necessary grace if the time of testing should ever come. Dying grace is for dying, not living. Grace to suffer persecution is for those who are suffering persecution, not for those who are at ease in Zion.

But the man who was exhorting the Philippians had every right to be heard on the question of persecution, as he reminded them. Many of them knew how he and Silas had suffered scourging and harsh imprisonment there in Philippi. We can imagine that as Paul's words were read, the jailer jumped to his feet and said, "I'll testify to that. I'm here, saved and in the fellowship, and my wife and children too, because of the way those dear men triumphed in prison and over pain!"

Paul was still suffering persecution as he wrote his letter. If for the moment the prospect of martyrdom had faded, it still remained a likelihood later on, for Paul was a man who stirred up not only friendship but also hostility everywhere he went.

PART II

Paul's Tremendous
Examples

Philippians 2:1-30

II. PAUL'S TREMENDOUS EXAMPLES (2:1-30)

The apostle Paul was a menace to the devil. Satan did not know what to do with him. *Lock him up in prison,* the evil one may have thought, *and he will win his jailers to Christ and write letters that will influence the thinking of millions for ages to come. Set him free and he will win whole continents to Christ. Kill him and he will win a martyr's crown.* Paul's triumphant spirit rang out in the first chapter of Philippians as he pealed the bells of our joy in Christ. In the second chapter he introduced other triumphant figures into his letter.

In Philippians 2 Paul approached more directly the problem that was marring the fellowship at Philippi. He had already shown the Philippians what a partisan spirit was doing at Rome, where some were preaching Christ out of contention, hoping to add affliction to his bonds. Now he urged the Philippians to put away the spirit of strife from their midst once and for all. He tried to persuade them by introducing three examples of the kind of spirit every Christian should display—the spirit displayed by Christ, Timothy, and Epaphroditus. Paul's first tremendous example was Christ.

A. Christ: Triumph in Sacrifice (2:1-18)

1. Paul's Approach to the Example of Christ (2:1-4)

In the first four verses Paul built up to the example of Christ by exhorting his Philippian friends not to add to his burdens by squabbling among themselves. His distress is evident in the first verse, their discord in verses 2-4.

a.   His Distress (2:1-2a)

(1) The Basis of His Appeal (2:1) "If there be therefore any consolation in Christ, if any comfort of love, if any fellowship of the Spirit, if any bowels and mercies…"

The basis of Paul's appeal is threefold. First there is *the supreme basis:* "Consolation in Christ…comfort of love." *Paraklesis,* the word translated "consolation" here, is akin to the word translated "Comforter" in John 14:16,26. And one of the names of the Lord Jesus is "the consolation of Israel" (Luke 2:25). Thus the word "consolation" carries with it thoughts of both the Holy Spirit and the Lord Jesus. Perhaps Paul also had in mind his friend Barnabas, who was called the "son of consolation" by the apostles in Jerusalem (Acts 4:36); he was a man addicted to helping others. (In Luke 6:24 the Lord used *paraklesis* to describe the satisfaction and solace people receive from temporal riches—a consolation received at the expense of true spiritual joy.)

Paramuthion, the word translated "comfort" in Philippians 2:1, occurs nowhere else in Scripture. *Paramuthion* means "stimulating force, incentive." Paul was appealing to his friends to keep to the fore the comforting, consoling power of the Lord Jesus and the stimulating power of love. The Philippians would bring joy to Paul's heart if they availed themselves of this power and settled their disputes.

Second there is *the supernatural basis:* "Fellowship of the Spirit"— that is, participation in the Spirit or sharing in the Spirit. Some conflicts are too violent to be resolved by natural means. The work of the Holy Spirit is needed. Witness the case of Peter and John. By nature their personalities clashed. Peter was a doer; John was a dreamer. When the Lord told Peter he would be called upon to die for Him, Peter pointed to John and demanded, "And what shall this man do?" (John 21:21) Jesus told Peter it was none of his business. But after Pentecost Peter and John enjoyed a harmonious relationship (Acts 3:1; 4:13; 8:14).

Third there is *the supporting basis:* "Bowels and mercies"—that is, heart and compassion. Paul was appealing to his friends' natural sympathy, tenderness, and feeling. Surely they of all people would not want to add to his bonds by giving him cause for grief.

The threefold basis of Paul's appeal is very broad. He was not going to leave any stone unturned in his quest for unity in the local church.

(2) The Burden of His Appeal (2:2a) "Fulfil ye my joy."

Paul's cup of joy was pretty well full. He had learned the secret of joy, that "joy unspeakable and full of glory" (1 Peter 1:8) which ought to be the lot in life of all who love the Lord. He had discovered the secret on the Damascus road when he had first looked into the face of Jesus. Paul had been surprised by joy, as was C. S. Lewis.

Lewis, who was a well-known scholar at Oxford and later held the Chair of Medieval and Renaissance English Literature at Cambridge, had lost his joy as a child when his mother died. Much of his life thereafter was a quest for that departed elusive, will-o'-the-wisp quality in life. With his father away at work and his brother at boarding school, he was alone in a big house full of books. For years he dwelled in a Tolkien-like never-never land of fantasy and make-believe. He gave up Christianity at the age of fourteen.

During years of schooling, military service, and teaching, his quest for joy continued. Although Lewis had several near encounters of a spiritual kind, all he saw was the ghost of joy. He read more and more books and became a materialist and an atheist.

Then God closed in on him. He met people who made an impact on his life. He discovered the writings of George McDonald. And Lewis became a theist. He started going to church, more as a statement against his former atheism than anything else. Finally he became a Christian—a real Christian. God said to him, "Put down your gun and we'll talk." Lewis's quest was over. His desire for joy was so satisfied that he entitled his autobiography *Surprised by Joy*.

Paul was surprised by joy on the Damascus road and he kept on adding to that joy. Joy is knowing Jesus, and Paul was getting to know Him better and better. Jesus had prayed to His Father, "Now come I to thee; and these things I speak in the world, that they might have my joy in themselves" (John 17:13).

Joy filled Paul's soul. His cup of joy was now full, but there was still room for a few more drops. In Philippians 2:2 we hear him pleading for a few more drops of joy to brim his cup. "Fulfil ye my joy," he said. And what would fill that cup of joy full to overflowing? The news that his quarreling friends had settled their differences forever at the foot of the cross.

b.   Their Discord (2:2b-4)

(1) The Need for Likemindedness (2:2b) "Be likeminded, having the same love, being of one accord, of one mind."

Paul piled up words and phrases to drive home his plea. He told the Philippians to be "likeminded." The word translated "likeminded" means "to mind or think the same thing." Paul wanted the Philippians to be likeminded *in what they thought.* A meeting of their minds would bring their petty squabbles to a logical, sensible, rational end.

Paul wanted the Philippians to be likeminded *in what they wrought*—that is, he wanted them to have the same love worked out in them as had been wrought out in his own life. Mental agreement would not last long if they did not put their hearts into it. A feeling of love and regard for each other was needed.

Paul wanted the Philippians to be likeminded *in what they sought.* He urged them to be "of one accord, of one mind"—in other words, of one purpose. The idea behind the word translated "of one accord" is "soul and soul together." Handley Moule suggested the rendering "possessed with the idea of sentiment of unity."

What Paul was after was not just a patching up of differences, but absolute unity of mind, heart, and purpose in the Lord. Nothing less would do. The Philippians must bury their disagreements so deep they could never dig them up again.

(2) The Need for Lowliness (2:3)

(a) The Cause of Their Discords (2:3a) "Let nothing be done through strife or vainglory."

Strife pulls the other person down; vainglory puts oneself up. Both produce discord in the local church. Even a little *contentiousness* and *conceit* can ruin a gathering of God's people.

In the wilderness the children of Israel were marred by a spirit of criticism and chronic complaining. This spirit was evident from the beginning and came to a head in the rebellion of Korah, Dathan, and Abiram, who challenged the right of Moses and Aaron to be the leaders of God's people. "Ye take too much upon you," the rebels said (Numbers 16:3). They wanted to pull Moses and Aaron down and put themselves up.

(b) The Cure for Their Discords (2:3b) "In lowliness of mind let each esteem other better than themselves."

Paul was not saying that we should consider everyone else to be more gifted or more capable than we are. It is a false humility that depreciates any acknowledgment of one's gifts. C. S. Lewis showed that true humility is evident when a man who designs the most beautiful cathedral in the world—and knows it is the most beautiful cathedral in the world—would have been just as pleased if someone else had designed it (Screwtape's Letter XIV).

To pretend not to have abilities we know we do have is not humility, but hypocrisy. If we esteem others better than ourselves, we do not consider everyone else to be superior to ourselves, but we do want everyone else to have preferential treatment.

Humility is the opposite of conceit and selfish ambition. Humility is concern for the advancement of others. The man who reigns in the affections of God's people is not the bossy, pushy man, but the quiet, godly, unassuming man who is always seeking the good of other people. Barnabas was such a man.

(3) The Need for Largeness (2:4) "Look not every man on his own things, but every man also on the things of others."

To seek one's own advancement is worldly. To seek the prosperity, good, and promotion of others is divine. Philippians 2:4 expresses the essence of the spirit of the Lord Jesus. Those who heed these words of Paul have the larger view of life. The view that seeks one's own things tends to narrowness, selfishness, bigotry, smallness, and meanness of soul. The view that seeks to promote the interests and well-being of others leads to largeness of life both here and hereafter.

Lot sought to promote his own interests when he chose the well-watered plains of Jordan. How shortsighted he was in his selfish desire to take the best and most fertile part of the country for himself. God could already see those green valleys and prosperous cities buried in salt and sulfur, a smoking ruin of desolation. Lot lost fortune and family in Sodom and almost lost his faith; certainly he lost his testimony.

All the land of Canaan had been deeded by God to Abraham, yet that noble unselfish servant of God simply stood there saying, "We be brethren," while Lot took what looked like the best. But when the separation was accomplished, who was the bigger man? Who was marked by largeness of heart?

And Abraham did not lose anything because of his largeness. Lot journeyed *east* and once his caravan had gone over the hill and down into the valley toward those well-watered plains, God spoke. He said to Abraham, "Lift up now thine eyes, and look from the place where thou art northward, and southward, *and eastward,* and westward: For *all* the land which thou seest, to thee will I give it, and to thy seed for ever" (Genesis 13:14-15, italics added).

All the comments in Philippians 2:1-4 are merely Paul's approach to the example of Christ. Verses 5-11 present the example itself, by far the greatest example of all.

2.   Paul's Appeal to the Example of Christ (2:5-11)

a.   The Person of Christ (2:5-7)

(1) As Sovereign: The Messiah (2:5) "Let this mind be in you, which was also in Christ Jesus."

Philippians 2:5-7 gives us, as Handley Moule said, "the most conspicuous and magnificent of the dogmatic utterances of the New Testament." He continued:

> Let us consider it for a few moments from that point of view alone. We have here a chain of assertions about our Lord Jesus Christ made within some thirty years of His death at Jerusalem, made in the open day of public Christian intercourse, and made (every reader must feel this) not in the least in the manner of controversy, of assertion against difficulties and denials, but in the tone of a settled, common and most living certainty. These assertions give us on the one hand the fullest possible assurance that He is man, man in nature, in circumstances and experience, and particularly in the sphere of relation to God the Father. But they also assure us, in precisely the same tone, and in a way which is equally vital to the argument in hand, that He is genuinely divine as He is genuinely human.[1]

Paul began by using the Messianic title "Christ Jesus" in Philippians 2:5. W. E. Vine pointed out that the order of the names and titles of the Lord is always a matter of precision in the New Testament. "Christ Jesus" places the emphasis on the exalted One who "emptied himself" (2:7, RSV). Vine said:

> "Jesus Christ" describes the despised and rejected One who was afterwards glorified (2:11), and testifies to His resurrection.

"Christ Jesus" suggests His grace, "Jesus Christ" suggests His glory.

In the Epistles of James, Peter, John and Jude, men who had companied with the Lord in the days of His flesh, "Jesus Christ" is the invariable order of the name and title, for this was the order of their experience: as "Jesus" they knew Him first; that He was Messiah they learnt finally in His resurrection. But Paul came to know Him first in the glory of Heaven (Acts 9:1-6), and, his experience being thus the reverse of theirs, the reverse order, "Christ Jesus," is of frequent occurrence in his letters, but, with the exception of Acts 24:24 [*sic*], does not occur elsewhere in the New Testament.[2]

As the Christ, Jesus was the anointed One, the Messiah so long promised in the Scriptures and awaited by the Jews. The Lord never gloried in His position, though He never denied it either.

Philippians 2:5 tells us that the mind of Christ is to be the mind of the Christian. The word translated "let (this) mind be" is *phroneō*, which means "to think of, to be mindful of." We are to think as He did. (Paul used the same word in 4:2, where he told Euodias and Syntyche to "be of the same mind in the Lord.")

(2) As Son: The Maker (2:6) "Who, being in the form of God, thought it not robbery to be equal with God."

In Philippians 2:6 Paul said of Christ that He was "in the form of God." The word translated "form" here is *morphē*, "the essential form." In almost the next statement (2:7) he said that Christ took "the form [same word] of a servant." The word translated "servant" here is *doulos*. Philippians 2:6 asserts that He who came to be man in every sense of the word, apart from sin, was also God *(theou)* in every sense of the word, with certain divine rights, attributes, qualities, and prerogatives. Philippians 2:7 asserts a real humanity that entailed certain human obligations to God. So Paul placed the two utterances side by side: *morphē theou; morphē doulos.* Christ's incarnation was not an emptying of Himself of His deity, but a clothing of Himself in humanity—in order to be a servant. His choosing to be a servant gives force to Paul's appeal to the example of Christ.

In view of the heretical interpretation of the incarnation that claims that Christ emptied Himself of His deity, it is important to note Gifford's statement regarding *morphē theou*. He said the expression refers to

> the nature or essence, not in the abstract, but as actually subsisting in the individual, and retained as long as the individual itself exists....Thus the passage before us *morphē theou* is the Divine nature actually and inseparably subsisting in the Person of Christ....For the interpretation of "the form of God" it is sufficient to say (1) it includes the whole nature and essence of Deity, and it is inseparable from them, since they could have no actual existence without it; and (2) that it does not include in itself anything "accidental" or separable, such as particular modes of manifestation, or conditions of glory and majesty, which may at one time be attached to the "form" or another separated from it.[3]

In other words, when Jesus became a man He did not and could not cease to be God. As God He was the eternal, uncreated, self-existing Creator of the universe, the One whom angels worshiped.

Because Christ was God and had always been God, He did not think it an act of robbery to be equal with God. The phrase translated "thought it not robbery" in the King James version was rendered "reckoned it no plunderer's prize" by Handley Moule. He pointed out that the word *harpagmos* ("robbery or prize") carries the idea of "to seize or to carry off by force."

Gifford commented on the words *to be* in the phrase "thought it not robbery to be equal with God." He said they are ambiguous and might give rise to the erroneous idea that to be equal with God was something to be attained as a prize in the future. He expressed preference for a rendering that is just as accurate and less ambiguous: "counted it not as a prize that He was on an equality with God." Gifford also explored the rendering of *harpagmos* and concluded that the passive "prize" is more correct than the active "robbery." Using the passive sense, one could translate Philippians 2:6 as follows: "Who, though He was subsisting in the essential form of God, yet did not regard His being on an equality of glory and majesty with God as a prize and a treasure to be held fast."[4]

Satan was the one who regarded the godhead as a plunderer's prize (Isaiah 14:12-15), to his own ruin. And it was he who, in the guise of a serpent, lured Eve into trying to grasp the same prize (Genesis 3:5).

(3) As Servant: The Minister (2:7a) "But made himself of no reputation, and took upon him the form of a servant."

Kenoō, the word translated "made of no reputation," means "emptied"; so the phrase "made himself of no reputation" means "emptied Himself." Some people think that Christ emptied Himself of His deity, but this idea is supported neither by this verse nor by the rest of the Bible.

In eternity past Christ was not only equal with God; He existed in the essential form *(morphē)* of God. In the act of becoming a servant, the Lord Jesus deliberately abandoned the glory and majesty He had with the Father before the worlds began. The Lord did not empty Himself of His divine attributes. He did not cease to be God even though He took upon Himself the outward characteristics of a servant. He assumed all that was essentially human without relinquishing anything that was essentially divine.

Doulos, the word translated "servant" here, usually means "slave." Jesus, however, became no man's slave. He became the bondservant of His Father. Jesus came to do always those things that pleased the Father (John 8:29), to live a life of perfect obedience to the Father. The Lord did not come to assert His own will, but to say, "Thy will be done" (Matthew 6:10). He came to be the perfect servant anticipated in the Messianic prophecies of the Old Testament (Isaiah 42:1-3; 52:13–53:12). "Behold my servant," said God in 42:1, and in the matchless fifty-third chapter we see Him becoming "obedient unto death, even the death of the cross" (Philippians 2:8).

(4) As Savior: The Man (2:7b) "And was made in the likeness of men."

When God said, "Let us make man," He added, "in our image, after our likeness" (Genesis 1:26). Man was created to be as much like God as a creature could be. God endowed man with intellect, emotions, and will; He gave him a body so that he could see, smell, taste, hear, and feel. Man's physical life was to be under the control of his mental, emotional, and volitional powers. Then God gave him something that set him apart from the animal creation: He gave him a spirit.

Man's body made him world-conscious and enabled him to live in a physical environment. His soul made him self-conscious— aware that he was a distinct individual with attributes, nature, personality, potential responsibilities, and accountability. His spirit made him God-conscious—aware that he existed to worship and serve his creator. Moreover the Holy Spirit indwelt his human spirit; he was a creature inhabited by God.

When God created the animals He gave each species its own particular behavior mechanism, rigidly controlled by what we call instinct. An animal does what it does because it is what it is. Dogs, eagles, salmon, bees, and all other creatures behave in certain ways because they are locked into those ways of behaving by instinctive inner drives.

God did not create man to be controlled by instinct; He created man to be inhabited by God. Indwelling the human spirit, the Holy Spirit supplied man's code of behavior. In man the human spirit, indwelt by the Holy Spirit, energized the intellect, emotions, and will, and monitored and controlled the senses. Thus man lived and moved and had his being in God (Acts 17:28). Man behaved as God would behave. Man existed to demonstrate what God is like.

When Adam sinned, the Holy Spirit vacated the human spirit and man was left with a sin principle in control of his behavior. His body became subject to disease and death; his senses were marred by imperfection and were subject to lust; his intellect, emotions, and will were impaired and became easy prey to evil and wrong; his spirit became the plaything of sinister spirits and the victim of false religion. Man in sin was not what God had in mind when He said, "Let us make man in our image, after our likeness." Man in sin is a distortion of man in the image of God.

No wonder Jesus said to Nicodemus, "Ye must be born again" (John 3:7). We are born of the flesh, born in sin, shapen in iniquity, spiritually dead. True, man in sin can be very clever. Evidences of his genius are everywhere. He can put men on the moon, but he cannot solve the problem of sinful behavior. Man in sin is capable of deep emotion; he can make great sacrifices, hold his lusts at bay, and impose incredible degrees of self-discipline; but he cannot cleanse himself of lust and sin and guilt. Man in sin can invent systems of religion, persuade millions to join a cause, and win countless converts to a creed, but he cannot win the approval of God. His sin still separates him from God. He needs to be born again.

"That which is born of the flesh is flesh," Jesus told Nicodemus, "and that which is born of the Spirit is spirit" (John 3:6). When a person comes to Christ and accepts Him as Savior, the blood of

Christ cleanses him from all sin. The Holy Spirit comes back into his human spirit and regenerates it. "As in Adam all die, even so in Christ shall all be made alive" (1 Corinthians 15:22). In Christ man is again man as God intended man to be: man inhabited by God.

All of this is important background information for a proper understanding of the phrase "and was made in the likeness of men." Man was made in the likeness of God; Jesus was made in the likeness of men; that is, He became truly human. People had no trouble accepting Him easily and naturally as a man. He was, however, man as God intended man to be: His spirit was always ruled by the Holy Spirit. Christ's intellect, emotions, will, nature, person, personality, senses, and physical powers were all under the control of the Holy Spirit moment by moment, day by day, year in and year out, from the moment He drew His first breath until the moment on the cross when He yielded up His Spirit to His Father. Christ's body, always under the control of God's Spirit, was the perfect vehicle for expressing all the fullness of the godhead bodily.

Now let us go back over Philippians 2:5-7 and view these verses from the standpoint of the four Gospels. We will begin with Paul's words in Philippians 2:5: "Let this mind be in you, which was also in Christ Jesus." There is much more here than meets the eye. The words "Christ Jesus" (Messiah Jesus) point us at once to the Gospel of Matthew, for Matthew wrote primarily to convince his country-men that Jesus was the Messiah; he wrote to show the Jews that the One they had cursed and crucified was the Christ they had awaited so long. He wanted to demonstrate that the long-promised Son of David was Jesus.

Matthew's objective is clearly discernible throughout his Gospel. He began by tracing the Lord's ancestry from David through Solomon. Then Matthew told of the coming of the wise men and their query that stirred Jerusalem: "Where is he that is born King of the Jews?" (2:2) Again and again he documented Christ's life with Old Testament quotations. Matthew's book is the royal Gospel—the Gospel of the sovereign, the Gospel of Christ Jesus, the Gospel of the Messiah.

Moving on to Philippians 2:6 we read that the Lord Jesus, "being in the form of God, thought it not robbery to be equal with God." These words of the Holy Spirit point us to the Gospel of John, for the Lord Jesus is depicted there as deity. John was writing toward the end of the first century when many heresies had taken root and were flourishing, and in one way or another all of these heresies attacked the deity of Christ. John wrote to the church to assure them that Jesus, being God in every sense of the word, had no need to grasp at deity as some kind of plunderer's prize.

John's objective is evident from his opening statement: "In the beginning was the Word [not a start but a state—the term translated 'was' is in the imperfect tense], and the Word was with God [an affirmation of His distinct personality within the godhead], and the Word was God [an avowal of His essential deity]. The same was in the beginning with God. All things were made by him; and without him was not any thing made that was made." The Word is One who transcends all *thought* (1:1), who transcends all *time* (1:2), and who transcends all *things* (1:3).

John went on to say that "the Word was made flesh, and dwelt [tabernacled, pitched His tent] among us, (and we beheld his glory, the glory as of the only begotten of the Father,) full of grace and truth" (1:14). Thus John described the incarnation. He used only five Greek words—Luke used about twenty-five hundred.

The idea that Christ "tabernacled" here is particularly appropriate. There was nothing very beautiful about the outside of the tabernacle, but the inside—with all its gold, costly fabrics, and rich colors—was ablaze with the abiding glory of God. When the golden furniture of the tabernacle was carried through the wilderness, it was always carefully covered. Similarly the glory of our Lord Jesus as He tabernacled on earth was a covered glory.

The theme of Christ's essential deity runs all through John's Gospel. He recorded Christ's "I am" statement to the Jews: "Before Abraham was, I am" (8:58) and selected miracles that declare His deity. Then John actually stated his reason for writing:

> Many other signs truly did Jesus in the presence of his disciples, which are not written in this book: But these are written, that ye might believe that Jesus is the Christ, the Son of God; and that believing ye might have life through his name (20:30-31).

Continuing in the Philippian passage, we read that Christ "took upon him the form of a servant." The coming of the Lord Jesus as God's perfect servant points us to the Gospel of Mark, since Mark, writing primarily for the Romans, depicted the Lord Jesus as the servant of Jehovah.

There is no genealogy of the Lord Jesus in the Gospel of Mark.

Neither is there one in the Gospel of John. Matthew and Luke both have genealogies, for in those Gospels we see Jesus as *the child born.* In John we see Him as *the Son given* (Isaiah 9:6). Taking us nowhere near the cradle, John announced in that grandest of all texts that "God so loved the world, that he gave his only begotten Son, that whosoever believeth in him should not perish, but have everlasting life" (John 3:16).

John, who stressed the deity of Christ, gave us no genealogy because as God, Jesus had no ancestry. Mark gave us no genealogy for quite a different reason. He was introducing a servant and no one is interested in the ancestors of a servant. The important information about a servant is what he can do. Thus in Mark's Gospel we see the Lord Jesus plunged into ceaseless activity.

The key words in Mark's portrayal of Christ are "immediately" and "straightway" and the key verse in the Gospel sums up Mark's point of view: "The Son of man came not to be ministered unto, but to minister [serve], and to give his life a ransom for many" (10:45). In the first part of the Gospel we see the Lord Jesus giving His life in *service* (He came not to be served but to serve, 10:45a); in the second part of the Gospel we see Him giving His life in *sacrifice* (He came to give His life a ransom for many, 10:45b).

It was particularly appropriate for John Mark to write the Gospel of the Servant because he himself had failed as a servant (Acts 13:5,13; 15:36-39) and had been recovered (2 Timothy 4:11). Perhaps it was Mark's writing of this Gospel that convinced Paul of Mark's recovery.

The Holy Spirit's final summation of the person of Christ in Philippians 2:5-7 is that He "was made in the likeness of men." The coming of the Lord Jesus as God's perfect man points us to the Gospel of Luke, since Luke, writing primarily for the Greeks, depicted the Lord Jesus as the perfect man and the wondrous Savior of men. The key verse in Luke's Gospel says, "The Son of man is come to seek and to save that which was lost" (19:10).[5]

The ideal of the Greek world was perfect humanity. The Greeks peopled mount Olympus with gods made in the image and likeness of men. They took the lines of human personality, projected them into infinity, and conceived of gods who were simply larger editions of themselves. Since the lines they projected were the lines of fallen human personality, the gods they conceived of were fallen gods. They were gods who lusted and warred and behaved like super sinners.

When Jesus came, God gave back to the human race a perfect man. Luke portrayed Him as a man who, while sinless, was full of love and compassion for sinners. While He was in constant touch with a world of evil, He remained holy. In Luke's Gospel we meet One who was loving and lowly, patient and kind, humble and holy, pure and undefiled. Jesus was very much a part of the human race, yet absolutely without sin.

We can take the lines of the Lord's human personality, project those lines into infinity, and have a perfect concept of God. If we want to know what God is like, we need only look at Jesus. He could say, "He that hath seen me hath seen the Father" (John 14:9).

Paul described Jesus as "the second man" (1 Corinthians 15:47). He is the second man for two reasons: (1) He is the second man because man in sin is not man as God intended man to be; so God calls Adam the first man, and Christ the second man. (2) He is the second man because He is not the last man. He is the last Adam (1 Corinthians 15:45) but not the last man. God intends to populate Heaven with a race of men and women just like Jesus. The Son of God became the Son of man so that the sons of men might become the sons of God. Man was made in the image and likeness of God; Jesus came in the image and likeness of men. Now we can be made anew in the image and likeness of Him: "We shall be like him; for we shall see him as he is" (1 John 3:2). Luke specialized in keeping before us the wondrous sinless humanity of Him who "was made in the likeness of men."

Having completed our review of Philippians 2:5-7 from a different perspective, we see that Paul's fourfold statement regarding the person of Christ captures the essence of the fourfold portrayal of Christ now found in the four Gospels that open the New Testament.

b.   The Passion of Christ (2:8) "Being found in fashion as a man, he humbled himself, and became obedient unto death, even the death of the cross."

What bothered Paul most before he was converted was the cross. Known then as Saul of Tarsus, he could not accept the claims of the church and subjected it to merciless persecution. To him the cross was the most *impossible* thing about Christianity.

Saul did not believe Jesus' claim to be God, but the concept was allowable. After all, the Old Testament idea of the Messiah included deity: "Thy throne, O God, is for ever and ever" (Psalm 45:6). And

Jesus' claim to be the Son of David could be easily verified by consulting the temple records. Even the fact that Jesus died was not the deciding factor for Saul, for Old Testament prophecy foretold the Messiah's death. What seemed most outrageous to Saul was that the One who claimed to be God manifest in flesh should die on a *cross*. The manner of His death is what rendered His claim impossible in Saul's mind.

The life, teachings, and miracles of Jesus were extraordinary, but Scripture said, "Cursed is every one that hangeth on a tree" (Galatians 3:13; Deuteronomy 21:23). The idea that the man who claimed to be Israel's Messiah should die an accursed death—cursed by the law, cursed by God—was not just outrageous; it was blasphemous.

Then one day Saul met the risen Christ—he was blinded by the brightness of His glory. Saul heard His voice and surrendered instantly to His claims. From then on, what had seemed the most impossible thing about Christianity became the most *impressive* thing about Christianity. The converted Paul wrote, "He…became obedient unto death, even the death of the cross." As the old children's hymn puts it:

> For such a cruel death He died,
> He was cast out and crucified;
> Those loving hands that did such good
> They nailed them to a cross of wood.

The horrors of death by crucifixion began with stabbing pain when nails were driven through hands and feet, and a sickening jolt when the cross was hauled upright and dropped into its socket so that the whole weight of the body tore the stab wounds. Then dizziness, cramps, raging thirst, starvation, and sleeplessness all added their torments. Gangrene, tetanus, and fever followed, and the heat of the sun and the torment of flies contributed to the suffering. The unnatural position resulted in cramps, the crushed tendons throbbed, and the arteries swelled. Every movement caused agony and the anguish gradually increased. For a strong man, death might not come for three days. The physical torture alone was terrible, but there was also the public shame of hanging naked and exposed.

For Jesus there was more. This glorious One was mocked by those He had come to save. And worst of all, He who knew no sin was made to be sin for us (2 Corinthians 5:21). At length out of the darkness came the dreadful cry, "My God, my God, why hast thou forsaken me?" (Mark 15:34) Well might we sing A. M. Kelly's hymn:

> Oh, make me understand it,
> Help me to take it in,
> What it meant to Thee, the Holy One,
> To bear away my sin.

Paul, with the Lord from Heaven filling his vision, could not get over Christ's death on the cross. With his Bible open before him, he could grasp some of the meaning of the cross, but the wonder of it was beyond him.

c.   The Position of Christ (2:9-11)

(1) Exalted (2:9-10)

(a) Why Every Knee Will Bow (2:9-10a) "Wherefore God also hath highly exalted him, and given him a name which is above every name: That at the name of Jesus every knee should bow."

We must never leave Jesus on the cross. Some churches, in their zeal to keep before their people the great stoop Christ took and the sufferings He endured, portray Him either as a helpless infant in His mother's arms or as a helpless victim on a cross. But He is no longer in the cradle! He is no longer on the cross! He is seated now in the place of power.

God never leaves Jesus subject to His mother, never leaves Him hanging on the tree. His Word always carries our thoughts up to the throne. God has highly exalted Him. He is the Lord from Heaven. He is God over all, blessed for evermore. The day is coming when every tongue will confess Him and every knee will bow before Him. Calvary was not the end of the story. God has no intention of letting the cross be the last word in the record of the way people treat His Son.

(b) Where Every Knee Will Bow (2:10b-d)

i.   In Heaven (2:10b) "Of things in heaven."

Heaven is the eternal abode of God. First Peter 3:22 tells us that the Lord Jesus "is gone into heaven, and is on the right hand of

God." Heaven is now the place of His presence, the scene of His
activity. It is from Heaven that the Holy Spirit came. And it is the
dwelling place of the angels.

"Of things in heaven" is a translation of *epouranios,* which means
"what pertains to or is in heaven." The word refers to those whose
sphere of activity or existence is above, in contrast to those whose
sphere of activity or existence is here below, on the earth. Thus
epouranios is used to describe Satan's present sphere of activity, the
sphere haunted by principalities and powers. This sphere is referred to in Ephesians as the "heavenly places" (the heavenlies) or
"high places." There the spiritual hosts of wickedness manifest
themselves, and in those same heavenlies we who are born into the
family of God can begin to enter into our possessions in Christ. (See
Ephesians 1:3,20; 2:6; 6:12.)

The Lord Jesus is exalted "far above all heavens" (Ephesians
4:10) and is made "higher than the heavens" (Hebrews 7:26). All
those whose realm is high above the earth will bend the knee to
Him: angels and archangels, cherubim and seraphim, thrones and
dominions—the heavenly host who love and serve Him, worship in
adoration at His feet, wait on His words, and rush to do His bidding.
And all the fallen hosts will bow to Him—those who today are the
dark denizens of the heavenlies: Satan and his angels, demons, evil
spirits, principalities, and powers.

In the Old Testament all Israel's battles and blessings were in
Canaan—a truth so evident in the book of Joshua. In the New Testa-
ment all the church's battles and blessings are in the heavenlies.
Christ rules in the heavenlies even as He rules in Heaven itself
(Hebrews 1:3).

ii.   Down Here (2:10c) "Things in earth."

The masses of mankind today offer Jesus no homage at all.
Millions are enslaved by soul-destroying systems such as communism, humanism, and false religions. In comparison with the
world's population, few own His sway. And all too often, we who
do belong to Him allow our lives to become so cluttered with
temporal things that we scarcely give Him the time of day. But a
change is coming: every man, woman, and child down here on
this planet will own Jesus as Lord; every knee on earth will bow
to Him.

The battle of Armageddon will put an end to armed resistance, and the judgment of the valley of Jehoshaphat will purge the planet of His surviving foes. The Christ-rejecting millions, all branded with the mark of the beast, will bend the knee before Him here on earth before being banished forever from the scene. The millennium will dawn and all men everywhere will gladly worship at His feet in the opening centuries of that golden age. Yet, sadly, so incorrigible is the rebellious nature of the unregenerate heart that as time goes on and millennial conditions become commonplace, many will render Him only "feigned obedience," as the psalmists put it in the original text (Psalm 18:44; 66:3; 81:15). But those who remain stubbornly unregenerate will not dare to display or openly voice their secret dislike of His holiness and His iron rule—not until Satan is released for that "little season" of which the Apocalypse speaks (Revelation 20:3).

iii.   In Hell (2:10d) "Things under the earth."

The dead—the unsaved dead—will be raised, summoned to the great white throne, and made to bow the knee. The founders of the world's false religions will be summoned to that judgment. Those who spawned devilish doctrines, fearful philosophies, and wicked ideologies will be there. Those who dyed the earth with the blood of the innocent will be there. Would-be world rulers, those who sinned with a high hand and on a vast scale, will be there. Those who hated Christ will be there. People whose grubby little lives were tainted by petty, mean, nasty little sins will be there. "The fearful, and unbelieving, and the abominable, and murderers, and whoremongers, and sorcerers, and idolaters, and all liars" (Revelation 21:8) will bow the knee to Him—forever.

Colossians 1:20 speaks of reconciliation of all things unto God—"whether they be things in earth, or things in heaven." But whereas the *reconciliation* embraces all things, the *rule* embraces Hell as well. Here we touch on the ultimate tragedy of the Christ-rejecter. God has given us the right to decide whether or not we will own the Lord Jesus as Savior; but God has given no one the right to decide whether or not he will own Jesus Christ as Lord. Hell will be populated by hosts of lost people who eternally own Him as Lord. The supreme irony and the endless gnawing torment of the lake of fire will be that they could have known Him as both Savior and Lord.

(2) Extolled (2:11)

(a) The Universal Confession (2:11a) "Every tongue should confess that Jesus Christ is Lord."

The word translated "confess" here means "to confess openly"—that is, to confess in the sense of agreeing with someone. The day will come when all created intelligences will have to agree with God that what He has done in exalting His Son to the highest pinnacle of power is right; that what He has done in providing redemption for all mankind through the shed blood of His Son is a marvelous exhibition of His immeasurable wisdom, love, and grace; and that what He has done in executing His wrath on all those who have rebelled against His throne or spurned His grace is an example of proper justice.

(b) The Universal Consequence (2:11b) "To the glory of God the Father."

God does all things for His own glory. This is the one satisfactory and adequate unifying factor in a consistent hermeneutic. In other words, the fact that God does all things for His own glory explains why God does what He does. This fact is the one essential that must underlie our interpretation of the Bible. God's grace and God's government, by themselves or both together, do not really explain all the truths in the Bible about God and His ways; but God's glory does.

God does nothing that detracts from His glory. At times that glory may seem obscured—as the sun is sometimes hidden by clouds—but it is always there. The day is coming when that glory will shine forth in all its brightest rays. God the Father will be seen, in the light of the Lord's person, passion, and position, to be infinitely and eternally worthy of universal and unceasing praise. The glory of the Father will seem to all to be the most obvious fact in the universe and a thunder of praise will ascend to Him from every creature sprung from His almighty hands. Would that it were so even now!

3.   Paul's Application of the Example of Christ (2:12-18)

a.   Transformation in Our Conduct (2:12-13)

(1) Full Surrender (2:12) "Wherefore, my beloved, as ye have always obeyed, not as in my presence only, but now much more in my absence, work out your own salvation with fear and trembling."

With the example of Christ before us, how could we consider anything less than obedience to God's will as acceptable service?

When Paul was in Philippi, the believers, influenced by his uncompromising dedication to the Lord and his unflinching obedience to His will, fell readily into step with him. They too learned obedience; they learned to surrender joyfully to the Father's "good, and acceptable, and perfect, will" (Romans 12:2). Now that Paul was no longer with them, they had to find and follow God's will on their own. It was imperative that they continue to tread the path of obedience, and this they were doing—with fear and trembling.

Paul understood the fear and trembling of the Philippians, for when he first went to Corinth he was "in fear, and in much trembling" (1 Corinthians 2:3). Leaving behind him a trail of flogging, imprisonment, persecution, and mockery in Philippi, Thessalonica, Berea, and Athens, he arrived with the intention of taking the city for Christ. Corinth, not as small as some of the other cities and not a university town like Athens, was a great seaport. It was a prosperous commercial center renowned (like San Francisco and New York) not only for its wealth and sophistication, but also for its sin. Armed only with the power of the gospel, Paul was going to take on Sin City, the Vanity Fair of the ancient world. He was afraid, but not of what man could do to him. Having long since conquered that fear, he could face being "killed all the day long" and "accounted as sheep for the slaughter" (Romans 8:36). He was in fear and trembling lest he let his Lord down by inadequately representing Him in that needy city.

Paul wanted the Philippians to have the same concern. We too should be afraid of letting the Lord down. His love for us is so great that we dare not act or speak or think in a way that would detract from God's glory.

With fear and trembling we are to work out our salvation. Salvation is a gift; it is not earned by any effort of ours; Paul is not contradicting that basic fact of the gospel. But we could liken the gift of salvation to the gift of a gold mine. If someone were to give you a gold mine of incalculable worth, you would have a treasure, but the gold would not do you any practical good unless you worked it out of the mine. Likewise we need to get busy and set to work on our salvation.

Aside from the Bible, the best exposition of the concept of working out one's salvation is found in the story "All Gold Canyon" by Jack London, who spent part of his early life prospecting for gold in Alaska. The story details the labors of a prospector named Bill.

Arriving in the "green heart" of All Gold Canyon, Bill lay down to drink water from the pool. London wrote:

> The sidehill attracted his attention. Still lying on his stomach, he studied the hill formation long and carefully. It was a practiced eye that traveled up the slope to the crumbling canyon wall and back down again to the edge of the pool. He scrambled to his feet and favored the sidehill with a second survey.
>
> "Looks good to me," he concluded, picking up his pick and shovel and gold pan.
>
> He crossed the stream below the pool...dug up a shovelful of dirt and put it into the gold pan.

London went on to describe the painstaking process of panning for gold. If you have read the story you will recall how Bill held the pan in both hands and dipped it in the water. He swirled the water around and around the pan, working the larger and lighter particles of dirt and gravel out and over the edge. At length only fine dirt and small bits of gravel remained. He swirled more carefully, keenly scrutinizing every specimen. When the pan seemed empty of all but water he spilled it out, leaving a residue of black sand on the bottom. There was not much left, just a thin streak, but in the midst of it was a small speck of gold. After a few more careful swirls of water he saw another. He was not finished. With great care he worked the rest of the black sand, a little at a time, to the pan's shallow rim. Watching for further signs of gold, he dribbled the sand carefully out of the pan. At last the final residue of dirt was gone and the prospector took stock of his find: seven specks of gold, not worth keeping but enough to exult over. There was gold in that sidehill.

Bill moved downstream and panned again with the same meticulous care. This time he counted five specks of gold. Farther and farther downstream he went, panning with a jealous eye on his meager gains: five, four, three, two grains of gold. When he garnered but a single speck of gold he stopped, lit a fire, and blackened the inside of his pan. No elusive golden grain would slip by him now. Still moving downstream he panned again—one grain. He tried again and again and again, three times in all, taking shovels of dirt within a foot of one another. Now each panning proved barren. He was going the wrong way.

The prospector returned to where he had commenced his operations and began to pan his way upstream. At first great success crowned his efforts. He garnered a dozen golden grains, then eighteen, twenty, two dozen. Just above the pool he was rewarded with thirty-five specks of gold.

The sun climbed higher in the sky. Still the man labored on, working his way upstream, but now the results were steadily decreasing. Yet the prospector was not discouraged, for he was working according to a plan. When he found no specks at all in several pans, he straightened up and surveyed the hillside with a satisfaction that would have puzzled a greenhorn.

A few feet above his first line of test pans Bill started a second line. The sun moved toward the west and began to slide down toward the horizon. Still the miner labored on. He began a third line of test pans. An observer might have noticed he was crosscutting the hillside line by line as he worked his way up. The center of each line produced the best results; the ends of each line were barren. As he ascended the hill the lines grew shorter. They were growing shorter in a regular way, indicating that somewhere up the slope the last few lines would be very short indeed. The shortest line would actually only be a point. A design like an inverted V was beginning to emerge. The converging sides of this V marked the edge where the pans no longer showed gold. The apex of the inverted V was the prospector's goal.

The work was arduous and getting harder, for each pan of dirt had to be carried down to the water to be washed. But the rewards were becoming greater. As Bill went higher up the hill, the pans yielded more and more specks of gold. They were now worth saving, so he put them in an empty baking-powder can. He toiled on, oblivious to the passing of time. Even the need to take precautions against snoopers slipped out of his mind. As the work progressed, he begrudged the time needed for food and rest.

By the third day the prospector was working a hundred yards uphill from the water. The outline of the inverted V was becoming more pronounced. As the crosscuts decreased in length, the depth of the *V* increased. Now Bill had to dig down thirty inches to find anything. Way back down at the water's edge he had found gold at grass-root level. The higher he went, the deeper the gold dipped into the hill. Soon he was digging down three feet and carrying his dirt an ever greater distance to be panned. Between him and the apex of his inverted *V* remained many more deep holes to be dug. Nor was there any way to know whether or not the gold farther up the hill might not lie even deeper. His back ached, his muscles protested, and the toil was endless. By the fourth day he was sinking his test holes six feet before the pans showed the desired trace of gold. And so the hard work went on. Patience and dedication were needed for working out a gold mine.

At one point Bill tried a short cut. He conjectured where the converging lines of the *V* would meet. He yielded to temptation, abandoned his laborious crosscutting, and climbed to where the apex had to be. He filled a pan and carried it down the hill to wash it. No gold. He climbed to the imagined apex again. He dug deep; he dug shallow. He filled and washed pan after pan without the slightest reward. Finally he rebuked himself for being such a fool, went down the hill, and resumed the crosscutting.

"Slow an' certain, Bill," he told himself. "Short cuts to fortune ain't in your line....Get wise. Slow an' certain."[6]

"Slow an' certain" must be our clue to how to work out our salvation. There are no shortcuts and we should be suspicious of those who think there are. We cannot work *for* our salvation, but we must work *at* it. Our goal is clear. The apex of our inverted *V* is Christlike obedience and a Christlike quality of life.

We must work out this great salvation of ours with fear and trembling because there are enemies—as Bill found out when the coveted prize was within his grasp. In the end he had to fight for what was his, and we can be quite sure we will have to do the same.

(2) Faithful Service (2:13) "It is God which worketh in you both to will and to do of his good pleasure."

God does not expect us to work out this gold mine of salvation on our own, relying on our own resources, opinions, and initiative. God expects nothing of us but failure. He has given us His Holy Spirit to indwell us, fill us, anoint us, and lead us into all truth.

In verse 12 Paul used the word *katergazomai* ("work out") to emphasize our responsibility. This word would be used, for instance, in speaking of a student working out a problem in arithmetic. He carries the problem through the various stages of its solution to its proper conclusion. Salvation has to be worked out to its proper conclusion, not in justification (settled once and for all when we believe) but in sanctification—in learning to live a life that is pleasing to God.

In verse 13 Paul used a different word, *energeō* ("worketh"), which means "to energize or work effectively." *Energeō* has more to do with God's enablement than with our resources.

The words "to will" in verse 13 are a translation of a Greek word meaning "to desire" and thus refer to a desire emanating from the emotions rather than from the intellect. We are "to will and to do." The Holy Spirit plants in the believer's heart the *desire* and the *determination* to bring pleasure to God.

Sanctification involves our cooperation with the Holy Spirit in producing a holy life pleasing to God. The Holy Spirit does not do it all. He provides the desire and the enablement, and we do as He indicates. As we say no to the wrong and yes to the right, He releases the effective working of His power. This cooperation produces a transformation in our conduct that is essential in maintaining a good testimony in the world.

b.   Transformation in Our Character (2:14-16)

(1) A Christ-exemplifying Temperament (2:14) "Do all things without murmurings and disputings."

The word "without" suggests isolation, so Paul was saying that the believer is to be isolated from murmurings and disputings.

Murmuring arises in discontented souls. We can be discontented with our circumstances—someone seems to be getting ahead of us or things aren't working out as we planned—and as a result we murmur. Murmuring is one of the dispositional sins that grieve the Holy Spirit so much. It can easily overtake us, if we are not careful, and become an embittering habit.

The children of Israel almost drove Moses to distraction with their murmuring in the wilderness. They did nothing but criticize and complain. Their murmuring was an exhibition of carnality, the antithesis of the Christlikeness that God was seeking to develop in His people.

The night of redemption was barely over when Israel's murmuring and disputing began. Seeing themselves trapped between pharaoh's storm troops and the Red Sea, the Israelites sarcastically remarked to Moses, "Because there were no graves in Egypt [a reference to the Egyptian national preoccupation with death and the tomb], hast thou taken us away to die in the wilderness?" (Exodus 14:11) They did not know what Moses knew—that the situation had been ordained by God for the complete humiliation and final overthrow of the foe (14:3-4).

The Israelites murmured when they came to Marah and were thirsty (Exodus 15:23-24). They murmured when they came to the wilderness of Sin and were hungry (16:1-3). (Note how Moses rebuked them in 16:7-9 and the Lord responded in 16:12). The Israelites chided with Moses at Rephidim when they were thirsty (17:1-2). And when Moses stayed so long in the mount, they complained and forced Aaron to make them a golden calf (32:1).

Numbers 11:4-6 records how God's people complained about the manna. Even Aaron and Miriam found fault with Moses (12:1-2). Then when the ten spies turned in a negative report about the promised land, the Israelites murmured bitterly (14:1-4) and thereafter sealed for themselves the fate of a continuing wilderness experience. Korah, Dathan, and Abiram disputed with Moses (16:1-4) and when God's judgment fell on them, "all the congregation of the children of Israel murmured against Moses and against Aaron" (16:41). The Israelites complained at Meribah-Kadesh (20:1-5) and drove Moses to the point where he lost his temper and lost his hope of leading them into a better life in Canaan (20:12).

Finally in Numbers 21:5 the Holy Spirit stripped away the veneer and exposed the twin sins of murmuring and disputing for what they were: "The people *spake against God,* and against Moses" (italics added). The Lord sent fiery serpents to chastise the people of Israel for these sins (21:6).

Now the same kind of behavior was breaking out in the church. Murmurings and disputings had arisen before (Acts 6:1) and they were beginning to surface in Philippi. Paul had to nip the problem in the bud, for he wanted his friends to be of a Christ-exemplifying temperament.

(2) A Christ-exalting Testimony (2:15-16)

(a) The Truth Visualized (2:15) "That ye may be blameless and harmless, the sons of God, without rebuke, in the midst of a crooked and perverse nation, among whom ye shine as lights in the world."

We are living in a dark world. All around us are people whose lives are bent and warped by sin. We were once just as bent, just as selfish, and just as crooked as other people, but our lives have been rekindled with light from on high. God has set us in this dark world as lamps. Our lamps shine, for example, when we do all things without murmurings and disputings.

We get along well with others because we are blameless and harmless. The word translated "blameless" here is *amemptos*, which literally means "without reproach." Luke 1:6 uses the word to describe Zacharias and Elisabeth, who were chosen by God in their advancing years to be the parents of John the Baptist. The word translated "harmless" in Philippians 2:15 is *akeraios*. In Romans 16:19 it is translated "simple." There Paul was urging the Romans, who lived in one of the most sinful and sophisticated cities in the world, to be "simple concerning evil." In God's eyes there is no advantage for the Christian in being worldly wise. *Akeraios*, which can also be translated "guileless or sincere," was used by the Greeks in everyday conversation to refer to unalloyed metal or wine unmixed with water. In other words, *akeraios* speaks of the real thing, that which is genuine.

The only reason we can even contemplate living a blameless and harmless life in an environment like ours, is that we have become the sons of God. Since the Son of God lived such a life, we can live such a life. His life was beyond rebuke. The word translated "without rebuke" in Philippians 2:15 is said to be *amōmētos*, which means "without blemish." It is no small order to be called upon to live an unblemished life in a world of sin and shame. The degree to which our testimony for Christ approaches the standard set in Philippians 2:14-15 is the degree to which we have truly learned the principles of living our new life in Christ.

When a non-Christian sees a professing Christian (at work or at home) who is argumentative, hard to get along with, and worldly in his ambitions, conversation, and behavior, the unbeliever soon forms a poor opinion of Christianity. When a non-Christian comes into a congregation of Christians who are quarrelsome, complaining, and motivated by a carnal spirit, the unbeliever is not likely to remain long. Most likely he will say, "I don't see how these people are any different from anyone else."

When Hobab, Moses' brother-in-law, came to visit the children of Israel in the wilderness, he saw a people redeemed by blood, gathered out of the land of Egypt, baptized unto Moses, journeying to the promised land, and gathered around the shekinah glory cloud. Moses said to him, "We are journeying unto the place of which the Lord said, I will give it you: come thou with us, and we will do thee good: for the Lord hath spoken good concerning Israel." Hobab's answer was both sad and sobering. He said, "I will not go" (Numbers 10:29-30). Why did he refuse this invitation to make his decision for Christ and join the ranks of God's redeemed people? Because of the murmurings and disputings of the Israelites. He had seen an alloyed testimony. He could not deny that they had been saved, but he saw nothing in their behavior to commend their lifestyle to him. He had seen better behavior among some of the unsaved. If journeying to the promised land meant keeping company with the children of Israel, Hobab was not interested.

Christians should avoid repeating the sins of the Israelites. We are to show to a lost world that a wonderful change has been wrought in our lives since Jesus came into our hearts. We are to "shine as lights in the world."

(b) The Truth Verbalized (2:16) "Holding forth the word of life; that I may rejoice in the day of Christ, that I have not run in vain, neither laboured in vain."

"Holding forth the word of life" is to be an integral part of our manner of life in this dark world where death lays its blighting hand on all. But the walk comes before the talk. When people see us living the life, they will listen to what we have to say. If our lives are as attractive as that of our Lord, people will be eager to ask what makes us so different from other people. We will soon have opportunity to confess Christ to them.

Paul urged the Philippians to hold forth the word of life in their rough and ready Roman colony. He had his eye on the rapture ("the day of Christ") and the rewards at the judgment seat of Christ. He wanted to be a rejoicing man, thrilled to see his converts winning golden crowns and high praise from the Lord of glory.

On the pragmatic level we can liken Paul to a man who has just been appointed district sales representative for a new firm of perfume manufacturers. His income is to be a percentage of his district's sales. He can try to drum up business by going out to knock on doors and visit the cosmetic departments of stores by himself. But he will be more successful if he convinces a hundred people to go out selling for him. The more they sell, the higher his wages will be.

Paul wanted to be as successful as possible in spreading the gospel. He wanted to persuade people to accept Christ, and he wanted his converts to do the same. And he wanted his converts to teach their converts to spread the gospel. At the judgment seat of Christ their reward would be his reward. Paul's cup of rejoicing would overflow if those he had won to Christ were to hear the Lord say to them, "Well done." Then he would know he had not labored in vain.

Paul was afraid he had indeed labored in vain among the Galatians. They had so succumbed to deadening Judaistic teaching that he wrote to them, "I am afraid of you, lest I have bestowed upon you labour in vain" (Galatians 4:11).

c.   Transformation in Our Concepts (2:17-18)

(1) Paul's Example (2:17) "If I be offered upon the sacrifice and service of your faith, I joy, and rejoice with you all."

Paul saw his beloved Philippian converts as consecrated believers who had presented themselves to God as a living sacrifice (Romans 12:1-2). As a holocaust to God, they were being consumed on the altar of sacrifice and service. Upon that burnt offering he was pouring out, as a libation, the wine of his own life blood, which he anticipated would flow in martyrdom. More than once his blood had already flowed in the persecutions he had suffered for the cause of Christ.

In Old Testament times, when a person brought an animal sacrifice to God, he also brought wine to be poured out as an accompanying libation. The amount of wine depended on the value of the sacrifice. The more impressive sacrifices required greater amounts of wine (Numbers 15:4-12). And since wine is symbolic of joy and exhilaration in the Bible, we could say, "The greater the sacrifice, the greater the joy." The pouring of wine on the Old Testament sacrifice taught the truth that the way of sacrifice is the way of joy. This truth is what Paul was teaching the Philippians.

Remembering the symbolic meaning of wine, we think of the wedding in Cana of Galilee. The wine gave out, but Jesus was there to restore the joy with His "good wine" (John 2:10). We can lose the happiness that is centered in a success, a promotion, or even a marriage, for happiness is a very transient visitor. Happiness depends on what happens. Joy, on the other hand, is a fruit of the Spirit (Galatians 5:22). Since it is centered in the Lord Himself, it remains, come what may.

(2) Paul's Exclamation (2:18) "For the same cause also do ye joy, and rejoice with me."

Paul had a stake in the Philippians and they had a stake in him. They were supporting him, helping to supply his financial needs, and ministering to him in prison. They were to rejoice in him just as he rejoiced in them.

Summing up Philippians 2:1-18, we see the relevance of Paul's pointing to Christ as the supreme example of triumph in sacrifice. What Paul was getting at is clear. In effect he was saying to the Philippians: "Your petty squabbles will soon tear the heart out of your testimony. There needs to be a transformation in your conduct, in your character, and in your concepts. You need a whole new view of the Christian life. You need to keep Calvary in mind. You need to think about Jesus, who is the living secret of holiness. Think about the path He pursued from Heaven's heights, to the cross of shame, and back to the throne of power at God's right hand. Think of His inestimable offering on the altar of sacrifice and service. Think of the libation of His blood. Think about Him 'who for the joy that was set before him endured the cross, despising the shame' (Hebrews 12:2). Look at your lives in the light of His cross. You too should be burning up for God. I myself am likely to be martyred—in any case I am a living martyr, dying daily (1 Corinthians 15:31). When we live in the light of Calvary, how can there be any room for murmurings and disputings?"

B. Timothy: Triumph in Service (2:19-24)

1. An Example of True Service (2:19-20)

a. Timothy's Commission (2:19) "I trust in the Lord Jesus to send Timotheus shortly unto you, that I also may be of good comfort, when I know your state."

Clambering among the mountains, we have been watching the lightning flash from yonder glory where Christ sits at the right hand of God, and we have been listening to the low rumbling thunder of quarrelsome saints in the valley below. Now comes a calm interlude and we feel as if we are standing by a placid lake.

The Bible is full of such variety. After the wars of Joshua and Judges come the pastoral scenes of the book of Ruth. After the questions of the book of Job come the more peaceful introspection and confident intercession of the book of Psalms. After the rules of Proverbs and the gloom of Ecclesiastes come the love and loyalty of the Song of Solomon. Isaiah spreads the pinions of an eagle, and then Jeremiah hovers like a dove. Hosea's weeping is followed by Amos's warning. Ezekiel confronts us with mysteries of the Jewish religion, and Daniel follows with accounts of Gentile rule. The changes of mood, pace, viewpoint, style, circumstance, audience, and goal in the Scriptures help to make Bible study rich and rewarding.

Now we come to an interlude between the dogmatism and pragmatism of Philippians 2:1-18 and the warnings, wonders, and wisdom of Philippians 3–4. We come down from the mount and find ourselves in Paul's Roman prison. We see this ambassador in bonds reviewing the character and credentials of two colleagues he hopes to send as his delegates to Philippi. As he writes about these delegates, he sets before us two more examples of what the Christian life should be.

In Philippians 2:19 he wrote, "I trust in the Lord Jesus to send Timotheus shortly unto you." In other words Paul was saying, "I

105

am hoping to send Timothy to you soon." In the original Greek sentence, the position of the name *Timothy* implies a slight emphasis on the name, as though Paul were saying, "*I* can't come, but *he* is coming."

Timothy was one of the better known of Paul's companions. His mother and grandmother, both model Jewish women, were named in 2 Timothy 1:5. His father was Greek (Acts 16:1) but since he apparently died when Timothy was quite young, the boy was raised by his godly mother and grandmother, who gave him a good working knowledge of the Old Testament Scriptures (2 Timothy 3:15).

Timothy was Paul's child in the faith and seems to have been converted at the time of Paul's first missionary visit to Lystra and Iconium. Paul may have recovered from his stoning at Lystra in the house of Timothy's mother. When Paul chose Timothy to be one of his companions on his second missionary journey, the apostle circumcised him to make him more acceptable to the Jews—Paul always approached the synagogue congregation first when he entered a new town.

Timothy was with Paul at Philippi, Thessalonica, and Berea, but stayed behind at Berea with Silas when Paul went on to Athens. When Timothy joined Paul at Athens, the apostle immediately dispatched him to Thessalonica. Rejoining Paul at Corinth, Timothy brought good news about the young Thessalonian church.

On the third missionary journey he was with Paul during his long stay at Ephesus. Then Paul sent him to Macedonia and Corinth. Since his name appears in the letter Paul wrote to the Romans from Corinth (Romans 16:21), we know that Timothy was with Paul when the apostle returned to Corinth himself. As Paul started out for Asia and Jerusalem via Macedonia, Timothy was one of those who went ahead to wait for the apostle at Troas.

Timothy was with Paul during the time of his first imprisonment in Rome. After Paul's release his various activities and journeys are not clearly chronicled. Timothy seems to have accompanied him to Ephesus. Apparently Paul left him to attend to the needs of the church there (1 Timothy 1:3) while the apostle himself went on to Macedonia and Philippi, Asia Minor (Philemon 22), and probably Spain (Romans 15:24), instead of sending Timothy to Philippi as he had intended (Philippians 2:19-24). The last mention of Timothy comes after Paul's rearrest and rigid detention at Rome: with his execution pending, Paul wrote to Timothy and urged him to come before winter and bring the apostle's cloak and books (2 Timothy 4:13,21).

According to Eusebius, Timothy was the first bishop of Ephesus. According to Nicephorus, Timothy was clubbed to death at a feast of Diana for denouncing the licentiousness.

At the time Paul was writing to the Philippians, Paul was hoping to send Timothy to Philippi so that he could bring the apostle news of his friends there. Many of the Philippians had known Timothy since the time he had come to town with Paul to found their church. Paul could not have chosen a better man or one he loved and trusted more, and he set him before the Philippians as an example of triumph in service. Whether or not Paul actually did send Timothy is largely a matter of conjecture.

b.   Timothy's Commendation (2:20) "I have no man likeminded, who will naturally care for your state."

Men who think like Paul are rare in any age. So are men who share his genuine, painstaking, self-sacrificing care for the spiritual needs of others. Evidently in all of Rome, Paul could not find a single believer whom he could send to Philippi. There may have been some who had the necessary *talents,* but they did not have the necessary *time.* There may have been some who had the time and the talents, but not the *temperament.* But in Timothy Paul found someone who was likeminded. Timothy was spiritually gifted and he was available. His natural way of caring for people enabled him to triumph in service, true service. A true servant is ready, able, and willing.

2.   An Example of Total Service (2:21) "All seek their own, not the things which are Jesus Christ's."

The curse of the local church today is lack of commitment. So few are willing to make an out-and-out commitment to a task. Our churches are full on Sunday mornings and empty the rest of the time. The same faithful few do nearly all the work. It is difficult to find anyone who will make a long-range commitment to do anything, whether it be to teach a Sunday school class, help in the nursery, or do visitation.

Several years ago I heard a veteran missionary talking about his service in Africa—he had gone out as a young man and had stayed there for fifty years. He was also talking about the modern tendency to go on summer crusades or to serve two-year terms. While not necessarily depreciating the value of short-term efforts, he was lamenting the lack of long-term commitment. "Thy servant will go a little way," Barzillai said to David (2 Samuel 19:36). That statement sums up much of the spirit of the age—our age and Paul's.

When Paul wrote Philippians 2:21, he was indicting Laodiceanism—that is, the spirit that wants the best of both worlds, the spirit that says, "Me first." Once a man who was called to be a disciple said, "Suffer *me first* to go and bury my father," and another would-be disciple said, "Let *me first* go bid them farewell, which are at home"; the Lord rebuked them both (Luke 9:59,61, italics added). No one who has this "me first" attitude is equipped to be a true servant of God.

True service is total service. That should be obvious when we remember we are called to handle "the things which are Jesus Christ's." We are called to carry on the work of Him who "took upon him the form of a servant." He went *all* the way. How can we say, "I'll go a *little* way"?

Paul recognized Timothy as a loyal companion, ambassador, and fellow worker. We learn from the Epistles to Timothy, however, that he was intimidated by stronger characters. Paul had to stiffen Timothy's resolve and remind him that he must go all the way in his commitment to Christ (1 Timothy 4:12; 2 Timothy 1:6-8).

3.   An Example of Tested Service (2:22-24)

a.   Why Paul Was Sending Timothy (2:22) "Ye know the proof of him, that, as a son with the father, he hath served with me in the gospel."

When I was a boy my father owned an automobile business in Britain. Over the premises was a sign that read, "Leonard Phillips and Company." In the early days my father hoped that his two sons would one day follow him into the business and he would have to change the sign to "Leonard Phillips and Sons." But that change was never made, for one of us became a pathologist and the other a preacher.

Paul could have put up a sign reading, "The Apostle Paul and Son." Although Paul had great joy when he thought of all the people he knew who were engaged in the Lord's work, he experienced a special personal satisfaction when he thought of Timothy "as a son with the father." In Philippians 2:22 Paul was reminding his Philippian friends of his relationship with Timothy: "as a child with the father so he with me," as some have more tenderly rendered the phrase.

The Philippians would have no trouble remembering Paul's fatherly devotion. No doubt the apostle could easily have avoided the scourging at Philippi if he had announced his Roman status to the lictors. Instead he had kept his mouth shut and taken the punishment and imprisonment like a man. Probably he had feared that if he were to escape the wrath of the mob, its fury would be turned instead against his dear son Timothy.

The Philippians would also remember Timothy's care and concern for his beloved Paul. The younger man was here, there, and everywhere looking out for the interests of Paul and the fledgling church. Indeed when Paul wrote in Philippians 2:22 of Timothy's service, he used the word *douleuō*, which means "to serve as a bondman or to take up the slave's life." Timothy was a veritable bondslave in his devotion to Paul.

Timothy was no raw recruit, no novice at the business of serving the Lord by serving others. "Ye know the proof of him," Paul said. Timothy's service had passed the test.

b.   When Paul Was Sending Timothy (2:23-24)

(1) His Anticipation of Definite News Soon (2:23) "Him therefore I hope to send presently, so soon as I shall see how it will go with me."

A review of Paul's circumstances is in order here. It can be inferred from various comments and references in the Philippian Epistle that a later rather than an earlier date in Paul's first Roman imprisonment must be assigned to this letter. His imprisonment had become more restrictive. He was in the palace (1:13)—the praetorium, the barracks of the praetorian guard—rather than in his own hired house as at first (Acts 28:30). He had been in bonds long enough for the Philippians to have heard of his imprisonment, to have sent Epaphroditus, and to have heard of Epaphroditus's arrival and illness. Paul's bonds had become widely known and had furthered the gospel (Philippians 1:13). The Epistles to the Ephesians, Colossians, and Philemon had already been written. We can form an idea of Paul's circumstances from these inferences, and from secular history.

In the second year of Paul's imprisonment (A.D. 62) important changes took place at Rome. Burrus, the praetorian prefect (the captain of the guard), died. Nero divorced Octavia and married a Jewish proselyte named Poppaea. This unscrupulous woman arranged for the murder of Octavia, showed strong partiality to the Jewish people, and had little sympathy for Christianity. Nero appointed to the position of praetorian prefect the man who had promoted his marriage to Poppaea. This prefect was Tigellinus, a veritable monster of iniquity. So Paul wrote with some doubt, on the human level, about the ultimate outcome of his trial. The trial date was nearer, but the outcome was more uncertain—at least if one looked only at the circumstances.

In the praetorium attached to the palace Paul was kept under closer custody. But God shielded Paul from new dangers that threatened. Pallas, brother of Felix and a favorite of Nero, died, so one source of danger was removed. And Tigellinus ignored Paul's case; no doubt the prefect thought it was beneath his notice.

In the meantime in spite of all the gnawing suspense, Paul maintained his resolute trust in the Lord and continued as much as was possible to get on with the work of God. Since his own case might hang in the balance for a while and since he felt that someone ought to go to Philippi, and go soon, to deal with the squabbles in the church, he proposed to send Timothy.

(2) His Anticipation of Dramatic News Soon (2:24) "I trust in the Lord that I also myself shall come shortly."

Paul could write with such seeming confidence in spite of the drawing in of the net around him, because he walked so close to the Lord. He was not expressing mere human optimism, but a sense of the Lord's increasingly evident will for his life. While on the purely human level the storm clouds were gathering, there were still rifts of blue in the sky. In any case, Paul's eye was on Christ, not Nero. We surmise from the later letters to Timothy that Paul *was* set free for a season, so this final reading of his current circumstances was correct. He had the true discernment of one who kept his focus on the Lord.

Paul had no such bright view of his future when he wrote his second letter to Timothy. Paul wrote that letter during his second imprisonment in Rome when Nero was on the rampage persecuting the church. The apostle knew his martrydom was at hand.

There are other references to Paul's ability to sense the Lord's will. For example in Acts 20–21 he realized that he should go to Jerusalem, and although everyone tried to dissuade him, he refused to be deterred, having already counted the cost (20:22-24; 21:10-14).

When Paul wrote to the Philippians, he seemed to have the same mysterious inner awareness of what was going to happen—only this time the Holy Spirit witnessed to his spirit that all would be well. If we do not have an inner guiding light on the pathway ahead, we do not walk so close to the Lord as Paul walked and we do not cultivate fellowship with the Holy Spirit the way Paul did.

As has been suggested before, it seems that Paul did eventually visit Philippi, possibly instead of sending Timothy.

C. Epaphroditus: Triumph in Sickness (2:25-30)

1. His Ministry (2:25)

a. Sent to the Philippians by Paul (2:25a) "I supposed it necessary to send to you Epaphroditus, my brother, and companion in labour, and fellowsoldier."

Paul had nothing but praise for this otherwise unknown Christian. The apostle began his eulogy by calling him "my brother." Timothy was Paul's son; Epaphroditus was his brother. No one did more than Paul to spread the family spirit throughout the church.

Epaphroditus was not only a brother in the family; he was also a fellow worker in the field. He was not afraid to roll up his sleeves and do a good day's work in the service of the Lord. Moreover he was a fellow soldier in the fight. He was not afraid to take on the enemy. These high words of praise for Epaphroditus came from a man who maintained lofty standards for servants and soldiers of the Lord.

In the brief time Epaphroditus had been with Paul in Rome, he had proved himself diligent and valiant. He was a man after Paul's own heart, but the apostle felt obligated to send him back to Philippi. Probably Epaphroditus was the bearer of Paul's letter to the Philippians.

b. Sent by the Philippians to Paul (2:25b) "Your messenger, and he that ministered to my wants."

Paul chose his words carefully. The word "messenger" usually refers to an apostle or a missionary in the New Testament. The expression "he that ministered" is a translation of *leitourgos*, which means "one who serves in an office, a minister." In the Septuagint that expression is used of the specially consecrated priests and Levites (Exodus 29:30; Numbers 16:9; also see Hebrews 10:11). So Paul's choice of words here shows that he regarded Epaphroditus

113

as a missionary-minister sent by the Philippians to meet his needs. Epaphroditus was no mere agent to deliver their love-gift. He was sent to be a ministrant to Paul, just as Paul had once been God's apostle/minister/missionary to the Philippians.

Paul appreciated not only the gift that was sent, but also the way it was sent—in the hands of a delightful likeminded believer. To acknowledge the thoughtfulness of the Philippians in sending Epaphroditus, Paul chose words associated with the most sacred forms of ministry.

2.   His Malady (2:26-27)

a.   The Selflessness of His Suffering (2:26) "He longed after you all, and was full of heaviness, because that ye had heard that he had been sick."

It is bad enough to be sick; but it is worse to be sick far away from home. Homesickness can set in, and only those who have been in a distant foreign land know how spiritually debilitating homesickness can be.

Adēmoneō, the word translated "full of heaviness" here, means "full of anguish and distress, deeply weighed down or depressed." Elsewhere in the New Testament *adēmoneō* is only used to describe the feelings of the Lord Jesus as He approached the agony of the garden of Gethsemane (Matthew 26:37; Mark 14:33). The Lord was "sorrowful and very heavy." The sorrow that weighed upon the soul of the Savior and prompted Him to urge Peter, James, and John to pray with Him was the kind of sorrow that seized the soul of Epaphroditus.

But what interested Paul was the cause of this depression. Epaphroditus was not depressed because he was sick, away from home, and among strangers. What burdened him was his concern that his family and friends at Philippi would worry about him. In other words his depression was not caused by self-pity, the usual cause of so much of our heaviness of heart, but by an unselfish concern for others. He did not want others to be burdened with his troubles.

b.   The Seriousness of His Sickness (2:27) "Indeed he was sick nigh unto death: but God had mercy on him; and not on him only, but on me also, lest I should have sorrow upon sorrow."

The illness of Epaphroditus was serious; Paul wanted the Philippians to know that it had almost killed him. There is no intimation here, however, that Paul healed him or even considered healing him. Indeed the opposite can be inferred from Paul's relief that the recovery of Epaphroditus spared him from added sorrow. Paul had the gift of healing (Acts 14:8-10; 19:11-12; 28:8-9) but he seems to have used it sparingly.

As the apostolic age drew to a close, the gift of healing seems to have been less and less in evidence. It was one of the transient gifts given to accredit the messengers of the church, primarily in the eyes of the Jewish people, "for the Jews require a sign" (1 Corinthians 1:22).

Epaphroditus recovered from his desperate illness and Paul saw in his restoration to health another token of the mercy of God—His mercy to both Epaphroditus and Paul. Paul was spared the sorrow of losing the fellowship of a man with whom he felt a spiritual kinship. And the apostle escaped the sorrow he would have felt if Epaphroditus had lost his life because of his efforts to minister to him. Moreover Paul did not have to bear the additional grief of knowing that it was the Philippians' kindness to him that had caused them to lose a friend and brother.

3.   His Memory (2:28-30)

a.   What Paul Required of These Believers (2:28-29)

(1) Rejoice (2:28) "I sent him therefore the more carefully, that, when ye see him again, ye may rejoice, and that I may be the less sorrowful."

"I'm going to send you back home," Paul said as soon as it was evident that Epaphroditus was on the road to recovery. The apostle hated to part so soon from a man he had come to appreciate so much, but Paul was a selfless soul. He wanted the Philippians to be able to rejoice over Epaphroditus's homecoming and restored health.

And they would rejoice—not only because Epaphroditus arrived safely, but also because he was bursting with news of Paul. Many long talks with Paul were indelibly engraved on Epaphroditus's memory, and he would want to share Paul's words with his fellow Philippians. When Paul had told a particularly impressive anecdote or expounded a favorite verse of Scripture, Epaphroditus had probably said to himself, "I must remember that and tell it to Lydia, and the jailer, and all the others."

In those long talks Paul would have told Epaphroditus how God had directed him from Troas to Philippi and how Luke had come so dramatically into his life. He would have talked about his experiences at Thessalonica, Berea, Athens, and Corinth, and asked, "Did you get to read my two letters to the Thessalonians?" Reminiscing about Mars Hill, Paul would have exclaimed, "When I quoted their own poets, they mocked!" Paul would have spoken of so many names, dates, places, and experiences that when Epaphroditus finally did go back to Philippi, he must have been a veritable Pauline encyclopedia.

The departure of Epaphroditus would leave a tremendous void in Paul's life. "Thou shalt be missed, because thy seat will be empty," Jonathan had once said to David (1 Samuel 20:18). And many a time Paul would look at the corner in his prison where Epaphroditus had sat and would miss the dear man who was his brother in soul and spirit. But had Epaphroditus died, Paul's loss would have been greater. He would have had "sorrow upon sorrow," but now he would be "less sorrowful."

Paul was never selfish. He loved Epaphroditus and determined to do what was best for him. We can imagine Paul saying, "I can't keep you here, dear friend. Your fever could recur, and that would be fatal. Besides, my own situation is more uncertain than it was before. So you must go home." Paul's determination is captured in his words in Philippians 2:28: "I sent him therefore the more carefully [the more diligently, with more earnestness]."

(2) Receive (2:29a) "Receive him therefore in the Lord with all gladness."

Paul did not have any serious doubts about the kind of reception Epaphroditus would receive. His friends would all be down at the dock at Neapolis to meet the boat. He would be escorted into Philippi as Paul had once been escorted into Rome (Acts 28:15). There would be a reception in Epaphroditus's honor at the church or in Lydia's home. Then hour after hour the Philippians would hang on his words, listen to his story, and ply him with questions.

Paul knew how to rejoice with those who rejoiced (Romans 12:15). He did not want the Philippians to think he would be depressed over the departure of his friend. "In the Lord" they were all one, and "in the Lord" he would be overjoyed with their joy.

Paul knew he belonged to the family of God and all the members of the family belonged to one body. Years ago he had written to the Corinthians:

> God hath tempered the body together...that the members should have the same care one for another. And whether one member suffer, all the members suffer with it; or one member be honoured, all the members rejoice with it. Now ye are the body of Christ, and members in particular (1 Corinthians 12:24-27).

Paul was simply practicing what he preached. He would rejoice with the Philippians. He wanted them to receive Epaphroditus in the spirit of gladness.

(3) Reward (2:29b) "Hold such in reputation."

The word translated "in reputation" here is *entimos*. The word is translated "precious" in 1 Peter 2:4,6 where God's thoughts about His dear Son are contrasted with man's contemptuous thoughts about Him. There Christ is described as "a living stone, disallowed [rejected] indeed of men, but chosen of God, and *precious*.... Wherefore also it is contained in the scripture, Behold, I lay in Sion a chief corner stone, elect, *precious*" (italics added).

Epaphroditus was precious. He had won his spurs in Christ, as far as Paul was concerned. Paul was telling the believers back home to hold Epaphroditus in the same high regard Paul did. Aware that "a prophet is not without honour, save in his own country, and in his own house" (Matthew 13:57), Paul admonished the Philippians, "Hold in high value such men as he is" (Handley Moule's rendering).

b.   What Paul Remembered of This Brother (2:30)

(1) His Commitment (2:30a) "Because for the work of Christ he was nigh unto death, not regarding his life."

Parabouleuomai, the word translated "not regarding" here, means "disregarding." Epaphroditus gave no thought to sparing himself even though his service placed him in peril of death. He was exposed to the disapproving eye of a Nero under the influence of Poppaea. To be associated with Paul at all invited suspicion, and to be known as his confidant spelled danger. But Epaphroditus shrugged his shoulders. He was ready to die if need be.

Epaphroditus was in danger, but the meaning of Philippians 2:29 might be that he scorned giving up his work on account of his sickness. He had come to minister to Paul and a few aches and pains were not going to deter him. Even when he realized he was very ill, he persisted in his service. As Handley Moule's gripping rendering reads, "On account of Christ's work he was at death's very door, playing as it were the gambler with his life."

(2) His Companionship (2:30b) "To supply your lack of service toward me."

Paul was not complaining about a lack of concern for him on the part of the Philippians—that was not his idea at all. Far from it. Such an interpretation of this verse is contrary to the spirit of thankfulness that breathes through the entire letter. Paul was deeply appreciative of all the saints at Philippi had done for him. His joy in their kindness and thoughtful fellowship lacked only one thing: their personal presence. That would have filled his cup full.

This lack had been amply supplied by their messenger Epaphroditus. He had come to render the service the Philippians were unable to give. This was the reason Ephaphroditus was willing to take such chances with his life. He was determined to defy danger and to scorn sickness in order to fulfill his mission to Paul. He would minister to Paul on behalf of the church at Philippi even if it cost him his life.

These then are Paul's triumphant examples: the Lord Jesus, our example in sacrifice; Timothy, our example in service; and Epaphroditus, our example in sickness.

PART III

Paul's Typical Exhortations

Philippians 3:1–4:23

III. PAUL'S TYPICAL EXHORTATIONS (3:1–4:23)

Paul was more than conqueror despite his uncertain circumstances, so he gave a glorious testimony in his letter to his friends in Philippi. And he marveled as he wrote about the Lord Jesus descending from Heaven's heights, conquering death, and returning to the Father's throne on high. But he was coming closer perhaps to where the ordinary Philippian believers lived when he cited the example of Timothy, and closer still when he wrote about Epaphroditus, a man they rubbed shoulders with every day. Reading about one of their own, the ordinary believers would say, "What about us? How can we too live victorious lives? Is there a golden secret?"

Having aroused their interest, Paul proceeded to present his typical exhortations. Paul would not be Paul if he did not make an application of his great themes to the daily lives of his readers. So in Philippians 3:1–4:23 he showed his friends the practical value of proper theology, positive thinking, and perpetual thanksgiving.

A. You Cannot Defraud a Man Who Knows the Power of Proper Theology (3:1-21)

1.   The Christian and His Beliefs (3:1-3)

a.   The Dimensions of the Christian Life (3:1)

(1) Singing Fervently (3:1a) "Finally, my brethren, rejoice in the Lord."

Someone has said that Paul is the prince of all those preachers who, when they say "Finally, brethren," are really indicating the fact that they have now gotten their second wind. He is only halfway through his letter! But we can praise God for what follows; we would be greatly impoverished without it. In the subsequent verses we learn much about Paul and the secret of his victorious life.

Paul struck again the keynote of the Epistle: "Rejoice in the Lord"! We can imagine the reaction in Philippi when this exhortation was read to the congregation. A voice calls out, "Brother Epaphroditus, does Paul rejoice in that prison? Chained to a soldier night and day, he does not have a single moment of privacy, and he is going to have to appear before the caesar soon. Does Paul rejoice or is that line just a pious platitude?"

A booming voice breaks in: "Of course he does! And I'm here because he does, and so are my wife and children. I remember years ago when he and Silas were in our prison. A nice-looking pair they were when they were first handed over to me—they had been thoroughly thrashed by the lictors. I didn't have any sympathy for them at the time. 'It's the inner prison for you, my lads.' That's what I said to them. I forced their legs into the stocks, chained them down, slammed the door, locked them in, and left them in the dark. And do you know what they did? They sang! They sang fervently. Their singing shook me up. Ask my wife. And after the earthquake Paul and Silas were still singing—as though they already had their harps of gold. I saw myself as a sinner and I was saved that very night—and so was my family. I bet Paul is singing now. Come on, Epaphroditus. Tell them."

Epaphroditus tells the congregation how Paul's irrepressible joy is the talk of the imperial guard and a common topic of conversation in caesar's household. "Brothers," he says, "I went to Rome to cheer Paul up, but he cheered *me* up."

Another voice asks, "How can Paul be so happy about being in prison? How can I rejoice when I have such a tyrant for a master? He sold my little girl the other day to a lecherous old camel driver from Parthia. I'll never see her again. Who knows what is happening to her even now? How can I rejoice? I don't rejoice. I weep."

Epaphroditus replies, "Ah, dear brother, go ahead and weep. We all weep with you. But let me read again what Paul wrote: 'Rejoice *in the Lord*.' No matter how dark the day is, the Lord is still the Lord. He is still full of love and compassion, still concerned about us. Come what may, the Lord is still on the throne, still sovereignly in charge. He is still able to make all things work together for good—even for Paul as he faces Nero, and for us as we face heart-rending sorrows. The Lord is still mighty to save, mighty to keep. Let us focus our eyes on the Lord even though they are scalded with tears. He knows all about those tears. He cares! He is still the Lord who loved us enough to die for us. He is still the Lord, high over all."

Paul's exhortation is for us too. If we dwell on our sorrows, we will soon become depressed. If we feed our depression, it will grow until it sours all of life and renders us useless. The Lord taught my wife and me that lesson when one of our children was rebellious, far from home, and getting deeper and deeper into sin. We fasted and prayed. Every hour on the hour we gave ourselves to a round of fervent prayer that God would save that wayward one. And He did! But not until after He had taught us to rejoice *in the Lord,* no matter what.

Read again in 2 Chronicles 20:1-29 the account of that remarkable incident in the history of King Jehoshaphat when the Lord fought against his enemies. His country had been invaded by a powerful eastern coalition, so he proclaimed a fast and led his people in prayer. Verses 21-22 are particularly noteworthy:

> He appointed singers unto the Lord, and that should praise the beauty of holiness, as they went out before the army, and to say, Praise the Lord; for his mercy endureth for ever. And when they began to sing and to praise, the Lord set ambushments against the children of Ammon, Moab, and mount Seir, which were come against Judah; and they were smitten.

The praising man prevails. So let us rejoice in the Lord, in Him who sits on the throne of the universe. He controls all the factors of matter, space, and time, and He will make all things work together for good. How could it be otherwise when He is so good? As the hymn writer put it,

> I'll bless the hand that guided,
> I'll bless the heart that planned,
> When throned where glory dwelleth,
> In Immanuel's land.[1]

(2) Standing Firmly (3:1b) "To write the same things to you, to me indeed is not grievous, but for you it is safe."

This sentence may be a fragment of an ancient Greek poem, probably the work of a comic poet (perhaps Menander) who delighted in neatly turned expressions. To capture the underlying rhythm the sentence can be rendered:

> To write the same things to you
> Is not irksome to me but is safe for you.

Repetition is good pedagogy. Most of us learned the alphabet by repetition. We learned how to count and pronounce words the same way. We learned the multiplication tables by repeating them over and over again until they became so thoroughly embedded in our minds that they were part of our mental makeup. Now we can recall them instantly and without effort.

Paul was glad to repeat the great truths of the faith so that they would become second nature to the Philippians. "Christ only, always, living in me"[2] must be the truth that underlies all else in the conscious and subconscious mind of the child of God.

b.   The Dangers of the Christian Life (3:2) "Beware of dogs, beware of evil workers, beware of the concision."

There are dangers, so beware! Keep your eyes open for deceivers. Paul underlined *the character of the deceiver:* "Beware of dogs." Dogs bark and bite. In the Bible they are always regarded as unclean animals. In Paul's day they roamed in packs, rending, tearing, and devouring. God's people are not dogs, but sheep. Dogs wreak havoc among sheep. We gather from various New Testament Epistles that many deceivers were attacking the flock in the early church.

Paul also underlined *the conduct of the deceiver:* "Beware of evil workers." The false teachers Paul was referring to were up to no good. They were men of fair words and foul conduct. The word translated "evil" in Philippians 3:2 is *kakos,* which means "depraved, bad." Since *kakos* indicates viciousness of disposition and desire, we gather that the badness of these false teachers was inward.

Then Paul underlined *the claims of the deceiver:* "Beware of the concision." *Katatomē,* the word translated "concision," occurs only here in Scripture. The verb form occurs twice in the Septuagint: in Leviticus 21:5, which forbids any kind of heathenish cutting of the flesh; and in 1 Kings 18:28, which records how on mount Carmel the prophets of Baal "cut themselves after their manner with knives and lancets, till the blood gushed out." Paul regarded the Jewish ordinance of circumcision, when demanded of Gentile converts by Jewish zealots, to be no better than a heathenish cutting of the flesh. Circumcision on those terms was simply a mutilation of the body, because as a religious rite circumcision was part of that Old Testament Judaism which had been rendered null and void by the cross of Christ (Colossians 2:11).

c.   The Distinctives of the Christian Life (3:3) "We are the circumcision, which worship God in the spirit, and rejoice in Christ Jesus, and have no confidence in the flesh."

The Jews lost sight of the underlying meaning of circumcision, and the rite—as rituals so often do—degenerated into an end in itself. Circumcision came to symbolize being a Jew as opposed to being a Gentile. But true circumcision is of the heart.

The Old Testament act of circumcision was very painful and was normally administered when a boy was eight days old. Adult male converts to Judaism had to submit to the rite to be brought into the good of the Abrahamic covenant. This rite, symbolic of the Abrahamic covenant, was endorsed by the Mosaic covenant. Now we Christians come into the good of the *new* covenant. What circumcision did symbolically for the Jews, the cross does for us.

In the Old Testament type the knife was applied to the instrument of a man's creative power. Circumcision was a symbolic acknowledgment of the total inability of the flesh to produce spiritual seed or fruit for God. In the New Testament the symbolic rite is abolished. Under the new covenant we are circumcised, not in the cutting of the body with a knife, but in the death of Christ as the cutting edge of the cross is brought to bear upon our hearts. The "flesh" (Romans 7:18) is cut off—put in the place of death— so that our new life in Christ can produce spiritual seed and true fruit for God.

Paul had understood this truth for a long time, and his spirit was provoked when Jews in general and Jewish Christians in particular went around insisting that Gentile converts to Christ be forced to endure circumcision in order to become full citizens in the king- dom of God. Evidently these Judaizing false teachers had come to Philippi, so in his letter he reminded his friends that "we are the circumcision, which worship God in the spirit, and rejoice in Christ Jesus, and have no confidence in the flesh."

These false teachers dogged Paul's footsteps everywhere he went. He called them "dogs"—the term of contempt and scorn the Jews themselves reserved for uncircumcised Gentiles—and he used the word with the Holy Spirit's full approval.

The fallacy of having confidence in the flesh is exposed in the next section of Paul's letter. In Philippians 3:4-14 he embarked on one of those fascinating autobiographical passages that tell us so much about himself and at the same time so much about ourselves.

2.   The Christian and His Behavior (3:4-14)

a.   Paul's Past Glory (3:4-6)

(1) What Once He Had (3:4) "I might also have confidence in the flesh. If any other man thinketh that he hath whereof he might trust in the flesh, I more."

Paul took on the Judaizers on their own ground: their religiousness, which they mistook for righteousness. There was a time when Paul was more religious than any of them, more "Jewish" than them all. His attack on their confidence in the flesh was not merely academic. He had once been where they still were, sat where they still sat, thought as they still thought, done what they still did. But then he met Christ. One glimpse of the Lord from Heaven was all it took to strip mere religion away from his soul forever. The moment he encountered Christ on the Damascus road he realized what he had been doing and where his religious zeal had brought him. The Lord's words, "Saul, Saul, why persecutest thou me?" (Acts 9:4), stabbed his very soul. He discovered that everything in which he had trusted was not only worthless; it was also wicked because it made him an enemy of the Lord Jesus.

(2) What Once He Hailed (3:5-6)

(a) His Status as a Pure Jew (3:5a-b)

i.   He Was a Jew by Religion (3:5a) "Circumcised the eighth day."

When Paul was a baby, too small to have any say in what went on, a religious rite had been administered to him. Although the circumcision was done not by him, but for him, the rite made him, under the terms of the Abrahamic covenant, an accepted member of the Hebrew religious community.

Some people believe that infant baptism similarly brings a child into the good of the new covenant. The notion is erroneous and has led millions who have never been converted to believe themselves to be Christians. This Romish error, carried over into Protestantism by reformers who failed to distinguish between Judaism and Christianity, is supported by covenant theology, which portrays the church as spiritual Israel. Many portions of the Old Testament have to be allegorized and spiritualized to make this false premise sound reasonable.

If we interpret the Scriptures literally, culturally, and grammatically, we will quickly see the fallacy in making the church an extension of Israel and the fallacy in comparing Jewish circumcision with Christian baptism. The church is not Israel. An elementary principle of interpreting the Bible is that we must make a difference where God makes a difference.

Israel's destiny is plainly forecast in the Bible. As a prelude to end-time events, many Jews are to return in unbelief to their ancient homeland. They will suffer great tribulation at the hand of the beast, and a remnant will be rescued by Christ at His return to fight the battle of Armageddon. The Jewish survivors of the coming holocaust will be converted and will administer the millennial kingdom under Christ. Today when individual Jews accept Christ as personal Savior, they (like anyone else) become Christians and are added by the Holy Spirit to the church. (See Romans 9–11.)

The church is an entirely separate entity in the purposes of God. It was supernaturally injected into history on the day of Pentecost, and when its numbers are complete and its work is finished, the church will be supernaturally ejected out of history at the rapture. The origin, purpose, ministry, mystery, and destination of the church are all quite different from Israel's.

Christian baptism is never presented in the New Testament as an initiatory rite; neither do we read of its being administered to infants. Baptism is for believers, not for babies. The blood of Christ, not the water of baptism, joins us to the new covenant. An instrument of public confession rather than personal conversion, baptism is the outward expression of an inward experience. It is "the answer of a good conscience toward God" (1 Peter 3:21). Baptism is different from circumcision in purpose, form, and significance, and no more dangerous error could exist than to confuse or equate the two.

But for the purposes of his exposure of the Judaizers, Paul boasted of the fact that he was circumcised on the eighth day as was required by God (Genesis 17:10-14).

ii.   He Was a Jew by Race (3:5b) "Of the stock of Israel, of the tribe
      of Benjamin, an Hebrew of the Hebrews."

Paul could also make national, tribal, and parental claims as he
presented his credentials. First he stated *the national claim:* "[I am]
of the stock of Israel." He was born into a nation chosen and set
apart by God. No nation except Israel has ever had a treaty relationship with God (Romans 9:4-5). It was as great a privilege for Saul of
Tarsus to be born into a Jewish home as it is for a person today to
be born into a Christian home. The Jewish nation had many spiritual advantages that other nations did not have. Those advantages
have often been clouded by apostasy, apathy, and erroneous rabbinical exegesis, but the advantages have always been there. All of
history attests to the fact that God has a unique relationship with the
Jewish people and in a special way has kept His hand on their
nation.

Next Paul stated *the tribal claim:* "[I am] of the tribe of Benjamin."
The tribe of Benjamin had given Israel its first king, Saul. Just as that
illustrious Benjamite had persecuted David, so Saul of Tarsus had
persecuted David's greater Son. But unlike the Old Testament
Saul, the New Testament Saul ended up crowning Him Lord of his
life. The tribe to which both Sauls belonged remained true to the
throne of David at the time of the division of the Hebrew kingdom.
On the purely human level Paul was proud of being a Benjamite
since the name of that tribe appeared with honor on many a page
of Scripture. Doubtless as a boy he had pored over all the references
to Benjamin in his Bible; it was better to be a Benjamite than a
Danite or a Reubenite.

Then Paul stated *the parental claim:* "[I am] an Hebrew of the
Hebrews." The phrase in the original language can be translated,
"a Hebrew of Hebrews." In other words, both Paul's parents were
Hebrews. We would like to know more about them, especially as
there are hints that he was disinherited when he became a Christian. Be that as it may, these parents certainly saw to it that young
Saul was thoroughly grounded in the Scriptures. Their pride must
have been great when they saw the early signs of his genius, and
their satisfaction complete when he went off to Jerusalem to study
theology at the feet of the renowned rabbi Gamaliel. Paul's parents
successfully held their vigorous and strong-minded son against the
pull and tug of the Gentile world that surrounded him at Tarsus. A

lad with a mind and heart like his would have been fascinated by that world, but he was "a Hebrew of Hebrews."

If the King James wording is more accurate—"an Hebrew of the Hebrews"—Paul must have been saying that on the human level he could boast about his Jewishness. Just as we sometimes speak of a convert to Romanism being "more Catholic than the pope," Paul was "an Hebrew of the Hebrews," outstripping his colleagues and contemporaries in zeal and enthusiasm for things Jewish.

(b) His Stature as a Practicing Jew (3:5c-6) "As touching the law, a Pharisee; Concerning zeal, persecuting the church; touching the righteousness which is in the law, blameless."

Paul had been *a fundamentalist Jew:* "As touching the law, a Pharisee." The Pharisees were the avowed enemies of Christ in the Gospels, just as the Sadducees were the avowed foes of the church in the book of Acts. But at least the Pharisees believed the Bible— that is, they believed the Bible as interpreted (or rather misinterpreted) by their rabbis. In their zeal the rabbis added their interpretations and traditions to the Scriptures. (The Talmud began to emerge as these oral teachings were written down. By the time the Talmud was finished, it virtually replaced, to all practical purposes, the Torah.) The rabbinic traditions were a source of controversy between the Pharisees and Jesus. He set those traditions aside, repudiated their method of adding to the Scriptures, and called them hypocrites and a generation of vipers.

Raised as a Pharisee, Paul was trained to observe all the encrusted traditions. He learned to venerate the sabbath, fast, make long prayers, and tithe. He was taught all the shibboleths so dearly treasured by his sect—"the most straitest sect of our religion," as he described it in Acts 26:5.

Paul had also been *a fanatical Jew:* "Concerning zeal, persecuting the church." He had been "exceedingly mad" against the Christians (Acts 26:11). The Holy Spirit's comment is that Saul "made havock of the church" (8:3). The word translated "made havock of" is *lumainomai,* which conjures up pictures of a boar tearing up tender saplings to get at their roots. Saul went on a self-appointed though Sanhedrin-sanctioned mission to root out the church in Damascus. But on the way he met the Lord from Heaven and was soundly saved.

Moreover Paul had been *a fastidious Jew:* "Touching the right-eousness which is in the law, blameless." Not sinless, but blameless. He had in all good conscience sought to live up to a standard of behavior that God could accept. He had made a sincere effort to keep God's law. He had tried to do his best even though that best was never good enough.

Such was Paul's past glory. If anyone could have gloried in his religion, it was Paul. He had once thought himself to be the chief of saints, but when he saw the Son of God, he realized he was the chief of sinners.

b.   Paul's Present Gains (3:7-11)

(1) What He Discounted (3:7-8)

(a) He Wrote Off All His Human Religion (3:7) "What things were gain to me, those I counted loss for Christ."

Paul was looking at his religious balance sheet and counting up his gains. He spread out his bags of gold—seven in verses 5-6. The Judaizers would have been delighted with every one of them. He picked them up and put them on the scales and then he looked at Christ. He could have one or the other: his carefully accumulated gains as a religious man or Christ. He could not have both. As on the Damascus road, so now as an experienced Christian, he did not hesitate a moment. He picked up his once-treasured gains and threw them away as so much trash.

The word translated "gain" in Philippians 3:7 is *kerdos*, the same word used in 1:21—"to die is gain." The word translated "loss" in 3:7-8 is *zēmia*. The only other place *zēmia* occurs in Scripture is in Luke's record of Paul's shipwreck. When the captain and the centurion were debating about whether they should set sail from the Fair Havens anchorage, Paul warned, "Sirs, I perceive that this voyage will be with hurt and much damage *[zēmia]*" (Acts 27:10). When the storm was driving the ship headlong to disaster, Paul said, "Sirs, ye should have hearkened unto me, and not have loosed from Crete, and to have gained *[kerdainō,* akin to *kerdos]* this harm and loss *[zēmia]*" (27:21)—an ironic statement if there ever was one.

Paul used the same irony to describe his gains and losses as a religious man. All he had gained was loss. What he had con-sidered assets turned out to be liabilities. *Kerdos* is actually plural in Philippians 3:7 and *zēmia* is in the singular, indicating that Paul's one big debit consumed all his fancied credits. Since his one liability consumed his assets, he would have been left spiritually bankrupt if he had not gained Christ. Having Him changed the picture. Gladly Paul wrote off all his human religion for Christ.

(b) He Wrote Off All His Human Resources (3:8) "I count all things but loss for the excellency of the knowledge of Christ Jesus my Lord: for whom I have suffered the loss of all things, and do count them but dung, that I may win Christ."

Paul had given up everything for Christ: his home in Tarsus, his parents, all hope of a settled home life. He had given up his Jewish religion and his ambition to climb the ladder to the top so he could rule the Sanhedrin. He had given up his health to hardships, floggings, perils, and shipwrecks. He had given up the smile and favor of the Jerusalem church to minister to the Gentile world. He had given up his freedom and now he had just given up Epaphroditus. One day the apostle would even give up his life on the altar of Nero's hate.

But Paul gladly counted all things loss in order to know Christ. The apostle would allow nothing to come between him and his visions—the one on the Damascus road and another after his arrest in Jerusalem (Acts 23:11). Paul was prepared to write off as "dung," as worthless refuse, anything that might interpose itself between his soul and the Savior.

If we were able to ask Paul if he ever felt the loss of the things he gave up, he would look at us in astonishment and say: "Loss? Of trash? What loss? I have seen Christ face to face, bright as the morning, fairer than the day, lovely beyond all loveliness. I have looked into His eyes and that is all I ever see. I have heard His voice and that is all I ever hear. It rings like the sweetest music in my soul. I love Him with all my heart and with all my soul and with all my strength. I live only for Him. In the strength of the heavenly vision I live on and on, anticipating the day when I shall see that face and hear that voice again. All I want is to win Christ, to hear Him say, 'Well done, Paul!'"

No other call to consecration can compare with Philippians 3:8. Oh, that we might see Christ as Paul saw Him! This world would lose all its power to attract us or distract us. We would say what Paul had already said to his Philippian friends: "For to me to live is Christ, and to die is gain" (1:21).

(2) What He Desired (3:9-11)

(a) A Complete Appreciation of Salvation Truth (3:9)

i.   A Position to Enjoy (3:9a) "And be found in him."

Salvation is largely a matter of one's position. The unsaved man is without Christ, without God, without hope (Ephesians 2:12). The saved man is "found in him."

Years ago Dr. R. A. Torrey, the first president of Moody Bible Institute, was talking with a man about the need for him to be regenerated, to be born again. The gist of that conversation follows.

The man raised an objection: "I know some people," he said, "who make no pretense of being Christians, but live fine upright lives; they are kind and generous and exemplary. I also know people who say they are Christians, but live less exemplary lives."

Dr. Torrey replied, "It's all a matter of what state you are in." Then he drew two rectangles in the dust on the floor and pointing to one he said: "This rectangle represents the state of unregeneracy. Let's liken it to the state of Colorado. In the state of Colorado one man might live up here at 14,110 feet on Pike's Peak, another man might live down here at sea level, and another man might be down here working thousands of feet below the surface in a mine. But all three men are in the state of Colorado. Just so with the state of unregeneracy. One person might live on the mountains of morality, another might live a very ordinary kind of life, and yet another might live down in the darkness and dirt of a vile and wicked life; but they are all in the state of unregeneracy. We are all born in that state."

Dr. Torrey pointed to the other rectangle and continued: "This is the state of regeneracy. You get out of the state of unregeneracy and into the state of regeneracy by being born again. In the state of regeneracy one person might live on a very high spiritual plane, another might live a very average Christian life, and another might be backslidden and live a carnal worldly life. He might even fall into serious sin, but he is still in the state of regeneracy. Indeed his outward life might compare very unfavorably with the life of the man living on the mountains of morality in the state of unregeneracy. But one man is in a state of regeneracy and the other is not.

"The moral man living in a state of unregeneracy is devoid of spiritual life and is lost, no matter how moral he is. The backslider living in a state of regeneracy has spiritual life, even though for the time being it is not at all evident, and he will be saved in spite of his poor showing as a Christian. It all depends on which state you are in. If you are not born again, you can be. You can pass from a state of unregeneracy to a state of regeneracy by accepting Christ as your Savior."

To be found in Him is salvation truth; to have Christ found in us is sanctification truth. To be found in Him means that when God looks at me He sees Christ; to have Christ found in me means that when other people look at me they see Christ. To be found in Christ is an unassailable position.

ii.   A Possession to Enjoy (3:9b-c)

a.   Discarding a False Righteousness (3:9b) "Not having mine own righteousness, which is of the law."

Paul had once worked very hard to live up to a standard of behavior that God could accept. He had taken pride in his achievements. We can imagine him, before his conversion, naming the commandments one by one and evaluating his performance.

"'Thou shalt have no other gods before me.' Yes, I have kept that commandment. I have never turned aside to a false god. I have worshiped Elohim-Jehovah ever since I was old enough to know His name.

"'Thou shalt not make unto thee any graven image....Thou shalt not bow down thyself to them, nor serve them.' Yes, I have honored that demand of the law. I have never been involved in idolatry. As a boy in Tarsus, a pagan city where many idols were to be seen, I learned the abysmal folly of worshiping graven images.

"'Thou shalt not take the name of the Lord thy God in vain.' I have never done that! I have considered the name of God to be the ineffable name, a name to be revered. Never ever have I spoken that blessed name lightly, flippantly, or vainly.

"'Remember the sabbath day, to keep it holy.' I have kept the sabbath and kept it well. I have not worked on the sabbath day. I have studied the minute details the rabbis have added to sabbath-keeping. I approve of them and have sought to observe them.

"'Honour thy father and thy mother.' I have done that. My

parents have always reigned in my affections and I have sought to please, obey, and honor them at all times.

"'Thou shalt not kill. Thou shalt not commit adultery. Thou shalt not steal. Thou shalt not bear false witness.' All these I have kept from my youth up (see Luke 18:21). Nobody could accuse me of breaking these laws."

So far, so good. Paul sees he has kept the letter of the law. He thinks his efforts to build a judgment-proof righteousness have been successful. It is too bad there are not just nine commandments, for when he comes to number ten he runs into trouble.

"'Thou shalt not covet [thou shalt have no evil desire].'" At the end of his evaluation he has to make a sad confession: "I had not known sin, but by the law: for I had not known lust, except the law had said, Thou shalt not covet. But sin, taking occasion by the commandment, wrought in me all manner of concupiscence [lust]. For without the law sin was dead. For I was alive without the law once: but when the commandment came, sin revived, and I died. And the commandment, which was ordained to life, I found to be unto death. For sin, taking occasion by the commandment, deceived me, and by it slew me" (Romans 7:7-11).

When he wrote to the Romans, Paul looked back on his preconversion days. He showed how his supposedly judgment-proof righteousness had been breached. The *Titanic* of his own ability to sail triumphantly to Heaven by his own efforts struck the iceberg of the tenth commandment. An enormous gash was made in his "righteousness, which is of the law." The seas of sin came surging in and he was sunk. One gash was all it took to breach his self-confidence and leave him a sinner bereft of all hope in the law.

So Paul discarded a false righteousness. When he met Christ and understood the significance of those nailprints in His hands and the meaning of the cross, he realized there was a better way to achieve a perfect standing before God.

b.   Discovering a Flawless Righteousness (3:9c) "But that which is through the faith of Christ, the righteousness which is of God by faith."

The secret to a flawless righteousness is Christ. The Lord Jesus, by the life that He lived, produced a genuine righteousness, "the righteousness which is of God." He kept all the commandments. No lurking law leapt out of ambush to slay Him. Further, He kept the laws of God not only in the letter but also in the spirit—as expounded by Himself in the sermon on the mount. From the moment He first drew breath until the moment He said, "Father, into thy hands I commend my spirit," he did always those things that pleased the Father (Luke 23:46; also see John 8:29).

Then He laid down that sinless life as an atonement for our sin—to cancel the debt we had accumulated by our failure to produce behavior that God could accept. But that was not the end! He rose from the dead, He lives forever in the power of an endless life, and by His Holy Spirit He regenerates us and comes to live in us. As He once gave His life *for* us, He now gives His life *to* us so that we can stand before God, not in the tattered rags of our own righteousness but in the seamless robe of His righteousness.

(b) A Complete Appropriation of Sanctification Truth (3:10-11)

i.   The Personal Gain (3:10a) "That I may know him."

A consideration of salvation truth leads to a consideration of sanctification truth. Here we have the secret of a holy life: "That I may know him." No one can live a holy life without utter dedication to the life-purpose of knowing Christ.

People have lived with single-minded devotion to much lesser goals. For instance, Eliezer Ben Yehuda dedicated himself to the goal of reviving the Hebrew language; Sir Edmund Hillary devoted himself to pressing up steep and treacherous slopes to stand atop mount Everest; Christopher Columbus set his face like flint to sail westward, in spite of the threat of mutiny, to find a new world. Hundreds of other mariners had sailed westward, but none of them held on so obstinately or so long as Columbus. These verses from Joaquin Miller's poem capture the persistence of the man:

> Behind him lay the gray Azores,
> Behind the Gates of Hercules;
> Before him not the ghost of shores,
> Before him only shoreless seas.
> The good mate said: "Now must we pray,
> For lo! the very stars are gone.
> Brave Admiral, speak, what shall I say?"
> "Why, say 'Sail on! sail on! and on!'"

. . . .

> They sailed and sailed, as winds might blow,
> Until at last the blanched mate said:
> "Why, now not even God would know
> Should I and all my men fall dead.
> These very winds forget their way,
> For God from these dread seas is gone.
> Now speak, brave Admiral, speak and say"—
> He said: "Sail on! sail on! and on!"

What was the difference between Columbus and his crew? In times of testing they were ready to give up; he intended to see the voyage through to the destination.

Paul's goal, his master passion, was Christ. Paul had met Him and now he wanted to know Him. There is all the difference in the world between meeting someone and knowing someone. I have met thousands of people in the course of my ministry over the years. Some I have forgotten almost instantly; some I have come to know; a few I have come to know well.

I always have trouble remembering individuals I have met before, especially if our first meeting was long ago in a different setting. People will come up to me after a service and say, "Do you remember me?" It is most embarrassing. Sometime I hedge; sometimes I guess. Sometimes I simply say no and a momentary reaction of shock often follows.

My wife remembers better than I do, probably because she is more people-oriented. She studies people, asks them questions, and makes a determined effort to remember names, faces, and facts about children, grandchildren, employment, hobbies, and major and minor operations. It is amazing how often people confide in her and tell her about their aches and pains; they give her what I call "an organ recital." My mind, sad to say, is often miles away while they are giving her all these vital statistics.

If in the course of my ministry we return to a place we have been before and I notice a person who looks vaguely familiar, I'll whisper to my wife, "Who's that woman in the yellow dress?" My wife will answer, "That's Mrs. Mary Jones. You ought to know her. We stayed with her and Bill the last time we were here."

However some of the most unlikely people make an impression on me. I'll recall them instantly even after many years, perhaps because of a gesture or a voice inflection.

To know someone requires genuine interest. Getting to know a person well involves spending quality time with him. In a meaningful and progressive relationship, each person reveals himself—his likes and dislikes, his hopes and fears, his ambitions and history, his thoughts and feelings. Building an intimate relationship is not the work of a day or two; a lifetime association is involved.

Paul wanted to know Christ. Knowing Him was his main goal in life. What a wondrous goal it was! Paul wanted to know the One who created the stars; the One who controls the universe; the One who knows all there is to know about space technology, nuclear physics, biochemistry, and electronics; the One who has lived down here, experienced life to the full, and tasted its joys, sorrows, possibilities, and pains; the One who fully understands, loves and cares, encourages and forgives; the One who is good, patient, kind, and helpful. To know Him is life eternal (John 17:3).

Surely for us too there could be no greater goal in all the world, no greater joy in all eternity than to know Christ. To know Him we must spend time with Him, listen to Him, respond to Him, and talk to Him. As we do, our love for Him will grow and we will begin to be like Him. We will begin to think as He thinks, act as He acts, and say what He says. Then at last the day will break, the shadows will flee away, and we will see Him face to face. We will be with Him and like Him for all eternity.

"That I may know him." In considering this statement of Paul's consuming ambition, we have emphasized the word "know" and then the word "him." Now let each of us emphasize the word "I" and say, "May Paul's goal henceforth be my goal."

ii.   The Progressive Gain (3:10b-d) "And the power of his resurrection, and the fellowship of his sufferings, being made conformable unto his death."

The first result of knowing Him will be knowing something of *Christ's resurrection power.* We think of the effect resurrection power had on Peter and Thomas.

Before Jesus went to Gethsemane, Simon Peter in his self-confidence assured the Lord that no matter how many others denied Him, he never would. That boastful pride suffered a speedy fall when Peter, warming his hands at the world's fire, faced the challenge of a serving maid. He failed the test and was crushed and overwhelmed by his denial. With the Lord's last look haunting his soul, Peter went out and wept bitterly. One wonders where he went; perhaps he went to Gethsemane.

Then Peter entered into a knowledge of "the power of his resurrection." The risen Lord met him, but what happened at that interview is a well-kept secret. The Holy Spirit quietly drew the curtain over that scene, but let us see the later scene when Peter and the others were at the lakeside (John 21). Every detail is significant. The fire of coals, the Lord's use of the old name Simon, and the threefold question recalled Peter's failure. Jesus asked, "Simon, son of Jonas, lovest thou me?" With that question the Lord rekindled Peter's fervor. Then Jesus gave some instructions: "Feed my sheep....Follow me." With those commands the Lord reshaped Peter's future.

Peter never forgot that scene by the lakeside (compare John 21:18-19 with 2 Peter 1:14). The memory of the occasion gave him the power to face martyrdom. The source of Peter's power was Christ's resurrection. Peter had the confident assurance that Jesus was really and truly alive.

Before Thomas saw the risen Christ, he was plunged into the depression of unbelief by the tragedy of the crucifixion. He was so depressed that when the other disciples gathered in the upper room, he stayed away. Then when the other disciples told him they had seen the Lord, he stubbornly refused to accept their united word—but he made sure he missed no more meetings. Thomas was with the disciples the next time the Lord suddenly appeared. The Lord's greeting to Thomas proved that He had heard the disciple's doubting words. Jesus said, "Reach hither thy finger, and behold my hands; and reach hither thy hand, and thrust it into my side: and be not faithless, but believing" (John 20:27). Skepticism was immediately transformed into faith. In a moment Thomas was at the feet of Jesus. "My Lord and my God," he said (20:28)—in one breath putting Jesus on the throne of his heart and on the throne of the universe. The power of Christ's resurrection transformed Thomas.

The knowledge that Jesus is alive and that He has conquered the grave once and for all will make anyone a new person. Christ's death cancels the penalty of sin, and the power of His resurrection cancels the power of sin.

The second result of knowing Him will be knowing something of *Christ's rejected position.* "The fellowship of his sufferings" will make us willing to face the sneers and snubs of the world.

Jesus had to face the animosity of His family. His brothers did not believe in Him and on one occasion they wanted to restrain Him forcibly. They said He was beside Himself, a polite way of saying He was out of His mind. Jesus also had to face the alienation of His followers. After His teaching on the bread of life, many of His disciples left Him (John 6:66). As the pressure began to build against Him, more and more turned away. In the end "they all forsook him, and fled" (Mark 14:50). Then too Jesus had to face the accusation of His foes. They slandered His birth, charged Him with being in league with Satan, twisted His words, and hired false witnesses against Him.

"He is despised and rejected of men; a man of sorrows, and acquainted with grief" (Isaiah 53:3). Such were His sufferings and we can share in them. His rejected position will be ours if we identify ourselves with Him. But animosity of family, alienation from friends, and accusations of foes will only drive us closer to Him.

The third result of knowing Him will be knowing something of *Christ's redemptive passion.* We will be "made conformable unto his death." The heart of the Lord Jesus yearns over a lost world, a world for which He died. If we get to know Him and learn to lean on His breast as John did, we will know something of the beating of His heart for sinful men. We, like Paul, will find our attitude toward sinners conforming to His. With Christlike passion Paul wept and told God he would be willing to go to Hell if his going there could lead to the conversion of the Jewish people. In Romans 9:1-3 he wrote: "I say the truth in Christ, I lie not, my conscience also bearing me witness in the Holy Ghost, That I have great heaviness and continual sorrow in my heart. For I could wish that myself were accursed from Christ for my brethren, my kinsmen according to the flesh."

How unlike Christ we are! How little we know Him! Many of us have boys, girls, moms, dads, and close friends outside of Christ. We may briefly mention their names in our prayers. But where are the passion, the agony, the total sacrifice of pleasure, creature comfort, time, and sleep as we fast and pray for their salvation? Where are the "strong crying and tears" (Hebrews 5:7), the poured-out anguish, and the pains of Calvary? No wonder our loved ones go on day after day in their sins. Christ died for them, went to the cross for them, was made conformable to death for them. If we knew Him and were made conformable to His death, we would not rest, we would count no sacrifice too great, we would become partakers of His passion until they forsake their heedless ways and come to know Him too.

iii.   The Prospective Gain (3:11) "If by any means I might attain unto the resurrection of the dead."

In the New Testament the usual term translated "resurrection of the dead" is *anastasis nekrōn,* which refers to both the resurrection to life of the saved and the resurrection to judgment of the lost. Here, however, Paul added the preposition *ek* as a prefix to *anastasis,* forming the word *exanastasis.* The preposition *ek* means "out from." A circle with a line coming out from deep within it illustrates the significance of *ek.* A circle with a line coming away from the circumference would illustrate the significance of the dissimilar preposition *apo,* which means "away from" rather than "out from." The literal meaning of *exanastasis* is "out-resurrection"—that is, a resurrection out from the dead as distinguished from a resurrection of the dead. Since Philippians 3:11 is the only place Paul used *exanastasis* and since the context does not specifically elaborate on the meaning of the verse, we can do little more than surmise his reason for choosing the word.

Paul had no doubt whatsoever that he was going to be included in the general resurrection of the saved. He wrote at some length about that resurrection in 1 Thessalonians 4:15–5:11 and 1 Corinthians 15:35-58. Why then did he have any doubts about attaining the "out-resurrection"? What did he mean by "out-resurrection"?

Possibly Paul envisioned a group of people who will have a special position in the resurrection of the dead. This privileged group will be taken "out from" all the others rising from the dead. Those who are set apart will have attained a place of status. As we would say today, they will have "arrived."

The Greek word translated "attain" in Philippians 3:11 is *katantaō.* The same word is found in Acts 16:1 where Luke said of Paul, "Then *came* he to Derbe and Lystra" (italics added). In other words, Paul arrived at Derbe and Lystra. When Paul wrote to the Philippians he was not yet sure he had arrived at the "out-resurrection," but by the time he wrote 2 Timothy 4:7 he was sure, it seems, that he had attained the coveted position.

The context confirms this interpretation of Philippians 3:11 in a general sort of way, for a person can attain the place of honor by getting to know Christ the way Paul had been saying he wanted to know Christ (3:10). The "out-resurrection" will perhaps be the beginning of special honors for those who have learned something of "the power of his resurrection." Those who have known "the fellowship of his sufferings" will reign with Him. Those who have been "made conformable unto his death" down here will have a triumphant experience of His life over there. In the verses following Philippians 3:11, we see Paul straining every nerve to attain a prize he referred to as "the high calling of God."

c.   Paul's Projected Goals (3:12-14)

(1) Assessing His Situation (3:12)

(a) Realistically (3:12a) "Not as though I had already attained, either were already perfect."

Think of Paul's career up to the time he made this statement. Within a few weeks of his conversion he had made such an impact on Damascus and had stirred up such opposition that he was forced to flee the city (Acts 9:25). Paul went to Arabia where he thought through Old Testament revelation in the light of the cross of Christ. He formulated the essence of New Testament doctrine and actually coined many of the words and expressions that are now the common currency of Christian theology. While waiting for God to call him to his life work, Paul evangelized Arabia, Tarsus, and Cilicia. Then, moving to Syrian Antioch at the urging of Barnabas, the apostle made a great impact on that wicked city.

Paul evangelized the island of Cyprus and founded a string of churches in Galatia—at Antioch in Pisidia, at Iconium, at Lystra, at Derbe, and later in northern Galatia. He championed the cause of Christian liberty and helped the elders of the Jerusalem church understand that Gentiles did not have to become Jews in order to become Christians—a monumental achievement that set the church free from the shackles of Judaism.

Paul pioneered the work in Europe where he planted thriving churches in Philippi, Berea, Thessalonica, and Corinth. He made a memorable speech on Mars Hill before the intellectuals of the world. He evangelized Ephesus and left behind him a church which in turn reached out and planted other churches in western Asia Minor.

After years of traveling and preaching and teaching and exhorting, Paul arrived at Rome as a prisoner. Yet even there, while he lived in constant peril of death, he was winning converts in the ranks of the imperial guard and extending the cause of Christ into caesar's palace.

Paul had influenced scores of young men to follow his example and give themselves to evangelizing, pastoring, and teaching—Timothy, Titus, Luke, Silas, Sopater of Berea, Aristarchus, Secundus, Gaius, Tychicus, and Trophimus, to name a few. The apostle had performed miracles—healing the lame, casting out demons, banishing fever, curing the sick, raising the dead. He had suffered great hardships with joy in his heart and a song on his lips. He had been beaten, scourged, shipwrecked, imprisoned, stoned, mobbed, castigated, and mocked.

Yet Paul wrote, "Not as though I had already attained, either were already perfect." (The word translated "perfect" is *teleioō*, which means "perfected, to make a full end, consummated.") If Paul had to make a statement like that, wherever do *we* stand? He did not feel he had arrived nor did he dare rest on his laurels. He was assessing his situation realistically in the light of cold facts: the work of world evangelism was barely begun.

(b) Resolutely (3:12b) "I follow after, if that I may apprehend that for which also I am apprehended of Christ Jesus."

Borrowing the language of the athlete, Paul was saying, "I am pressing on with a view to seizing that for which I have been seized." The word translated "follow after, press on" is the same word translated "persecuting" in Philippians 3:6. The same kind of commitment that once drove Paul on to stamp out Christianity now drove him on to plant it everywhere. He had one consuming passion: to get hold of that for which Christ had gotten hold of him.

(2) Adjusting His Sights (3:13-14)

(a) A Full Stop (3:13a) "Brethren, I count not myself to have apprehended."

Paul had written letter after letter embodying the sublimest concepts of spiritual truth, the most exalted views of Christ, and the dynamics of Christian living and church growth. Indeed those letters documented the heart and soul of the faith. Yet the apostle was saying, "I do not think I have grasped all there is to grasp. I have not arrived yet."

(b) A Fresh Start (3:13b-14)

i.   The Plan (3:13b) "This one thing I do, forgetting those things which are behind, and reaching forth unto those things which are before."

The past was the past. Thank God for it, but it was the past. Paul had touched two continents for Christ, but what about Africa? And what about the continents not yet discovered?

Paul had reached Rome and now he wanted to go to Spain. Beyond Spain lay the unevangelized outposts of the empire. And what about the regions where Rome's proud eagles had never soared? Who was to take the gospel to the islands of Britain and the barbaric Picts and Scots, to Gaul, to the Huns and Goths, to Parthia beyond the Euphrates, to the Indus, and to the fabled land of Sinim? Were not these places and peoples part of Paul's great commission as apostle to the Gentiles? There remained much land to be possessed.

The task was quite unfinished—indeed, barely begun. Paul decided there was only one thing to do: begin again as though nothing at all had already been accomplished. His new plan was to put the past resolutely behind him and set his sights on new targets ahead.

In stating his new objectives, Paul used the memorable phrase "this one thing I do." D. L. Moody, almost as busy a man as Paul in the work of Christ, used to say, "It is better to say, 'This one thing I do,' than to say, 'These forty things I dabble with.'" Paul would agree. He concentrated all his energy on the one goal he had set for himself. Nothing could distract him.

ii.   The Prize (3:14) "I press toward the mark for the prize of the high calling of God in Christ Jesus."

Throughout this entire intense passage we see Paul as a man running a race. His head is thrust forward, his expression is set in fiercely determined lines, his body is straining toward the goal, his every nerve is tense, his breath is coming in gasps, and his whole being is stretched to the utmost. Every last ounce of energy and will power he has is being prodigally spent to win the prize.

What is the prize? "The high calling of God" or "the high call of God" or "the calling on high," as the original words have been variously rendered. Paul wanted to be a way-out-front winner. He wanted to be in the "out-resurrection." He wanted to be one of those called out from the rank and file of those ascending on high. He wanted the prize.

The bottom line of this uncompromising dedication, what motivated Paul, was Christ. It was the Master, not a map that held the apostle in his unswerving and unsparing race toward the goal. Always behind the visions of the lands and the lost was the vision of the Lord.

3.   The Christian and His Brethren (3:15-19)

a.   Faithful Brethren (3:15-17)

(1) An Exhortation (3:15-16) "Let us therefore, as many as be perfect, be thus minded: and if in any thing ye be otherwise minded, God shall reveal even this unto you. Nevertheless, whereto we have already attained, let us walk by the same rule, let us mind the same thing."

Paul came to his application. This astonishing piece of autobiography was not written to magnify his own dedication, but to motivate ours. He did not want us to applaud him, but to pass him.

Christianity is too often a spectator sport. We sit in the stands and applaud or deride the people who are in the arena. We say, "That was a good message," or "I never heard that truth before." We file sermons away in our minds as useful information we can exhibit to others or use in our own preaching. The thought that a sermon might perhaps have some personal, practical application rarely seems to occur to us.

Sometimes we spectators do not applaud. We say, "I never thought a preacher would act like that!" We forget that the best of us is human. If we lived in the arena, if our every move was being scrutinized, people would find reasons to gossip about us.

Paul challenged the Philippians to come down from the grandstand and get in the race. Some of them, of course, were already in it and were doing well; he described them as "perfect"—that is, mature or initiated. Paul encouraged these faithful brethren to be of the same mind as himself: to forget what had already been attained, to set new goals, to run to achieve them, and to keep their eyes fixed on Christ.

Not all the Philippians were "perfect." Some were "otherwise minded." Many of Paul's contemporaries did not cast him in the same heroic mold we do. To them he was a dangerous fanatic. They disliked what he stood for, feared his intellect, suspected his theology, were intimidated by his zeal, and resented his success. And among those who admired Paul and thanked God for him were those who were preoccupied with their own affairs and did not give their minds to the great themes that occupied his mind. They did not see the lost world as Paul saw it; they did not grasp sanctification truth as Paul grasped it; they did not see Christ as Paul saw Him.

Whether they were "perfect" or "otherwise minded," Paul wanted them all to "walk by the same rule...mind the same thing." No matter how far we have already come, let us all run on the same road.

(2) An Example (3:17) "Brethren, be followers together of me, and mark them which walk so as ye have us for an ensample."

Paul was saying, "Take me for your model. And take for models other men who are pursuing the same spiritual goals I am." He was not being egotistic. The Holy Spirit was guiding Paul's pen. The Holy Spirit had no better example to set before us than that of Paul. The example of Christ is of course taken for granted. But on the purely human level, Paul was the ideal missionary, the ideal soul-winner, the ideal pastor, the ideal Bible teacher, and the ideal practitioner of the faith. Paul's hesitation to put himself forward as an example was overruled by the Holy Spirit as false humility.

True humility does not consist in pretending we do not have gifts that we know we have and everyone else knows we have. It does not consist in depreciating our attainments as though they are inferior when they are obviously of a high order. To pretend we cannot do something we can do, or to pretend we have not done something we have done is not humility, but hypocrisy. Humility is acknowledging what God has done in our lives and giving Him the glory and praise.

In addition to Paul there are other faithful brethren—from the past and the present—we can take as examples of the Christian life. We can thank God for every man, woman, boy, and girl who inspires us to be more like Christ, more sincere, more earnest, and more committed.

b.   False Brethren (3:18-19)

(1) Their Number (3:18) "Many walk, of whom I have told you often, and now tell you even weeping, that they are the enemies of the cross of Christ."

When Paul arrived on the shores of Europe and came to Philippi, he was a veteran of foreign wars. He had already planted church after church in Galatia; he had seen how quickly Satan could mount a counterattack; he had seen what happened at Antioch; he had been to Jerusalem to challenge those in the church who wished to Judaize the Gentile believers; he had probably already written his Galatian Epistle.

It did not take Paul long to realize that wherever he went he would have to warn his new converts about false brethren. So when he came to Philippi he gave the warning. He was quite sure many false brethren would follow him there, for everywhere else they had dogged his steps, confused the issues, taught falsehoods, upset the saints, and caused divisions.

Paul wept over those who were enemies of the gospel. What a revelation of a Christlike heart! Paul wept, "with cries and tears" as one rendering puts it, for the enemies of the cross as much as he wept for the damage they did to those who fell under their evil spell. The cross offers a remedy for those who are enemies of Christ, but those who are enemies of the cross of Christ oppose the means of the salvation Christ procured for us at infinite cost. People who make themselves enemies of the cross put themselves beyond the reach of redemption.

Can you imagine the scene in the prison cell in Rome as Paul wrote Philippians 3:18? The jailer—chained to this enigmatic man with a patient disposition, brilliant inquiring mind, gentle heart, and indomitable will—sees tears well up in his prisoner's eyes and run down his cheeks. "Cheer up, sir," the soldier says. "Things aren't all that bad. After all, you are a Roman citizen and one of these days you'll be free. They don't crucify Romans. At least not here in Rome they don't."

Paul blinks away the tears, smiles, and looks at the jailer. "You misunderstand. It is not for myself I weep."

"Ah!" the companionable soldier says. "Then it's for your friends— or your wife—or your kids? I hope they're all right. You'll be free again soon and back with them. Mark my words. Cheer up. Everything is going to be all right."

"I am not weeping for my family or my friends. I am weeping for my foes."

"Well sir, they'll get their deserts one of these days. You wait and see. And I hope they get a good taste of the lash. Innocent you are. We all know that."

"You misunderstand, my friend. I am not weeping out of resentment. I am not weeping *because* of them. I am weeping *for* them."

(2) Their Nature (3:19)

(a) Their Doom (3:19a) "Whose end is destruction."

The word translated "destruction" is sometimes translated "perdition." Jesus used the word when he referred to Judas as "the son of perdition" (John 17:12). The word is first used in the New Testament in Matthew 7:13 where the Lord says, "Wide is the gate, and broad is the way, that leadeth to destruction [perdition], and many there be which go in thereat."

No wonder Paul wept for the false brethren. He knew they were lost and on their way to a Christless eternity. He found no consolation in that knowledge, in spite of all the damage they had done to him and his churches. The thought of where these men would spend eternity broke his heart.

(b) Their Desires (3:19b-d) "Whose God is their belly, and whose glory is in their shame, who mind earthly things."

The false brethren were ruled by the sensual, the shameful, and the secular. They set themselves up as religious teachers with a message more Scriptural than Paul's. And Paul showed that their robe of religion, righteousness, and respectability was nothing better than a cobweb coat spread over self-indulgence and materialism.

Of course they saw themselves differently. They saw themselves as zealous guardians of truth, as propagators of the true gospel, as

men who were willing to leave the comforts of home and family to
travel great distances to enlighten Paul's deluded converts. If along
the way they were hospitably received and royally entertained, they
thought, "The labourer is worthy of his hire" (Luke 10:7).

Their heirs and successors in professing Christendom have been
legion. Some were among the clergy of Father Chiniquy's acquaintance. In his classic autobiography he told of an incident that
reinforced his growing conviction that all was not well with the
church which he devoutly loved and served, the church in which he
had been raised and ordained a priest.[3]

According to the story there was a desperately poor widower
whose sole marketable possession was a pair of little pigs. He
wanted his parish priest to say masses for the soul of his departed
wife, but he could not afford to pay the fee. The priest, who refused
to be merciful and waive the fee, left the widower imagining his wife
longing for a priest to say the masses that would frank her through
the flames of purgatory. The widower could not live with the
knowledge that his beloved remained in anguish and torment in
the fire, but he had no money.

The next day Father Chiniquy and thirteen other priests attended a supper hosted by the father confessor of the widower. The
main dish was a succulent suckling pig. When the host jokingly
admitted that it was one of the widower's little pigs, Father Chiniquy
shoved away his plate in disgust and castigated the priest for his
heartlessness. The parish priest and the other guests, who had
laughed "to show their appreciation of their host's wit," reflected
the corruption and greed of their church.

The history of religion is replete with such stories. May we who
today serve the Lord keep our hearts open to the Holy Spirit's gaze.
May we keep our consciences tender lest we fall into the trap of
serving out of desire for gain and glory.

4.   The Christian and His Birthright (3:20-21)

a.   Our Position (3:20)

(1) Our Beloved Homeland (3:20a) "Our conversation is in heaven."

The word translated "conversation" is *politeuma*, which can be
rendered "citizenship." *Politeuma* refers to the seat of government
in the country of which we are citizens *(polites)* and in which we have

certain rights and responsibilities. Handley Moule rendered Paul's statement, "Our city-home subsists in the heavens."

Citizenship was highly prized in an empire made up mostly of slaves and freed men. Paul enjoyed the rare privilege of being a Roman citizen. Yet he was far more proud of being a citizen of glory.

Our citizenship too is in glory. This citizenship is open to all who will enthrone the King of glory as sovereign, Savior, and Lord. We Christians belong to the aristocracy of Heaven where our Lord reigns at the right hand of God, and we have a responsibility in this present world never to disgrace our homeland.

And what a homeland it is! In our country the streets are paved with gold, the walls are built of jasper, and the gates are made of pearl. A rainbow-circled throne, a crystal stream, foundations ablaze with gems, many mansions, and the tree of life are there. Sickness, death, and pain do not haunt our country's streets, and no hospitals, prisons, asylums, or retirement homes can be found. This land of fadeless day is eternally bathed in the sunshine of God's smile. No sobs or sighs are ever heard—just anthems of praise, doxologies of bliss, and songs expressing "joy unspeakable and full of glory" (1 Peter 1:8). The citizens—all most gloriously fair—are served by angels commissioned by the throne to minister to salvation's heirs.

Right now we are pilgrims and strangers in a foreign land. This world is not our final home. We are here as Heaven's ambassadors. Every night we pitch our tent a day's march nearer home. We are never to forget even for a moment where our citizenship lies. The thought of that fair land and its all-glorious King will influence our dress and our deportment. It will help determine what we say, where we go, how we behave, what pleasures we permit, how we invest our talent, what we do with our money, how we treat other people, and the amount of time we spend in worship, service, Bible study, and prayer.

(2) Our Blessed Hope (3:20b) "From whence also we look for the Saviour, the Lord Jesus Christ."

Our citizenship is in Heaven and the King of that country is coming back to earth. He came here once before and men crowned Him with mocking thorns and nailed Him to a tree, but He rose in triumph from the tomb and returned in a battle-scarred body to His home on high. He's coming back—soon. He's coming twice: first to the air to receive us unto Himself; then to the earth to deal with His foes and to right the wrongs of this world.

We are looking for Him. The word translated "look for" in Philippians 3:20 is *apekdechomai,* which means "to eagerly wait for." Paul used the word elsewhere to describe the eager anticipation with which all creation awaits His coming: "The earnest expectation of the creature waiteth for the manifestation of the sons of God" (Romans 8:19). The apostle pictured all nature standing, as it were, on tiptoe to catch a glimpse of the sons of God coming into their own.

Jesus said, "I go to prepare a place for you. And if I go and prepare a place for you, I will come again, and receive you unto myself; that where I am, there ye may be also" (John 14:2-3). The Christians of the first century anticipated that His coming would be in their lifetime. We too hope He will come in our generation. Never before have there been so many signs to herald His return: the rebirth of the state of Israel; the rise of Russia; the coming together of the nations of Europe in a collective consciousness not known since the fall of the Roman empire; the discovery of nuclear power; the spread of atheism and humanism; a permissive society; the widespread use of illegal drugs; the toleration of pornography and perversion; the increasing fascination of millions with the occult; the spread of false religion; apostasy in the church; widespread famines; the emergence of deadly diseases resistant to all known drugs; the seeming increase in earthquakes; terrorism; and persecution. Seeing all these signs, we—like those first-century Christians—should be living in eager expectation that His coming will be in our lifetime.

b.   Our Prospect (3:21)

(1) A Glorified Body (3:21a) "Who shall change our vile body, that it may be fashioned like unto his glorious body."

From the time He emerged from the womb, Jesus had a perfect body—free from any taint of sin, free from any disease or deformity. His body was a magnificent vehicle through which He could express in human terms the glorious life of God.

From the time He emerged from the tomb, Jesus had a glorified body. It could appear or disappear; it could come and go untrammeled by space, matter, or time. He could walk through a stone wall and then sit down and eat a meal as if He had come, like anyone else, through the door. His glorified body still bore the scars of Calvary, but now it was engineered for eternity. One day we will have bodies like His.

Right now we have what Paul calls "our vile body." Another translation reads "our body of humiliation." This body is inseparably linked with the burdens and abasements of its daily functions, frequent infirmities, and final dissolution into dust. We are humbled by this body's needs and limitations. And we are humbled by the fact that all too often this body is the handmaiden of lust and sin.

But "our vile body" is going to be changed—not thrown away, but changed. It is to be transfigured. Jesus did not abandon His body and leave it in the tomb. He reunited His soul and spirit with His body (which had been miraculously preserved from corruption) and transfigured it.

Our bodies are to be "fashioned" like His; they are to be conformed to His glorious body. In 1 Corinthians 15 Paul told of seven changes that will take place in our present bodies to make them like Christ's body. All these changes will take place "in a moment, in the twinkling of an eye" when Christ comes (15:52).

(2) A Guaranteed Belief (3:21b) "According to the working whereby he is able even to subdue all things unto himself."

Unbelief stares at the corpse in the coffin or the skeleton in the unearthed ancient grave, bows to the finality of death, and reasons: *The body becomes a mass of corruption. It rots and eventually returns to dust; or it is thrown into the sea and eaten by sharks; or it is reduced to ashes on a funeral pyre. What could be more final? Death is the utter end of physical life. The soul conceivably could survive the disaster of death and wander ghostlike through realms unknown. But the body is irretrievably lost to the process of decay and decomposition.* Then Faith steps in, grits its teeth, and nobly says, "Lord, I believe; help thou mine unbelief" (Mark 9:24). With faith Martha faced the incontrovertible fact that her brother's body was already rotting in the grave. When Jesus said, "Thy brother shall rise again," she could bravely reply, "I know that he shall rise again in the resurrection at the last day."

Then with a sublime consciousness of a reality greater than the grave, Jesus added, "I am the resurrection, and the life: he that believeth in me, though he were dead, yet shall he live: And whosoever liveth and believeth in me shall never die. Believest thou this?" Martha looked into the matchless face of Jesus and staked all on what He was, more than on what He said. She answered, "Yea, Lord: I believe that thou art the Christ, the Son of God, which should come into the world" (John 11:23-27). Within the hour Lazarus was alive from the dead.

Paul was bidding us to take our stand with Martha, not with the world that looks at the cold corpse and says, "That's the end." Paul looked at the living Christ and said, "He is able even to subdue all things unto himself." He is able! That is faith's answer to unbelief.

When Paul bore testimony of the truth of the gospel to King Agrippa, the apostle threw down this challenge: "Why should it be thought a thing incredible with you, that God should raise the dead?" (Acts 26:8) The fact that we will live again is no more incredible than the fact that we live at all. Think of the complexity of a single human body or even a single cell. One molecule of hemoglobin—the protein in blood that carries oxygen to every part of the body—contains 3032 atoms of carbon, 4812 atoms of hydrogen, 780 atoms of nitrogen, 4 atoms of iron, 880 atoms of oxygen, and 12 atoms of sulfur. All 9520 atoms have to be hooked to each other in a certain order and in exactly the right way—just to make one molecule essential to physical life.

The more science unravels the mystery of the human body, the more awesomely complex it is seen to be. For example, every living thing is made up of microscopic cells so small that the letter *o* on this page could contain up to forty thousand. Yet each individual cell is a world in itself with a specialized function and an intricate timetable that tells the cell when to grow, when to divide, when to make hormones, and when to die. In a human body some three billion cells die and are replaced every minute. The human brain contains some thirty billion cells; the skin has about a million cells per square inch; and in the veins some twenty trillion cells go about their business.

All cells reproduce by dividing, and when a cell divides, each new cell receives a complete copy of the blueprint, the code of life. The code determines whether the cell will be that of a cockroach, camel, maggot, or man. The code also determines the differences between brothers in the same family.

The nucleus of each cell is dominated by chromosomes, which carry in their chemistry every characteristic of the living creature being formed. Each chromosome is made up of genes. Each gene is a distinct strand of DNA and contains the code for making one particular kind of protein, the basic building block of life. The code itself uses twenty amino acids in a protein chain. These amino acids can be arranged in different ways to make the assortment of proteins needed to build a human body. The diameter of the nucleus of the cell is less than four ten-thousandths of an inch. Components of any given cell are enclosed in a membrane only one-half of a millionth of an inch thick.

That we should live at all is a miracle. That we should live again is no greater miracle. The God who made us once can easily make us again "according to the working whereby he is able even to subdue all things unto himself." Unbelief looks at the corpse; faith looks at the Creator. Unbelief sees a dead body in a coffin; faith sees a risen, triumphant, omnipotent Christ. He is the unconditional guarantee of our belief.

B. You Cannot Defile a Man Who Knows the Power of Positive Thinking (4:1-9)

1.   Thinking about One's Spiritual Life (4:1-5)

a.   Paul's Positive Thoughts about the Philippians (4:1-2)

(1) His Pleasure As He Thought How Dear They Were (4:1) "My brethren dearly beloved and longed for, my joy and crown, so stand fast in the Lord."

In chapter 4 Paul once more came back down to earth. He intended to grasp the nettle that had been stinging him ever since his initial heart-to-heart talk with Epaphroditus in Rome. But first Paul wanted to assure the Philippians of the unique place they all held in his heart. They were his "dearly beloved." He did not just like them; he loved them. And he did not just love them; he loved them dearly.

Paul longed for his Philippian friends; he yearned to be with them. He was homesick for them. Conjuring up pictures of them in his mind's eye, he remembered their facial expressions and their gestures. Paul visualized them at home and at work. He could see where each one sat when the church assembled. He could feel the bearhug of the jailer and the friendly handshake of Lydia. Oh, how he missed them!

The Philippian believers were his joy and crown. The drabness of his prison was relieved by the joy he felt when his thoughts turned to his friends gathered in the Lord's name at Philippi. As he thought of them, the prison walls melted away. Time seemed to change into eternity. Earth receded and Heaven appeared. Picturing himself answering to his name at the roll call of the judgment seat of Christ, he heard the Lord's "Well done!" and saw himself receiving a crown. Emblazoned on the gleaming diadem was the word *Philippi*. The scene faded and the walls of the Roman jail closed in on him, but the glow lingered in his soul.

Paul's reveries never lasted long. He had a thorn in his flesh, a messenger of Satan to buffet him—to keep him solidly anchored to earth and time (2 Corinthians 12:7). The thorn reminded him he had not yet received his crown, and so he wrote, "Stand fast." He remembered the one sad item in the report Epaphroditus brought from Philippi. And he remembered that enemies of the cross of Christ were prowling among his churches.

If we give any ground to Satan, he will press his advantage. He will send his forces through the breach in our defenses. A mere skirmish in the battle, if not contained, will quickly escalate into a crisis of major proportions. If we allow a little indulgence here, a little carelessness there, a sneak peep at a questionable book on the shelf of a bookstore, battalions of evil thoughts and lustful desires will seize our imaginations and entrench themselves in our minds. Only a long and determined effort will dislodge them, and even then some will lurk in the recesses of the soul to regroup and attack again and again—often in life's holiest moments. So Paul's exhortation is for us too: "Stand fast in the Lord."

(2) His Plea As He Thought How Divided They Were (4:2) "I beseech Euodias, and beseech Syntyche, that they be of the same mind in the Lord."

Brought out in the open at last is the disagreement between two sisters in the assembly of God's people. Paul needed no one to tell him the miserable details.

The pattern is familiar to us as well. Words pass between two people over something quite inconsequential, such as a difference of opinion about the color of the drapes over the baptistery. Soon the two are not on speaking terms at all. They look the other way when they pass each other on the street. Spouses are drawn into the squabble. Sympathizers are recruited and the church takes sides. Personality differences, doctrinal differences, and procedural differences are fuel for the fire. With the whole church at loggerheads, its testimony suffers as the unsaved witness (and sometimes referee) the argument. The work of the church comes to a halt because nobody can agree on anything. Every issue, every suggestion for furthering the ministry of the church, becomes the football of church politics. The more spiritual members of the fellowship make a few attempts to bring order, sanity, and Christian charity back to the fore and then either retire sadly into their shells or leave in search of more congenial gatherings.

Paul named names. In the end the only way to deal with some of these problems is to name names and force the two people causing the trouble to face their personal responsibility for what has happened. Paul was no longer skirting around the issue; he was no longer giving veiled hints, appeals, and suggestions. He suddenly and bluntly confronted the parties involved. After eighty-two verses he finally nailed the problem down.

We can imagine the reaction in Philippi. The church had welcomed Epaphroditus back home, and he had called a meeting for the first reading of Paul's letter. Everyone was there; the place was packed. Epaphroditus or one of the other elders broke the seal on the scroll to show that the letter had not been tampered with, and he began to read. Sentence by sentence the Epistle unfolded. Here and there were hints that Paul knew about the squabble. Euodias and Syntyche looked furtively at one another and just as uneasily looked away. They darted angry looks at Epaphroditus. *Did he go and blab to Paul?* one of them wondered. *I'll give him a piece of my mind.* Then they heard Paul's words regarding Epaphroditus: "Receive him therefore in the Lord."

And suddenly like a bolt from the blue the two ladies heard their own names being read: "I beseech Euodias, and beseech Syntyche, that they be of the same mind in the Lord." Like a flash of lightning and a thunderclap the squabbling pair were named—bluntly, inescapably, shockingly. Every eye was on them. They felt like curling up and dying on the spot; they wished the ground would open and swallow them up. The atmosphere in the meeting room was charged. A deathly hush fell on the gathering. One of the ladies flushed a crimson red and burst into tears. The other bit her lips and turned as white as a sheet.

As we recreate the scene in Philippi, we can surmise that the tender pleading of Paul was reflected in the tone of the reader. Instead of an apostolic command accompanied by a warning of dire penalties to come, the Philippians heard a gentle plea linked to the name of the Lord whom Paul had been exalting all through the letter. Mercifully the reference to Euodias and Syntyche was brief, leaving much unsaid.

Paul swiftly changed the subject, but how unerring was his aim! And his words apply to us as well as the Philippians. We do not have to be of the same mind about politics. We do not have to be of the same mind about whether to embrace the steady-state or the big-bang theory concerning the nature of the universe. We do not have to be of the same mind about dress, diet, sports, books, music, or speakers. But we do have to be of the same mind in the Lord. Being of the same mind in the Lord does not necessarily mean that we cannot have differing ideas about doctrinal matters within the framework of given fundamentals. But it does mean that we cannot squabble about our differences.

Being of one mind does not mean that we tolerate doctrinal error concerning the person of Christ, the person and work of the Holy Spirit, or other essentials of the faith. When writing to Rome, Paul enjoined wide accommodation of other people's views on eating ritually unclean food, but he was prepared to fight tooth and nail for the freedom of Gentile Christians from Judaistic legalism.

b.   Paul's Positive Thoughts about His Partners (4:3-5)

(1) He Wanted Them to Be Helpful (4:3) "I intreat thee also, true yokefellow, help those women which laboured with me in the gospel, with Clement also, and with other my fellowlabourers, whose names are in the book of life."

Paul was realistic enough to recognize that even though he was an apostle and the spiritual father of the assembly at Philippi, his exhortation to Euodias and Syntyche was not sufficient in itself to solve the problem. The women were going to need additional help to resolve their differences. If the disagreement had been long-standing and particularly acrimonious, there would be deep scars.

Added to those scars would be the effect of the shock Euodias and Syntyche felt when they heard their names being read publicly in the church. (How utterly humiliated they would have been if they had known that for all the rest of time, wherever the gospel went and this letter followed, their names would be read in connection with a quarrel that had contributed a sour note to an otherwise happy and Christlike fellowship of God's people!) Paul knew that an overwhelming sense of shame could inhibit Euodias and Syntyche from further service. Their feelings of disgrace might cause them to hide, unable ever again to face their fellow believers or continue in the Lord's work. Or the ladies might react in anger and be furious with Paul and Epaphroditus. In any case, Paul commissioned his "true yokefellow"—probably Epaphroditus—to do what he could to soften the blow.

Indeed Paul tried to soften the blow himself by mentioning how these two women had once worked with him, with Clement, and with other "fellowlabourers"—perhaps a reference to Silas, Timothy, Luke, and Lydia, who had thrown themselves wholeheartedly into the Lord's work.

As was typical of Paul, he did not dwell on the problem. He dealt with it, but then sought to lift his readers' thoughts immediately to higher ground. Having given honorable mention to Euodias, Syntyche, and Clement, he added, "Whose names are in the book of life," thus lifting them from the sordid to the sublime, from the paltry to the eternal. In that heavenly atmosphere all quarrels must cease. In the realization of God's love for His own, all sense of our worthlessness must die. Thoughts of God knowing each of us by name, turning our names over in His mind, and lovingly writing those names down must lead Christians from petty motives to noble aspirations.

In *Pilgrim's Progress* John Bunyan portrayed a man who occupied himself with the paltry and missed the eternal. He thought of nothing else but turning the mire over and over with his muck rake. Behind him, proffering a golden crown, stood an angel, but the man kept his eyes on his muck rake. As we imagine the scene, we are reminded of these words someone has so aptly phrased:

> Could'st thou in vision see
> The man God meant
> Thou never more could'st be
> The man thou art, content.

In Philippians 4:3 Paul, like Bunyan, was saying in effect: "Look up! Don't miss the glory. Throw away your muck rake. Reach for the crown."

(2) He Wanted Them to Be Happy (4:4) "Rejoice in the Lord alway: and again I say, Rejoice."

Paul's answer to all of life's problems is the Lord. In an atmosphere of rejoicing in the Lord, all discord dies. Distressing thoughts are overcome by thoughts of the Lord and His love, goodness, wisdom, power, and care. The Lord is too wise to make any mistakes, too loving to be unkind, too powerful to be thwarted, and too involved in all that concerns us to be aloof. How can we think of the Lord and not rejoice?

In this sad world of sin, tears may scald our eyes, but thoughts of Him, beaming like sunshine through the rain, will make rainbows of our tears. David thought of the Lord and sang: "Yea, though I walk through the valley of the shadow of death, I will fear no evil: for thou art with me; thy rod and thy staff they comfort me" (Psalm 23:4).

Life can be grim. Sometimes we are called to bear burdens that crush us to the dust. Painful bereavements may cause us to long for death. Regrets and remorse may tear out our hearts, and haunt us and torment us until we groan in agony of soul. Paul's answer is always the same: think about the Lord. We are not to rejoice in what overwhelms us—that would be foolish. We are to rejoice in the Lord.

The Lord can restore the years the locusts have eaten (Joel 2:25). He can bind up the brokenhearted (Isaiah 61:1). He can make evil become a means of grace. "As for you," said Joseph to his brothers, "ye thought evil against me; but God meant it unto good" (Genesis 50:20). In Paul's words, "He is able even to subdue all things unto himself" (Philippians 3:21). The Lord has the power. We may have to limp like Jacob to the end of our days on earth. We may be broken by God because of our past, but in eternity a wise and loving Lord will give us back what we so wantonly threw away.

(3) He Wanted Them to Be Holy (4:5) "Let your moderation be known unto all men. The Lord is at hand."

The word translated "moderation" can also be translated "forbearance" or "yieldedness." The word speaks of selflessness, of a spirit ready to yield in anything that is simply of self—for the Lord's sake.

The classic Biblical example of yieldedness is the attitude of Abraham when strife arose between his herdsmen and Lot's herdsmen because there was not enough pasture for all their flocks and cattle. "Let there be no strife, I pray thee, between me and thee," said Abraham, "for we be brethren" (Genesis 13:8). He simply yielded and allowed Lot to have his own way. If the conflict between the two groups of herdsmen was a bad testimony to the Canaanites and Perizzites (13:7), Abraham's solution was a good testimony.

We must remember that the context of Philippians 4:5 is the conflict between Euodias and Syntyche. Paul was urging them to be selfless and he added, "The Lord is at hand." Who would want to be caught away in the rapture from the middle of a bitter argument with another Christian?

While rejoicing in the Lord is Paul's general recipe for a *happy* life, expecting the second coming of Christ is his general recipe for a *holy* life. Who would want to be overtaken by the Lord's coming when he was watching a questionable movie or depositing money acquired dishonestly? Understanding the power of positive thinking, Paul made "The Lord is at hand" his watchword, the guardian he set at every door.

2.   Thinking about One's Secular Life (4:6)

a.   Our Worries (4:6a) "Be careful for nothing."

The word translated "careful" means "anxious." The Lord Himself introduced the idea behind this verse in the sermon on the mount: "Take no thought [be not careful, full of care, overanxious] for your life, what ye shall eat, or what ye shall drink; nor yet for your body, what ye shall put on. Is not the life more than meat, and the body than raiment?" (Matthew 6:25) The Lord pointed to the birds and the grass as evidence that God providentially cares for His creatures.

The Gentiles, He said, were preoccupied with material things, but those who know God as their Father should be occupied with the affairs of His kingdom. Then "all these things" will be added to them (Matthew 6:33). We are not to worry. A children's rhyme teaches us not to be anxious:

> Said a robin to a sparrow:
> "I should really like to know
> Why these anxious human beings
> Rush about and worry so."
>
> Said the sparrow to the robin:
> "I suppose that it must be
> That they have no heavenly Father
> Such as cares for you and me."
> (Elizabeth Cheney)

b. Our Wants (4:6b) "In every thing by prayer and supplication with thanksgiving let your requests be made known unto God."

Our requests are known to God already, yet He loves to hear us ask. Prayer is one of many mysterious factors in God's administration of the universe. We do not know how prayer works, but God arranged it to encourage us to come to Him. He longs for us to come, come often, and linger long. He longs for us to talk to Him, tell Him all about our troubles, and make our requests known to Him.

A British minister once told me a quaint story (actually about himself) that illustrates God's desire to hear our requests: A couple who did a lot of entertaining in their home had a little boy. Usually visitors would acknowledge him by pressing a few coins into his hand. These small gifts he put in his money box. One day a guest seemed to be unaware of the social courtesy customarily extended to the child, so the boy fetched his money box and rattled it in front of the visitor. The expected contribution was supplied, but afterward the father took the boy aside and said, "Son, you are never again to ask a stranger for anything. You are to ask me. I'll never tell you off for asking me." And he added, "Because I'm your dad."

Like the father in the story, God says to us, "If you need anything, you are to come to Me. I am your Father." Nothing is more dishonoring to God than His children begging someone else for what is His joy and responsibility to provide. Ministries that rely on massive begging appeals to all and sundry do great dishonor to the name of God and the cause of Christ. On a personal level, the trouble with making our requests known to others is that they often give grudgingly; or they give from an ulterior motive; or they give ignorantly, not knowing whether our requests are the kind that God Himself would honor.

We are to come to God about everything. Our heavenly Father is interested in every detail of our lives. He has flung wide the gates to His presence. "Come," He says, "tell me all about it." When we come to God, let us remember the words of the old hymn:

> Thou art coming to a King;
> Large petitions with thee bring;
> For His grace and power are such,
> None can ever ask too much.[4]

3.   Thinking about One's Secret Life (4:7-9)

a.   What Paul Shared with the Philippians (4:7-8)

(1) The Secret of a Guarded Thought Life (4:7) "The peace of
    God, which passeth all understanding, shall keep your hearts
    and minds through Christ Jesus."

What can disturb God's peace? Could some happening in a
remote part of the galaxy disturb His peace? Of course not. He is
omnipresent, always on the spot. Nothing can take place behind
His back. He is right there, no matter where, all the time.
    Could some diabolical thought of Satan disturb God's peace?
Could some mystery, some obscure idea, some crafty twist of error,
or some plot hatched in the demented soul of Lucifer to thwart
God's beneficent purposes and bring new forms of suffering into
the universe disturb God's peace? Of course not. God is omniscient. He knows all the wiles of the evil one and in His infallible
wisdom has anticipated and annulled every one of them. Satan's
deep counsels are just so much gibberish to God, however clever
and sophisticated they may seem to us.
    Can all the might of the gates of Hell (Matthew 16:18) disturb
God's peace? Of course not. He is omnipotent. He can command
galaxies and create atoms. He can toss stars into space and hold
satellites whirling at inconceivable velocities on their orbits. There
is no physical, moral, or spiritual power that He does not rule with
consummate skill and tireless ease—not in Heaven or earth or Hell,
not now or ever.
    Nothing can ruffle the peace of God. It is a calm beyond all
storms, a rest beyond all strife, a haven beyond all tempestuous seas.
The peace of God is majestic and sublime.
    Did Soviet atheism and militarism disturb God's peace? Was He
intimidated by the size of the Russian army, by the success of Soviet
propaganda, or by the worldwide presence of the KGB? Of course
not. Long ago He wrote Russia's doom into His Book.
    In Paul's day, was God upset by Nero? When that evil man
burned Rome, blamed the Christians, and began a persecution
rarely surpassed in history, did he take God by surprise? Did God
hastily cut short the day of grace and summon Michael to usher in
Armageddon then and there? No. His peace was undisturbed. All

was foreknown. We do not know why God held back His hand then or why He holds it back now, but "we'll understand it better by and by."[5]

The unfathomable peace of the God who controls the universe and pursues a faultless purpose, is the peace that Paul commended to his Philippian friends. Their arguing should vanish in the infinite calm of God's peace.

This divine peace kept Paul's mind and heart. The word translated "keep" in Philippians 4:7 is *phroureō*, which is translated "kept with a garrison" in 2 Corinthians 11:32. *Phroureō* means "to keep in custody." Between Paul and threatening circumstances stood a garrison. God's peace had him in custody. A great river of peace was thrown like a moat around the citadel of his soul.

God's peace was the antidote Paul offered for disturbing thoughts and emotions. The apostle was not writing about a mere theory or a theological proposition removed from daily reality, but an operating principle of dynamic Christian life. Paul was a living testimony that the principle worked. It was the secret of his calmness of soul in both the Philippian jail and the caesar's cell.

How does the principle work? How can we hope to be garrisoned by God's peace? Philippians 4:7 provides the answer: "Through Christ Jesus." We are kept not through our strength of will, not through our sublimation of thought, not through our resolution of heart, but "through Christ Jesus." Years before, Paul had sent this glorious formula for living the Christian life to the believers in Rome (Romans 5:1; 6:23; 7:25) and now he was putting the principle into practice as a prisoner in their midst.

It was Christ Jesus who brought the peace of God down to earth. Heralding His birth across the Judean hills, the heavenly host said, "Glory to God in the highest, and on earth peace, good will toward men" (Luke 2:14). That imperturbable peace hushed the storm-tossed sea of Galilee and gave rest to the tormented soul of the Gadarene demoniac. That peace remained unshaken by conflict, criticism, crisis, and cross. At all times, in all places, under all circumstances, Christ reposed in His Father's good and acceptable and perfect will (Romans 12:2). And when Jesus appeared in the upper room on resurrection evening, His greeting to the disciples was "Peace" (John 20:19).

"Through Christ Jesus" was the secret of Paul's own peace of soul. God's peace was established in him by the indwelling Christ. Paul experienced the peace of God because Christ lived His life in Paul.

Christ would live His life in the Philippians too if they would let Him, and He is willing to live His life in us as well. Satan would like to take our minds and hearts by storm, but God offers His peace as a garrison to stand guard against all attacks.

(2) The Secret of a Guided Thought Life (4:8)

(a) The Choices (4:8a)

i.   Thoughts That Promote Inner Character "Whatsoever things are true, whatsoever things are honest, whatsoever things are just."

A guarded thought life has to be accompanied by a guided thought life. God expects our active cooperation. When we find our thoughts wandering down questionable paths, we must resolutely take them in hand. We must practice deliberate cultivation of positive thinking—and we must not surrender this Pauline concept just because "psychology preachers" have made wrong use of it. Positive thinking is possible only because Christ lives His life in us.

We are constituted to be able to think consciously of only one thing at a time. If we are thinking of something good, we cannot be thinking of something bad at the same time. So we can avoid unprofitable thoughts by choosing to think of their alternatives. Paul listed some of these alternatives, beginning with those that promote inner character. We should heed Paul's advice because all too easily and all too often unprofitable thoughts gain dominion over our souls.

We can begin by *excluding that which is false* and thinking about "whatsoever things are true." Some people argue that we ought to be conversant with all the subtleties of falsehood so that we will be able to deal with it when it arises, but the argument itself is false. The simplest way to expose a crooked line is to place a straight edge alongside it. Law enforcement agents who specialize in the detection of counterfeit money do not spend much time studying all the varieties of counterfeit bills; rather they make themselves thoroughly familiar with genuine bills circulated by the mint.

Study Paul's approach to error in Galatians, Colossians, 2 Thessalonians, and other Epistles. He said as little as possible about the sophistries of a false teaching—just enough to highlight its general outlines. Then he simply expounded the truth. He brought his readers back to the One who is the truth, back to Christ. Paul was too well instructed by the Holy Spirit to waste time wandering in mazes of error built by the evil one. Too often we lose ourselves in research into communism, Mormonism, humanism, or whatever the current "ism" is, when what we need to be doing is staying close to Christ. All the cults betray themselves in their answers to the question, "What think ye of Christ? whose son is he?" (Matthew 22:42)

A ship was threading its way through inshore islands when a lady on board asked the captain of the vessel if he knew where all the rocks and shoals were. "No Madam," he replied, "but I know where the deep water is." Likewise, instead of being preoccupied with religious or any other kind of falsehood, we should turn our thoughts to things that are true.

We can continue choosing alternatives that promote inner character by *extolling that which is fine* and thinking about "whatsoever things are honest." The word translated "honest" in Philippians 4:8 is *semnos,* which can also be rendered "honorable" or "venerable" or "grave." *Semnos* is translated "grave" in 1 Timothy 3:8,11, where Paul was writing about the characteristics deacons and their wives should possess. The translation is "grave" again in Titus 2:2, where Paul was writing about attributes becoming to older men. In Philippians Paul was advocating that we think about things that are respectable.

Today people tend to be occupied with tawdry things. They "spill it all out," shamelessly making the most intimate details of life a matter of open conversation. The advent of the "talk show" on radio and television has resulted in all kinds of topics being discussed and dissected without any regard for propriety. Problems formerly reserved for the ears of one's doctor or minister are shared publicly.

Paul advised us to concentrate our thoughts on nobler themes. Crudeness and coarseness should have no place in a Christian's thought life. We are to cultivate refinement and respect for the finer things of life. We are to train our minds to dwell on them. "As [a man] thinketh in his heart, so is he" (Proverbs 23:7).

The Word of God does not read like a Victorian composition. The Bible does not avoid mentioning the facts of life, but it avoids giving offense. The "realism" of modern writing with its constant barrage of four-letter words and explicit sexual details does nothing but pander to man's lower nature. The Bible never does that. We should pattern our thoughts after the Scriptures. We should extol the fine, avoid the base, emphasize the respectable, and cultivate the decorous and honorable.

As we pursue the path of positive thinking we can also promote inner character by *exalting that which is fair*. We can choose to think of "whatsoever things are just." The word translated "just" in Philippians 4:8 means "righteous" and comes from the root meaning "right." Many things in this world are not right, not just. We could easily dwell on what is not right, especially if we ourselves have been victims of injustice. We could build cases against people and seek revenge. We could allow our thoughts about what is unfair to sour our souls.

Paul would rather have us dwell on more profitable subjects. Even in a world of sin many things are right and proper. Paul managed to think positively when he was the victim of gross injustice. When he was arrested in Philippi, he responded by singing in his prison.

When Paul wrote to the Philippians, he had been in prison for years, first in Caesarea and then in Rome—on a wholly unjust charge. In fact one prominent Roman official had pronounced him guiltless (Acts 26:31-32). Another had kept Paul in custody in the vain hope that he would pay a bribe for his release (Acts 24:26). No man had been the victim of more injustice than Paul. But if he had brooded over the wrongs done to him, he would have become bitter—and useless in the service of the Lord.

We have all met people who have not responded to ill treatment the way Paul did. They have "a chip on their shoulder." Not being very positive individuals, they bore us to the point that we try to avoid their company.

ii.   Thoughts That Promote Inner Cleanliness "Whatsoever things are pure, whatsoever things are lovely, whatsoever things are of good report."

Nothing can be more detrimental to inner health and a Christian testimony than unclean thoughts. Paul told us the best way to combat such thoughts. We are to begin by *excluding that which besmirches*. We are to think on "whatsoever things are pure."

How timely is this exhortation! In our day secular society gives free reign to pornography, perversion, and all things impure. It is hard to find a modern book or television program that does not befoul the mind. School children are assigned to read books that would have been regarded as "dirty" a generation ago.

How does a person in our day keep his thoughts pure? By excluding the impure. Once given a lodging, impure thoughts are virtually impossible to evict. They lurk in the hidden recesses of the mind and make their presence known at the most unexpected times. They may show up when we are trying to worship or when we are engaged in an innocent conversation with someone who has no idea that we are suddenly entertaining lascivious thoughts. If a person once lets his thoughts wander down some impure path, hidden legions joyfully emerge and stampede, pushing the mind into all kinds of sin.

Only the blood of Christ can cleanse the mind. Then we must follow Paul's formula and deliberately think on "whatsoever things are pure." We must exclude that which besmirches by keeping our minds away from things that breed impure thoughts. We must stay away from "dirty" books and suggestive pictures and fill our minds with thoughts from untainted sources, particularly the Word of God.

Paul would also have us promote inner cleanliness by *extolling that which beautifies.* We are to think on "whatsoever things are lovely"—things that are gracious and kindly.

My father is a good example of someone who filled his mind with good things. His memory was full of poetry and hymns as well as Bible passages and commentary. He left school when he was nine or ten years old, but thereafter he educated himself; he would have qualified for a college degree in the classics. Often a phrase from Shakespeare or Bunyan would come out in my father's prayers and sermons, and even in casual conversation. He read only the best; he had no time for anything that fell below his standard. Only that which beautified, only that which was lovely was allowed space in his large library.

My father was a traveling preacher who spent long hours in other people's homes. He filled those hours by reading the best books and writing in notebooks ideas that captured his imagination. I have seen preachers listening to my father seize their pens and write as fast they could to capture the truths that were hurrying from a seemingly inexhaustible source. What they were hearing was the best of Campbell Morgan, Archbishop Trench, Handley Moule, C. H. Spurgeon, Griffith Thomas, and Graham Scroggie.

I have heard many preachers, but never one who could surpass my father in elegance of language and eloquence of speech when the Spirit was upon him. He could expound any passage in the Bible. I have seen him hand his Bible to someone in a Bible class and say, "What would you like to have me preach on today?" The person would open the Bible to Deuteronomy 28 or Psalm 31 or John 15 and hand it back to my father. He would begin to read a verse at a time and before long his thoughts would begin to flow until a Niagara of truths was pouring out.

In keeping with my father's dedication to pursuing lovely thoughts, he gave away many excellent commentaries to young men who had a propensity for the ministry.

Concluding his list of alternatives to unprofitable thoughts, Paul wrote, "whatsoever things are of good report." He would have us combat unclean thoughts by *exalting that which builds*. We are to think about things that lead to edifying, ennobling conversation. How many times we come away from a conversation with regrets! Too often our table talk degenerates into gossip or idle chitchat. We may not be vulgar or crude, but our words do not build character because we have not cultivated the habit of meditating on things that are noble—things that stretch the mind, enlarge mental horizons, open up new vistas of thought.

We have to make deliberate choices to think profitable thoughts. Our minds will not automatically drift into these channels. Most of us are mentally lazy. And because of the fall, we have a bias toward the degenerate. The secret of a guided thought life is an active assertion of the will, in cooperation with the Holy Spirit, to "think on these things."

(b) The Challenge (4:8b) "If there be any virtue, and if there be any praise, think on these things."

The hypotheses are assumed to be true. There really is no question as to the existence of virtue and praise.

Paul was challenging us to "think on"—think out, take account of—things that are true, honorable, just, pure, lovely, and of good report. And where will such thoughts lead us? To Jesus! In Him all these abstracts are translated into a warm and wonderful personality, a noble and inspiring person.

We cannot think of Christ ever being anything but true. We

cannot conceive of Him telling a lie or being deceitful or under-handed. We cannot think of Him being anything less than honorable. With David Livingstone, we think of Him as "a Gentlemen of the strictest and most sacred honor."[6] On this earth Christ was always just and fair, whether dealing with a fallen woman or a self-righteous Pharisee. How lovely He was! He was attractive both to strong men and in the noblest sense to women. We cannot imagine Him ever doing an unlovely thing. He had a good report even as a boy. At His trial nobody could think of anything He had said or done that could be used against Him. His enemies had to hire false witnesses, twist His words, and resort to mob psychology and highly-charged political slogans to get Him condemned.

Before laying the choices and challenge of Philippians 4:8 before us, Paul penned two words at the end of verse 7: "Christ Jesus." Verse 8 stems directly out of thoughts of Jesus and leads us directly back to thoughts of Jesus. We must think of Christ. That is the ultimate secret of a positive thought life. All unworthy thoughts perish in His presence.

b.   What Paul Showed to the Philippians (4:9) "Those things, which ye have both learned, and received, and heard, and seen in me, do: and the God of peace shall be with you."

Paul's friends at Philippi knew that Paul practiced what he preached. If someone should object that the standard set by Jesus was too high, Paul could say, "Very well, then what about me? You saw me live the Christ-life before you. How do you think I did it? I'm made of the same stuff you are. My back bled when thrashed by lictors; my flesh cringed from pain; my limbs became cramped in the stocks. I knew what it was to be afraid, disappointed, depressed. Only I didn't moan and complain and give up. I sang! How did I do it? By accentuating the positive and filling my heart and mind and soul with thoughts of Christ."

C. You Cannot Defeat a Man Who Knows the Power of Perpetual Thanksgiving (4:10-23)

In his letter to the Philippians Paul introduced us to three secrets for triumphant living: proper theology (3:1-21), positive thinking (4:1-9), and now perpetual thanksgiving (4:10-23). Thanksgiving is an essential characteristic of the victorious Christian life.

1. The Experiences Connected with This Kind of Life (4:10-13)

a. Knowing How to Wait (4:10)

(1) Paul Acknowledged the Final Coming of the Philippians' Gift (4:10a) "I rejoiced in the Lord greatly, that now at the last your care of me hath flourished again."

In Paul's day people under arrest were not cared for by the state. It was up to the prisoners themselves to see that their physical needs were met. Paul had no visible means of support. He was cast wholly on the Lord and hence on the Lord's people.

The Lord's people in Philippi had sent Paul a financial gift. (Their thoughtfulness of him is a good example of positive thinking!) Evidently this gift was not their first, for the apostle said their care of him had "flourished again."

Paul did not take their gift for granted. One of the purposes of his Epistle to the Philippians was to express his thanks. His acknowledgment of their gift was not a perfunctory note, but a letter full of heartfelt appreciation and spiritual instruction. They had ministered to his physical needs; his response was to minister to their spiritual needs.

The word translated "hath flourished again" can also be rendered "blossomed out" or "revived." The original word suggests a sudden, spontaneous, natural flowering of the Philippians' love for Paul. He was reminded of the thought behind the gift and it touched a responsive chord of praise in his soul. "I rejoiced in the Lord greatly," he told them. Paul's rejoicing was always in the Lord.

Why did Paul interject, "Now at the last"? Perhaps his circumstances had been particularly straitened lately. Perhaps he had been praying with increased importunity for his financial needs to be met. Perhaps God had been saying to him (as He so often says to us), "Wait!" Perhaps Paul had been waiting for a long time as God tested his patience and trust to the utmost. "At last!" Paul burst out.

The Philippians sent a gift to Paul, but where were all the other churches during his time of need? Where were all the other Christians, Paul's children in the faith? Where were all the other apostles?

Where was the Jerusalem church? They especially should have had at least some concern for Paul's financial needs. He had ministered lavishly to their needs; he had urged churches he had planted to be forward in sending their gifts to the Christians in Jerusalem. And it was largely due to the elders of the Jerusalem church that he was in prison. If they had not been so insistent that Paul demonstrate his Jewishness, he would never have been in the temple area where he was arrested. That church seemed to have washed its hands of him altogether.

But at last the Lord had answered Paul's prayer. And the apostle rejoiced that He had used a group particularly dear to him as His instrument.

(2) Paul Acknowledged the Faithful Character of the Philippians' Giving (4:10b) "Ye were also careful, but ye lacked opportunity."

The Philippians had wanted for some time to send help, but the opportunity to forward a gift had not come. Mail service was not available in those days and travel, even along the celebrated Roman roads, was not a light undertaking. And who would want to seek out a man in prison in Rome under the suspicious eye of Nero? Paul's address might cause even the more generous of his friends to pause before volunteering. Thus finding a way to send a gift was a spiritual exercise for the Christians at Philippi.

Today it is common to receive registered letters outlining dire circumstances and pleading for an instant and generous response, but the Philippians had not received any begging letters from Paul. Paul told his needs to the Lord. The Lord impressed those needs on certain of His people, and the result was spiritual giving rather than high-pressure giving.

b.   Knowing How to Want (4:11-13)

(1) What Paul Denied (4:11a) "Not that I speak in respect of want."

The word translated "want" here, *husterēsis,* occurs in only one other place in the New Testament: Mark 12:44. We read between the lines of Mark's graphic account of a now-famous incident: One day when the Lord was sitting near the treasury in the temple in Jerusalem, He watched as with fanfare and flourish the rich cast in their donations. Presently along came a widow, obviously poor. For a long time she hesitated, debating about her contribution. It was not that she was hesitant to give—she had already decided to part with the mite in her hand. The problem was that there were two boxes—one marked "For the Lord" and other marked "For the Poor."

She approached the box marked "For the Lord." That was where she wanted to put her money. She wanted to express her gratitude to the Lord for His love and care. Then she felt drawn to the box marked "For the Poor." She knew all about being poor. It would be so nice to think that even in an infinitesimal way she had helped the poor. But if she put her money in that box, she would not be able to support the more spiritual side of the work of the Lord. She was in a dilemma: one small coin and two great needs.

Then to the delight of the watchful Lord, she fished in her robe and uncovered another small coin, just like the other. Now she had two mites. Quick as a flash one went into the Lord's box, the other went into the box for the poor, and away she went, melting into the crowd. She had nothing left in the world and expected to go to bed supperless that night, but I like to think that the Lord, who is no man's debtor, had a surprise waiting for her when she arrived home.

The Lord drew the disciples' attention to the woman. "This poor widow," He said, "hath cast more in, than all they which have cast into the treasury: For all they did cast in of their abundance; but she of her want [*husterēsis,* 'destitution'] did cast in all that she had, even all her living" (Mark 12:43-44).

Paul was not as poor as the widow in Mark 12. In Philippians 4:11 he was saying, "Please don't think I was down to my last penny; I had not arrived at the point of destitution. Please don't think I am complaining or criticizing or begging for more. God has never let me down."

(2) What Paul Declared (4:11b-13)

(a) The Serenity of Contentment (4:11b-12)

i.   The Apprehension of the Lesson (4:11b) "I have learned, in whatsoever state I am, therewith to be content."

Later Paul expressed a similar thought to his young colleague Timothy: "Godliness with contentment is great gain" (1 Timothy 6:6). Whatever his circumstances were, Paul was content.

When he was hailed enthusiastically upon his return to churches he had planted, Paul was content. When he was chained to a particularly impatient and unsympathetic Roman soldier, Paul was content. When he and his friends were on their way to Jerusalem to deliver a generous gift from Gentile converts on the mission field, Paul was content. When he was preaching to scholars in the intellectual capital of the world, Paul was content. When he was leading a runaway slave to Christ, Paul was content. When he was preaching to a king, Paul was content. When he was writing a theological masterpiece, Paul was content. When he was waiting to appear before a court that could sentence him to death, Paul was content.

Paul had learned to live in complete detachment from his circumstances. Since his circumstances were all ordered by the Lord, all was well. God's will was "good, and acceptable, and perfect" (Romans 12:2). Paul's state of soul is enviable and is attainable only when one has a perfect trust in God. Such trust can only be cultivated at the feet of Jesus.

ii.   The Application of the Lesson (4:12) "I know both how to be abased, and I know how to abound: every where and in all things I am instructed both to be full and to be hungry, both to abound and to suffer need."

Most of us know what it is to be abased. The word translated "abased" here is used elsewhere in the Greek language to describe a river in a time of drought. So Paul's words can be rendered, "I know how to run low." Most of us have learned what it is to run low, but have we learned *how* to run low? We have perhaps also learned what it is to abound (to overflow), but have we learned *how* to abound? Paul had learned *how*.

Have we learned how to face poverty without panicking? Have we learned how to face sickness or rejection or disappointment? Have we learned how to face prosperity without pride? Have we learned how to face success, applause, and exuberant well-being? Many have succumbed to life's adversities because they never learned how to handle them. Probably more people have succumbed to life's advancements because success went to their heads.

Joseph is the classic Biblical example of a man who learned how to face a life of abasement in prison and a life of abundance in the palace. The Holy Spirit sets him before us as the most Christlike man in the Old Testament. The secret of Joseph's victory over both frowning and felicitous circumstances was his implicit faith in God.

In his hour of testing in Potiphar's house, in his hour of travail in prison when even the chief butler forgot him, and in his hour of triumph as the grand vizier of Egypt, Joseph was always the same—Christlike. Neither lust nor lies, neither abasement nor abandonment, neither prosperity nor power could spoil him. Joseph learned how to face both a cross and a crown, and he emerged as a magnificent type of Christ.

In the New Testament Joseph is rivaled only by Paul. No matter why, no matter where, no matter what—Paul was in on the secret of an all-victorious Christian life.

No matter why! The *why* did not bother Paul. His interest was in learning *how*. He was like Nicodemus. When Jesus told that moral, respected, and religious man he needed to be born again if he wanted to see the kingdom of God, Nicodemus did not ask *why*. He asked, *"How* can a man be born when he is old?" (John 3:4, italics added) Paul knew that the *why* was always to be found in the will of an all-wise, all-loving, all-sovereign God.

No matter where! Paul said, "Every where." Everywhere included the prison in which Paul sat as he wrote Philippians 4:12, and other prisons in which he had been chained and held under lock and key for years. Everywhere included "the deep" where he spent "a night and a day" (2 Corinthians 11:25). We are left to imagine for ourselves what Paul was like as he rode the troughs and foaming crests of a stormy sea. Hanging onto a spar or plank of wood, he was adrift in shark-infested waters, but he was abiding and abounding in Christ. Perhaps other passengers, desperately clinging to some scrap of wreckage, heard a voice singing words like these:

We have an anchor that keeps the soul
Steadfast and sure while the billows roll,
Fastened to the Rock which cannot move,
Grounded firm and deep in the Savior's love.[7]

No matter what! Paul was victorious "in all things," even in chains. He was a man made for high seas, distant horizons, and far countries. He had a restless, roaming spirit and would have understood the cowboy who sang, "Don't fence me in." Yet he was content in prison.

Paul was a "military" strategist of the widest vision. In another age, under different circumstances, if he had been born a Greek or Roman Gentile, he would have been an Alexander or a caesar. Instead he was born a Jew and born again a Christian, and his soaring ambition saw a world to be conquered and brought captive to the feet of Jesus. Paul had plans to conquer Spain, plans to go where the caesar's legions had not gone, plans to cross the Rhine, plans to invade the islands of Britannia, plans to bring wild ungovernable tribes to Christ—but he was in prison. Who can tell how his captivity must have galled his soul? Eventually imprisonment would have crushed even his proud spirit if he had not known how to be content "in all things."

In Philippians 4:12 Paul also said, "I am instructed." The word translated "am instructed" is *mueō*, which means "to initiate." A derivative of *mueō* is *musterion*, which means "mystery." So Paul was saying, "I have been let into the secret; I have been initiated into the mystery."

In Paul's day the "mystery religions" claimed to have deep, divine secrets that were revealed only to those who were properly initiated. Even deeper secrets were revealed to those who could pass the various levels of further initiation. Those mysteries, which were jealously guarded so that they could be kept from the masses, beckoned to all kinds of people from the emperor on down. Just as people today join the Masonic orders or occult societies in the hope of finding the key to success and the ultimate answers to life's questions, people in Paul's day were drawn to those fraudulent mystery religions. Those religions were fraudulent because their deepest secrets were only lies, deceptions of the evil one. The Holy Spirit calls such revelations "the deep things of Satan."[8]

But the secret Paul knew was gloriously true. It was God's secret and Paul was going to share it with everyone. "I am instructed," he said, "both to be full and to be hungry, both to abound [to run over] and to suffer need [to run short]." Feast or famine, he knew how to live above his circumstances. He had learned the serenity of contentment.

(b) The Secret of Contentment (4:13) "I can do all things through Christ which strengtheneth me."

How could Paul be content whether full or hungry? Knowing Paul, we can anticipate the answer. The secret, he said, is Christ! It was Christ who strengthened him.

Paul's strengthening began early in his Christian life. Soon after Ananias restored his sight and commanded him to be full of the Holy Spirit, Paul began to show that he knew the secret of victorious Christian life. Luke wrote:

> Then was Saul certain days with the disciples which were at Damascus. And straightway he preached Christ in the synagogues, that he is the Son of God. But all that heard him were amazed....But Saul increased the more in strength [endunamoō], and confounded the Jews which dwelt at Damascus, proving that this is very Christ (Acts 9:19-22).

Endunamoo also occurs in Philippians 4:13 where it is translated "strengtheneth." This verse is Paul's testimony at the other end of his life. He had learned how to handle all of life's ups and downs not in his own strength, but in Christ's strength.

Jesus faced all that human life has to offer. He was born in a Bethlehem stable and raised in a humble home. He went to school and worked at manual labor to earn His daily bread. He knew what it was to tramp the highways and not have anywhere to lay His head at night. He knew bereavement, suffering, and pain. He died an agonizing death after being falsely accused, scorned by enemies, and forsaken by friends. In his darkest hour He was conscious of being abandoned even by God.

Yet He always trusted God implicitly and dwelled in His love. He knew that God was His Father and the Holy Spirit was His constant companion. Even in the dreadful hour when He became sin for us and that orphan cry was wrung from His lips, He knew that He, through the eternal Spirit, was offering Himself without spot unto

God. He had strength enough to blot out the sun, rend creation's rocks, burst open sepulchers, and tear the temple veil. He had strength enough to die in the will of God on a cross of shame.

Christ's strength was the source of Paul's strength. The apostle exhibited Christ's strength, not his own. "I can do all things *through Christ*," he said (italics added). The formula in Philippians 4:13 is the same as the formula in 4:7: "Through Christ." Christ, living His life in Paul, made all the difference. Paul commended the secret to his friends in Philippi and to us wherever we are today.

2.   The Exercises Connected with This Kind of Life (4:14-23)

a.   Personal Needs (4:14-20)

(1)   Explanation (4:14-16)

(a)   The Reason for Paul's Past Financial Need (4:14-15a) "Ye have well done, that ye did communicate with my affliction....In the beginning of the gospel, when I departed from Macedonia..."

Paul had been in desperate financial need before. He had been short of funds when he had more or less been forced to leave Philippi at the time the work in Europe first began. He had gone on to Thessalonica, and when driven out of Thessalonica, he had gone on to Berea and then Athens. The reason for his need for money at that time was the pressure of open doors for evangelism along with the pressure of persecution.

Under normal conditions when funds dried up, Paul had a simple remedy: work! Paul scorned the idea of sending out urgent appeals for money. He went back to making tents. He did not stop his soul-winning, church-planting, and disciple-training activities; he simply added secular work to his evangelistic activities. And even as he plied his needle, he would have taught gospel truths to customers, suppliers, and passers-by.

But after Paul left Philippi and Macedonia (northern Greece) for Achaia (southern Greece), the work of evangelism flourished so greatly that he could not spare the time to do secular work. Apparently he had two options: (1) go hungry while doing spiritual work; or (2) ease up on spiritual work in order to have time to do secular work to earn money to buy food. Paul chose to go hungry. He chose to fast.

When Paul fasted, no doubt he remembered the Lord's instructions: "When thou fastest, anoint thine head, and wash thy face; That thou appear not unto men to fast" (Matthew 6:17-18). Not a soul knew that Paul was starving. He did not even think of sending broad hints in a letter to Lydia. He was ashamed to beg—begging seemed to him to be a betrayal of trust. God knew his needs and that was enough. Since Jesus went hungry for forty days in the will of God and resolutely resisted Satan's temptation to turn stones into bread (Matthew 4:1-4), Paul felt that he could go without food for the sake of the gospel. He knew that God, in His own good time and way, would take care of his financial needs as long as he was in the will of God.

Turning our thoughts to Paul's present situation, we notice that he commended the Philippians for their practical Christian kindness. Certainly he had been let into the secret of how to face hunger; he knew how to draw on the resources of the indwelling Christ to accept hunger with equanimity. But Paul was no mystic, no fanatic, no ascetic. He could cheerfully accept hunger and poverty in the will of God, but he did not like being hungry any more than anyone else does. He would willingly have starved to death for the cause of Christ, but he was glad that the Philippian aid came when it did.

(b) The Relief of Paul's Present Financial Need (4:15b-16)

i.   The Lacking Concern of the Churches (4:15b) "No church communicated with me as concerning giving and receiving, but ye only."

Paul showed how deeply he felt the other churches' lack of concern "in the beginning of the gospel." The many churches he had planted and the thousands of people he had led to Christ did not seem to care about his financial needs when he "departed from Macedonia." The church in Syrian Antioch had sent him forward as a missionary to the regions beyond. Why had not they remembered him? What about the churches of Galatia? They had once received him "as an angel of God"; they would have plucked out their own eyes and given them to him (Galatians 4:14-15). But they had not helped him when he had needed financial aid. The one bright spot had been the church at Philippi. Only they had sent him relief.

Now that Paul was at Rome, history was repeating itself. Paul, a prisoner in the cause of Christ, was being left to starve. The churches he had founded had forgotten him. The church at Rome had forgotten him too. Where was the "well-beloved Epaenetus"? Where were Mary, Andronicus, Junia, Amplias, Urbane, Stachys, and all the others (Romans 16:1-16)? Perhaps they had died or moved far away. All Paul knew was that he had been forgotten. But the Lord had not forgotten him!

ii.   The Loving Concern of Their Church (4:15c-16) "But ye only. For even in Thessalonica ye sent once and again unto my necessity."

Paul was still remembering the former generosity of the Philippians. Twice they had helped him while he was at Thessalonica. Thessalonica was nearly a hundred miles down the Egnatian way, a considerable distance in those days. (When I was a boy in rural Britain, people could live and die and never go farther than twenty miles from home. I can remember when a trip on the train from my hometown of Newport in South Wales to London, which was a hundred miles away, was a notable event.)

So when Paul was a hundred miles away and the Philippians were still babes in Christ, they had reached out to him twice—and he was only in Thessalonica a scant three weeks. Now they had reached out to him all the way to Rome. Every memory of their loving concern warmed his heart.

(2) Exhortation (4:17) "Not because I desire a gift: but I desire fruit that may abound to your account."

Paul was not one to dwell for long on the temporal side of an issue. He was grateful of course for the financial relief that had come, but he was even more pleased by the spiritual implications of the Philippians' gift. They were laying up treasure in Heaven! As a preacher friend of mine used to say, "If you want treasure in Heaven, you'd better give some money to someone who's going there!"

"Not because I desire a gift," Paul hastened to say. Another rendering states, "Not that I am hunting for a gift." We might say, "I am not fishing for a gift." (The writers of a great many prayer-letters today could not make that claim.) Paul had long since learned to trust the Lord to supply all he needed.

He explained, "I desire fruit that may abound to your account." He was really "in quest of the interest that is accumulating to your account," as Handley Moule rendered the statement. Paul was concerned above all else that his converts build up their spiritual assets against the day when they would be rewarded at the judgment seat of Christ. Far from giving a sordid hint that he would like another gift, Paul was lifting the whole concept of financial support to the heights. His exhortation referred to their bank account in Heaven, not his bank account down here.

(3) Exultation (4:18)

(a) Paul's Delight in Their Gift (4:18a) "I have all, and abound: I am full, having received of Epaphroditus the things which were sent from you."

This verse puts an end to any suggestion that Paul might have been hinting for more gifts.

Like Paul, George Muller trusted the Lord entirely. This famous Christian philanthropist wanted his orphan homes in Bristol, England, to be a tangible testimony to an unbelieving world that God was alive and well and still very much in business. To achieve this goal, he refused to make any need known to anyone but God.

Muller would not accept a financial gift from a person he knew to be in debt; such a donation was always courteously but firmly refused. Another of his principles was to give a full accounting of what he did with all the money he received. Therefore he developed the habit of circulating an annual statement called "The Chronicle of the Lord's Dealings with George Muller." Because this annual statement, which listed every gift, might be misconstrued as a subtle way of hinting for support for the work entrusted to him, Muller never released "The Chronicle" to the public until there were more than ample funds in the bank. Never was an issue published when funds were low.

Similarly Paul was "full" when he wrote to the Philippians. Epaphroditus had delivered their gift. Now he had plenty. He had need of no more.

(b) Paul's Description of Their Gift (4:18b) "An odour of a sweet smell, a sacrifice acceptable, wellpleasing to God."

J. B. Phillips's rendering of this verse is delightful: "Now I have everything I want—in fact I am rich....Such generosity is like a lovely fragrance, a sacrifice that pleases the very heart of God."[9] Many a time I have borrowed his phraseology in acknowledging some dear saint's kindly ministry to me.

The more familiar King James wording is helpful too, for it carries us back to the offerings of the Old Testament. All of those offerings were intended to speak of Christ, but three especially delighted the heart of God: the meal offering, the peace offering, and the burnt offering. In the giving of the law in Leviticus, God began with these three offerings (Leviticus 1–3). The meal offering spoke of Christ in the glory of His flawless humanity. The peace offering spoke of Christ as the peacemaker bringing God's people into happy fellowship and communion with God and each other. The burnt offering spoke of Christ as being all for God in a way only God Himself could fully appreciate. These three sweet-savor offerings brought special pleasure to God.

Paul viewed the financial gift of the Philippians as a kind of New Testament equivalent of a sweet-savor offering. Their gift was not something God required or demanded; it was the overflow of grateful hearts, "a sacrifice acceptable, wellpleasing to God."

(4) Expectation (4:19-20)

(a) Their Temporal Gain (4:19) "My God shall supply all your need according to his riches in glory by Christ Jesus."

The Philippian church probably was not wealthy. Looking at the size of the offering he had just received, Paul perhaps did some mental arithmetic and came to the conclusion that the total amount represented sacrificial giving on the part of many. They had given more than they could really afford. Now instead of his having need, some of the donors may have had need.

But Paul knew that his God was their God and no one could outgive Him. his God was rich in glory and would allow nothing to happen that might diminish His glory. Out of His unfailing treasury

He would supply their need. The Philippians had a double guarantee: the guarantee of God's character and the guarantee of God's Son. Even on the temporal level they were bound to be gainers by giving to God.

(b) God's Eternal Glory (4:20) "Now unto God and our Father be glory for ever and ever. Amen"

The thought of God's eternal glory and His guaranteed response to the Philippians' gift brought forth a doxology from Paul. (How characteristic of Paul!) When he thought of the inexhaustible riches of the God who is our Father, what more could he say than "Amen"?

Temporal riches are so often a source of quarrels, covetousness, greed, and materialism. One day the temporal will be replaced with the eternal. All need or desire for present gain will be swallowed up in the glory of God. A new heaven, a new earth, and vast new empires in space will whirl and dance around a new galactic center: the new Jerusalem, the capital city of a new creation that knows neither measure nor end. And all will be bathed in God's glory. Who would have thought that an ordinary gift to a servant of God would suggest such vistas as this?

Just like the gift given to Paul, our gifts have eternal consequences. Money given to one of the Lord's own is money given to God. The next time we consider giving financial help to a servant of God, let us remember that God's glory is involved.

b.   Parting Notes (4:21-23)

(1) Greetings (4:21-22)

(a) From the Apostle (4:21a) "Salute every saint in Christ Jesus."

Paul could see them in his mind's eye: those he had won to Christ and those won to Christ after he had left (Epaphroditus had described them to him). Paul made no attempt to name the saints. In acknowledging a gift he could not name some and not others. His heart went out to them all and he gathered them up in his warm embrace. "Salute them all," he said.

(b) From the Assembly (4:21b-22)

i.   Paul's Circle of Friends (4:21b) "The brethren which are with
     me greet you."

No doubt these brethren were Paul's personal friends who,
daring to be identified with him, visited him in prison. Most of them
were probably as poor as he was. Again Paul did not give names,
perhaps out of consideration for their safety.

ii. Paul's Circle of Fellowship (4:22) "All the saints salute you,
     chiefly they that are of Caesar's household."

There were numerous Christian congregations at Rome by this
time and Paul without doubt was in constant touch with them all.
Many of them, while perhaps keeping a discreet distance from
Paul, would have been interested in churches in the provinces,
outposts, and colonial cities such as Philippi. One group in particular, however, sent greetings to the Philippians: "they that are of
Caesar's household."

The group of Christians belonging to the household of the
emperor seems to have included his slaves, former slaves, and
people who filled all kinds of offices connected with his domestic
establishment. Paul's reference to this group gives an interesting
sidelight on the progress the gospel had made at Rome. In Nero's
own court, within the chambers of his palace, were numerous
Christians! They were the salt of the earth, the light of the world,
the aristocracy of Heaven. There is little doubt that conversions in
the caesar's own household were linked to Paul's presence in Rome
and the impact he had made on the imperial guard.

(2) Grace (4:23) "The grace of our Lord Jesus Christ be with you
     all. Amen."

The Epistle begins with grace and ends with grace. It begins with
the Lord Jesus Christ and ends with the Lord Jesus Christ. Christ is
the theme of the letter from beginning to end—His name occurs
more than forty times, an average of once in every two or three
verses. Christianity, after all, is about Christ. It is not simply a creed;
it is Christ. It is not just precept and principle; it is a person—the

most wonderful, glorious person in the universe. Christ had captured Paul's heart years ago on the Damascus road and had reigned there ever since. In one of the highlights of the letter Paul exclaimed, "To me to live is Christ, and to die is gain" (1:21). And his parting word is "The grace of our Lord Jesus Christ be with you all." All we can do is echo his final "Amen."

NOTES

Introduction

1. W. J. Conybeare and J. S. Howson, *The Life and Epistles of St. Paul* (Reprint, Grand Rapids: Eerdmans, 1959).
2. See John Phillips, *Exploring Acts* (Neptune, NJ: Loizeaux, 1986).

Part I

1. Two examples are *Jehovah Shalom,* "the God of peace," and *El Shaddai,* "the giver of grace, the all-bountiful, the One who supplies all our needs."
2. See 1 Corinthians 1:8; 5:5; 2 Corinthians 1:14; Philippians 1:6,10; 2:16.
3. See John 14:2-3; 1 Thessalonians 4:13–5:1 and 5:3-11; 2 Thessalonians 2:1.
4. See Romans 14:10; 1 Corinthians 3:11-15.
5. Dean Henry Alford, *The New Testament for English Readers* (Chicago: Moody Press, n.d.) 1257.
6. Author unknown.
7. J. B. Phillips, *The New Testament in Modern English* (New York: Macmillan, 1972) 324.
8. Ibid., 387.
9. Author unknown.

Part II

1. H. C. G. Moule, *Philippian Studies* (London: Hodder and Stoughton, 1897) 96-97.
2. W. E. Vine, *The Epistles to the Philippians and Colossians* (London: Oliphants, 1955) 16. Note: "Christ Jesus" appears in Acts 19:4, not Acts 24:24; it also occurs in 1 Peter 5:10,14 as well as in Paul's letters.
3. Gifford. Quoted by W. E. Vine in *An Expository Dictionary of New Testament Words* (Nashville: Nelson, 1984) 453-454.
4. Ibid., 887-888.

5. Note that in the King James text, much vilified in our day as being archaic and too hard to understand, there is not a single word with more than one syllable in this verse. The difficulties with the King James text are grossly overstated. Those who bypass this peer of Bible versions deny themselves acquaintance with the grandest and sublimest masterpiece in the English language. For centuries it was the Bible of the English-speaking world. It made England and America great. Men and women who could barely read pored over its pages, imbibed its teaching, understood its message, and enriched their lives—gaining an education in the process. Its cadences ring with a richness not found in other versions. It is a tragedy that many have so readily set it aside for lesser substitutes.

6. Jack London, "All Gold Canyon" (The Century Company, 1905). Reprinted in *Jack London's Tales of Adventure*, ed. Irving Shepard (Garden City, NY: Hanover House, 1956) 340-352.

Part III

1. From "Immanuel's Land" by Anne Ross Cousin.
2. From the hymn "Have Thine Own Way, Lord" by Adelaide A. Pollard.
3. Charles Chiniquy, *Fifty Years in the Church of Rome* (Reprint, London: Protestant Truth Society, 1885) 264-270.
4. From "Come, My Soul, Thy Suit Prepare" by John Newton.
5. From hymn by Charles A. Tindley.
6. F. W. Boreham, *A Bunch of Everlastings* (London: Epworth, 1920) 118.
7. From the hymn "Will Your Anchor Hold?" by Priscilla J. Owens.
8. Revelation 2:24, RSV. "Depths" in the King James version is a translation of *bathos*, which means "deep." The plural is used to describe the deep, nefarious designs of Satan.
9. J. B. Phillips, *The New Testament in Modern English*, 417.

Explore the

BIBLE

in greater depth with the
John Phillips
Commentary Series!